T0373423

A

Philip E. Lilienthal *(signature)*

■   ■   ■

B O O K

The Philip E. Lilienthal imprint
honors special books
in commemoration of a man whose work
at University of California Press from 1954 to 1979
was marked by dedication to young authors
and to high standards in the field of Asian Studies.
Friends, family, authors, and foundations have together
endowed the Lilienthal Fund, which enables UC Press
to publish under this imprint selected books
in a way that reflects the taste and judgment
of a great and beloved editor.

The publisher and the University of California Press Foundation gratefully acknowledge the generous support of the Philip E. Lilienthal Imprint in Asian Studies, established by a major gift from Sally Lilienthal.

Rivers of Iron

Rivers of Iron

Railroads and Chinese Power
in Southeast Asia

David M. Lampton, Selina Ho,
and Cheng-Chwee Kuik

UNIVERSITY OF CALIFORNIA PRESS

University of California Press
Oakland, California

© 2020 by David M. Lampton, Selina Ho, and
Cheng-Chwee Kuik

Library of Congress Cataloging-in-Publication Data

Names: Lampton, David M., author. | Ho, Selina, author. |
    Kuik, Cheng-Chwee, author.
Title: Rivers of iron : railroads and Chinese power in
    Southeast Asia / David M. Lampton, Selina Ho,
    Cheng-Chwee Kuik.
Description: Oakland, California : University of
    California Press, [2020] | Includes bibliographical
    references and index.
Identifiers: LCCN 2019057897 (print) | LCCN 2019057898
    (ebook) | ISBN 9780520372993 (cloth) |
    ISBN 9780520976160 (ebook)
Subjects: LCSH: Railroads—Political aspects—China—
    21st century. | Southeast Asia—Foreign relations—
    China—21st century. | China—Foreign relations—
    Southeast Asia—21st century.
Classification: LCC HE3288 .L35 2020 (print) |
    LCC HE3288 (ebook) | DDC 385.0959—dc23
LC record available at https://lccn.loc.gov/2019057897
LC ebook record available at https://lccn.loc
    .gov/2019057898

Manufactured in the United States of America

29 28 27 26 25 24 23 22 21 20
10 9 8 7 6 5 4 3 2 1

Dedicated to the proposition that building connections is the future

And building walls is the past

Contents

Illustrations

Preface

Setting the Stage

This volume explores China's current effort to join with its continental Southeast Asian neighbors and Singapore to realize a broadly shared vision of connecting the People's Republic of China (PRC) to its southern neighbors by a high- and conventional-speed rail network. This effort needs to be understood from many perspectives, one of which is the context of the last four decades' accumulated economic, political, and policy developments in China that have made this effort possible and driven it forward. This undertaking in Southeast Asia also needs to be viewed in the context of Beijing's broader national purposes, namely to sustain growth at home and change the political and economic geography of the PRC's entire periphery in a direction favorable to China's economic and strategic interests. These past developments and current purposes and interests predictably create reactions among other states in the region and beyond that are important considerations throughout this book.

Looking back to the time of Chairman Mao Zedong's 1976 death, the PRC was economically impoverished and unable to effectively project economic, military, or intellectual power much beyond its own borders. To address the gigantic challenges facing the nation that Mao had bequeathed to his successors, beginning from the late 1970s Deng Xiaoping focused on domestic economic development energized by market incentives, human and institutional capacity building, and reassurances to the world that China would be benign as its power grew. By pairing gains in modernization with foreign policy reassurances, Deng fostered a pacific external environment that provided a strategic window of opportunity for China to grow unmolested. Much like George Washington, Deng wanted to free his country of premature and costly entanglements that might detract from the task at hand—modernization.

To this end, Deng was more than willing to have his country temporarily play the part of student to more "modern" countries, notably the United States. He even instructed his officials to "learn from Singapore," a small city-state.[1] For the next three decades, Beijing was often a seemingly passive participant in an increasing range of international organizations and bilateral relationships, allergic to assuming heavy international burdens and responsibilities prematurely. Deng and his two immediate successors (Jiang Zemin and Hu Jintao) seized the resulting strategic window of opportunity to usher in three-plus decades of high-speed domestic economic expansion and societal change that enormously improved welfare across the entire population, albeit with some segments of society gaining more than others. Between 1978 and 2009, China's gross domestic product (GDP) per capita grew from about US$300 to about $4,100 (or more than thirteen times),[2] and after a costly 1979 border war with Vietnam the PRC waged no other large-scale bloodlettings, though there were a few territorial skirmishes along the way, including South China Sea encounters with Vietnam. All in all, Deng's two immediate successors carried on the broad modernization strategy of "reform and opening" (*gaige kaifang*) in ways largely compatible with Deng's vision. Indeed, Deng had chosen *both* Jiang Zemin *and* Hu Jintao as his sequential successors in order to enhance the prospects of policy continuity, something entirely absent from the tumultuous Mao era.

By 2010, however, in the last one-fifth of Hu Jintao's period in office, the PRC's comprehensive national power had multiplied and Washington had become distracted, if not hobbled, by prolonged post-9/11 conflicts (Afghanistan, Iraq, and smaller-scale operations in Africa, Central Asia, and the Middle East), the global financial crisis of 2008–9, and political gridlock in Washington born of domestic economic inequality and political polarization. In Beijing, Hu Jintao's successor, Xi Jinping, came to power in 2012–13 and concluded that the combination of China's enormous growth and America's unexpected faltering had combined to create an opportunity for China to step out of the international shadows and resume a great power role after more than 150 years. For their part, the Chinese people are proud of their accomplishments and anxious to play a greater and more respected role in the world. China's military wants to be a key instrument of the nation's further renewal, to more assertively defend sovereignty claims, and to protect the PRC's expanding equities in its region and globally.

The birth of the Belt and Road Initiative and reactions to it. A signal event heralding in this new era was Xi Jinping's announcement in late 2013 of the "One Belt, One Road" (*yidai yilu*) initiative (later rebranded as "BRI," or the Belt and Road Initiative), an effort to construct infrastructure linking the PRC to its land and sea periphery at all compass points. In two speeches in 2013, one in Kazakhstan in September and the other in Indonesia in October, President Xi proposed creating a "Silk Road Economic Belt" and a "Maritime Silk Road Initiative." The grand vision was to create both land and sea connectivity by constructing a web of infrastructure (roads, ports, pipelines, air, rail, cyber, power grids, etc.) as well as people-to-people and other connectivity. Despite the linguistic confusion of land "belts" and watery "roads," this broad policy umbrella has subsequently provided a hook upon which a very dynamic Chinese system can hang an endless number of infrastructure-building and connectivity projects, provide considerable financing to kick-start them, and promote the export of materials and human resources that China has in abundance. This effort also holds out the prospect of constructing an economic and strategic system with China as its hub. Its essence is the creation of economic and other power projection platforms at 360 degrees from China itself.[3]

In May 2014, in remarks that have not been authoritatively repeated since, Xi signaled the underlying impulse of this overall effort, calling for letting "the people of Asia run the affairs of Asia, solve the problems of Asia and uphold the security of Asia."[4] Thereafter, at October 2017's Nineteenth Party Congress, Xi had pursuit of the BRI written into the Party Constitution and at the subsequent National People's Congress held the following spring, Xi engineered the elimination of term limits that applied to him as China's head of state. By early 2018, therefore, one could clearly see that China had entered the post-Deng era both domestically and in terms of its foreign policy. China was no longer hiding the bright light of its national ambitions under a bushel (*tao guang yang hui*), it now had a leader who had the will, constitutional sanction, and potential longevity to pursue a massive international infrastructure-building effort, and the PRC now had much greater resources and advanced technologies with which to pursue those ambitions.

These ambitions, some clearly articulated and others less so, have aroused economic hopes and a sense of opportunity in many parts of the world, as they also have spawned economic and security anxieties. Beijing's proposal to build a regional and global connectivity network is effectively a move to tie the strategic "backyards" of many other powers into the PRC's own network. India has asked itself what tying in Pakistan, the smaller South Asian states, and Myanmar to China means for New Delhi. Russia asks what increasing Chinese integration with "its" so-called near abroad means for Moscow. Japan asks itself what tighter economic and strategic integration between China and Southeast Asia implies for its interests in a region central to its supply chains and critical to its maritime security. Likewise, Europe wonders how greater Chinese investment in and connection to its southern flank (Italy, Greece, and Serbia) will affect European standards, governance, economic interests, and rules-based international order. Vietnam ponders what China tying in Hanoi's Southeast Asian neighbors will mean for its own economic, cultural, and political autonomy. And, the United States similarly worries about what a growing Chinese sphere of influence in East, Southeast, and South Asia means for its security, maritime, trading, and resource interests, as well as its five post–World War II alliances and its regional preeminence. In short, the BRI has and will continue to set off a globally diverse set of ruminations and reactions, many strategic and geoeconomic in character.

The organization and financing of the BRI. Looking at the effort organizationally, as Nadege Rolland does in her research,[5] this policy initiative is one to which Chinese President Xi Jinping and Premier Li Keqiang have devoted enormous personal attention, travel time, and words. Beneath them is a complex array of central planning, coordination, and implementing institutions (and subordinate counterpart units in the localities), primary among which are: The Leading Small Group on Advancing the Construction of the Belt and Road, its Office of the Leading Small Group, and the ubiquitous National Development and Reform Commission (NDRC).

In terms of the anticipated government budget and capital available for this enormous overall undertaking with fuzzy geographic, bureaucratic, financial, and economic sector boundaries, the Xi administration has not released authoritative total figures about aggregate anticipated expenditures, what actually has been committed, or what may be committed in the future. Indeed, as we see throughout this volume, the very concept of commitment is an indeterminate notion when dealing with the PRC in this zone of activity. Chinese figures often conflate actual investment, contemplated investment, and the value of China's commercial contracts for projects when the PRC often has little or no role financing an undertaking. The vice-chairman of the NDRC, Ning Jizhe, said in May 2017 that BRI investments would be about $120–$130 billion annually for five years.[6] But we do not know which countries, nor which activities of various levels of administration and sectors of the Chinese economy are included in this figure, much less what percentages of these "investments" are grants, loans, joint ventures, contracts, and so forth. The China Development Bank in January 2018 committed $250 billion for BRI loans,[7] but this does not enlighten us about the activities and commitments of other financial actors including China's Export-Import (Exim) Bank, nor of the more seemingly commercial financial institutions in the PRC. Of course, there is always the problem that current promises fail to be realized in an uncertain future. The future is uncertain not only because Beijing may fail to deliver, but also because partners change their minds.

In 2017, the Asian Development Bank (ADB) estimated that a total of about $26 trillion would be required to meet Asia's infrastructure needs by 2030.[8] Therefore, whatever the figure for Chinese expenditures on BRI eventually proves to be, even the PRC's ambitious plans leave enormous room for the activities of other governments, multilateral development organizations, or the global private sector.[9] Equally important, it is far from self-evident that the Chinese people and leaders will sustain large external commitments, given the huge domestic needs that remain unmet.

The Southeast Asia railroad dimension of BRI. This book examines one part of this overall Asian (indeed global) effort and reactions to it: high- and conventional-speed rail construction in Southeast Asia. In the chapters to follow we tell the story of how this undertaking has unfolded, what it reveals about Chinese power, and how and why the PRC's smaller neighbors are reacting as they are to their huge, dynamic neighbor.

Fed in no small part by domestic efforts to lionize Chinese leader Xi Jinping, as well as by tendencies among outside observers to see the PRC as a juggernaut, almost any economic development or infrastructure project undertaken by Beijing and its state enterprises, localities, or private interests is immediately viewed as a PRC initiative under the signboard of the BRI. In fact, many projects around the world and in

Southeast Asia in which the PRC is involved are not Chinese ideas or initiatives, but rather the ideas, visions, and aspirations of others, the pursuit of which China now can energize with its technology, human resources, and financing, as well as simply competing for contracts. This is certainly the case in Southeast Asia with railroad development.

Under Xi Jinping, there has been a conjunction of long-standing regional aspirations for connectivity, China's desire to play a more robust global role strategically and economically, and the PRC's growing capacity to do so. The PRC has veritable mountains of steel and concrete to sell abroad, a substantial body of personnel to employ overseas, and considerable foreign exchange that Beijing needs to productively deploy internationally. For their part, China's neighbors want the infrastructure these Chinese exports, capital, and engineering talent can construct, even as they fear the dependencies and competitive pressure that such connectivity will entail. All China's neighbors, not least in Southeast Asia, wish to reap the benefits of Chinese involvement while avoiding the many risks they perceive.

Assessing BRI and the focus on Southeast Asia. Because BRI is a vast undertaking, involving many actors at home and abroad, involving uncertain commitments, with many long-term and short-term effects, it is difficult to make an overall assessment of individual projects, much less the overall endeavor. Predictably, implementation of specific undertakings has been highly variable, with some stopped entirely, others long delayed, still others encountering societal counterreactions in partner countries, some being built but subsequently proving unsustainable, and still others being reasonably successful. There is also the fact that because most infrastructure projects around the world come in over budget and behind schedule, one should view all this comparatively— infrastructure is not easy anywhere.

A big part of the story is how and why individual countries decide to join with Beijing while others prefer to remain aloof. Some countries are enthusiastic in their embrace, others are reluctant, while some prefer to explore other partnerships. Almost everyone is looking for ways to benefit from Beijing's initiative while minimizing downsides such as strategic dependence, cultural and societal conflict, economic dependency or disruption, and the negative reaction of other big powers and neighbors.

If one tried to consider BRI as a whole, one could easily lose focus and never move beyond superficial generalization. This book, therefore, examines in detail the PRC's efforts in one important sector of connectivity in a very promising and strategically important area—high-speed and conventional-speed rail construction in Southeast Asia. Exploring rail construction in this region makes sense for several reasons. To start, Southeast Asia is critical strategically to the PRC. Both China's "Continentalists" and its "Maritime Interests" view the region as a space important to the nation's future in which to build land routes to reduce vulnerability from shipping lanes through the Persian Gulf, Indian Ocean, and the archipelago around Singapore and Indonesia. Second, both interest groups also see Southeast Asia as a relatively secure place to establish value-added production chains centered on China and to access growing consumer markets as Southeast Asia's middle class grows rapidly. The region also has rich and relatively skilled human capital to which the PRC can offload the lower value-added components of its manufacturing chains as China's domestic costs of production increase. Further, by building the pathways of North-South commerce, China directs future economic activity in its direction. And finally, Southeast Asia is a region with lagging infrastructure in which China can seize first-mover advantages to establish its technical and construction standards early in the development process, placing itself in an advantageous position to win future economic competitions.

In short, Southeast Asia is important to the major interest groups that drive Chinese domestic and foreign policy. If it is important to China, it should be important to the rest of the world in the competitive age upon which we have embarked. America and other powers should consider how to benefit from this undertaking, while remaining cognizant of the pitfalls, by seeking to build *balanced connectivity* in this critical region.

Acknowledgments

In late 2015, this book's three coauthors agreed to collaborate in order to first describe, and then explain the larger meaning of, a region-changing development—the construction of a high-speed and conventional railroad network that gradually is creating a web of interconnectivity linking China to its seven Southeast Asian neighbors down to Singapore. This project is immense, ongoing, and the precise shape of the system that will evolve is indeterminate. Conducting the field and documentary research necessary to write this book has required covering a diverse expanse of territory embracing distinctive political and economic systems, cultures, languages and dialects, and histories, in a region in which nations are each at a different economic level. If one considers only countries, this ambitious project involves eight, and if one disaggregates each of these heterogeneous states into subcomponents, the number of actors becomes staggering. Finally, though not part of the continental system that is the focus of this study, the experience of Indonesia dealing with Beijing on rail development has been an important reference point that we have had to consider too.

The complexity, scope, and more than four-year duration of the necessary research has required the assistance of many talented people. Our team has involved numerous research assistants, drawn upon the knowledge of hundreds of interviewees across many nations, and required extensive documentary research. Beyond the eight immediately involved countries (plus Indonesia) we also had to contact international multilateral organizations, multinational corporations, and countries well beyond the region. This research has involved many trips to China and Southeast Asia by our team, the first of which, in the summer of 2016, was to Singapore and Malaysia, where we interviewed then retired Prime Minister Mahathir. Another extensive field trip occurred in the summer of 2017, a two-week overland journey from Bangkok along the prospective rail line through northeastern Thailand, Laos, and on to the People's Republic of China (PRC) border at Boten, Laos. Subsequently, in May–June 2018, the team spent considerable time in Singapore and Malaysia, where we took a field trip from Kuala Lumpur up to near the Thai border on the east coast of Malaysia, following the route of the East Coast Rail Link. Construction had been suspended during our field trip, but it was subsequently resumed after Malaysia and China succeeded in renegotiating the deal in April 2019. During our time in Malaysia, we also met with His Royal Highness Sultan Nazrin Muizzuddin Shah, the Sultan of Perak, whose territory north of Kuala Lumpur hosts the China Railway Rolling Stock Corp. (CRRC) manufacturing center. Finally, in August 2018, we undertook field research, again in Thailand, thereafter visiting Cambodia.

Our purpose in these acknowledgments, therefore, is to identify and thank those whose intellectual, informational, organizational, and monetary assistance made this undertaking possible. The authors express great appreciation to the Smith Richardson Foundation for its multi-year grant to the principal investigator (PI) for this project, then Professor and Director of China Studies at Johns Hopkins—School of Advanced International Studies (SAIS), David M. Lampton. The authors appreciate the foundation's deliberative process for helping refine the initial proposal and for being flexible as the project unfolded in an extraordinarily complex setting. In particular, the PI wishes to thank Allan Song, Esq., Senior Program Officer for International Security & Foreign Policy at the foundation, for his help and encouragement.

Also critical to the success of this project has been the support of SAIS in the form of research funds and research assistants, and the encouragement of then SAIS Dean Vali Nasr and then Associate Dean for Administration Myron Kunka. This project also owes a debt of gratitude to the Lee Kuan Yew School of Public Policy in Singapore, not least the then Dean Kishore Mahbubani, and the National University of Malaysia (UKM) in Bangi, for their supportive attitudes. The authors also wish to thank the following research assistants: Kevin Dong, Lan Peiyuan, Lei Yingdi, Liu Zongyuan (Zoe), Zhaojin Ji, and Zhu Mingqi, all in various capacities at SAIS; Ms. Alicia R. Chen at Stanford University; Jing Bo-jiun and Xu Shengwei at the Lee Kuan Yew School of Public Policy in Singapore; and Ithrana Lawrence and Intan Baizura at UKM in Malaysia. Ithrana helped on field visits and in many other ways. Finally, we acknowledge and thank Susan Lampton for the photographs taken during the 2017 summer fieldwork in Laos.

In the latter phase of this project David Lampton assumed the position of Research Scholar and Oksenberg-Rohlen Fellow at Stanford University's Shorenstein Asia-Pacific Research Center (APARC) within the Freeman Spogli Institute. All of our team express appreciation to APARC and its director Gi-Wook Shin for the support, encouragement, and productive environment that permitted completion of this project, including the provision of research assistance.

The authors' intellectual and other debts extend beyond the institutions, individuals, and splendid research assistants mentioned above. Throughout the period of research, individuals and organizations throughout China and Southeast Asia assisted our team by convening workshops and meetings in the region, introducing us to interviewees, and accompanying us on field visits. The authors particularly wish to express their deepest gratitude to Professor Jantima Kheokao and her assistant Ms. Natnicha Krirkgulthorn. They made possible the trip (on and off road) from Bangkok to the Chinese border at Boten, a trip that took us the length of northeastern Thailand and Laos and back to Luang Prabang. Professor Jantima made arrangements and helped with interpretation, also intellectually contributing to the project by drawing on her deep wellspring of local and regional knowledge of both Thailand and Laos.

With respect to introducing our team to individual interviewees and arranging group meetings and seminars in China and Southeast Asia, we wish to thank Dr. Zhou Qi, executive director of the Tsinghua University National Strategy Institute; Director Wang Wen of the Chongyang Institute of Financial Studies at Renda (People's University in Beijing); representative of the Ford Foundation in China Elizabeth Knup; The Stanford Center at Peking University and Professor Jean C. Oi, Lee Shau Kee Director of the Center; Professor and Vice Dean Phouphet Kyophilavong at the National University of Laos; Datuk Dr. Ruhanie Ahmad, former member of Parliament (Malaysia); Mr. Kuik Cheng Kang, editor-in-chief of Sin Chew Daily (Malaysia); Professor and Director Anuson Chinvanno at Rangsit University (Thailand); Dr. Chanintira Na Thalang of Thammasat University; H. E. Sok Siphana, advisor to the Royal Government of Cambodia; and H. E. Academician Sok Touch, president of the Royal Academy of Cambodia, along with Director General at the Academy

Dr. Kin Phea; Ambassador Pou Sothirak, Executive Director of the Cambodian Institute for Cooperation and Peace, and Dr. Vannarith Chheang, President of the Asian Vision Institute. Our team also expresses great appreciation to various country offices of The Asia Foundation in Southeast Asia, China, and Washington, D.C. The foundation's offices throughout Asia provided our team suggestions as to whom we might contact and briefed us on local knowledge. We particularly must thank the foundation's country representatives, Vice President Nancy Yuan, Senior Director for International Relations Programs John Brandon, and President David Arnold.

Given the business, commercial, intellectual property, and other proprietary interests involved, not to mention political and security sensitivities within and among all the countries involved, we have had to protect the identities of most of the informants who have shared their knowledge with us. Many persons assisted us greatly, but prudence dictates that they remain anonymous. This research has complied with all the human subject protections that are part of the Institutional Review Board (IRB) procedures at Johns Hopkins University as well as the protections that simple decency and common sense dictate.

Our research team sometimes met with interviewees one on one, while in other circumstances we met with groups (sometimes large groups) in almost conference- or seminar-like settings. Across the eight countries (plus Indonesia) in the region we met with government officials (both national and local), think tank and university personnel, companies, international multilateral organizations, and senior representatives of foreign governments. Altogether, our team members, singly and as a group, spoke with hundreds of persons in well over 150 organizations. These interviewees included a former prime minister of Malaysia, a former prime minister of Thailand, a vice premier in China, a senior executive branch official in Thailand, a minister of transport and a minister of commerce in Southeast Asia, a former minister of foreign affairs in Thailand and one in Malaysia, a former defense minister in Malaysia, foreign ministry personnel in several countries, planners in several countries, Chamber of Commerce, industrial, and business leaders in China and Southeast Asia, nongovernmental organization leaders, parliamentarians, and dozens of academics, think tank executives, and research personnel across China and the region. One interesting group of interviewees comprised local rail station masters and railroad administration personnel along the right-of-way moving from Bangkok to Isan, the northeastern region of Thailand.

The authors are in debt to each of these informants, but we respect their desire to remain unacknowledged. We have sought to convey accurately what our interlocutors told us. Nonetheless, all conclusions are those of our research team. Those individuals who shared their knowledge with us are not responsible for any errors of fact or interpretation that we may have inadvertently committed.

Throughout this volume, we liberally quote from interviews, observing the following convention. Long quotes are indented in the text. Words without quotation marks are close to verbatim, but not exact word-for-word recapitulations. Words with quotation marks represent the exact words. With respect to the romanization of Chinese names, we employ Pinyin throughout, unless some other rendering is widely used for those characters, often a personal or place name. With respect to the rendering of names of persons in Taiwan, we use the local spelling.

Turning to administrative support for this project, the authors express their gratitude to Ms. Zhaojin Ji, senior program coordinator for China Studies at SAIS. This project would not have lifted off the launch pad administratively without her deep knowledge of the inner workings of Johns Hopkins University. Also, of great help in her capacity as Associate Director of China Studies and SAIS-China was Ms. Madelyn Ross, preceded in this post by Dr. Carla Freeman. On the financial administration end, Ms. Vivian Walker at SAIS has our gratitude, having pushed through the paperwork necessary to handle a complex project spanning eight countries and having employees in three different nations. For her cooperation on accounting and report issues for the Smith Richardson Foundation, we wish to thank Ms. Kathy Lavery.

The authors express their overwhelming appreciation to Ms. Krista Forsgren, the manuscript's initial editor. She brought order and clarity to our writing and improved the book enormously. Once we submitted the manuscript to the University of California Press, we were the beneficiaries of constructive suggestions made by anonymous reviewers. We thank them for their guidance, with our only regret being that their anonymity precludes us from thanking them directly. At the University of California Press we also express our appreciation to all the editors and others involved in this volume's production and marketing, not least the Acquisitions Editor Reed Malcolm, who provided encouragement and guidance throughout this project. Beth Chapple did a superb job copyediting the manuscript, and the authors thank Archna Patel and Francisco Reinking for shepherding the manuscript through the production process. We thank Susan Stone for indexing.

In conclusion, each of this volume's coauthors wishes to thank family members who have supported each of us in so many ways, not least by forgoing the time together that we otherwise would have had.

David M. Lampton, Selina Ho, and Cheng-Chwee Kuik

February 2020

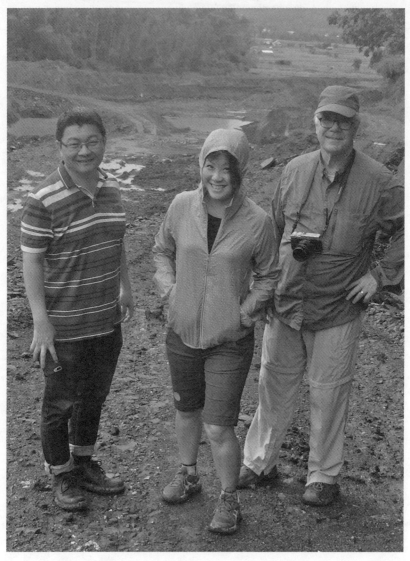

FIGURE 1. Authors (*left to right*) Cheng-Chwee Kuik, Selina Ho, and David Lampton at construction site, railway tunneling, Northern Laos, June 2017. Photo by Susan S. Lampton.

CHAPTER 1

Chinese Power Is as
Chinese Power Does

Rivers of Iron tells the story of China's unfolding role in realizing the regionwide dream of building an intercountry railroad system connecting Southwest China and its seven Southeast Asian neighbors. This system is gradually taking shape with construction of Chinese-backed projects underway in several of the countries. Progress is being made. Nonetheless, while the People's Republic of China (PRC) is strong, it is not a goliath bestriding the world, even in this region where China looms over its small and medium-size neighbors.

This book illuminates the strengths and weaknesses of China's demonstration of power during President Xi Jinping's self-styled "New Era" as well as the capacity of its smaller neighbors to resist, shape, and at times even take advantage of China's actions. Utilizing frameworks from the fields of international relations and comparative politics, this book seeks to explain how domestic politics in all eight of the involved nations affects their external behavior. Finally, *Rivers of Iron* addresses a fundamental development issue in what is emerging globally as a new age of infrastructure—How should we understand the role of infrastructure in development, and how do policy makers and analysts balance the long-term value and prospective gains of investments with the sometimes huge short- and medium-term costs?

In June 2017, while our multinational research team was in Laos deep in interviews, Chinese engineers and laborers, organized in multiple construction brigades, were burrowing tunnels through the impoverished country's karst mountains and building bridges to span many of its innumerable rivers and streams to prepare the path for the construction of a relatively high-speed rail (HSR) line from the Lao People's Democratic Republic's border with China at Boten southward to Vientiane (Thanaleng) on the Mekong River, a distance of 414 kilometers.[1] This was the first segment of China's envisioned "Central Line" running from Kunming to Bangkok, and eventually on to Singapore via Kuala Lumpur. In the most expansive vision of the evolving rail network, the Central Line would eventually be flanked by lines to the east (through Vietnam and Cambodia) and to the west (through Myanmar), with all three meeting in Bangkok and thereafter shooting down Peninsular Malaysia to Singapore. At the time we were in Laos, the border town of Boten was towered over by a golden gateway marking the entry point into China. It was a bit incongruous given the surroundings of the dusty town choked with trucks.

When we asked a senior Lao official during this 2017 visit why his country was proceeding with a project that would create a heavy national debt burden (more than half of Laos's 2015 GDP) for its less than seven million population, indebtedness that might compromise the small nation's sovereignty, he offered a two-part explanation. He started by saying that most thriving civilizations historically have developed along rivers or near oceans, going on to contrast that pattern with his country's circumstance—Laos is landlocked, poor, isolated, and mountainous. While Laos is on a great river, the Mekong, it is upstream and much of its territory is not on the waterway. Moreover, the Mekong basin has large seasonal fluctuations in precipitation that dramatically impact flows and therefore river transport. Unlike every other country in continental Southeast Asia, Laos has no direct maritime access; oceans are accessible only by passing through contiguous states—China, Vietnam, Myanmar (Burma), Cambodia, or Thailand. As the official put it, in close paraphrase: China is on the coast. We need to build an Iron River. Other countries' civilizations had rivers for transport. We have to build our own Iron River—a railroad.[2]

The second part of his explanation was a realistic assessment of how Laos's circumstances shaped the decision to permit PRC companies to finance and start constructing the mammoth railroad project. The Lao PDR had the choice of refusing to move ahead with the railroad and thereby remaining a poor island in a sea of more rapidly developing neighbors, or assuming a weighty debt burden in the hope that the rail project would create new economic and social opportunities, and possibly a brighter future. Beijing, he recounted, made it clear that if Vientiane did not move ahead with the Central Line, alternate routes to both the east and west would be available. Lao leaders weighed the pros and cons of being bypassed, making what amounted to a leap of faith:

> As you know we are in the middle, a landlocked country. Others have better opportunity. Cambodia has sea; they have railways. Thailand also has good infrastructure. But for us, we don't have good infrastructure. For us, if we don't take the steps we will lose the opportunity to connect to China, Vietnam, Thailand, Malaysia, and Singapore. The research indicates that the closest route from China to Southeast Asia is through Laos; but if we are not ready, then we will lose the opportunity. We need to take the decision, whether we will accept or not to accept. The [Lao] government thinks [that] if we don't accept, then we will lose the opportunity. [If we don't accept], we won't have any debt. But then we will [continue to] be poor like this. We must try to manage, to leverage on our location. We look at Singapore. They are surrounded by sea; no resources, no land. How do they manage to do that? With a big seaport, the ships have to pass Singapore. So we want to take the opportunity [to leverage our location]. Our biggest market is China. Through railways from Singapore, Malaysia, and Thailand, we can benefit from them. We can gain from trade and so on. So this is very crucial. We know there will be debt. If we don't know how to manage the debt, it is no good. But if we know how to manage the debt, then okay.[3]

THE IDEA OF A PAN-ASIA RAILWAY

Rivers of Iron is about China's endeavor to work with its seven Southeast Asian neighbors to construct what is envisioned to eventually be an integrated three-line, high- and medium-speed, standard (1.435 m) gauge, rail network running from Kunming, in Yunnan Province (southwestern China), to Singapore at the southern tip of the Malay Peninsula.[4] This idea of a Pan-Asia Railway was *not* a Chinese idea (see chapter 2). Rather, the vision had its genesis with British and French colonialists in the late 1800s and early twentieth century, then subsequently was pushed by Japan during World War II. Thereafter, the PRC's neighbors to the south and in the Association of Southeast Asian Nations (ASEAN) seized the baton. Beijing has embraced this more than century-old idea and is now taking an active role to make it a reality. President Xi Jinping made a state visit to Laos in November 2017, whereupon leaders of both countries pledged to accelerate the already ongoing efforts on the first stage of the overall network.[5] As of this writing, construction in Laos is advanced and due for completion in late 2021.

The distance from Kunming to Singapore via each of the three envisioned lines is longer than the Transcontinental Railroad's 1,776 miles laid across the United States' midriff from Council Bluffs, Iowa, to Sacramento, California between 1863 and 1869. That monumental undertaking played a catalytic role in establishing America as a Pacific power. Upon completion, the United States was able to use its iron river to move its agricultural, natural, and industrial products across an enormous continent, develop its western reaches, and extend its growing power across the Pacific Ocean.

Now, 150 years later, Southeast Asia and southwestern China (Yunnan and Sichuan provinces and the Guangxi-Zhuang Autonomous Region) hope this ongoing effort can do as much for them as the Transcontinental did for America. Xi Jinping's "China Dream" (中国梦, *Zhongguo Meng*) of continental influence meshes with the dreams of China's landlocked and isolated southwestern provinces, as well as the dreams of the seven Southeast Asian countries hoping to connect to the dynamic and growing powerhouse of China. Though anxieties exist, these shared aspirations are moving toward realization, in part, because China, for the first time, has the technology, human resources, and capital to drive the process forward. In terms of power, Beijing's elite aspires to make China the hub of an enormous regional economic system, build their country ever more tightly and strategically into value and production chains, and connect all modes of transportation to ports around the fringes of maritime Asia for commercial and military power projection.

The American experience offers some perspective on this undertaking. In *Nothing Like It in the World,* his classic study on the building of the Transcontinental Railroad in the United States, Stephen E. Ambrose cataloged the messy, corrupt, problem-plagued, violent process of its construction. Since the two railroad construction companies building the line (the Union Pacific and the Central Pacific) were paid per mile of track put down, and the two companies started from opposite ends of the route—competing to see which could lay the most rail—it is little wonder that much of the initial construction was shoddy and completed very rapidly. Given the need for congressional support in Washington, sweetheart securities deals were rampant. Land giveaways were legion. Working conditions for Chinese laborers were appalling.[6] In *The Beautiful Country and the Middle Kingdom,* John Pomfret cites reports documenting "teams of Chinese bone collectors" that "followed the railroad, collecting the remains of the dead workers so they could be shipped back to China for burial among their ancestors. They were . . . 'the caravan of the dead.'"[7]

Ambrose concluded his volume by saying that despite all the debates, problems, uncertainties, tragedies, shenanigans, and missteps during

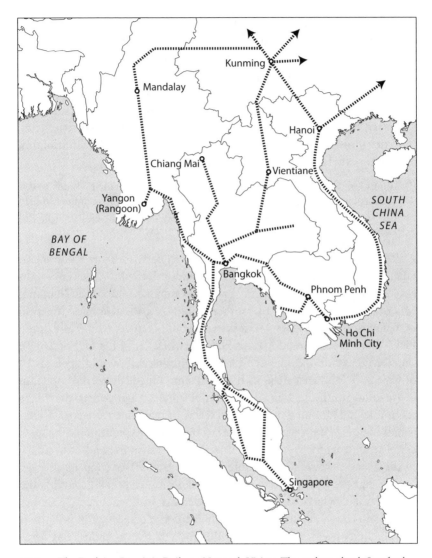

MAP 1. The Evolving Pan-Asia Railway Network Vision. The authors thank Stanford University Press for the rights to reproduce this map, which appears in David M. Lampton, "All (High-Speed Rail) Roads Lead to China," *Fateful Decisions: Choices That Will Shape China's Future*, ed. Thomas Fingar and Jean C. Oi (Stanford, CA: Stanford University Press, 2020).

the Transcontinental's creation, from the vantage point of a few decades after the project's completion, no one doubted that the undertaking had been a transformative investment by the American public and private sectors. This undertaking represented the joint efforts of Abraham Lincoln, the northern states in the context of the Civil War and its aftermath, the US Congress, and a concatenation of oversize personalities ("robber barons") who were visionary and unbridled entrepreneurs (Charles Crocker, Leland Stanford, Mark Hopkins, Collis Huntington, and many others). Ambrose concluded:

> Things happened as they happened. It is possible to imagine all kinds of different routes across the continent, or a better way for the government to help private industry, or maybe to have the government build and own it. But those things didn't happen, and what did take place is grand.[8]

If the entire three trunk-line pan-Asian rail network from Kunming to Singapore is eventually completed, it would link the PRC's seven Southeast Asian neighbors (Vietnam, Laos, Myanmar, Cambodia, Thailand, Malaysia, and Singapore) to southern China. At the Kunming junction in Yunnan, the Southeast Asian system would connect to the rest of the PRC's 29,000 km long domestic HSR network (as of the end of 2018), slated to be 38,000 km by 2025.[9] The Kunming hub would open up all of China to Southeast Asia, as it would simultaneously further open up continental Southeast Asia and the island state of Singapore to the PRC's economic and human dynamism. In terms of maritime transport, China is making deals with regional states to build and expand ports that will connect with highways, industrial parks, air transport, and railroads—so the broader vision is a new intermodal network (see Map 1).

The first component of the three-route vision to break ground is the Central Line, which has been well underway in Laos since December 2016. The Laos stretch was the first link to start construction because it was the most politically feasible of the three pathways under consideration. The segment should be operational (to the Thai border) by the end of 2021.[10] In February 2018, Thailand and China started to discuss a sequence of agreements that, if consummated, would have Chinese firms contract with the Thai Transport Ministry to continue building the Central Line from Nong Khai (on the Thai side of the border with Laos) 615 km to Bangkok via Nakhon Ratchasima. If plans hold, the intention is to "complete the railway in 2023 as well as to connect it with the China-Laos railway."[11] At the February 2018 meeting, Thailand and China agreed to engage in three-way talks (China, the Lao PDR, and Thailand) to facilitate a smooth hookup with the Lao line and establish protocols for customs and immigration.[12] Modest technology transfer from the PRC would be part of the deal with Bangkok. Two years prior to this meeting, in March 2016, the Thai military government announced that it would entirely finance the Thai section of the project itself. A short test rail link, a 3.5 km pilot stretch between Klang Dong and Pang Asok in Khorat's Pak Chong District, was under construction in December 2017.[13] Thus, the Thai portion of the Central Line is likely to materialize, with the timing, allocation of responsibilities, and myriad other details remaining to be worked out as of early 2019.

In addition, as of early 2018, at the other end of the Central Line, Singapore and Malaysia were close to soliciting tenders for the segment connecting Singapore to Kuala Lumpur. Both Malaysia and Singapore initially aimed to complete construction of the Kuala Lumpur (KL)–Singapore high-speed rail by 2026, but the mid-2018 election in Malaysia caused a deferral in soliciting tenders.[14] Overall, if (when) completed, the Central Line would tie together China, Laos, Thailand, Malaysia, and Singapore. The two segments of the Central Line that are most uncertain are those in Thailand (south of Bangkok) and Malaysia (north of Kuala Lumpur). After the 2018 Malaysian elections, some new uncertainties about the KL-Singapore stretch surfaced as well, as discussed in chapters 4, 5, and 6. In Thailand, the sometimes-violent separatist movements in southern provinces pose a challenge to connectivity in that region. In October 2017, the then Malaysian Transport Minister Liow Tiong Lai said that Thailand has expressed interest in holding talks with Malaysia about constructing an HSR line from Kuala Lumpur to Bangkok, but he added that the proposal is "still at the early stages."[15]

If the envisioned "Western Line" of the three-route vision starting in Kunming is constructed as well (and this is uncertain), Myanmar would be added to the system, with the track starting in Kunming and going through Mandalay and Yangon before reaching Bangkok. Were the "Eastern Line" to be constructed, Vietnam and Cambodia would join an integrated network. Each of the three component lines, not to mention the overall network, is extraordinarily complex and ambitious, whether viewed from an engineering, financial, international, or domestic political perspective. If completed, these undertakings (individually or as a whole) would change the economic, urban, demographic, and strategic landscape of the entire region. Indeed, even if only the Central Line (now under construction) is completed in the near- to medium-term, it would have transformative impacts.

Looking around the world for economic growth potential, there are few more promising regions than southern China and its neighbors in Southeast Asia. The seven Southeast Asian nations potentially involved in these projects (Myanmar, Laos, Vietnam, Thailand, Cambodia, Malaysia, and Singapore) have a combined population of over 282 million (86 percent of the US population), with the combined regional population expanding at more than the world population growth rate[16] and average GDP growth rates at roughly twice the world average in 2017.[17] By 2050, ASEAN as a whole (ten nations) will likely represent the fourth largest economy in the world.[18] Considering land area, continental Southeast Asia is only 23 percent as large as the United States,[19] meaning that its population densities are much higher than America's—a consideration (when taken in isolation) that favors railroad development. Considering the increase in interconnectivity with China (with its huge population, landmass, and economic growth), this project will create productive synergies within a total population of about 1.7 billion persons, not quite one-fourth of the world's people.

Scanning the world's highest potential emerging markets, Southeast Asia stands out. It has a rapidly growing middle class: the size of the middle class in ASEAN (ten nations) in 2012 was 190 million, and by 2020 that population likely will reach 400 million.[20] If one compares daily wage costs per manufacturing employee, in 2016, China had reached $37.20 per day per manufacturing worker, while rates in Vietnam and Thailand were one-quarter to one-half of that rate.[21] Lower-end assembly and manufacturing has been migrating from the PRC south for some time. The seven ASEAN countries potentially involved in this set of rail projects are strategically located as China off-loads labor-intensive industry to its southern neighbors and continues to move up value-added chains, further developing its own international production chains.[22] Haier, the Chinese white goods manufacturer, for instance, has been off-loading manufacturing to Southeast Asia since 1996. Sweater production has been moving from China to Yangon, Myanmar.[23] With mounting Sino-American trade frictions in 2018–19, this shift of value chains south has been given added impetus as foreign direct investors began to move components of the value chain (and make new investments) outside the PRC to reduce exposure to US tariffs and other protectionist measures aimed at Beijing.[24]

In short, the high- and conventional-speed rail developments described and explained in this volume are unfolding against the backdrop of a rising China, a growing Southeast Asia, and a United States of relatively diminished international dominance. The United States should not be counted out, but in order to change reality, Americans first must understand it and then commit the resources necessary to shape it.

SIGNIFICANCE OF THIS STUDY

Against the backdrop of the developments outlined above, what are the significant policy and theoretical questions that form the intellectual backbone of this comparative, multi-nation research project? What general conclusions germane to social scientists as well as policy practitioners emerge from this research? We hope that this book serves as a positive example of multinational collaborative research.

Five Context-Setting Issues

1. What is the role and timing of big infrastructure projects in economic and social development? For many years US foreign assistance policy and the lending practices of international multilateral organizations have downplayed grand infrastructure projects in their portfolios, instead favoring human and institutional capacity-building endeavors (chapter 8).[25] This approach of state institution building has its roots in a human resource and institution-centered perspective on development that takes a skeptical view of the financial, human, and ecological costs of large infrastructure projects.[26] Many grand infrastructure projects have modest revenue flows that extend payback periods to such an extent that few commercial enterprises are interested in financing them, because they require subsidies as far as the eye can see. With big infrastructure, the gains are diffuse and long term, and while positive externalities may be significant, they are not easy to quantify; immediate costs are concentrated and often highly visible politically. Projects such as the Aswan High Dam in Egypt, built with considerable Soviet help in the 1960s, and the Three Gorges Dam, built later in the PRC, come to mind. Completing big infrastructure projects requires large and sustained involvement by the public sector, and leaders must invest serious political capital for a protracted duration. The downside risks of enormous failures are ever-present.

China and many of its neighbors have a different view of development, a view in which infrastructure catalyzes growth and has many positive externalities. Theirs is a "field of dreams, build it and they will come" mindset. In economic terms, this is "supply-driven" growth fueled by the belief that the supply of infrastructure will create its own demand. Their inclination is to build infrastructure in order to stimulate growth and development, the idea being that they will grow into their systems. Japan, through the "Partnership for Quality Infrastructure,"[27] and the United States more recently through its Build Act (2018), along with multilateral institutions such as the World Bank, Asian Development Bank, and of course the Asian Infrastructure Investment Bank (AIIB) that Beijing founded in 2016, are bending in this direction and taking a more forward-leaning attitude toward infrastructure. But these organizations have cultures as well, and they are slow to change. This book addresses the issue of how China under Xi Jinping sees the development process, how questions about the wisdom of this approach trigger debates within the PRC itself, and the impact this approach has on other strategic and economic players in the region and beyond.

2. Does Beijing's export of HSR and conventional rail systems represent a Grand Strategy or is it reflective of an entrepreneurial PRC system going in several directions simultaneously? The strategic intent of Beijing's policy is to make China an economic hub for its vast periphery, provide connectivity nodes for military power projection, drive China's move up the value-added ladder, and increase its neighbors' dependence on the PRC. The Belt and Road Initiative (BRI) is the broad signboard under which these objectives are articulated and advanced. However, the individual projects making up the overall effort, and their successes and travails, reflect a much more dynamic system in which PRC state-owned enterprises (SOEs), various central bureaucracies, provinces, localities, and interest groups at home and abroad seek to use the overall banner of BRI to achieve their own parochial goals. Beijing can become saddled with projects lacking a sound development rationale, stuck with long-term money losers, and confronted with backlash by affected communities abroad. Concisely, there is a broad underlying national strategy undergirding BRI (explained in chapter 3), but the actual shape this strategy assumes in the course of implementation is indeterminate and its execution often haphazard, as chapters 4 and 6 demonstrate. It will take decades to assess the balance sheet of this overall undertaking. However, if even a significant fraction of the rail and other projects currently underway or contemplated are implemented soundly, the effects will be far-reaching.[28] Of course, the failures will also leave their own legacy.

3. How is strategic economic competition shaping the future? Since the first decade of the twenty-first century, China's rapid development and construction of HSR and conventional-speed systems (both at home and abroad) has given birth to a technology-forcing industry that has required the creation of sophisticated domestic and foreign supply chains, thereby driving China's entire industrial base forward. HSR may become to China what the Boeing Company has been to America in terms of both its pervasive influence in the domestic economy and as an export producer. In the March 2018 session of the National People's Congress (NPC), for instance, among key points in "The Report on the Work of the Government" was the following observation: "In high-speed rail, e-commerce, mobile payments and the sharing economy, China is leading the world."[29] HSR energizes China's move up the value-added ladder in many industries, with the PRC working feverishly to further improve its core HSR technology and develop super-fast magnetic-levitating and conventional trains that it hopes will travel upward of 370 miles per hour (nearly 600 kmph).

Equally important, the more the PRC gets export contracts early in the development process in various parts of the world, the more it will set the standards for subsequent projects and development. As Beijing explains, "the [BRI] Initiative will help *align* and coordinate the development strategies of the countries along the Belt and Road . . ." (emphasis added).[30] Getting Laos, currently with almost no rail built, to adopt the Chinese standard for its projects made it likely that Thailand will have to adopt the same standard if it wants to seamlessly connect to Laos. The building of domestic and foreign supply chains and setting standards increase Beijing's power in the global and regional economic, military, and diplomatic systems. Power exists when a country is able to tilt the international business and development playing fields in its direction—China is seeking to do just that.

These trends and their strategic implications have also energized Japan to compete with China on rail projects on the Indian subcontinent, in Southeast Asia, and elsewhere around the world.[31] Other countries such as France, Germany, Canada, and the Republic of Korea also are part of this international competitive dynamic. It is important that this international competition not lead to a race to the bottom in terms of environment, financing, and other standards.

There is another aspect to this geoeconomic competition. Beijing seeks to construct a regional system that will channel freight and passenger flows along a north-south axis, making the PRC the economic hub for

Southeast Asia. This would represent a huge step forward for China's economic dominance in a region where the PRC already is the largest import source for each of the ten ASEAN countries and a major export absorber for the region. Japan, India, and the United States are interested in creating an east-west counterbalancing flow of people and goods, linking together India, Myanmar, Laos, Cambodia, and Vietnam and funneling goods to the Pacific and Indian Oceans for maritime movement to Japan, the Pacific Basin, and elsewhere. This thinking is compatible with the vague, emerging "Indo-Pacific Strategy" that the United States began to articulate in 2017–2018. One way forward for the United States is to think in terms of what we call *balanced connectivity*. This approach implies accepting the utility of China's north-south efforts, as well as creating a more stable and balanced overall structure (network) by fashioning complementary east-west connectivity in Southeast Asia.

4. Is the PRC's industrial policy conducive to building an innovative and competitive economic system, and is it "fair"? Because the PRC built an entire domestic HSR network and globally competitive export industry with remarkable speed, this book speaks to fundamental controversies over industrial policy. Industrial policy is at the heart of the trade friction and broader economic friction between Washington and Beijing in the era of Donald Trump and Xi Jinping. In the realm of scholarly debate, Ling Chen, in her book *Manipulating Globalization*, asks under what conditions Beijing's attempts to use industrial policy to stimulate industrial innovation are effectively implemented locally.[32]

Arguably, in the HSR case we have an instance in which Beijing has identified a key emerging industry and technology, leveraged access to its domestic market to acquire foreign technology, focused resources on developing and adapting that technology, and used subsidies and provided cheap capital to create both domestic and foreign markets for these systems. At least superficially, the HSR example challenges the comfortable assumption that industrial policy and state intervention retard innovation and produce second-rate systems. Of course, there are other important considerations, not least the domestic and international debt implications.[33]

Industrial policy also raises other questions. What damage does Beijing do to relations with others in its attempts to push ahead with its industrial policy? What are the implications for economic "fairness" and a level playing field in international trade? Do the massive subsidies central to such a system represent unfair competition and/or reduce overall system efficiency? How long will Chinese citizens be willing to subsidize others who buy their products, whether they be steel or high-speed trains? Will China end up with industries that cannot compete outside an insulated bubble of protection and industrial favoritism? Beijing's "Made in China 2025" initiative and earlier efforts to identify strategic emerging industries, of which HSR is a stunning example, speak to this underlying debate.[34] China's rapid development of a domestic and export HSR industry, and a similar development of the civil nuclear power sector,[35] indicate that exceedingly rapid progress is achievable, though the damage to efficiency and the underlying global competitive system remain problematic.[36] This type of system is vulnerable to bad decisions made because of poor risk assessment. Failed projects affect borrowers and lenders alike, as well as ripple through the global financial system.

5. Can connectivity and a high degree of social control coexist? Beijing is betting its economic future on connectivity and external links to drive growth as its own domestic economic expansion slows. To foster this connectivity means facilitating cross-border flows of almost everything and reducing the friction costs of crossing international boundaries. However, the party-state in Beijing under Xi Jinping is, at the same time, trying to control politically relevant interconnections of all sorts, particularly cross-border connections. Big data, increased domestic security expenditures (which overtook external defense expenditures in 2009),[37] and new technology are being found and created in order to gain greater internal control. Consider the concept of "Internet Sovereignty." The question is, "Can the PRC efficiently connect regionally and globally, greatly accelerate the exchange of goods and people, foster innovation, and at the same time seek to control what information its citizens can access?" At the outset of "reform and opening" (*gaige kaifang*), Deng Xiaoping talked about the need to put up "screens" to keep ideological flies out as the windows of China opened to the world. On June 4, 1989, the bloodshed in Tiananmen Square demonstrated how hard that would be. This new world of international economic connectivity that China is building makes putting up screens yet more difficult.[38] Nonetheless, in his speech to the Nineteenth Party Congress in October 2017, Xi Jinping said that China did have a successful model to share with others, in which a high degree of sociopolitical control, innovation, and high growth all were compatible objectives. As he put it, "With this we have seen a further rise in China's international influence, ability to inspire, and power to shape; and China has made great new contributions to global peace and development."[39]

This study of the development of HSR, therefore, occurs against a backdrop of issues much broader than simply transportation and construction contracts, important as they are. This volume is relevant to future industrial competitiveness, standards setting in emerging industries, shaping development approaches globally, the PRC's prospects for domestic stability, and maintaining strategic balance in an increasingly central and dynamic part of the world. Militarily, the development of interconnecting rail, highway, airline, pipeline, and port infrastructure built and financed by Beijing will provide China new bases of power projection, the likes of which it has never before possessed. For China's southern neighbors, the issue is how they can extract the benefits from these developments without sacrificing too much autonomy. For China a core issue is whether its appetite for risk is going to exceed its capacity to absorb risk.

Having identified several backdrops against which this research assumes broader significance, which lines of social science inquiry does this study draw upon for inspiration and insight, and to which areas of inquiry does it contribute?

Core Questions for Social Science

How should we understand power and Chinese power? There is a vast literature on the power of nations, organizations, groups, and individuals. Theorists and practitioners have written about power from earliest times, concerned with its types, origins, acquisition, exercise, limitations, and consequences. Plato, Confucius, Aristotle, Sun Tzu, Machiavelli, Mao Zedong, and contemporary social scientists such as Max Weber, John Mearsheimer, Kenneth Waltz, Joseph Nye, Amitai Etzioni, Robert Dahl, Edward Banfield, Michael Mann, and Michael Barnett and Raymond Duvall, among others, have contributed to this rich literature. In *The Three Faces of Chinese Power: Might, Money, and Minds,* David Lampton described power in a manner that serves the purposes of this volume.

> Exercising power is to be distinguished from merely having an impact. A mindless brute has impact, but the exercise of power involves the purposeful use of resources to achieve goals efficiently . . . A powerful nation is one that authoritatively sets its own agenda as well as the international agenda over a broad range of issues, wins support for (or compliance with) its policies both internally and externally, influences the implementation process so that there is a high degree of correspondence between initial intentions and actual outcomes, and desists from pursuing policies that prove ineffective or counterproductive.[40]

In the context of China's rail connectivity building effort, this definition requires several questions be addressed: How much of the connectivity vision outlined above will the PRC, in fact, be able to achieve through
sequential negotiations (chapter 5) with often-skeptical neighbors (chapters 4 and 7)? Can Beijing win over (or sideline) other skeptical powers
(Japan, India, and the United States, for example)? Is it possible for Beijing to sustain the growing resource requirements of its external commitments, or, will its citizens demand a greater share of wealth for themselves
(chapters 3 and 8)? Will China's firms and government at various levels
coherently implement policies across so many borders, adapt to the varied conditions in the seven transit countries, and learn from mistakes
(chapter 6)? What domestic political and bureaucratic struggles must be
resolved within and between the PRC and its partner countries to realize
these undertakings? Simply put, can China do it? What does all this tell
us about Chinese power and about power more broadly?

As impressive and daunting as the physical engineering for these
projects is, the difficulty of getting so many national and local actors
even remotely on the same page politically is a still bigger challenge, not
least because China and its neighbors have a checkered history together.
While the progress of the overall set of projects described above has
been significant and even surprising thus far, they are not destined to
succeed. Smaller rail schemes have failed for Beijing elsewhere in the
world. Should large chunks of this vision fail to materialize or prove
value-subtracting over the long haul, the causes of these setbacks will
prove as interesting and important as the causes of success.

The PRC has sharp elbows as a power; its people are entrepreneurial
and energetic. The citizens of countries south of China know what it
means to be pushed around by the Middle Kingdom. This observation
brings us to another major issue of concern to international relations
research. How do small nations on the periphery of much larger and
more powerful ones protect their interests and sometimes even manage
to manipulate big powers? To what degree do small and medium nations
have agency in their dealings with big, strong nations?

How do small states deal with big, powerful states? In sixteenth-century
Florence, Italy, Niccolò Machiavelli addressed this generic problem in
the practical guidance he offered his prince, Lorenzo De' Medici, concerning how to maintain domestic political power and survive when surrounded by predatory principalities.[41] In China about two centuries earlier, Lo Kuan-chung (Luo Guanzhong) wrote about the Three Kingdoms

period (AD 220–280),[42] recounting how three states (Wei, Shu, and Wu) vied for dominance in a period of disorder. In recent history, the leaders of two Asian states important to the story of this volume—Lee Kuan Yew of Singapore and Tun Dr. Mahathir Mohamad in Malaysia—described in their autobiographies how they balanced between an assertive China and more distant powers (not least the United States) to maintain their young nations' degrees of freedom.[43] The point is, throughout history small states and societies have been concerned with survival, sometimes even aspiring to achieve prosperity, while flanked by stronger neighbors who did not have their best interests at heart.

Contemporary international relations scholarship is no less concerned with this issue of how small states deal with stronger powers in the interstate system. Though this book focuses on one set of undertakings, building rail connectivity between one overwhelmingly large country and several smaller neighboring nations, it is a concrete example of this larger challenge. Social science inquiry on the topic of asymmetric power relations is highly germane to these practical and theoretical concerns. This literature asks, How is it that smaller states seek to maintain freedom to maneuver, maximize benefits, and minimize risks when dealing with larger, often assertive states?

A central contributor to this line of inquiry has been Brantly Womack and his book *Asymmetry and International Relationships*.[44] Among many studies, one that speaks directly to power asymmetry and the behavior of small and medium states is Andrew Mertha's book on China's foreign assistance relationship with Cambodia's Khmer Rouge.[45] Mertha demonstrates how in the late 1970s a desperately poor and in many ways dependent Cambodian leadership managed to resist forms of assistance from Beijing that would have compromised its freedom and created dangerous dependencies.

Broader, more theoretical studies, most importantly the works of Kenneth Waltz and Stephen Walt, identify the cooperation and balancing strategies available to small states. Smaller bandwagoners can (in effect) throw up their hands and join with the stronger actor (or threat) to gain security, albeit at the cost of losing autonomy. Alternatively, the weaker player can align with other powers in the international system to balance a stronger threat, thereby securing some measure of protection.[46] Along this line of theorizing and comparative analysis, several scholars have pointed to a third approach heavily employed in Southeast Asia—"hedging."[47] Hedging involves the smaller, weaker party adopting strategies that seek to achieve benefits from the stronger party, on the one hand, while preparing for worst-case self-defense contingencies on the other hand.[48] The hedging approach is the default setting for Southeast Asian nations, with some hedges heavier than others.[49] In the final analysis, some weaker states lean more heavily toward not agitating Beijing, while some employ a harder balancing approach, and still others unapologetically hedge. Nations can change their foreign policy mix over time in response to changing domestic and external circumstances.

In short, China's neighbors want reassurance from, and beneficial ties to, the PRC, but they are committed to guarding against intimidation by building fallback arrangements with others. This almost schizophrenic Southeast Asian posture toward the PRC is evident in almost every chapter to follow, most notably chapters 4–8.

What is evident in these interactions between China and its Southeast Asian neighbors is that smaller, weaker states have agency. Constructivists emphasize how states are socialized into conforming to a set of norms, rules, and behavior. For instance, Alastair Iain Johnston has noted that as a result of engagement initiated by the much smaller states of ASEAN, post-Mao China has been socialized into international regimes and multilateral organizations.[50] Big states are also concerned about whether they are "socially acceptable."[51] Alice Ba notes that for states to lead, there must be followers. This means that leading states need acceptance as such.[52] In his work on hierarchy in international relations, David A. Lake emphasizes that hegemons often restrain their behavior toward smaller states because they need to gain goodwill, win friends, and influence others.[53]

That smaller and weaker states can exercise such influence on big powers often results from the fact that they pose little threat. Such asymmetrical relations give smaller states maneuvering space vis-à-vis larger powers, in contrast to realist approaches that tend to devalue the role of secondary states. Smaller states are able to resist and modify the actions of larger powers, and even sometimes shape the policies of these more powerful actors.

How does the PRC negotiate in complex games? Another expansive area of inquiry germane to the literature on Chinese foreign policy concerns PRC negotiating strategies and tactics (chapter 5). Most of the research on Chinese negotiating strategy has concerned China's modus operandi in *bilateral,* single-issue negotiations.[54] Indeed, much of the literature focuses on Beijing's negotiating record and practice with just one major actor, the United States.[55] This book, however, addresses an open-ended sequence of negotiations concerning one main issue, in which earlier rounds with one national interlocutor (i.e., Laos or Indonesia) create the context for subsequent negotiations with the next state (i.e., Thailand or Malaysia). To further complicate matters, in the final analysis the outcomes of the series of individual negotiations must result in one integrated system.

Prior successful negotiations may increase the odds of reaching agreement with subsequent parties—a domino effect (see chapter 5). For example, once Laos reached agreement with Beijing in 2016 to extend the Central Line to the Thai border, this made the allure of reaching agreement with Beijing greater for Bangkok, though uncertainties remained. From Beijing's perspective, given the investment of time and money to get to the Lao-Thai border, the economic incentive to reach a deal with Thailand accordingly became greater. Yet when Indonesia won relatively favorable financial terms from Beijing to build a railroad from Jakarta to Bandung, Thailand demanded equal or better terms from Beijing for the Central Line through its territory. Similarly, when China agreed with Indonesia not to require sovereign guarantees for its financing, Japan subsequently loosened up its financing approach as seen in its push to (successfully) obtain a rail contract with India.[56] This study illuminates China's bargaining behavior in the context of overlapping negotiations with a great number of players unfolding over a protracted period, with each outcome shaping subsequent negotiations, often in unforeseen ways.

What is the relationship between domestic and foreign policy behavior? Robert Putnam, in his classic piece on two-level games, explains how a nation's behavior in the international arena reflects domestic political and constitutional calculations and, reciprocally, how the international arena shapes domestic politics in individual nations.[57] Throughout *Rivers of Iron*, one sees the PRC's fragmented authoritarian system affecting its external behavior—with the right hand often not knowing what the left is doing.[58] Since his assumption of power in 2012–13, Xi Jinping's drive to consolidate control represents his gargantuan effort to enhance coordination in a fragmented system that is not fully responsive to his will.

Many entities in China (central bureaucracies, localities, and public and private enterprises) compete for central funding, vie to dump excess inventories abroad, and compete for contracts. This dynamic often results in PRC firms engaging in cutthroat competition, over-promising foreign customers, and subsequently underperforming on projects. Several scholars, including Czeslaw Tubilewicz and Kanishka Jayasuriya, along with Selina Ho, argue that with respect to China's involvement in the entire Mekong River Basin set of projects (including railroad development), Yunnan Province has played a central role.[59] Tubilewicz and Jayasuriya also argue that a key driver has been a "state capital and national-subnational alliance."[60] Former Australian Ambassador to China Geoff Raby explains: "It [attaching projects to the BRI brand] is a way within the system people can get brownie points and get projects approved."[61] Thus, the behavior of Chinese actors abroad derives from the character, opportunities, and necessities of their domestic system (chapter 3). A central fact is that subnational actors such as local bureaucrats have agency— they build local, national, and sometimes international coalitions that reflect their resources, objectives, interests, and preexistent conditions, sometimes with passing regard for central intentions.[62]

Likewise, Southeast Asian nations' behaviors toward China must be understood in the context of varied domestic dynamics in each of the relevant nations, as highlighted in chapters 4–7. For instance, varying land acquisition policies, practices, and conditions in Thailand and Malaysia help account for why railroad politics in these two settings are poles apart, requiring completely different PRC playbooks as Beijing and its agents move between countries to negotiate deals. In Malaysia and Indonesia, dealing with powerful local authorities is a major consideration, whereas in Thailand, the national government and Thai Rail Authority are crucial allies if Beijing wants to move forward.

In Chinese domestic politics (chapter 3) the PRC's growing commitments to large-scale projects in Southeast Asia (and elsewhere) increasingly conflict with Chinese popular sentiment that resents such huge expenditures abroad. Chinese bankers have also warned about the high risk inherent in loans provided for some projects. Consequently, Beijing increasingly seeks to drive ever more advantageous deals with its potential partners to keep growing domestic resentment at bay. Predictably, political forces in Southeast Asian partner countries resent what they see as the PRC's strong-arm tactics and sometimes onerous terms. Moreover, in several countries where Beijing has worked on HSR and conventional-speed rail projects, their leaders have had to be careful to avoid the charge of compromising sovereignty in their quest to get Beijing involved in building badly needed infrastructure. Some of these leaders, such as former Prime Minister Najib Razak in Malaysia, ultimately failed in this endeavor, being portrayed at home as a handmaid to China after Beijing came to his rescue to bail out the troubled state fund 1MDB (discussed in chapter 4). This is one of the reasons that led to the political resurrection of Mahathir in mid-2018. The new prime minister immediately put some of the projects agreed to by Najib and underway (or contemplated) with China on hold in order to solidify national finances and drive a harder bargain with Beijing, thereby boosting his domestic legitimacy.

In the past, some of Beijing's initial negotiating positions have been extreme with respect to the terms proposed to neighbors (e.g., Thailand and Laos) for financing and development rights.[63] These muscular negotiating positions have their origin in the coalition politics necessary to win support within the PRC, as well as a healthy dose of greed. Finally, China's southern neighbors are themselves industrializing to various degrees. While they see advantages in participating in the Chinese economic juggernaut, at the same time they fear their local economies will be overwhelmed by a tsunami of products flowing into their domestic markets from the PRC. This fear is very strong in Vietnam in particular, as indicated by the public protests in early 2018 resulting from Hanoi's decision to allow 99-year leases on concessions granted to foreign investors, many of whom are Chinese. How ably will Beijing address these concerns?

Questions of single system and cross-system policy implementation. In the 1970s and 1980s, political scientists seriously addressed the challenge of "policy implementation" around the world, including in China.[64] They sought explanations for why, in almost all systems irrespective of political type, there existed a wide gap between the initial intentions of central government policy formulators and the subsequent results once policy had been implemented in specific localities. Jeffrey Pressman and Aaron Wildavsky identified the core challenge as "the complexity of joint action,"[65] that is, the addition of each political actor to an implementation process reduces the probability that policy implementation will move forward unscathed. In complex national systems, many players are involved in each undertaking; it does not take the addition of many actors to dramatically reduce the correspondence between intention and outcome. As Barry Naughton explained, there is an "implementation bias" in which players at every level of a system (in this case, in China, the transit countries, and their subordinate administrative and territorial units) deflect policy in the direction of their own interests. As policy directives move downward in complex systems, this produces cumulative distortions, delays, or failures of policy.[66]

It is very hard to move policies—and therefore projects—through any *single* national system, as these earlier studies uniformly indicate. In the age of globalization, where complex programs such as infrastructure construction span several national systems (in this case, eight), the implementation problem is much more difficult. In fact, it is a small miracle that anything happens amidst the problems, distortions, and missteps that hobble the process.

In this volume, we investigate a rolling set of developments rather than choosing one story with a clear beginning and a definitive ending. Studies about policy implementation and negotiation generally start with a clear government decision to undertake a single, discrete project, such as a dam or a particular civilian nuclear power plant. The research then follows the story of that single undertaking through to completion ("process tracing"), looking for systematic and idiosyncratic factors affecting the eventual outcome. There is a beginning and a clear conclusion.

This volume breaks innovative ground, inasmuch as it starts with a guiding vision, a broad intention to enhance connectivity, not a single decision. It traces the evolution of this vision and its implementation, recognizing that the undertaking is open-ended, and that each prior decision nudges the overall trajectory along an ever-adjusting path. This vision is an unfolding process in its early stages. Part of the complexity of analyzing this undertaking is that each of the eight parties who are a part of this vision (not to mention international organizations and powers in the larger international system) shares the broad goal of connectivity, while each gives specificity to that aspiration in the process of its own unfolding domestic politics, international negotiations, and policy implementation. This circumstance reflects the nature of both politics and policy making, within and between nations. Policy making is a dynamic process in which goals shift and prior outcomes set the stage for later directions; negotiation often occurs amidst policy implementation, and the process may never come to a clear-cut conclusion.

David Lampton was doing research in 1982 in the Yangzi River Valley. Upon concluding his research, he was given a March 1959 (Great Leap Forward–era) map drawn up by the Yangzi River Valley Planning Commission (*Chang Jiang Liuyu Guihua Bangongshi*), graphically displaying ongoing and contemplated projects in the river basin that drains one-third of China (dams, diversion areas, canals, and irrigation projects). Looking back at that map drafted more than six decades ago (as of this writing), it is staggering how much had been built by the late 2010s, though projects were not built in the order initially contemplated, many underwent significant design or specification changes, costs often went through the roof, and some simply failed in their basic mission. The rail vision studied here is an analogous undertaking, except that it is international in scope and therefore more complex still. The rail maps outlining today's vague aspirations may very well become some version of reality thirty or more years in the future.

In short, this is an unusual policy study, and herein lies its value. This study does not simplify reality to such an extent that the quest to define a discrete, completed case prevents us from understanding the nature of the actual process involved in cross-national policy implementation of enormous projects. Even partial completion of the overall vision will have transformative effects.

RESEARCH FOUNDATIONS

The research for this book presented numerous challenges. The emerging rail network that is the subject of this book potentially embraces eight sovereign countries and innumerable local jurisdictions of various degrees of autonomy ranging from a sultanates in Malaysia to the city-state of Singapore, and even encompasses ungoverned areas in the outlying border regions of several countries. Planning travel in parts of several of the countries in Southeast Asia today still elicits warnings about personal risk when visiting some of the remote regions traversed by the proposed lines; Cambodia, Thailand, and Myanmar all have such marginally governed regions. The design, planning, and building of overall connectivity in the region also involves international multilateral organizations such as the World Bank (WB), Asian Development Bank (ADB), ASEAN, and organizational offshoots. Many subregional and special-purpose cross-national organizations are involved, such as the Greater Mekong Subregion (GMS) program involving Yunnan Province and the Guangxi Zhuang Autonomous Region, with the ADB playing a coordinating role,[67] and the US government-led Lower Mekong Initiative. Also, there are both private and government corporations and commercial entities from the eight directly involved nations and from all over the world, as well as national and international nongovernmental organizations. Our small multinational research team has had a challenging task given the number of actors and the sprawling geographical and organizational ground covered. In understanding and assessing infrastructure projects, there is no substitute for researchers knowing the physical, organizational, and human elements on the ground. It is not until a scholar actually sees all such elements of an undertaking that one begins to appreciate the challenges. Throughout this huge and diverse region there are unstable geological, social, and political structures shaping development and implementation of these projects at every stage.

Even before landing on the ground to begin field research, the job of preparing for what our team would see required extensive documentary research. An indispensable precondition for effective interviewing is to know as much as possible about the subject beforehand.[68] Prior knowledge is essential to establish credibility with subjects/interviewees, to economize on scarce time, and to enable one to fill in the blanks and assess the accuracy of the documentary record through on-the-ground visits. To prepare, we scoured available documentation (such as the local press in each country), government and international organization documents, and international commentary on the progress and problems of these efforts by the Chinese (and others) to construct these projects. This volume's coauthors speak several of the languages of the region, and in the cases of Thailand, Vietnam, and Laos we had local experts accompany us into the field. Two of this volume's authors live in the region (Singapore and Malaysia), bringing to this project the perspective of people very much affected by the unfolding effort(s).

Once we had the basic documentary resources under control, we began a multiyear research effort involving field trips and interviews—carried out singly and together as two- and three-person teams—speaking with various geographic, corporate, societal, multilateral, and government actors throughout all eight countries and beyond, as explained in detail in the acknowledgements section of this book. Our team conducted field trips to many project sites and national capitals in Southeast Asia. Some locations that we visited included the East Coast Rail Link (ECRL) in Malaysia, the Malacca Gateway project south of Kuala Lumpur, the entire lengths of the prospective rail lines in Thailand and Laos, and major projects in Cambodia. Our most extensive on-the-ground interactions and exposures were in China (Beijing, Yunnan, and Sichuan), Laos, Thailand, Singapore, Malaysia, and Vietnam, with one trip each to Myanmar and Cambodia. In Cambodia we visited Sihanoukville, where Japan has financed port development and modernization and the Chinese-invested Special Economic Zone outside the city center, a project involving many countries, notably China, the Republic of Korea, and Japan. Our interaction with international organizations in Southeast Asian countries was in the context of meetings with individual country representatives rather than administrators at their regional or global headquarters. Altogether, our research team spoke with hundreds of persons in well over 150 organizations (many "interviews" involved groups of people). Some interviews involved extensive discussions, while others were less exhaustive. We conducted some interviews in isolated field locations with single individuals (such as station masters in Thailand), and many other interviews took place in urban centers with government, corporate, think-tank, and educational leaders or entities. Quite simply, this project could not have been undertaken by a solo researcher either in terms of physical capacity or breadth of knowledge. This has been a team effort in the deepest sense of the word.

Looking critically at the interview sources as a whole, all interviewees (and interviewers) have blind spots or limitations stemming from their particular vantage point and life experiences. This is unsurprising, given the large number of actors playing a role or having a stake in the future of these multifaceted and enormous undertakings. The rail projects of interest here involved billions of dollars and took shape through rolling negotiations as our team was conducting interviews. A lot was at stake. Many interviewees were constrained, wanting to preserve every negotiating advantage they could for their organizations and countries. Prudence required not releasing information that might undermine their own bargaining positions. Beyond the money, jobs, and development gains at stake, constraints derived from the fact that "interviews" often occurred with many people in the room. In the more authoritarian systems in which we conducted research, regimes sometimes permitted their experts to interact with us only when other compatriots were present, both for reasons of internal security and to expose as many of their people to the conversation as possible. This circumstance created its own boundaries of the permissible for everyone involved, including interviewers. On the other hand, even in big settings people go off script.

A further consideration was that several of the nations had military or authoritarian regimes that were relatively circumspect in dealing with foreigners in all settings. In Myanmar, for instance, we had access to civilians but not the underlying military governing structure. In Thailand this was true as well, except in one case. For their part, companies did not want to divulge or erode their commercial positions and were often reluctant to discuss any delicate challenges they faced. Entities such as the China Development Bank (CDB) and the Export-Import Bank of China (Exim Bank) are policy arms of the PRC government, creating obvious constraints. More broadly, both within and outside

China, state-owned and controlled enterprises further blur the distinction between government and market-based enterprises.

With respect to international multilateral organizations, interviewing their staff who consider themselves international civil servants (rising above loyalty to a particular country) was in some ways easier than interviewing either government or business respondents. Nonetheless, their need to be fair and avoid dragging their organization into controversy meant that they often were reluctant to wade into tendentious issues. As to nongovernmental and civil society organizations, they always are walking on thin ice in most of these countries, so they need to be cautious. Elected or appointed officials, whether executive or legislative, desire reappointment or election and hence are reluctant to offend superiors or constituents. This all adds up to the fact that in this type of research, rarely is the interviewer in a neutral, entirely objective, or transparent setting.

In short, our team endeavored to discern the overall picture from the insights provided by a myriad of written and human sources. Each of our respondents may have seen only a small part of the overall picture or were more or less reluctant to share what they did know. Thus, we sought to synthesize fragmentary information as best we could. In the end, a fairly fine-grained picture emerges from this wide-ranging research.

BOOK OUTLINE

The architecture of this book is unembroidered. Following this introduction, chapter 2 addresses the long-gestating idea of rail connectivity between China and Southeast Asia (the Pan-Asia Railway idea), and the recent development of a regional vision that Southeast Asia could embrace as its own, and to which China was in a position to contribute, if not energize. We also provide background on Beijing's experience in developing HSR technology, constructing its own domestic HSR system, and constructing rail systems outside of China. Chapter 2 provides varied contexts for understanding where China is today and where it is headed in building a Pan-Asia Railway.

Chapter 3 is about domestic politics in the PRC with respect to rail development abroad, focusing on the drivers of this international effort, the politics of securing and implementing projects, and debates over future policies. Succinctly, this chapter describes the grand conceptual and interest group–motivated debate that the Pan-Asia Railway vision has unleashed in China itself. Chapter 3 locates China's behavior toward its neighbors and these projects in the nature and operation of the Chinese political system.

Chapter 4 then analyzes the domestic politics in the partner countries that unfolds as each of the Southeast Asian neighbors considers and shapes the distinctive relationship it wishes to establish within the grand vision. This chapter addresses how each country's developmental needs interact with its ruling elites' domestic political calculations, their need for legitimation, and special interests at various levels. These needs, in turn, lead the seven Southeast Asian national governments to *react variably* to China's rail proposals. Competing groups either emphasize benefits or costs and risks, all in the service of attempting to acquire or defend power at home. Throughout the book, but in this chapter especially, what comes through is just how sensitive China's involvement in these countries is and how, even in those nations most dependent on Beijing (such as Laos and Cambodia), PRC activities are very controversial. Beijing needs political acumen as well as to learn from history and listen carefully today, in order to make these relationships work. Political dexterity in Beijing is needed and not always evident.

Chapter 5 assesses the general character and specifics of the PRC's negotiations with its neighbors on this issue, analyzing how and why they have been far more successful and smooth with some countries than others. This discussion adds to a rich literature on PRC bilateral negotiating strategy, by enlarging consideration to an interconnected sequence of multilateral and bilateral negotiations over an extended period. Overall, as China's commitments have grown over time, internal pressures are pushing Beijing to become more discriminating in its commitments and more exacting in its negotiations.

Chapter 6 addresses the challenges of policy implementation. We pay particular attention to the political, financial, sociocultural, and technical dimensions, seeking to examine how clusters of issues arise in the course of implementation and how initial agreement on a project is only the first step in a long, arduous journey toward completion. The first stretch of the Central Line is under construction in Laos, and Thailand is moving haltingly forward, meaning that connectivity from Kunming to Bangkok is in sight, albeit not absolutely certain. And although the initial agreement has been deferred in the case of the Singapore to Kuala Lumpur link, our team anticipates that this line will materialize within a decade or so.

Chapter 7 deals with international dynamics, tracing and assessing how the interplay of geoeconomic and geopolitical factors shape the evolving patterns of Southeast Asia–China engagement on rail connectivity projects. In the region, while geoeconomics was the driving force in the 1990s and first decade of the twenty-first century, as we moved into the second decade, geopolitics and strategic concerns have risen in importance for all parties. These projects, with their mix of economic, diplomatic, and military rationales, have bearing on state-to-state competition and on competition among global business enterprises. Assuming that considerable rail connectivity is established among China and its neighbors, this will dramatically change the region's competitive landscape— diplomatically, militarily, and economically. The United States, Japan, India, and others cannot remain indifferent to these commercially and strategically significant developments, and they are beginning to react.

Finally, chapter 8 assesses what this set of actual and prospective projects means for China, the region, and the world. What does this study tell us about PRC power and China's ability to sustain internal support for a very ambitious effort over a prolonged period? What does it tell us about the capacity of China's smaller neighbors to shape their own destinies? Among key issues in this respect are the burdens that massive infrastructure projects may heap on countries with low carrying capacity.[69] Looking beyond the challenges of this mammoth undertaking, we also must consider its transformative potential, if implemented with reasonable intelligence and sensitivity over the coming decades. America and like-minded countries should strive to create balanced connectivity. This constructive approach would have positive impacts that reverberate far beyond the region.

CHAPTER 2

The Grand Vision

China is changing from a country exporting clothes, shoes,
and hats to one exporting high-speed trains.[1]
—China Daily, October 26, 2015

A prominent and influential Chinese social scientist was waxing eloquent
in a November 2015 interview, explaining his thinking that there are two
locomotives of the global economy—China and the United States. China,
he argued, had 20 million companies and they invested at home, and
increasingly abroad. "Chinese move. Moving very rapidly . . . They used
to say that all roads lead to Rome. Rome had 18,000 [actually 80,000]
kilometers of roads. Nowadays every road leads to China in an economic
sense. Railroads carry one-quarter of our passengers now."[2]

Though it is not yet true that all economic roads lead to China (and
this somewhat presumptuous view of China's ascent is under attack in
China, as we will see in chapter 3), PRC leaders are endeavoring to
make this a reality. Its companies and localities grasp at every economic
opportunity. This chapter provides the context and background for this
vision as it pertains to Southeast Asia—an entrepreneurial China connected by rail to seven of its southern neighbors, terminating in the city-
state island of Singapore. Progress on this huge project has been genuine
since 2013, when Chinese President Xi Jinping first articulated what has
become known as the Belt and Road Initiative (BRI), or *yi dai yi lu* in
Chinese. Where did this vision come from and what are its dimensions?
How did the PRC acquire the technology, build the industry, and lay
the domestic high-speed rail system that makes realization of this vision
of going far beyond China's borders possible? The background history
recounted in this chapter provides needed perspective, making it clear

that the vision of interconnectivity is not an alien one imposed by a powerhouse on its passive neighbors. The railroad projects under construction and in the planning stages could not have happened without dramatic economic and technological development in the PRC, nor without the opportunities provided by great economic and social development in Southeast Asia in the last four decades. Southeast Asians themselves have been planning for connectivity for a long time, as we see in this chapter and again in chapter 7. History, which has brought us to a moment of opportunity and risk for China and its neighbors, is thus vital to take into account.

EARLY RAIL DEVELOPMENT IN SOUTHEAST ASIA

The twenty-first-century vision of railroads binding China to its immediate neighbors in South and Southeast Asia can be traced back to the dreams and interests of British and French colonialists in the region.[3] In the late nineteenth and early twentieth centuries, the British in India, Burma, and the Malay Peninsula,[4] and the French in Indochina, sought to secure economic and strategic advantage by developing both East-West connectivity (e.g., between Burma and Siam) and connections to China's southwest. The immediate goal in China was Yunnan Province, since it bordered many of these colonies, but Sichuan Province, Yunnan's neighbor, was the ultimate prize—large, populous, China's breadbasket and a place with great, unexploited potential. With coastal China already extensively penetrated by more than a few big powers (including themselves) ensconced in coastal treaty ports, Britain and France had direct access to potentially lucrative inland parts of China by approaching the Middle Kingdom from their colonial perches to the south and coming up through China's soft underbelly. The Red River Valley, connecting Yunnan Province to Vietnam, is a natural north-to-south transportation corridor, thus creating an opportunity for the French to build north-south economic links to isolated southwestern China. With the completion of the French Railway in 1910, which connected Kunming, Hanoi, and Haiphong, Yunnan was linked by rail to Vietnam well before it was connected to the rest of China.[5] Indeed, the Chengdu to Kunming line within China itself was started only in 1958 and completed in 1970.

By the beginning of the twentieth century, with China's defeat in the Sino-Japanese War (1894–95), the ongoing rot of the Qing Dynasty, and the suppression of the Boxer Rebellion (1899–1901) by the punitive Eight-Power Expeditionary Force, China was mortally wounded.

The Qing Dynasty granted 12,000 km of railroad concessions to various powers between 1895 and 1901.[6] This was during the first age of railroads; the twenty-first century is the second age.[7]

Foretelling twenty-first-century debates over railroad development linking China and Southeast Asia, the European colonial authorities pushing for Southeast Asian rail construction in the late nineteenth and early twentieth centuries had to explain to their skeptical domestic audiences how a decision to invest in these proposed projects was wise in light of the costs and the political, strategic, and economic risks. Yunnan and Sichuan Provinces, though rich in potential, were, in fact, extremely poor and undeveloped. Huge investment and massive engineering would be required to traverse vast, rough terrain with little prospect of short or even medium-term economic returns. British and French citizens (and politicians) asked whether or not these were wasteful colonial vanity projects.

Parenthetically, it is worth observing that Laos was so poor that the French never seriously contemplated building a rail route there, and to this day the poor, landlocked, mountainous country has virtually no rail line (beyond about 3.5 km on the north bank of the Mekong River). As one Lao Foreign Ministry employee explained to our research team, "During the French colonial time, we only had one kilometer of railroad. The French saw Laos as a small country. Not profitable for them . . . That is why there is a need but also it is challenging for us to build the train."[8]

With respect to historical rail development in Vietnam, when short-term economic rationales for big undertakings failed to persuade skeptics, the railroad promoters used the long-term development argument. As Jean-François Rousseau explains, the French governor-general in Indochina in the late 1800s, Paul Doumer, argued (to his doubtful countrymen in Paris) that "civilization follows the locomotive." Doumer pointed to the positive developmental effects railroad construction had produced on France itself, in the United States (multiplying American wealth "ten times"), and in Australia.[9] He argued that rail development would have similar positive economic and cultural impacts in Indochina. As it happened, Doumer and his fellow rail promoters also found powerful political allies in Paris, not least the French steelmakers who needed an outlet for their excess output—an interest that also drives powerful economic interests in today's PRC. Grandiose plans abroad can become ways to infuse vitality into anemic industries at home.

Reflecting on the problems of implementing nineteenth- and early twentieth-century projects in the same region provides essential perspective for all of the implementation problems being encountered in current efforts (discussed in chapter 6). In late 1898 the initial segment of railroad from Haiphong to the Chinese border at Lao Cai (in what is today Vietnam) was approved, but a series of problems and debates continually intruded even as construction proceeded. The main issues included political unrest in parts of the terrain through which the rail line would pass; financing problems of all description, including private financiers wanting government-guaranteed loans; unanticipated engineering and construction challenges in turn multiplying costs; and issues of long-term ownership. Additionally, there was the challenge of how to use the Indochina portion of the railroad to leverage capital for the future section of the railroad running from the Chinese border with Indochina to Kunming. Finally, there was the very real human cost of the construction itself—tragically, somewhere between 12,000 and 24,000 "coolies" (mostly from China) perished in the construction effort, along with 44 of the 929 European personnel.[10] Selda Öztürk reports that death and disease took a massive toll on workers recruited from Canton (Guangzhou), with only seven of the initial eight hundred recruits even getting to the construction site of Lao Cai. The French representatives of the railroad company referred to them as "waste population" from Canton.[11] The records count to the last individual each European who perished, while history only reveals a sickeningly broad range of Asian laborers who died in the construction. Setting these tragic human costs aside, these cumulative challenges slowed things down and drove the material costs beyond projections.

Turning to actual results of this effort, "The Indochina-Yunnan Railway was a financial bottomless pit,"[12] not measuring up to projections in terms of freight volumes, revenues, or strategic benefits, except on the Haiphong-Hanoi rail segment.[13]

On a more positive note, the French colonialists did the hard work of identifying a feasible route between Southeast Asia and China and built something that became an engineering marvel of its age. Many decades later, transport plans and projects still build upon this early engineering legacy. The Long Bien River Bridge crossing the Red River in Hanoi, for example, remains an engineering triumph as well as a very aesthetically pleasing structure that North Vietnam managed to keep marginally operational throughout the war against the United States, despite persistent and heavy American aerial bombardment in the 1960s and 1970s.

Rousseau suggests that a powerful domestic coalition in France was the political foundation for these early colonial rail projects. Politicians built domestic support by promising jobs and profits from abroad; colonial country construction firms were, in effect, given cost-plus contracts. Private and state banks were initially reluctant to lend (in the absence of sovereign guarantees), seeing no way the project could generate the necessary returns. And ultimately taxpayers got stuck with the guarantees, but the builders prospered. Then too there was nationalism, justifying costly projects using the currency of national and civilizational greatness— France's *mission civilisatrice, la grandeur de la France.* In American civilizational discourse a resonant idea was "Manifest Destiny." And in twenty-first-century China, the echo of such calls is heard in the phrases "The China Dream" (*Zhongguo Meng*) and Xi Jinping's signature calls to greatness, "the rejuvenation of the great Chinese nation" and "community of common destiny," the attainment of which will be marked by the ever-wider international currency of the so-called China model of development. In short, many political dynamics evident in the late nineteenth and early twentieth centuries are at work in the greatly changed context of the twenty-first century—only now the Chinese, not the Western colonial powers, are driving the train, literally and figuratively.

JAPAN AND ITS IMPERIAL MISADVENTURES

The second incarnation of a pan-Asian railroad was born of necessity and involved Japan. As we will explain in chapters 4, 5, and 7, Japan is now seeking to play a major role in the rail development that is the topic of this book, for both strategic and economic reasons. Today's efforts, however, were preceded by its ultimately unsuccessful efforts seven decades ago.

By late 1943 to early 1944, as World War II dragged on in the Pacific, Tokyo was having trouble safely using the shipping routes extending from its home islands to Southeast Asia, because US naval forces were sinking its ships at an unsustainable rate—the rising sun's merchant marine fleet was reduced to about three-quarters of its prewar size.[14] Japan sought to bypass the maritime dangers by building a railroad line that would extend from Manchuria to Rangoon and on to Singapore, traversing China from north to south, proceeding across the northern tier of Southeast Asia, then down the Malay Peninsula, and eventually reaching Singapore.

From April to December 1944, Tokyo launched Operation *Ichi-go,* a massive assault on central, southern, and southwestern China designed to clear and secure the path for this railroad and, in the process of combat, cut off Allied supplies reaching Chiang Kai-shek's embattled forces in southwestern China.[15] Major targets were US-Nationalist airfields in southern China. Japan also had a large number of troops dug in fighting the British and Americans in Burma.[16]

Ultimately, the bloody battles in Burma that sapped Japan's energies and Tokyo's huge losses during *Ichi-go* itself, the fact that Chiang Kai-shek was able to sustain his battered forces with US assistance in southwestern China, General MacArthur's ability to regain bases in the Philippines from which to attack Japan directly, and the collapse of Germany in mid-1945, which freed the Allies to focus on Japan alone, all combined to foil *Ichi-go* and the rail plan. Indeed, it would be a long time before the vision of a Pan-Asia Railway could again be seriously contemplated.

SOUTHEAST ASIAN POST–WORLD WAR II VISIONS

In the aftermath of the Second World War, the turbulent era of decolonization swept through India, much of South Asia, Indonesia, Vietnam, and Burma. Then came the founding of the People's Republic of China on October 1, 1949. Painful domestic turmoil and nation and institution building accompanied the formation of these new and reconfigured states (with major civil unrest and dislocations such as China's Great Leap Forward and then the Great Proletarian Cultural Revolution, from 1958 into the second half of the 1970s, occurring along the way). Development proceeded at various rates and with varying degrees of volatility in each country throughout continental Southeast Asia and in China. In the 1950s and well into the 1960s, China was widely viewed as a destabilizing force in the region, supporting Malayan insurgents, the Indochinese Communist Party led by Ho Chi Minh, and the Indonesian Communist Party (PKI), among others. Nonetheless, economic growth eventually began to take off throughout the region, starting in the 1970s in many places and accelerating at varying rates into the second decade of the twenty-first century.

One other international development important to railroad development that intruded in this period was the Sino-Soviet dispute that fully emerged in the 1960s and lasted for two-plus decades. This conflict was born of the competition between Beijing and Moscow for the affections and mantle of ideological leadership of other communist and developing countries. Vietnam is a prime example of this competition for such influence. Even before the last Americans had withdrawn from South Vietnam in April 1975, the USSR was boosting ties with Hanoi, helping restore the French-built (1936) rail link between Hanoi and Saigon (now Ho Chi Minh City). As one Vietnamese transportation bureaucrat put it to our research team, "So, the Russians helped us get two parts of our country together in 1974 to 1975."[17]

The death of Mao Zedong in September 1976 and the swift transition to Deng Xiaoping's leadership was a cornerstone development that finally allowed the PRC to start upon a path toward economic modernization. By 1978–79, Deng Xiaoping had launched the PRC's transformational "reform and opening" (gaige kaifang) modernization effort. Domestically, Deng's push was built on material incentives and market reform, and firmly anchored in an international economic policy grounded in comparative advantage. His foreign policy promoted external cooperation in order to provide breathing space for domestic economic development. The PRC's dramatic economic performance in the post-Mao era, combined with parallel and mutually reinforcing rapid economic growth in the region around China from the 1980s on, provided the political space and economic wherewithal to consider broader, grander visions.

Another highly relevant development was the creation of the Association of Southeast Asian Nations (ASEAN) in 1967, a multilateral regional body focused on creating economic growth, political stability, national resilience, and peace among its member states (five members at first, now ten) and in the broader Asian region. Railroads were part of the ASEAN vision, particularly among the continental member states and Singapore, since the 1990s. The initial driving forces for pan-Asian railroad development were Malaysia, ASEAN itself, and the Asian Development Bank (ADB). China did not take the lead.

In December 1995, the Fifth ASEAN Summit called for construction of the SKRL [Singapore-Kunming Rail Link] flagship project that would cover "several routes through Singapore-Malaysia, Thailand-Cambodia-Vietnam-China (Kunming) and spur lines in Thailand-Myanmar, and Thailand–Lao PDR," scheduled for completion by 2015.[18] In December 1996, a Special Working Group (SWG) meeting, with participation by seven ASEAN countries (Cambodia, Laos, Malaysia, Myanmar, Singapore, Thailand, and Vietnam) and China was held in Kuala Lumpur. The SKRL SWG, chaired by Malaysia and supported by the ASEAN Secretariat, meets annually to monitor the progress on the SKRL in each country (see chapter 7 for more).[19]

Notwithstanding China's participation in the annual SWG meeting and Malaysian proposals to Chinese leaders, it was not until recently that China was in a position to take initiative in any regionwide connectivity-building effort, lacking as it did the capital, technology, and vision. In a conversation with then Premier Zhu Rongji in the late 1990s that revealed his own desires to push regional rail connectivity forward, then Prime Minister Mahathir (who again became prime minister in a surprise May 2018 election victory) recounted:

> Zhu Rongji showed interest, but China was not that economically capable at that time, not that rich, so he was interested but China could not afford it at that time—now [2016] they have the money.[20]

One Chinese banker involved in separate discussions at this time said, "Zhu Rongji did not show interest in building railways outside China; he wanted internal construction."[21]

Despite the annual ASEAN SKRL SWG meetings since 1996, it wasn't until 2010 that ASEAN put forth its own connectivity plan (later expanded into the "Master Plan on ASEAN Connectivity").[22] Then, in 2012, the Southeast Asian leaders and Beijing agreed to form the ASEAN-China Connectivity Cooperation Committee.[23] Thereafter, the Asian Development Bank Institute published *Connecting Asia: Infrastructure for Integrating South and Southeast Asia* in 2016.[24] In the set of actual and envisioned rail projects linking China and Southeast Asia that is the topic of this book, the PRC is aligning itself with a preexistent regional vision (of a conventional rail network) and then negotiating country by country to build segments of its own envisioned HSR network. This is a Southeast Asian train that Beijing has hopped onto. But before Beijing could take initiative, it first had to build out its own domestic system and amass the technological, industrial, organizational, and financial resources to be effective. It is to the story of building these capacities that we now turn.

CHINA DEVELOPS ITS TECHNOLOGY AND RAIL SYSTEM, AND AMASSES CAPITAL

When Prime Minister Mahathir exchanged views with Zhu Rongji in the late 1990s about rail connectivity with China and inquired as to Beijing's possible interest, the PRC had its own wrenching domestic economic challenges. At this time, on Premier Zhu's watch, "more than 30 million [state-owned enterprise workers] were laid off or given early retirement, and 18 million were working in restructured corporations that were no longer considered SOEs . . ."[25] All this was done in order to kick-start SOE reform and push industrial China along a path of

TABLE 1   CHINA NET FOREIGN DIRECT INVESTMENT
INFLOWS, 1990–1997

Year	Net FDI Inflows (in current USD billions)
1990	3.487
1991	4.366
1992	11.156
1993	27.515
1994	33.787
1995	35.849
1996	40.180
1997	45.439

SOURCE: World Bank.

TABLE 2   CHINA FOREIGN EXCHANGE HOLDINGS

Year	Foreign Exchange Holdings (in USD millions)
1990	28,594
1991	42,664
1992	19,443
1993	21,199
1994	51,520
1995	73,579
1996	10,500
1997	14,000
2017 (as comparison)	3,140,000

SOURCE: Trading Economics.

greater efficiency. In 1997, the PRC was a large net debtor to the World
Bank, a large net recipient of foreign direct investment amounting to
$45.439 billion, and had very small foreign exchange holdings of $14
billion (as compared to $3.140 trillion in 2017).[26] More to the point,
China had virtually no technology to export and had relatively backward domestic rail and highway systems. As recently as 2006, the PRC
only had 43,339 km of public highways, a number that had almost tripled by 2016.[27] China had to grow in strength and infrastructure before
it had much to offer others or its leaders could think about ambitious
ventures abroad.

Moreover, a lot of other things had to happen domestically before building any high-speed rail (HSR) in China, much less abroad, would become remotely possible. Among those were the development of continually improving rail technology and production of globally competitive products; the creation of a technical and engineering workforce that could imagine, design, and implement such projects; and a PRC commercial and diplomatic presence abroad that would make Beijing a salient partner. These things did happen, and they occurred with remarkable speed, but it would not be until just prior to the ascension to power of Xi Jinping in 2012–13 that the pieces fell into place. Supreme Leader Xi benefited from the actions of prior leaders (particularly Jiang Zemin, Zhu Rongji, Hu Jintao, and Wen Jiabao), to whom he gives scant credit. Accordingly, our narrative needs to go back in time to provide an abbreviated account of the development of railroad technology and infrastructure in the PRC preceding Xi Jinping.

RAILROAD DEVELOPMENT IN CHINA

In the late nineteenth and early twentieth centuries, railroads were not universally welcome in China. Jonathan Spence explains: "Of the new technologies confronting the Qing [Dynasty], the railways proved to be the most troublesome. Many Chinese considered railways disruptive to the harmony of nature and of man: they sliced across the land, disturbing its normal rhythms and displacing its benevolent forces; they put road and canal workers out of jobs and altered established market patterns."[28] Nonetheless, ensconced in Shanghai, the British (Jardine Matheson & Company) built the first short, commercial railroad in China in 1876, only to have it ripped up in 1877 by a recalcitrant Chinese local official.[29] The first Chinese-constructed line (Kaiping Tramway and Imperial Railways of North China) was built in 1881 in Tangshan in what was then called Chihli (now Hebei Province).[30] Tangshan was where the Kaiping Coal Mine was growing and where a future president of the United States, Herbert Hoover was a mining engineer during 1899–1900.[31] The thirty-first president-to-be was about twenty-five then. China's defeat in the Sino-Japanese War and the aftermath of the subsequent Boxer Rebellion set off a scramble among foreign powers to build many rail lines as they each tried to strengthen their footholds in a China teetering on the brink of collapse.[32] Amidst all this activity, an entirely Chinese-designed and Chinese-constructed rail project was built in Beijing in 1909.[33] As Evan Osnos recounts, "When the Empress Dowager was given a miniature engine to bear her about the Imperial City, she found the 'fire cart' [*huo che*] so insulting to the natural order that she banished it and insisted that her carriage be dragged by eunuchs."[34] This was not an auspicious beginning for Chinese railroad engineering.

By the collapse of the Qing Dynasty in 1911, 9,854 km of rail line had been installed in China by various entities. Among the contributing factors to the dynasty's collapse in October 1911 was the development of a movement (in Wuhan and elsewhere) to reject the Qing's decision to nationalize all railroads, thereby removing them from the hands of some provinces as well as private Chinese and foreign investors. Chinese leaders had rather self-contradictorily proposed to take control of national rail development, even though this meant seeking railroad finance (loans) from foreigners—with foreign governments lurking behind these foreign companies. By nationalizing the railroads, the Qing managed to simultaneously alienate key provinces and private investors at home, thereby mobilizing nationalists who resented any foreign role in building China's modern infrastructure.[35]

Following the Qing Dynasty's collapse, more than three decades were punctuated by civil unrest, warlord rule, civil wars between the Chinese Communist Party (CCP) and the Kuomintang (Guomindang [GMD], or Nationalists), Japanese invasion and rule, massive famine, and revolution. Some warlords (e.g., Yan Xishan in Shanxi Province) built railroads, while Chiang Kai-shek and Mao Zedong destroyed rail lines, first to stem the tide of Japanese invaders in the War of Resistance against Japanese Aggression (1937–1945), and later to prevail in the civil war against each other. In the end, by 1948, China had expanded its rail length very little, reaching a national total of only 12,768 km, which works out to an average annual addition to rail length of 78 km throughout the entire 1911–1948 period.

With the founding of the PRC in October 1949 and Mao's increasingly erratic rule thereafter, rail expansion proceeded episodically, so that thirty years later in 1977–78, when Deng Xiaoping assumed power, the nationwide system totaled only 47,400 km of rail line (or 29,459 miles, about the mileage the United States had in 1860[36]). For a country the size of the PRC, this was very small. Deng was concerned about poor rail system performance, and in 1975 (during a brief return to favor and power after his first Cultural Revolution ousting), he issued directives on improving rail performance.[37]

The initiation of "reform and opening" by Deng Xiaoping upon his final assumption of power, and the relatively continuous policies pursued by his successors Jiang Zemin and Hu Jintao thereafter, greatly augmented China's economic and technological base. Some summary statistics serve to illustrate what Deng's revolution produced in terms of technological foundations that made vigorous rail and HSR progress in the new millennium possible. In 1994, China granted 9,120 industrial and transportation patents; in 2010, it granted 105,243.[38] Similarly, in 1994 China graduated 229,922 engineers, with that number rising to 2,120,361 in 2010.[39] One can quibble about quality differentials in terms of international comparisons of intellectual property and human resources, but at some point sheer numbers do matter. In 1994 there were 59,000 km of rail line; by 2010 that number had grown to 91,178.[40]

HIGH-SPEED RAIL ENTERS THE PICTURE

In the wake of the June 4, 1989, tragic violence in Beijing and elsewhere in China, PRC leaders were looking for ways to move ahead with economic reform and find ways to restore confidence in China's modernization trajectory.[41] In this context, in 1990 the Ministry of Railways (MOR)[42] put forth for discussion its "Beijing-Shanghai High-Speed Railway Program Concept Report" to that year's National People's Congress (NPC) session.[43] Thereafter, conditions favorable to HSR developed along the following three dimensions, with the Ninth Five-Year Plan (1996–2000) being a particularly important signpost along the way:

1. The MOR sought to wring as much efficiency and speed out of the existing domestic conventional rail system as possible, selectively implementing upgrades, such as the "Speed-Up" program.

2. The MOR began to selectively introduce foreign components and rolling stock where possible, and to electrify systems. By 1995 some Japanese and Swiss technology was brought in, followed in the second half of the 1990s by Swedish technology, especially the X2000 tilting electric multiple unit (EMU),[44] which ran on the Guangzhou-Shenzhen line for a number of years.

3. HSR research and development (R & D) was accelerated, with indigenous EMUs developed, the most important of which was the "Blue Arrow" which began runs in December 2000 from Guangzhou to Shenzhen.[45]

Beginning to pick up steam in 2002 by ramping up the acquisition of foreign technology,[46] China's drive for HSR began in earnest in January 2004, when the "Mid- and Long-Term Railway Network Plan" was approved under newly installed Minister of Railways Liu Zhijun.[47] With the revision in 2008, this plan came to include "new lines to connect Yunnan with Laos, Myanmar, and Vietnam."[48] The 465 km Guiyang-Kunming link opened December 28, 2016.[49] The core feature of this domestic plan was the construction of four east-west and four north-south dedicated high-speed trunk lines—a national grid spanning almost all of the PRC.

This evolving infrastructure plan reflected six parallel developments. To start, there was an explosion of domestic passenger demand (more below). Second, there was increasing demand for limited track space for both passenger trains and freight trains—each trying to handle more business. The only way out of the direct competition between freight and passenger trains seemed to be to create separate passenger and freight lines, which in turn would dramatically increase the average achievable speed on dedicated passenger lines.[50] Growing incomes, rising middle-class aspirations, and the PRC's increasing participation in global production chains fueled the surge in demand for both passenger and freight rail services. The swelling need for freight capacity for mounting export volumes spiked due to China's entry into the World Trade Organization in December 2001.[51] John Scales, of the World Bank, believes that by separating freight and passenger lines, the gains in freight revenues would go a considerable distance toward financing possible losses in building the high-speed passenger systems.[52]

A third consideration motivating the emphasis given to HSR was the desire to showcase modern China to the worldwide audience for the Beijing 2008 Olympic Games (announced in 2001). Fourth, when the global financial crisis hit in 2008–9, Beijing's macroeconomic planners sought to stimulate sagging aggregate demand by accelerating public works, with HSR being an important component of that effort. Fifth, the availability of newly developed technology, initially imported (or appropriated without payment) but soon indigenized, was a critical development. In 2010, around 90 percent of HSR technology had its origins abroad.[53] Finally, leadership was decisive, not least Minister of Railways Liu Zhijun (in office March 2003–February 2011), who was an indispensable and highly effective HSR project champion.

Behind all of this was a national political leadership looking for new flagship, national-champion enterprises with export potential. Civil nuclear power plants held similar promise and followed the same pattern as HSR: advanced technology was acquired abroad (in exchange for limited foreign access to the PRC's domestic market), that technology was adapted and improved upon, a domestic system was built to gain experience, and exports of the technology could then begin, all the while building on perhaps China's greatest comparative advantage—the ability to organize and implement huge infrastructure projects. Financing and the commitment of the central government were critical. Joining the central government, which played the lead financial role, were local governments, foreign investors, and banks (domestic, state, and other). Railroad bonds were issued in profusion. Zhenhua Chen and Kingsley E. Haynes, using Chinese Railway Audit Reports, tell us that "The Railway Bond, which is commonly known as the Railway Construction Bond, is another key source of financing for Chinese railway infrastructure expansion. . . . By the end of 2014, the amount of all immature bonds had reached 902.5 billion *yuan* (US$146.92 billion), most of which was used for national HSR railway network expansion."[54]

In 2013, Xi Jinping, in effect, adopted a successful domestic industry created by his predecessors, Jiang Zemin and Hu Jintao, as a centerpiece of his own signature outward initiative: "One Belt, One Road" (OBOR), later rebranded the Belt and Road Initiative (BRI). The revisionist history being written in China that ascribes all progress to Xi Jinping underplays the enormous progress made and groundwork laid by his predecessors. Often successors try to paint their predecessors as do-nothings; Xi's predecessors were decidedly not that.

Examining several driving forces behind conventional rail and HSR development, passenger demand was decisive. In 2004, China moved about 600 million passengers by train annually; by 2009, the number had nearly doubled to 1.2 billion.[55] During the same period, as measured by billions of person-kilometers traveled by train, that number also doubled. To cope with this exploding demand, ever more people had to be moved ever faster on ever-expanding dedicated passenger lines, because comingling passenger and freight trains on the same tracks slowed down everything and was therefore tremendously inefficient. In 1993, trains in China chugged along at an average speed of 30 kmph and, as Evan Osnos recounts, "travel for ordinary people remained a misery of delayed, overcrowded trains nicknamed for the soot-stained color of the carriages. . . . China lagged behind, with what the state press bemoaned as two inches of track per person—'less than the length of a cigarette.'"[56] Then, two decades later, China Railway was "contemplating testing a train at 600 km/h."[57]

Another key driver was rapid technological development. As Murray Hughes explains,

In the early 2000s it became clear just how serious China was about high speed. Missions to study high-speed operations in Europe and Japan were sent out to gather data. While European and Japanese suppliers were keen to win contracts, they were also wary about giving away their expertise. On the other hand, the size of the potential market dwarfed anything in Europe or elsewhere, but the price was to give the Chinese the technical knowledge that they sought—the Chinese insisted on setting up joint ventures with local companies having a majority interest.[58]

The PRC successfully leveraged its domestic market's size to acquire a massive volume of technology. Thereafter, China improved on this technology and indigenized it. The PRC built not only a domestic high-speed rail system but also a globally competitive export industry. The first intercity HSR for passengers commenced service between Beijing and Tianjin on August 1, 2008, exactly one week before the opening ceremony of the Beijing Olympics, a lockstep synchronized drum-roll program of 2,008 drummers that seemed a metaphor for the discipline displayed in building the first HSR. The 113 km long Beijing-Tianjin line was rated at a speed of 350 kmph.

To build this system, develop the technology, and fashion a globally competitive manufacturing industry, in 2000–2 the preexisting, fragmented Chinese railroad and rolling stock manufacturing industry was consolidated into two corporate entities: China Northern (CNR) and China South (CSR).[59] By June 2015, because of cutthroat competition between the two companies abroad, and in order to consolidate R & D efforts and to present a unified front to foreign countries, these two companies merged to form CRRC Corp., Ltd. (Zhongguo Zhong Che). The new entity had 183,061 employees the year following the merger, and the corporation was valued at $26 billion.[60] Fundamentally, for the HSR effort to succeed it required leadership commitment, money, and enormous engineering and management talent, as well as repeated organizational reengineering of multiple bureaucratic and commercial structures.

Looking at the R & D dimension of this undertaking and the implications for building an export industry, Hughes explains:

> Within China, a huge program to develop high-speed technology was simultaneously put in place by the Ministry of Railways and the Ministry of Science & Technology. . . . According to Duan Liren, who was Deputy Director-General of Transport Management in Beijing . . . it was 'the biggest research project ever undertaken by the Ministry of Science & Technology' and covered ten major fields of research. Also involved were twenty-five of China's leading universities, eleven top research institutions and fifty-one national laboratories. . . . All these resources were pooled to assimilate the

[foreign and domestic] technology and implement it on an industrial scale. . . . Many of the world's high-speed train suppliers took part in this process: [Kawasaki, Siemens, Bombardier, and Alstom]. . . . There is no doubt that China wants to sell its own high-speed rail products on the world market. . . . [I]t has also assimilated track and signaling technology, giving it the ability to bid for almost any type of high-speed rail contract.[61]

There were of course many vicissitudes and a major calamity along the way—the July 23, 2011, collision of two high-speed trains at Wenzhou, Zhejiang Province, carrying a combined total of 1,630 passengers. Chinese authorities stated that 40 died and 192 were injured in the accident.[62] Subsequent forensic analysis indicated that the pile-up was the result of a combination of signal problems, electrical system failure, design flaws, and poor management. To make matters worse, political authorities immediately (in the minutes and hours after the crash) intervened to *literally* bury the wreckage and try to enforce a news blackout, with the Propaganda Department telling the PRC mass media and journalists: "Do not question, do not elaborate."[63] That directive failed in no small part because of social media and the instantaneous dissemination of images. The credibility of the government and the HSR program itself was brought into question.[64] Liu Zhijun, who already was under investigation for various felonious misdeeds, was among fifty-four persons held accountable for the tragedy. In the aftermath of the Wenzhou wreck, there was a reorganization of the entire railroad bureaucratic structure, dividing rule making (now located in the Transport Ministry), from system operation and construction (placed in the China Railway Corporation, CRC), from inspection (housed in the National Railway Administration, under the Transport Ministry), as explained earlier.[65]

Beyond issues of technology acquisition, industrial development, and bureaucratic organization, there were fundamental economic issues that needed to be addressed and remain controversial. One important recurrent issue concerned the economic soundness of the system and opportunity costs: Could capital have been deployed in more efficient and beneficial ways, such as to build highways? Slower trains? Air travel? Moreover, there was the question of organizational culture in the MOR under Minister Liu—for him, speed of everything was paramount—both trains and construction. One reason for the Wenzhou crash was that controllers were afraid to stop the trains to ensure safety. After all, Minister Liu had the nickname "Great Leap Liu."[66] Incidentally, after his purge, critics outside the railroad system felt free to criticize him, with one of our informants calling him "a stupid man" and another saying that during his tenure he dominated railroad public relations to assure uniformity of message.[67] Ironically, it was the very qualities of power, purpose, drive, and unorthodox methods that account for both Liu's success and his subsequent downfall, when greed was compounded by arrogance.

Challenges and economic issues aside, in 2018 China had a national HSR grid of 25,000 km of track, and that length was slated to reach 38,000 km by 2025; this high-speed rail grid hauled 1.71 billion persons in 2017;[68] and the system has a safety record rivaling that of the world's safest airlines.[69] Moreover, the PRC has created a globally competitive export industry. In a very short time span China acquired and improved the technology, built the industry to manufacture the equipment, laid the railroad network itself, and modified government agencies to bring all this about.

By way of comparison, the United States has reconfigured its rail ownership and management system repeatedly across the decades (Amtrak was created in 1971 to consolidate disparate, money-losing lines) and fifty years later has still not been able to develop a reliable, rapid, high-performing, and financially viable passenger system—breakdowns and derailments on its signature Northeast Corridor Line are almost commonplace.[70] In contrast, by 2020 China announced plans to have HSR service to 80 percent of its major cities (urban areas with populations over 1 million), and total track distance covered by the system will be 30,000 km.[71]

THE ROLE OF LEADERSHIP AND THE IMPORTANCE OF A BUREAUCRATIC CHAMPION

While it is incorrect to attribute all success (or failure) to the will, insight, or personal qualities of a strong, decisive leader, it is equally misguided to ignore the role of a driven, goal-oriented leader who is skilled in building coalitions to promote their objectives. The PRC's successful and rapid HSR push owes much to the now scorned Minister of Railways Liu Zhijun. It is doubtful that China would have the HSR system it has today without the lubricant of Liu's extensive connections (albeit many corrupt ones) and his political guile. His guile included mobilizing family members and mistresses, making massive payoffs, and strategically building the least economically viable parts of a project before the most economically profitable pieces, in order to preclude investors turning back on funding once a project commenced. Leland

Stanford displayed the same skill set as he played a pivotal role in building the Transcontinental Railroad. In James Scott's terminology, Minister Liu was a "bureaucratic capitalist." Scott explains:

> [I]t is axiomatic that officials with political power are able to manipulate that power in a way that maximizes their own wealth. The translation of power into wealth may occur in either of two ways. First, politicians and bureaucrats may enter business directly—in public or private firms—and take direct advantage of legal monopolies, state subsidies or quotas, and government contracts to amass private fortunes. . . . I would call such individuals "bureaucratic capitalists." Alternatively, politicians and bureaucrats may simply exploit an existing commercial elite by systematically extorting benefits from it and "selling protection." I would call such individuals "bureaucratic extortionists." . . . This distinction is an analytical one, inasmuch as a particular official can, and often does, take advantage of both roles.[72]

Minister Liu was born into a modest peasant household in 1953, grew up in Hunan and Hubei Provinces in China's heartland, and left middle school early, working himself up over the course of his nearly four-decade-long career in the MOR and advancing his education at various Party schools along the way. As Liu made his way up the ladder, the MOR was a vast empire in China, with tentacles reaching into every province-level entity (except Macau) once the Qinghai-Tibet line opened in 2006. The ministry even had its own independent phone systems and sociopolitical institutions; it was basically an expansive, self-contained fiefdom. Given the enormous procurement requirements of the MOR, the vast rights-of-way subject to Liu's control, and the interests of local leaders in getting rail service (or upgraded service), the minister had unlimited ways to build support for his vision within the upper echelons of the Chinese party-state, as well as unlimited opportunities to personally enrich himself, family, friends, and those whose cooperation he needed. Local leaders, for example, regularly had to plead with the MOR in order to get boxcar space to haul in essential supplies for their cities and transport their products out. One of the most important such commodities, a staple of life in China, was coal. One coauthor of this book had a conversation with a mayor of a major coastal city in which that person recounted that he literally had to travel to coal mining areas and negotiate for the shipment of supplies to his coal-short municipality.

In his time in the leadership of the MOR, Liu Zhijun built a vast "ecosystem almost perfectly hospitable to corruption"[73] involving his brother and assorted personalities connected to webs of subcontractors. They prospered by taking a slice of every transaction that occurred in the process of building and operating both the HSR system and the conventional rail system. Opportunities to adulterate concrete, skimp on reinforcing bar, or speed-up construction to boost profit margins were commonplace occurrences. Unfortunately, as the HSR system ages, it is predictable that an unknown but significant fraction of the construction will prove substandard and far from solid; what Chinese refer to as "*doufujiang*" [bean curd remnant] projects. Beyond these real safety and corruption issues, cost overruns were titanic. Perhaps with some hyperbole, Liao Ran at Transparency International summed it up as follows: "At least 700 billion *renminbi* [about $110 billion] went to the high-speed rail system in 2010 alone, with 'no independent oversight or regulation.' . . . [This rail project may be] the biggest single financial scandal not just in China, but perhaps in the world."[74] We say this "may be" hyperbole only because the Crédit Mobilier Transcontinental Railroad financing scam involving Union Pacific directors was truly astronomical in its era in the United States, eventually coming to involve members of Congress, a US Secretary of the Treasury, and the Speaker of the House.

Underpinning and amplifying this corruption and waste was the explosion of economic stimulus money poured into the Chinese economy ($625 billion) to boost aggregate demand at the beginning of the global economic crisis of 2008–9. Much of this went into rail projects.[75] Even before the Wenzhou collision, Liu Zhijun was placed under investigation and dismissed as party secretary of the MOR in February 2011 (and replaced as minister shortly thereafter). After the collision, he was convicted and given a death sentence subject to reprieve in 2013.

Notwithstanding all of this corruption and mess, one fact should not be obscured: Liu's key insight was his belief that the first Chinese high-speed rail grid should not initially rely upon indigenous, autarchic innovation but rather liberally use foreign technology and trade access to China's HSR market for Beijing's right to acquire, use, improve, own, and eventually export the resultant HSR technology, eventually developing the PRC's own brand name. This is an example of what Western leaders like President Trump refer to as "forced technology transfer," and what China's economic negotiators call "business": trading domestic market access for technology.

A key policy decision was made on April 1, 2004, not long after Liu became minister, when the State Council adopted the following policy principle: "Introduce advanced technology through joint design and manufacturing to build the Chinese brand."[76] At Liu's direction, foreign firms were invited to make project bids that were subject to three stipulations: technology must be transferred to the PRC, pricing must be acceptable, and the final product must be a Chinese brand. This bidding process was used to create competition among foreign firms in order to minimize cost and win the most favorable terms for technology transfer. Strict schedules of production localization were enforced. Throughout the decade, this foreign technology was absorbed, modified, and the China Railway High-Speed (CRH) or *"He Xie"* (Harmony) brand emerged. By 2019, China had further upgraded and improved its brands with the "Fu Xing" (Renaissance) fleet in widespread use.

Core to Liu's thinking was that once this initial foreign technology had been improved, indigenized, and production localized (as had happened by about 2012–13), the PRC could export it, eventually becoming a global competitor for market share and competing with the initial developers and providers of the technology from Japan, Europe, and Canada. In the process, China created an industrial champion that could drive the development and upgrading of domestic supplier firms throughout the country. Parenthetically, this was also the strategy that Beijing employed in dealing with Westinghouse and Toshiba's AP-1000 civil nuclear power plants, with their innovative modular construction and gravity-fed cooling technology.[77]

The underlying fact is that China is good at replicating, improving, and manufacturing existent technology, but not yet as skillful at fundamental discovery and building transformative technology prototypes. Liu's idea was to let the foreigners pour resources into initial R & D and then let the PRC do what it does best—replicate, improve, and manufacture. Moreover, China's capacity to make significant domestically developed improvements is growing. Yoshiyuki Kasai, chairman of Central Japan Railway, notes ruefully that he cautioned Japan's KHI, which provided original high-tech trains to the PRC, not to pursue deals that might end up creating a global competitor with a price advantage: "They didn't take our advice. I think it's been a bitter experience for them. . . . The Chinese catch-up speed was so fast; they could not have imagined they would be competing [with the Chinese] for contracts in the US."[78]

So why would presumably savvy international competitors make the mistake of giving China critical technology for them, in turn, to use in direct competition against themselves? As Siemens President and CEO Heinrich von Pierer put it, "the risk of not being in China is bigger than the risk of being in China."[79] Moreover, because China was clearly going to build systems abroad, each of the foreign competitors hoped that by being quiet in the short term, they would be attractive partners in future Chinese-led consortia. China's foreign competitors also made the assessment that the PRC would be more lumbering and less adaptable, allowing them (the foreign originators of the technology) to keep ahead of the PRC on the innovation curve. In short, greed and complacency contributed to this outcome. From the vantage point of 2019, it is fair to say the race is not over—Japan prevailed over China in winning an agreement with New Delhi to build an HSR line from Mumbai to Ahmedabad (December 2015), and China prevailed in a contest with Japan to build an HSR line from Jakarta to Bandung in Indonesia in 2017 (see chapter 6 for more detail).

In understanding the reason technologically advanced powers would share their proprietary technology with China, one consideration is paramount. In the real world *large domestic markets* have more leverage over foreign suppliers than small ones, and Beijing has played this card masterfully. Consider the "Walmart price" and what that has meant for supplier pricing capacity around the world. Moreover, it also may be true that China's innovative capacity was underestimated, or that outsiders gave insufficient attention to the difference between "invention" and "innovation" capacity in manufacturing and product adaptation. Although there are vast invention and innovation deserts in China, there are also deep pockets of innovation excellence (particularly in manufacturing and product adaptation) that foreign competitors can easily underestimate. First and foremost, China has put dramatic emphasis on training engineering talent at home. Add to this the influx of returning students from degree-work around the world, along with the infusion of Taiwan talent coming to the mainland, and one sees a dramatic increase in national capacity since 2000. Finally, there is the ever-present problem of outright intellectual property theft that represents another considerable danger.

GLOBAL EXPORT AMBITIONS: SUCCESSES AND VICISSITUDES

A central feature of the high-speed rail vision in the PRC has been the creation of a globally competitive, leading, new industry that indicates China's emergence as a global technological power. While the path to exporting rail systems for Beijing has not been without challenges (see chapters 5 and 6), and assessments should remain balanced because we are still in the early days of this global development, Beijing employs its HSR accomplishments as a door opener when trying to win rail business around the world. Yet in each particular negotiation China has been flexible in adapting its pitch for high-speed rail to selling and installing somewhat slower systems more appropriate to the circumstances found in many less-developed areas around the world.[80] The ability to build HSR may get Beijing in the door, even if China ends up building slower and less costly systems.

Although it is often unclear when a binding deal has been reached between the PRC and a partner, since around 2005 China has reached a number of international railroad construction agreements of various sorts. Some have been completed (e.g., Ethiopia to Djibouti), others have been off-and-on or canceled entirely (e.g., Mexico), some postponed pending renegotiation (Malaysia), and still others have been over budget and behind schedule (e.g., Vietnam's first urban railroad in Hanoi). Beyond Southeast Asia, China's efforts to build conventional and high-speed systems have included many regions of the world: Eastern Europe, Latin America, Central Asia and Russia, Turkey, the Middle East, and Africa.[81] An HSR project between Ankara and Istanbul in Turkey was completed in 2014, making it the first (and, as of 2018, only) Chinese HSR project completed abroad. One marquee project has been a multination rail network project aimed at tying together seven nations in East Africa by conventional-speed standard-gauge railroad, the first stage of which was the 470 km (290–mile) Nairobi-Mombasa line in Kenya, costing $3.8 billion (the cost and associated debt have been subjects of criticism within Kenya), and completed eighteen months ahead of schedule in May 2017.[82] Also in Africa, in January 2018, a 759 km (472-mile) Chinese-built railroad connecting Djibouti and Addis Ababa started operating—it appears that the budget was at least $500 million over initial estimates, and Ethiopia started repaying loans even before the project was completed.[83]

China's experience in building high-speed and conventional standard-gauge lines abroad has been quite variable—ranging from a lot of hype about plans that came to naught (e.g., the California-Nevada gamblers' high-speed express) to relatively smooth implementation (Kenya), or reaching initial agreements but hitting serious snags shortly after starting (Indonesia, where land acquisition has been a problem, as chapter 6 explains), to projects that have potential financial problems (potentially Laos). Notably, some projects have been subject to client-country political discontinuities (such as election outcomes) that suddenly undermine the consensus for a project—one notable case being Malaysia in May-June 2018, when a shift in party rule led to the postponement of plans to solicit bids for a Singapore–Kuala Lumpur HSR.[84] Finally, there is the proposed construction of a 349 km (217-mile) HSR line from Belgrade to Budapest, which became entangled in European Union procurement that produced delays.[85] Why some projects succeed smoothly while others flounder or fail is an important analytic question addressed in both chapter 5 on negotiation and chapter 6 on implementation.

Irrespective of launch and implementation problems, there is a distinctive character to China's efforts to promote its rail construction and systems abroad.

1. PRC rail projects usually involve a coalition of its policy banks, sovereign funds, multilateral institutions such as the Asian Infrastructure Investment Bank (AIIB), localities, SOEs, backing and promotion by China's diplomatic establishment, and smaller Chinese entrepreneurs involved with the commercial development aspects of a project.

2. There is flexibility in offering standard-gauge rail systems of different speeds and capacities, not just true HSR systems.

3. Financing arrangements often do not require purchaser government guarantees, meaning Beijing often bears the risk of nonpayment or finds other collateral for the debt.

4. There are many ways in which these projects are financed (loans, grants, almost barter-like arrangements, and build-operate-transfer, to mention a few), including revenues from accompanying commercial development along rights-of-way being calculated into the project's total cash flow.

5. There are creative ways to inject other value into the total deal by the Chinese side investing in collateral production capacity (e.g., rolling stock production in the host country), technology transfer, staff training, subcontracts to local companies, and local employment guarantees.

6. China gives value *in the short term,* which means the cheapest price and fastest delivery, which is *not the same as total life-cycle costs,* where Japan often may have the edge. As one Malaysian transport official explained:

> A lot of people say Japan is expensive. In my view, when you look at costs, you shouldn't [just] look at the cost upfront; "you should look at life-cycle costs." We find the life-cycle costs in terms of Japanese technology: lighter [rolling stock], there is savings not just on maintenance but also energy costs.

In a life cycle of 25–30 years, Japan is cheaper. In Japanese philosophy, [a] crash is to be avoided entirely. They take a long time to put out trains, lots of meticulous parts. . . . China tends to pay attention on speed. . . . They want to finish things fast; they are more customer-driven. At one of the HSR fairs here, we asked how fast they could do it and the Chinese told me "how fast do you want to build?"[86]

Or, as a Singaporean observer put it, the Chinese practice is to "sign first, and solve problems later."[87]

It is obligatory to note, however, that big railroad and other capital projects around the world often run dramatically over budget, which is a problem not limited to PRC infrastructure initiatives—think of the "Big Dig" in Boston that ran years behind schedule: in 1982, when the project was started, cost estimates were $2.8 billion; when completed twenty-five years later, its cost had reached $14.78 billion.[88]

CONCLUSIONS: HISTORY, LEADERSHIP, AND A MODEL

In their volume *Chinese Railways in the Era of High-Speed,* Chen and Haynes sum up the principal factors contributing to the stunning creation of a nationwide, high-performing, and transformative industry.[89] To start, sustained and massive central government support and a politically strong bureaucratic champion were essential. Strong and sustained central government support translates into expedited land acquisition, priority provision of bank loans and other human and financial resources, and Beijing's ability to compel unsupportive bureaucracies, localities, and societal groups to cooperate overall. In addition, Minister of Railways Liu Zhijun was very important during the years 2003–11. Second, it was critical that China was building on a relatively solid preexistent research and manufacturing base in the rail sector. While unable to develop cutting-edge technology on its own from the start, the PRC could rapidly absorb, manufacture, and improve the technology of others, particularly in collaboration with foreign firms anxious to get a slice of the Chinese domestic pie. Finally, this brings us to the critical importance of the "exchanging market for technology" strategy.[90]

A core finding of this chapter is that Beijing has developed a multi-pronged approach to both domestic development and achieving international competitiveness in key industries such as building railroads. The prongs consist of (1) identifying and concentrating R & D efforts on specific core industries for the future and pouring in institutional, human, and financial resources; (2) mobilizing resources to acquire foreign technology through conventional purchase, joint ventures, mergers and acquisition of foreign technology firms, and (in some cases) theft; (3) offering the enticement of China's enormous domestic market to induce foreigners to part with their proprietary technology; (4) marshaling China's considerable and growing science and technology capacities to improve the acquired technology; and (5) providing PRC financing capacity to make promotion of its export products (i.e., HSR) attractive to purchasers. The twofold fact that China has enormous foreign currency reserves and can mobilize the high savings rate of a domestic population with still relatively few outlets for its capital (financial repression) contributes to the PRC's ability to put relatively cheap money behind selected development priorities and come in at a lower export price than more market-embedded competitors.[91] Nicholas R. Lardy reports: "In 2004–13 the average real deposit rate [in China] was more than 300 basis points below the average deposit rate in 1997–2003."[92] That is, capital for the Chinese government and others was particularly cheap at the height of the HSR building effort.

This five-part model creates many challenges for, and frictions with, international competitors, as well as with those who join China in these projects. For Beijing, the risks include: overextension, betting on what may prove to be losing technologies, alienating purchasers of Chinese systems who find Beijing overpromising and underperforming, and alienating Chinese citizens who can see that projects abroad mean fewer resources spent at home to meet domestic needs. Nonetheless, when Beijing has a good concept and guesses right, it can be a formidable competitive force against foreign firms. The most impressive thing, overall, is the speed with which this industry has been created and now is being promoted abroad.

By starting this book with an assessment of the historical antecedents of the vision of railroads linking China with seven of its Southeast Asian neighbors, we essentially have asked: "Where did this idea come from?" The short answer is neither from Xi Jinping nor from the PRC. Rather, this vision has been long-incubating, starting with the British and French colonial powers, then the Japanese given the exigencies of the Pacific War in the 1940s, subsequently embraced by local leaders such as then Malaysian Prime Minister Mahathir in the 1990s into the 2000s, and reinforced by multilateral and regional organizations such as ASEAN and the ADB in particular.

Only in this century's first decade did Beijing begin to have the resources, technology, and overarching vision of China as the hub of economic development in Asia to serve as a driving force in railroad development. Beijing and its entrepreneurial local actors and SOEs seized the vision created by others and have been negotiating country by country to be builder, financier, and developer of the vision to the degree that the PRC is able to reach a satisfactory agreement with each of its seven Southeast Asian neighbors. Each country Beijing negotiates with has its own ideas, resources, vulnerabilities, anxieties, unanticipated political and economic discontinuities, and negotiating leverage—each presents its own profile of risk and opportunity. As one lead engineer in the Chinese railroad sector put it to us,

> "The plan [of three rail lines to Singapore] hasn't exactly been adopted. People were thinking, China was thinking of linkage with neighbors and they were thinking of it, but it was not possible financially for a long time and only recently with China's development is it possible—still there are many difficulties. There are many different countries with many different systems—Thailand, the military. Sometimes there are geopolitical concerns, or outside powers. The US doesn't want to see these countries connected to China—harsh words by you [the United States].[93]

Moreover, this corresponds with the ascension of Xi Jinping to power in Beijing in 2012–13. In 2017, as he began his second term in office (and rapidly eliminated the requirement that he relinquish power at the end of that second term), Xi claimed Beijing's global infrastructure effort as his own by embedding it in the constitution of the Communist Party of China.[94] Xi has sought to anchor his legitimacy to the regional and world economy and global power structure. The basic story of the creation of China's HSR system and its extension to Southeast Asia is a story of the convergence of a preexisting idea, with the creation of financial and technological capability over a rather short period of time, and the political needs for legitimation of a new generation of Chinese leaders bent on making China the hub of the regional, and eventually the global, economy. This is China's grand vision, and one that the West may continue to underestimate at its own peril, even as outside observers remain sober about the problems ahead.

CHAPTER 3

China's Debates

The "invisible hand" of the market and the "visible hand" of
government (i.e., strategy, planning, and policy in a broad
perspective) can jointly shape economic geography and create
mutual sharing and [a] win-win development mode among
regions and nations.
—Chinese researcher[1]

The "Flying Geese [Formation]" was a good idea—before it
was Japan, but now it is China.
—Chinese banker[2]

The West is coming to see ever more clearly that under Xi Jinping the
PRC aims to increase state guidance in core and future-oriented economic and development activities, both at home and abroad[3]—what
Barry Naughton has called the "grand steerage."[4] The development of
HSR described in chapter 2 is just one example. In this vision the state
plays a major role in identifying new industries, working actively to
develop and acquire technology through a variety of conventional and
unconventional means, driving R & D, subsidizing ventures at home
and abroad with inexpensive capital, fencing out competitors, and vigorously promoting business opportunities through intimate cooperation among Chinese firms, Beijing's diplomats abroad, and China's
state-owned banks, most particularly the China Development Bank
(CDB) and the China Exim Bank. Moreover, Beijing self-consciously
and explicitly seeks to reconfigure regional, indeed global economic
geography to China's benefit, arguing that this is good for its region, the
Global South, and even the historically dominant economies of the
West. Beijing nonetheless realizes that, in its own words, the West

"sharply criticizes the China-proposed B&R initiative [BRI] and describes it as being 'designed to hamper free trade and put Chinese companies at an advantage.'"[5]

While acknowledging the centralized dimension of what is occurring, analysts also need to appreciate the parallel decentralized, bottom-up character of much of what happens in the PRC. This bottom-up dimension can arise in two broad ways, the first being that localities simply launch off in a direction on their own initiative, thereafter trying to get Beijing (known as the center) to buy in. The other approach occurs when the center launches a vague initiative and localities try to squeeze their pet projects under the wide umbrella. Either way, local initiatives account for much of the system's dynamism. Then, as one think-tank researcher put it: These initiatives from below "shape the responses of [institutions] like the *Fagaiwei* [National Development and Reform Commission, or NDRC] and line ministries as they try to shape, stop, or promote various activities, and it is the experience of these upper-level actors in finding what works and what does not that can change, reinforce, or diminish their priorities."[6] The attempt is to lash together the focus that centralism can provide with the dynamism of localities, bureaucracies, and firms. This often is an undisciplined process—messy and vulnerable to excessive exuberance.

As seen in the preceding chapter, dealing with the rapid development of a domestic HSR system and a set of globally competitive enterprises, Beijing views its state-directed approach as having been remarkably successful to date. As one very senior Chinese foreign policy adviser put it to our team in April 2018: "You [the United States] are a market economy and we have a situation where our most important enterprises are state-owned enterprises. That is the foundation of our economy, and it is not going to change."[7] To the degree that the United States, or broader Western policy, aims to dismantle this structure in the name of free trade and market-economy norms, that is the extent to which Western firms and governments are likely to be rebuffed for the foreseeable future. As a Chinese Trade Ministry official put it in June 2018, quoting Mao Zedong, "You fight your war your way, and I will fight mine my way."[8] China is in a triumphalist moment, even as it recognizes and is disconcerted by its own numerous weaknesses. As one young Chinese educator and researcher put it, "What can the US learn from China? Infrastructure and nonmilitary going abroad—the internet, Alibaba, investment. We are in a mutual learning period. It is time for the US to learn from China."[9]

PRC leaders know that this state-centric approach (one aspect of which is what Beijing calls "Made in China 2025" industrial policy) is becoming a raw point of contention with the world's principal market-based economies. We see the mounting friction in the reactions of industrial associations in the West,[10] governments in Europe,[11] and in concerted and protracted US efforts to get Beijing to retreat from its industrial policies. This will undoubtedly generate Sino-American friction, as evidenced in the growing, dangerous trade frictions that were escalated to an entirely new level in mid-2018 by the Trump Administration. Within China, this triumphalism and the conflicts it spawns are becoming a key aspect of domestic debate as well, a story to which we will turn momentarily.

Core to American thinking, indeed much of Western thinking, has been the idea of a level playing field. In contrast, an active party-government role in state enterprises in frontier industries is key to PRC thinking under Xi Jinping. BRI is founded on the assumption that state capitalism can work as a dynamic and competitive economic system and that well-conceived government action, planning, and focused resource allocation can propel China's society and economy forward by incubating future-oriented industries, developing human resources, and shaping the economic geography of its periphery and beyond.

Nonetheless, the above ideas, particularly their application in specific instances, are not only questioned and debated abroad but also subjects of vigorous controversy within China itself. This chapter is about these internal debates. We have to keep two opposed ideas simultaneously in mind: Xi Jinping has considerable consensus behind him in China that major strategic decisions cannot simply be left to the free market. Simultaneously, there is enormous internal disagreement and friction over which specific endeavors to bet on and which kinds of resources to put behind them. There also is recognition that markets can enforce discipline, foster innovation, and achieve efficiencies that bureaucracies cannot. Setting industrial policy means setting national priorities, and there almost always is disagreement over what those priorities should be. Above all, there is a growing debate in China as to how strong China really is, how much strength it has compared to the United States and others, and how many competitors it can take on simultaneously. There is worry that pushing too hard is encouraging others in the international system to band against China. In short, there are those who see Xi Jinping's grand vision and sharp elbows as not in China's best interests.

The last four decades of reform and opening have produced intellectual and interest group pluralization that is evident as these internal debates unfold, particularly debates germane to HSR and conventional rail development at home and abroad. The range of PRC opinion about rail development in Southeast Asia (indeed with respect to BRI) runs the gamut from assessing it as a visionary idea on a par with the Marshall Plan[12] to "not going to happen—impossible. Too many actors, too many countries, not economical."[13] One analyst said, "Xi Jinping has a layman's understanding of economic things, no strategy. Just reacts to advisers."[14] The viability, feasibility, sustainability, and profitability of rail projects are also questioned by bankers and other experts.[15] China's realists are dubious about grand visions and great leaps.

Nonetheless, four admirable core ideas undergird Beijing's push toward connectivity with its periphery, in this case Southeast Asia through HSR (and conventional-speed) development:

- Infrastructure provides the pathways along which power in its coercive, economic, persuasive, and ideational forms moves. Infrastructure is the grid through which all forms of power move.[16] Infrastructure lies at the core of China's future power and welfare.

- Infrastructure expansion propels broad-based economic growth and *needs to run ahead of actual demand* for it. Infrastructure drives growth—its construction should not await growth and demand. High-speed rail and other similar infrastructure is what the economist Lawrence Lau calls *development leading infrastructure*, as distinct from *development lagging infrastructure*.[17]

- China improves its own economic and geostrategic position by improving its surrounding neighborhood and tying a rapidly growing periphery into its own value chains, transportation networks, production, and marketing. Frederick Ma, chairman of the MTR (Mass Transit Railway) Corporation in Hong Kong, calls this the "parallel development of various economic systems."[18] The idea is that it is easier to succeed in a "good neighborhood" than a "poor one."[19] As one senior planner in Beijing said, we have "a much greater vision—'grow through neighbors and even the EU and Eurasia.'"[20] So, for example, Beijing and Guangdong Province are treating the urban agglomeration of Hong Kong, Macau, and Guangdong's entire Pearl River Delta as one developmental unit in many respects ("The Greater Bay Area") and the construction of infrastructure in one jurisdiction of this agglomeration is seen as enhancing the welfare and growth potential of each of the other localities, creating a virtuous upward spiral for all. We see an international example of this concept applied in the cooperation of Kuantan, capital of the state of Pahang, along the east coast of peninsular Malaysia, and China's Guangxi Autonomous Region, where together they are forging a common growth strategy in the forms of The Malaysia-China Kuantan Industrial Park and the Kuantan Port's linkages with Guangxi's Qinzhou Port. Even before the above developments, these ideas were gestating in China, given impetus by a widely read 2009 World Bank report entitled *Reshaping Economic Geography*. The report argued for economic integration within and between countries, calling for efforts to "integrate lagging and leading provinces within a nation" and to "integrate isolated and well-connected countries."[21] One can see China's sequence of first building its own comprehensive domestic HSR network among provinces, then extending this system to its periphery, as an expression of this broader concept.

- Finally, people in the PRC's periphery are increasingly accepting the inevitability of China's rise and economic dominance. As one scholar from Myanmar put it in early 2018, "The 21st century will be, one way or another, the century of Asia under the economic lead of China and India. . . . The West, even though it is trying to catch up with the rapid growth of China, will have to try to survive economically and politically."[22] If the region around China assumes (and however ambivalently accepts) Beijing's primacy, and if the Western share of the global economic pie continues to decline, China's periphery will adapt itself to what it sees as inevitable. Influential (though not universally accepted) voices in China immodestly reinforce this thinking, saying, "The reason why changes have taken place in Sino-US relations is that the comprehensive national powers of both countries have fundamentally changed. In the past decade, China's comprehensive national power has surpassed that of the United States. This new discovery was way beyond the estimation and prediction of the US and China."[23] Success, and talking like a winner, tends to produce more success. There are voices in China that are more modest, individuals who see China as having substantial vulnerabilities and uncertainties, but their cautionary urgings are not in the ascendancy in the "new era" of Xi Jinping.

Each of these four ideas are subject to debate both within and outside the PRC. Although the dominant coalition in Beijing has been able to forge ahead with this overall vision built on these assumptions, each step in the policy formulation and implementation stages has been subject to political and bureaucratic debate nationally and locally. Even if everyone in the PRC agreed about the basic assumptions listed above, in practice there would still be fierce struggle over the allocation of resources among an almost infinite number of claimants. There is also fierce debate over how to implement such a vast vision and how to deal with the unanticipated challenges. As the future unfolds, China's current ambitious grasp may exceed its reach. There is political struggle every step of the way, at all levels, within China itself and among China and its prospective project partners.

BRI: AMBITIONS AND ASSUMPTIONS

BRI, as a concept and strategy, was adopted as a party decision at the Third Plenum of the Eighteenth Central Committee on November 12, 2013, a plenum that boldly declared that the market will play a "decisive role in allocating resources," but which somewhat contradictorily also promoted industrial policy, the flagship of which became BRI itself.[24] A year later, General Secretary Xi Jinping chaired the Eighth Meeting of the Central Leading Group for Finance and Economics, a meeting devoted to BRI. In December 2014, the Central Economic Work Conference named BRI a key strategy to be promoted in 2015. And, in March of 2015, "the NDRC, the Ministry of Foreign Affairs, and the Ministry of Commerce jointly released the *Vision and Actions on Jointly Building the Silk Road Economic Belt and 21st Century Maritime Silk Road*, setting forth guiding principles, defined routes and cooperation priorities for the BRI."[25] A banker from one of China's major infrastructure lending institutions put it this way: "When we made this plan we also seriously considered goods, logistics systems in this area [Southeast Asia]. . . . The reason that we thought it reasonable to have north-south rather than east-west connectivity [in Southeast Asia] was because China's economy is dominant. China's economy is what they rely upon and there is a north-south supply chain, more of a supply chain than East-West, Thailand, Cambodia, and Vietnam."[26]

By 2016, Beijing was launching its fourth broad approach to development since the First Five-Year Plan of 1953–57, according to Tsinghua University's Professor Hu Angang. This vision, what Hu calls "the

4.0 strategy," is by far the most globally ambitious of the PRC's post-1949 development approaches, seeking to link each of China's domestic economic regions to one another and to their respective international "hinterlands." The aim is to drive not only China's domestic growth, but also to catalyze growth abroad and funnel much of that expanding external economic activity toward China.[27]

This endeavor is nothing less than an effort to reshape regional economic geography, to make China central to its ever more prosperous periphery, and to help its own interior provinces escape their status as landlocked, isolated backwaters—ideas fully consistent with the World Bank recommendations in the 2009 study mentioned earlier.[28] Having fourteen immediate land neighbors and many significant maritime nations and societies proximate to the PRC's long shoreline energizes this ambition. By June 30, 2016, Beijing claimed to have "issued joint proposals and statements with 56 countries and regional organizations."[29] "The transport network consisting of railways, highways, sea routes and air routes, together with the electric power transmission and telecommunication networks, and oil and gas pipelines, creates a connectivity network that provides the physical infrastructure of the six economic corridors," one of which is the "China-Indochina Peninsula Economic Corridor,"[30] the corridor in which this study's railroad projects are contemplated and underway.

The aim of connectivity is to reduce transaction costs, increase urbanization, and foster regional economic integration through infrastructure construction. As pithily put in a Chinese saying—"If you want to get rich, build a road" (yao xiang fu, xian xiu lu). As the scholar Hu Angang put it,

> The Version 4.0 strategy is designed to redefine the development pattern for the regional economy in China, *as well as to promote interconnection with surrounding countries.* . . . This version will not only help to reshape the economic geography pattern of surrounding countries, but also affect the world economic geography. . . . Consequently, this strategy will greatly influence the current world economic map and promote the formation of a new world political and economic order.[31]

If we were to state a definition of the China Dream in developmental terms, this 4.0 version of national development strategy is at its conceptual core. This vision was enshrined in the revised party constitution adopted in October 2017.[32]

Traditionally, social scientists have considered that there are three broad forms of power—coercive, remunerative, and normative [or ideational].[33] If we draw an analogy, power in all its forms is the electricity of governance; infrastructure is the grid through which (coercive, economic, and intellectual) power moves. To exert power, one must be able to reach out and touch other parties, whether that "touch" is accomplished via the pathways of cyberspace, electric power grids, or transportation and communications in all their variants. No connectivity, no political power. For more than two thousand years, the Chinese have been builders, big builders (think of the mammoth gravity-fed Dujiangyan Irrigation System in Sichuan, built in 256 BC). Beijing is turning this long-standing comparative advantage to the service of building modern infrastructure that not only provides the opportunity for direct exports but more fundamentally constructs future pathways of power with China at the center and provides the pathways by which human and material resources will flow toward the PRC. This gives potential new meaning to the moniker Middle Kingdom.

In the Thirteenth Five-Year Plan (2016–20), the broad BRI vision was articulated, the core feature of which was *six* "international economic cooperation corridors": China–Russia–Mongolia, China–Central Asia–West Asia, China–Indochina Peninsula (into which this book's southern China–Southeast Asia HSR and conventional rail projects fit), the "Eurasian Continental Bridge," China-Pakistan (CPEC), and Bangladesh-China-India-Myanmar. The plan also calls for "the development of multi-modal transportation that integrates expressways, railways, waterways, and airways, build[ing] international logistics thoroughfares, and strengthen[ing] infrastructure development along major routes and at major ports of entry."[34] This is the infrastructure component of a broader strategy to make China a principal maritime and land power in the modern era.

Also important is giving "full play to the role of Overseas Chinese, returned Overseas Chinese, and the relatives of Overseas Chinese who live in China in fostering bridges of communication and bonds of friendship [in BRI project countries]."[35] In Southeast Asia, the explicit role for overseas Chinese is a two-edged sword inasmuch as the economic and political roles of resident and nonresident ethnic Chinese have often been nerve-racking issues, sometimes leading to fearsome anti-Chinese violence, notable examples of which occurred in Indonesia in 1965 and 1998, as well as in Vietnam on more than one occasion. Burmese and Thais alike resent the almost autonomous political control exerted by ethnic Chinese populations in the northern reaches of their countries. Go to the small but active border town of Boten on the Lao side of the border with the PRC and it takes considerable discernment to detect that this is not a part of China.

An important dimension of BRI relates to tourism and the flow of ideas—soft power. Cambodia is a good example. Given Cambodia's cultural riches and its poverty, tourism is relatively low-hanging fruit for economic growth, boosting access to hard currencies relatively quickly and heightening Cambodia's visibility on the global economic map. Investment follows tourists. Tourism played an important part in China's initial economic launch (hooking China into global corporate networks and training a predominantly rural workforce to conform to global economic and workforce practices). Now, with cash and experience, PRC interests are investing mightily in Cambodia, a destination for Chinese tourists.

Tekreth Samrach, chair of Cambodia's state airline, said: "To be frank, everyone goes to China to make money. . . . So we have to go to China to make money too."[36] Of two airport projects anticipated to be financed and built by PRC interests in Cambodia, one deal reflects the initiative of local interests in Yunnan Province, and the second, larger airport project has China's State Secretariat of Civil Aviation as the driver on the Chinese side. These planned projects illustrate a key feature of BRI—each project represents its own mix of local versus central initiative and finance.

Part of the motivation for Chinese investment in the transport sector in Cambodia is the 10 percent annual growth in air passenger loads. In 2017, tourism accounted for 12.3 percent of Cambodia's GDP, with a million Chinese visiting that year—more than two million were expected for 2020.[37] Chinese investors follow the tourists, land prices increase, thereupon drawing in PRC developers of all descriptions. Nonetheless, there are many cautionary notes—47.5 percent of Cambodia's total debt was owed to PRC creditors in 2017.[38] Incidentally, 40 percent of Myanmar's external debt was owed to the PRC at the end of 2017.[39]

Another often-overlooked objective of BRI is ensuring that Chinese technical and other standards are the ones that surrounding nations adopt as they lay the foundations for their own modernization with China's involvement. Adopting Chinese standards means locking the PRC's neighbors and others into Beijing's hardware and software standards/specifications which, in turn, inclines future purchases in the PRC's direction. Once basic systems are established, future sales by non-Chinese suppliers must be compatible with the initial Chinese standards.[40] Accordingly, huge future revenues may flow toward China as owner of the underlying standards and technologies. As the PRC's Thirteenth

Five-Year Plan put it, "We will increase cohesion between development plans and [the] technological standards of China and those of other countries along the routes of the Belt and Road Initiative."[41] Andrew Polk explains in greater detail:

> Most analyses of the Belt and Road initiative focus on whether individual projects will become profitable or will leave China further mired in debt. Yet the return on investment for a port in Sri Lanka or a rail line in Thailand matters less to Chinese officials than the ability to push participating countries to adopt Chinese standards on everything from construction to finance to data management. For just one example, China is exporting key technical standards for the construction of high-speed rail through these projects—in large part to circumvent standards set by Western players.[42]

One final aspect of this BRI vision is the creation of globalized corporate cultures within Chinese firms to promote values and narratives associated with the BRI. During field research in Malaysia in mid-2018, our team went to the Section One Base Camp of the China Communications Construction Corporation's (Zhongguo Jiao Jian, or CCCC) East Coast Rail Link (ECRL) Project in Kota Bharu, state capital of Kelantan. There the firm conspicuously displayed approved slogans that conveyed to workers and visitors alike the firm's aspirational corporate culture or corporate vision (*qiye yuanjing*). Successful organizations link their employees' daily exertions to more existential, indeed noble, objectives. The slogans convey the ethos this corporation seeks to instill internally and convey externally: Integrating the Whole World; The Builder Knows No Borders; We Build a Better Connected World; We Make Cities More Livable; and We Create Better Life for People.

FROM VISION TO DEBATE

Articulating an expansive, indeed grandiose, vision is the easiest step in a very long journey through China's domestic political terrain. Moreover, winning cooperation in potential partner countries and assuring that projects get implemented in modestly efficient ways reflective of the initial intentions of policy makers is a massive undertaking. These intrinsic challenges generate intense political debate among Beijing's central leaders, bureaucracies, provinces and localities, corporations, a broad range of interest groups, and sometimes the public at large. This debate plays out at two levels: (a) as part of broad societal politics and (b) among constituencies more directly engaged in the realm of infrastructure and China's HSR and conventional rail initiatives abroad.

Societal Debate

As of this writing, it remains to be seen how dissatisfactions at the popular level may be expressed and how effective opposition may become, but one thing is clear—there is a powerful current of opinion within China, particularly among intellectuals, that views the export of HSR and conventional-speed rail systems (and other national largesse of this kind, and foreign aid more generally) on not strictly commercial terms, as an expression of a basic problem with the Communist Party and its leadership. As well, there is broad resentment that policy decisions are being made by a small coterie of advisers disconnected from broader publics. These advisers are too anxious to satisfy their political masters.

The line of attack runs something as follows: China still has 100 million people living below the poverty level; China has many pressing domestic problems itself; this massive, global BRI effort is reflective of a "Great Leap" mentality built on ill-founded hopes rather than serious research; overestimating China's strength is alienating powers near and far because they are concerned that Beijing may act on the basis of its inflated sense of itself and nationalistic impulses; the supreme leader is using vanity projects abroad to bolster legitimacy at home and win support among self-interested state enterprises; and the propaganda system is pushing programs that can't stand up to serious analysis. This indictment is searing and has resonance with an undetermined fraction of Chinese society.

In describing the dominant vision and rationale for building interconnectivity and the overall BRI initiative above, we drew liberally from the writings and research of Tsinghua University's Professor Hu Angang, a long-time and close adviser to China's senior leaders on China's development, most particularly China's rapidly growing comprehensive national power. His basic policy point of view has been that the PRC has been growing rapidly, its comprehensive national power recently surpassed that of the United States, and that Beijing should take this opportunity to reshape the economic geography of the PRC's region and beyond. In short, seize the day, seize the hour!

In reaction, in an early August 2018 blog post, a long list of Tsinghua alumni (the university being a principal technical training ground for future leaders, many of whom are engineers) attacked Professor Hu's research methods, his conclusions, and the harmful international effects of his work, which they branded a "laughable" exaggeration of China's national capabilities. On top of misdirecting national leaders, his work had aroused, they argued, concern abroad about China's national intentions given such an exaggerated sense of China's capacities. The resulting anxieties being generated abroad fed containment policies in foreign capitals, not least in Washington.[43] This posture of geostrategic, geoeconomic, and industrial policy assertiveness had helped produce a trade war and deteriorating strategic trust with the United States.

PRC central authorities reacted almost immediately, saying that "while being vigilant against Chinese society's arrogance, they [presumably the Tsinghua alumni writing the blog post] should help the country rid itself of the fear of the US and encourage Chinese people to fight US hegemony."[44]

Just prior to this, on July 24, 2018, Xu Zhangrun, professor of law at Tsinghua University, published a broadside against current political directions in the PRC. Xu denounced what he and many other PRC citizens see as Beijing's financial profligacy on foreign aid and show projects abroad. Parenthetically, one is reminded of the important role Tsinghua University students and faculty played in the Cultural Revolution's course five decades ago.[45] Now, at least some of its students, faculty, and alumni appear to be turning their analytic powers, platform, and connections against many of the university's own graduates now in leadership and policy positions in Beijing and throughout the country. After taking aim at many targets, including the "tendency towards overweening self-confidence" and "buddying up to failed and totalitarian states like North Korea and Venezuela," Xu took aim at "Excessive International Aid."

> Over-investment in international aid could possibly result in deprivations at home. . . . Its cash-splashes are counted in billions or tens of billions of dollars. For a developing country with a large population many of whom still live in a pre-modern economy, such behaviour is outrageously disproportionate. Such policies are born of our "Vanity Politics." . . . The nation's wealth—including China's three trillion dollars in foreign reserves—has been accumulated over the past four decades using the blood and sweat of working people. . . . "Fuck you," you hear people say. "What the hell does that have to do with anything?" Such sentiments reflect popular sentiment; they can't be duped like the hapless and uncomplaining subjects of yesteryear.[46]

In short, national arrogance, excessive largesse abroad, and fears that China's muscular push abroad has engendered unnecessary pushback against Beijing all have the potential to become explosive domestic issues. The HSR vision abroad could become entangled in this broader debate. The way Beijing could to some degree insulate itself from this volatile debate is to make sure the bulk of its projects abroad are on a firm commercial footing.

Expert-Level Debate

Among the recurring and important issues debated among more directly involved participants in the HSR undertaking are the following:

- How does the central government allocate resources among many competing and urgent priorities? There is a fierce competition for resources. A most pressing issue is the division of total government revenues among the central and local governments.

- How does one think about the relative weight of costs and benefits, over what time frame? How does one assess positive and negative externalities from such massive undertakings?

- What kinds of projects, in what specific locations, make the most developmental sense?

- How should one value strategic or geopolitical gains versus more immediate economic losses? Or, as explained by one Beijing expert informant, "China is trying to balance different goals: economic and foreign policy goals."[47]

- What strategic and other risks are being assumed in constructing immovable infrastructure in geologically, geographically, and politically unstable places, and what are the levels of acceptable risk?

- How does one unleash, and at the same time rein in, the entrepreneurial impulses of Chinese firms and localities, while controlling corruption?

- How does one encourage neighboring countries to be interested in BRI-related cooperation without Beijing making vacuous promises resulting in unfulfilled expectations?

- What lessons should be learned from past undertakings to improve future performance? Can the PRC avoid becoming just the next heavy-handed imperial power dealing with its periphery or reinforcing the image of a chauvinist power seeking to restore a previously existing "tribute system"?

All these questions can be subsumed under several broad areas of ongoing debate in China that are fundamental to the politics of China's rail and infrastructure ambitions domestically and abroad.

"Overinvestment" on Infrastructure and the PRC Fiscal System. If one is to understand bureaucratic behavior and political debate, a productive place to start is with the budgetary process. A signal year for the Chinese budgetary/fiscal system was 1994, fundamentally changing the central-local split of total government revenue in China from 22 percent for the central government in 1993 to 55 percent for the central government in 1994—the local government share was the reciprocal, declining dramatically.[48] Yet local governments still carried the responsibility for most government spending (health and education services, infrastructure, and law and order), despite their dramatically reduced share of total government revenue.[49] The resulting local revenue gap was to be made up by fiscal transfers (of three types: earmarked, lump sum, and tax rebates) from the central government to local governments. As Ziyang Fan and Guanghua Wan explain,

> Fiscal transfers from the central to local governments also increased. In 2012, for example, among the 5.6 trillion [RMB] in central fiscal revenue, 4.5 trillion were directly transferred to local governments, accounting for up to 74% of the total local fiscal revenue. . . . Considering that local PRC governments paid more attention to the [economic] development, with marked enhancement of fiscal strength after receiving lump-sum transfers, the most obvious benefit was for the local infrastructure [through "earmarked transfers"], which further improved their competitiveness in attracting investment, and finally promoted the rapid growth of the local economy, in a short period of time.[50]

To strip a complex story down to its bare essentials, this 1994 fiscal change had a number of effects, the most relevant to our story being Fan and Wan's finding that "every 1% increase in earmarked transfers [is] associated with a 5% increase in local spending on infrastructure. These fiscal transfers also increased the size of local government spending such that a 1% increase of fiscal transfer would increase the ratio of local fiscal spending to gross domestic product by 1%."[51] The results have been that "The PRC's level of infrastructure seems to exceed its level of economic development."[52] They further argue this pattern of local government expenditure is not sustainable and that the entire budgetary system needs to stop reinforcing excessive infrastructure investment. Instead, fiscal policy needs to weigh more heavily the provision of social services by local governments, improve avenues for local government taxation and finance, and adopt more market-based mechanisms to finance infrastructure.

All these budgetary and financial minutiae are profoundly important and vigorously debated in China, because it means that China has built a huge infrastructure industry that results in excess capacity and generates incentives for massive infrastructure exports. It also means that China's province-level and subordinate regions have been drivers in building infrastructure (along with relevant central ministries and allied state-owned enterprises) and, further, provinces along the PRC's international boundaries have been promoters of connectivity with their neighbors in order to accelerate their own development. As Fan and Wan put it, "PRC local governments are not only service-oriented but can also be considered governments of developing states."[53]

This means that infrastructure development (of which HSR and conventional rail projects are a notable component) lies near the core of fundamental political, budgetary, and policy debates in China: What should be local government responsibilities? Is China's investment in infrastructure excessive and unsustainable? And how should infrastructure projects be financed so as to better tap the benefits of market discipline and spread costs across generations? The resulting excess capacity of the infrastructure-related sector and its distorting effects on both exports and BRI itself need to be considered too. A final implication of all this is that an image of China's political process as just top-down ignores the considerable initiative of Chinese localities in promoting infrastructure in both their own areas and expanding connectivity with cross-border neighbors, in this case in Southeast Asia. Nor is the role of overseas Chinese communities to be overlooked in creating demand for projects outside the PRC (discussed in greater detail in chapter 5).

Assessing Project Costs and Benefits. A fundamental and politically divisive issue in building big infrastructure domestically or internationally is that the political and economic costs of constructing a project are hard to forecast. Project promoters tend to greatly underestimate costs in initial tenders. A project's costs are disproportionately up front, and important benefits are hard to measure and generally accrue over long periods. This is certainly the case for HSR projects, where costs are frontloaded while benefits are uncertain and profits are likely only after several decades. Infrastructure undertakings generate a mix of tangible and intangible gains. The challenge is to find ways to compellingly specify and quantify the costs and gains (over what time horizon?) so they can be compared. Thereafter, financing mechanisms have to be devised that place reasonable burdens on future generations of citizens that will benefit from the project(s). This is a core problem in all economic and political systems when it comes to infrastructure—concentrated pain for a relative few (those dislocated who are motivated to articulate grievances), diffused gain for many over generations, massive up-front costs, often long payback periods that need to be financed, and difficulty specifying all the positive and negative externalities with precision.

This character of infrastructure (in this case HSR and conventional rail) creates a political pattern in which present and future beneficiaries of the final project focus on the long-term gains (faster trips, new settlements along the right of way, speedier and more efficient logistics in production chains, and taking polluting automobiles off roadways that may not need to be built). Those who bear the immediate burdens and risks of financing, and those elements of society that prefer alternative expenditures or no project at all, argue that anticipated revenues will not (may never) pay for the initial expenditures, running costs, depreciation, and opportunity costs, in addition to all the painfully obvious immediate dislocations big projects inevitably inflict on some subset of current citizens.

The arguments can become ethereal, because many of the benefits are intangible or have different weights in the eyes of varied political constituencies or interest groups. As one analyst in a Beijing think tank put it: "One set of ideas is long term, market based, commercial interest, with emphasis on the role of enterprises and the interests of investors. But, on the other hand, others have a long-term view, so balancing of these two views is necessary. . . . We, all the stakeholders, invite all the players to create balance." This informant went on to explain how these perspectives were reconciled in the Chinese political process:

> There are lots of processes. These involve China's various bodies, stakeholders, shareholders of different projects, unilateral, bilateral, multilateral; different players. We have been involved in some negotiations. As observers, we notice every deal is not easy. There are different stakeholders; different levels of agreements among agencies. Infrastructure projects usually take a long time and are complex, involve different stages.[54]

Central to all this is societal and bureaucratic fragmentation. Fragmentation starts with the fact that, as one PRC observer put it, "Every

department has its own ideas, plans."[55] These ideas and plans derive
from normal bureaucratic friction stemming from mission competition,
budget scarcities ("budget wars"), divergent central-local perspectives,
each bureaucracy's distinctive organizational culture, and public-
private sector divisions. China's foreign aid, for example, is largely controlled by the Ministry of Commerce, but the Foreign Ministry would
like to control the foreign aid function with an eye to longer-term diplomatic interests and national strategies.[56] The Foreign Ministry, and its
embassies and consulates in nations around the world, often wants Chinese financial entities and funding agencies (the Ministry of Finance,
Exim Bank, and CDB, among others)[57] to fund projects in partner
nations that may make foreign policy sense, but virtually no economic
sense. We asked a Foreign Ministry official which bureaucracies were
skeptical of the railroad in Laos and which bureaucracies supported it:
"Basically, the Ministry of Commerce and the Ministry of Foreign
Affairs favored the Laos project, but the Ministry of Finance opposed
it."[58] This can give rise to bureaucratic slugfests, sometimes reaching all
the way to Zhongnanhai, the leadership command center in Beijing.

Equally fundamental, however, is the clash between two fundamental perspectives in China as it pertains to HSR and conventional rail
(and other infrastructure) construction. One perspective is embraced by
those advocating a "long-term point of view." The core idea, para-
phrased, is as follows. Yes, if one adopts a short-term, cash-flow perspective with market costs attached to capital, many of these HSR and
conventional rail projects probably will not pay for themselves in the
foreseeable future—perhaps ever. But if one considers the future growth
this infrastructure catalyzes, employment increases, China's building of
frontier industries for its competitive future, a tourist flow replete with
opportunities for small and medium-sized Chinese firms, and the geostrategic, geopolitical, and geoeconomic gains Beijing makes in power
projection and transportation diversification, not to mention positive
externalities such as fewer cars on roads and the efficient use of executive travel hours, then BRI projects such as those discussed in this volume could be viewed as sound—indeed visionary. More tangibly, building a network produces growth because of "network effects." As
Nicholas Lardy explains:

> High-speed passenger rail is a good example of long-lived infrastructure
> investment that will generate returns for generations. High-speed rail also
> has important network effects, i.e., the gains are not entirely captured until
> the network is more fully developed, allowing increasing amounts of freight

to move onto the preexisting rail system and move continuously over longer distances as a larger share of passenger traffic is carried on the dedicated high-speed rail network.[59]

From this perspective, infrastructure causes growth. Construction should not await growth. A very senior PRC leader put it this way in a group meeting in late 2017: "The market is so powerful that once a road is built, and toll roads, which are not our creation, it drives economic growth."[60] As another PRC interlocutor said, "Implementation of those projects over the next three to five years will be challenging, but if we look at the next twenty to thirty years, implementation will not be an issue. Look at 'Opening and Reform.' If you look at the last forty years, many of those challenges were resolved."[61] The coauthors of this book call this the "field of dreams approach." Build it, and they will come! As one senior Chinese rail construction official put it, "The beauty of this railway line is that we will do development along the line and develop the economy and generate traffic for the railway. This is not just a railway, it is a development plan for the underdeveloped, landlocked country [Laos], which will remain that way without the railway."[62] A senior think-tank researcher said, "China can import Southeast Asian resources into China and we can develop the region into an area like Europe. . . . This has political/development motivation."[63]

The other view is that if a project does not have a secure and sufficient revenue stream and a sound business plan, it doesn't pay—period. As one think-tank researcher in Beijing put it, "Some in China say we don't need these railways that much, so if they [Southeast Asia transit nations] don't make it feasible cost wise, we don't do it. We have got to get our own money back. . . . It should be feasible economically."[64] As one Chinese analyst summed it up, "High-speed railway is two hundred fifty kilometers per hour and up. HSR is a really stupid idea," going on to say that, "The population scale and density in these countries won't generate enough passenger revenue." Leaving no doubt where this individual stood, the person concluded: "This is not just stupid economically, but politically as well, because the Southeast Asians will see it as a threat to their sovereignty. They will nationalize our investment and we will lose."[65]

It is these two perspectives on assessing costs and benefits that lie at the heart of China's own domestic debate over HSR and simultaneously at the heart of China's neighbors' assessments of whether or not HSR and conventional rail are reasonable undertakings for them,[66] in addition to their rightful worries about being saddled with unsustainable debt burdens,[67] not to mention various dislocation concerns. Displaying an understanding of the fears of China's poorer neighbors, one Chinese academic informant referred to some Chinese financiers and the NDRC as "sharks that want to push these projects."[68]

Looking at the domestic politics within China of the PRC's initiatives abroad, one senior and well-placed Chinese academic explained:

> "There are three sets of interests, not just two: business interests, strategic interests, and the third is the countries themselves, particularly Cambodia, Vietnam, Laos, and to a degree Myanmar. Significant voices in these latter three or so countries . . . want prestige projects, turnkey projects they can turn on as free gifts. They count as lobbyists [here in China]. These voices are not restricted to the governments but include political elites in those countries, and also ethnic Chinese in these countries [the Chinese diaspora]— they complicate things. These interests and the Chinese are the pull force."[69]

Concisely, some sentiment exists in the PRC that poorer neighbors have their hands outstretched, looking for gifts from China. Further, there is some sentiment in the PRC that it can ill afford to meet all the external demands. The above informant asserted: "We have no business building up these societies [to our south]."[70] This same informant concluded: "Our real problem is that there is too much foreign policy that is too much abstract talk and not enough hard-nosed cost-benefit analysis."[71]

This clash of perspectives in the PRC easily segues into a related and serious topic of debate—risks abroad and risks at home.

Debates over Risk. Inside and outside China there are critics of both the domestic and foreign HSR endeavor (and other infrastructure undertakings associated with BRI) who raise questions about risks. Internal cautionary voices have come from the chairperson of China's Exim Bank ("Current international conditions are very uncertain, with lots of economic risks and large fluctuations for interest rates in newly emerged markets.") and from the People's Bank of China's Governor Yi Gang ("Ensuring debt sustainability—that is very important.").[72] China has enormous systemic risks related to total national indebtedness. According to the International Monetary Fund, the PRC's domestic debt–to-GDP ratio is reaching concerning levels, particularly corporate debt. In December 2017, an IMF report said: "Credit growth has outpaced GDP growth, leading to a large credit overhang. The credit-to-GDP ratio is now about 25% above the long-term trend, very high by international standards and consistent with a high probability of financial distress."[73]

With respect to debt germane to HSR domestically, in 2005, 50 percent of rail construction was financed by debt, while in 2009 the corresponding figure was 70 percent. Anderlini and Dickie reported in 2010 that the Ministry of Railways alone accounted for 10 percent of China's entire outstanding debt.[74] Beijing Jiaotong University Professor Zhao Jian argued: "This is a real debt crisis building up for the government and it is going to break at some point."[75] Justifiably, there is genuine domestic concern over how far Beijing can and should go in financing hugely expensive projects, both at home and abroad, that have long payback periods, if indeed they ever will be repaid (or endlessly rolled over).

For example, the PRC held nearly half of Cambodia's total debt in 2017 and the indebtedness to China of countries from Pakistan to Venezuela is worrisome to many Chinese and foreigners. For example, Beijing assumed management rights (for 99 years) of the Port of Hambantota in Sri Lanka after the city of Sri Jayawardenepura Kotte (Sri Lanka's capital in the Colombo metropolitan area) could not make the debt payments.[76] The PRC is experiencing generally slowing domestic economic growth amidst the need to shift to a new growth model driven by domestic consumption rather than exports, and more recently amid disruptions in the international trade system by the imposition of tariffs and other harmful interventions by nations on both sides of the Pacific (but notably the Trump Administration). Many in the PRC worry that making massive external commitments against the backdrop of growing domestic debt may be unwise. In the Sri Lanka case, many Chinese wonder how taking over an underutilized port could be a wise investment. Conversely, strategically suspicious foreigners can look at the acquisition of that very same port as a strategic windfall for PRC power projection—a fire-sale takeover.[77]

A second set of risks derives from the fact that infrastructure projects require huge upfront outlays of capital by both China and the recipient countries. Often these projects are to be constructed in areas of moderate to high financial and political risk. One respondent specifically mentioned the risks of unrest, saying "There is disorder in southern Thailand."[78] Should, indeed can, China shoulder these risks? About this, there is vigorous debate in the PRC. One PRC representative at a 2018 conference in Southeast Asia said: "People have a lot of suspicions about China's strategic intention. [Chinese] Lenders should be more fiscally disciplined. China has to cancel a lot of bad debts and aid to other countries. . . . We [China] have to be very careful about our lending and investments overseas. There are people who are unhappy with our money disrupting their lives. China has to be very careful."[79] Another Chinese respondent expressed worry about getting so involved in actual physical projects that can create so many forms of backlash, saying, "We should just invest in these economies."[80] The idea here is that the PRC needs to stay more liquid, not nailed to the ground with immovable projects, dubious debt, and scant local support. A *New York Times* report summed it up: "Chinese officials themselves are sounding a cautious note, voicing worries that Chinese institutions need to be careful how much they lend under the program—and make sure their international borrowers can pay it back." Chairwoman of the PRC's Exim Bank Hu Xiaolian concluded the article, "Our enterprises and Belt and Road Initiative countries will face financing difficulties."[81]

Related risks include insufficient government revenues in partner countries to service the debt (e.g., Pakistan and the CPEC, to which China has pledged US$57 billion; Islamabad is hemorrhaging foreign exchange and continually needing to borrow from Beijing and the IMF to pay previous debts).[82] Moreover, government instability or simply normal electoral change can dramatically alter prospects for a project, as was the case in Malaysia when in May 2018 Prime Minister Najib, a major ally of Beijing's BRI partnership in his country, was suddenly replaced in an election that brought former Prime Minister Mahathir back to power. Immediately upon his election, Mahathir declared that he would reassess the viability of two rail projects key to Beijing—the HSR line and the ECRL.[83] Dramatic changes in a country's economic conditions also can undermine prior financial commitments and plans (e.g., Venezuela and the decline in oil prices undermined Beijing's heavy investment in its oil industry). COVID-19 compounds all risks.

Nor should we ignore backlashes by governments and societies reacting to Beijing's sometimes heavy-handed approach to various projects, as has occurred in Mozambique, Myanmar, and Vietnam. One danger is that China becomes viewed as an actual or aspiring regional hegemon, in effect an updated version of the nineteenth- and twentieth-century imperial, colonial powers. Projects can be, and have been, stopped or "postponed" midway, losing sunk costs (e.g., the Myitsone Dam in Myanmar). Such projects can become the object of violence and resentment by locals. Backlash can occur because outside labor is brought in, due to environmental impacts or displacement and relocation issues, among many other factors. Also, friction has sometimes resulted from Chinese demands (open or covert) for onerous side payments or demands for development rights and/or barter arrangements should the initial financing arrangements falter. In the Thai rail case, for example, there was negative popular reaction to Beijing's demand for a very wide right-of-way that PRC interests could commercially develop to generate cash flow. In Laos, tangible assets had to be pledged if debt payments were not made.[84]

Then there is the consideration that with the proposed rail network ultimately envisioned as traversing seven Southeast Asian nations at various levels of economic and social development (with Myanmar, Cambodia, and Laos being the poorest), China is proposing projects that exceed the capacities of many localities to sustain or contribute to. As one PRC academic respondent put it: "How many of the [Laotians] have been sent to China for training [thus far]? NONE. If the Chinese run the whole thing it will be very costly; [what is the] benefit?"[85] In a related vein, one PRC informant frustrated with calls to use local workers with allegedly lower productivity said: "One Chinese worker equals five in Vietnam and ten in Laos."[86]

Another nonfinancial risk could actually stem from success with BRI. Chinese and foreigners are used to thinking of the PRC as a place citizens leave, not a place to which outsiders go to take up long-term residence and seek a better life. However, people on railroads can move in two directions. As labor costs in China rise, some of China's poorer neighbors may become a source of population movement toward the PRC, a possible development that some PRC citizens would not welcome. As one respondent put it: "We will have hundreds of thousands of Laotians in China. In Laos, [there will be] few Chinese [because China is aging so fast and young workers are in demand in China] . . . lots of things are changing."[87]

For reform-minded economists in the PRC, another area of concern is that BRI may take the PRC economy further from the objective of having the market play a "decisive role in allocating resources," an official call that was made at the late 2013 Third Plenum of the Eighteenth Party Congress.[88] Chinese observers are quite clear that even China's seniormost officials, starting with President Xi Jinping and Premier Li Keqiang themselves, have differing commitments to market-based economic change, with one respondent saying, "Xi and Li Keqiang are giving different emphases in economic policy."[89] One PRC think–tank researcher put it as follows in 2016: "Li Keqiang is for small government and less intervention. Xi Jinping is for big government, big state enterprises. Li Keqiang has tried innovation, but the political environment does not really permit him to do so."[90] To those with more of a market-economy bent, BRI has the smell of picking technological and economic winners and losers and ending up with bridges to nowhere. Barry Naughton talks about China's "unprecedented gamble" in an economy-wide framework. This is the "grand steerage," which he believes is deeply problematic.[91] Stanford's Andrew Walder explains, in a similar vein:

> In this context the Belt and Road Initiative (BRI), hailed within China as a major strategy foray, does not address these core problems, and in some respects is yet another way to delay reform and may be exposing China to more problems. . . . However impressive as geopolitical strategy, the initiative is mobilizing capital for projects with little prospect for financial returns in the near-term and in fact appears to be motivated in part by desire to absorb excess capacity in loss-making state corporations. Further extending the credit boom into financially risky projects, the BRI delays state-sector reform by propping up overcapacity sectors that are already the most in need of restructuring.[92]

"Birth Control" for Projects and Rising Foreign Expectations. Administrators, politicians, planners, and businesspeople all pay lip service at the altar of "coordination." In actuality, however, localities and organizations resist being coordinated unless it means making the behavior of others conform to one's own preferences. The very nature of China's administrative and political structure creates conflicts among vertical functional systems and horizontal territorial administrative levels.[93] Moreover, given China's promotion system, which generally rewards those who achieve economic growth and political order goals, there is *always* competition among leaders at all levels to be evaluated positively—to demonstrate career-enhancing performance.[94] This generates competitive behavior among leaders at all levels and across functional systems. Chinese officials are entrepreneurial. They resist coordination that does not serve their purposes.

This basic dynamic gives rise to a problem with BRI, and much else. BRI is a central initiative that involves huge amounts of money, embraces an almost unlimited number of potential projects, and whets the appetite of leaders at every level, a large number of functional bureaucracies, and particularly in SOEs. They are all in search of projects that can win central financial support, and they seek resources and endorsement for their schemes. It is with this perspective in mind that three years into BRI, a Beijing think tank undertook an evaluation of BRI and was quite direct about the problems associated with setting project priorities and making sure that a feasible number of projects was undertaken. The report's conclusion? China needed birth control for projects.

Currently the overall coordination mechanism among ministries, provinces and cities still remain[s] to be further reinforced. The lack of a mechanism for coordinating Chinese enterprises' overseas investment has negative effects on the development of the BRI that relies on market-oriented operation. . . . Therefore, great attention should be attached to institutional design as well as exploring and establishing an efficient and powerful nationwide coordination mechanism, so as to offer overall planning and coordination for the BRI. On the one hand, a "positive list" for the construction of the Belt and Road could be introduced to guide all sides to identify the trends in building the Belt and Road and promote more reasonable policy expectations to be formed at different levels of governments. On the other hand, a "negative list" for the construction of the Belt and Road should also be issued to confirm forbidden fields. . . .[95]

Closely paraphrasing one Chinese strategic analyst in Beijing talking about BRI, he wished it had "more of a strategic foundation—what were its goals, and how would success be measured?" It is an initiative, not a strategy, he said. A bit like a basket into which everyone threw their own disconnected ideas.[96] Dr. Lee Jones of the Queen Mary University of London testified with colleagues before a parliamentary inquiry in London, saying, "In reality, BRI is not a coherent geopolitical plan but an agglomeration of many competing interests and schemes. . . . It will unfold not according to some grand strategic master plan designed in Beijing but the often competing and incoherent interests of Chinese provinces, state-owned/private enterprises, policy and commercial banks, and recipient states."[97]

The stark fact is that China has a systemic problem with overcommitment that was exacerbated by President Xi Jinping, particularly in his first term in office (2012–13 to 2017–18).[98] As one respondent put it, Xi is "being criticized left and right for overpromising. The joke here is that Xi is trying to grow the GDP abroad. The media is hyping this. It is showing off China's wealth."[99] However, limiting initiatives and creating feasible expectations among prospective beneficiaries is a big problem. Whereas in a market system, financial markets and bankruptcy enforce some degree of control, in China, particularly when big projects and big SOEs are involved and there is industrial policy, it is difficult to enforce discipline. Ironically, an autocratic system has a discipline problem. Why?

This excessive appetite for big numbers and risk in both domestic and external projects stems from the nature of the Chinese political process, two aspects of which are central. First, there are many sources of initiative in the Chinese system. And second, while the party-state has many tools to promote projects (e.g., bank loans and grants, cadre promotions, directed R & D funds, and directives from party central, central planning agencies, and line bureaucracies), the center's most important power is creating broad policy umbrellas under which myriad SOEs and localities compete to ensconce their pet projects under the protective cover of the broad central mandate. The center creates policy space, policy opportunities that entrepreneurial firms and localities seek to exploit. Chinese localities have an army of lobbyists in Beijing pushing local priorities by linking them to broad central initiatives, and provinces often have substantial sources of revenue that they can mobilize to get a project started. Then, once the sunk costs are substantial, they present Beijing with a fait accompli and pleas for central help. As one government official in Beijing put it, "Yunnan already set up a railway even before there was an overall plan."[100] In Laos, a Western ambassador said to our team, "Not all of this is China's 'bad intentions,'—they [the central government in Beijing] can't control the spillover from Yunnan."[101] Another Western diplomat in southwestern China said that "Everyone is trying to get in on the act" of BRI.[102]

This bubble-up dynamic leads to the predictable result that with considerable frequency projects get started without adequate central coordination and without sufficient thought given to sustainable long-term financing or negative externalities. This dynamic applies to purely domestic projects but increasingly extends to cross-border undertakings as part of the "going out" initiative. The center then finds itself in the position of engaging in cleanup operations and reining in projects.[103] As one Chinese professor put it, "There are differences in central government, local government, and commercial [projects]. Each province/county has its own projects, and no uniform feasibility, environmental assessment."[104]

One illustrative example of these phenomena relates to the desire of small- and medium-size cities in China to obtain HSR lines and stations because they have seen the economic improvements these projects have produced in major cities elsewhere. This has set off a virtual stampede among smaller and medium-size cities. "The investment and economic activity that high-speed rail has brought to big cities has led to a fight among smaller ones to win the right to build a station along routes that pass nearby," according to *Caixin* magazine.[105]

This appetite often produces negotiations among localities and between them and the Ministry of Railways, China Railway Corporation, and NDRC. In the Thirteenth Five-Year Plan (2016–20), China is spending about $549.5 billion to expand the PRC's rail network—this is a huge trough at which most localities want to feed. "Competition between cities has often led provincial-level governments to make compromises on routes. . . . In Henan Province, for example, a feud between Dengzhou and Xinye resulted in the high-speed rail station being built 16 kilometers from Dengzhou and 14 kilometers from Xinye."[106] Local officials often want stations built outside of city centers, so they provide new foci for growth, while the railroad builders, investors, and operators prefer a guaranteed ridership by having lines and stations located in the existing city center. The NDRC, for instance, has "warned" local authorities "to be aware of the social and economic risks relating to high-speed rail developments, such as low appeal to businesses and residents, and required them to ensure that the debts taken on to fund such projects do not lead to higher financial risks."[107] Smaller cities want stations, often grandiose structures that reflect their outsize visions. These require huge upfront sunk costs that take a long time to recoup. This dynamic also is obvious among small cities and towns outside China that want to be hooked into this rail network.

In short, plans are always trying to keep up with the dynamic local reality; plans, once made, are continually spoiled by ongoing political and implementation processes at the local level.

Debate over China's Foreign and Security Policy and Role of the Military. Outside of the PRC there is debate about the degree to which China's connectivity drive is motivated primarily by economic objectives or by strategic/security aims. In actuality, both objectives are intimately intertwined. Within China, when considering the strategic component itself, there is debate over what the national security strategy should be, how it should be conceived. Basically there are two contending approaches—the continentalist[108] and the maritime. HSR (and conventional rail) connectivity in Southeast Asia serves both of these contending lines of thinking, thereby making it relatively politically durable.

The continentalist argument can be heard clearly in the voice of Southwest Jiaotong University's Professor Gao Bai, whom Agatha Kratz and Dragan Pavlićević describe as holding the following view: "The U.S. might be gathering maritime forces in the Pacific and promoting an economic integration partnership excluding China, but China's greater connectivity and infrastructure investment will make it the stronger power in political and economic terms in Asia."[109] The earliest public, comprehensive, and clear formulation of this approach was articulated by Peking University's Professor Wang Jisi in a seminal article entitled

"'Marching Westwards': The Rebalancing of China's Geostrategy."[110] Just as China's capacity to contribute to connectivity with its periphery was maturing, just as Xi Jinping began his consolidation of power, and just as the vision of BRI was taking shape, Wang wrote:

> China should not limit its sights to its own coasts and borders, or to traditional competitors and partners, but should make strategic plans to "look westwards" and "march westwards." . . . China does not have an international geostrategy in print, but as China's eastern regions have traditional development advantages, threats to China's sovereignty and territorial integrity have mainly come from the east. Since the founding of the PRC, foreign policy strategy and military deployments have always focused on East Asia and the Pacific Ocean. Up to now, this has been necessary. However, following the introduction of the "12th Five-Year Plan [2011–2015]: Western Development Strategy" and the corresponding domestic development strategies, China needs to put into practice an appropriate geostrategy to support this. . . . Firstly, China needs to make an overall plan and cooperate with many other countries, with a view to ensuring that the supply channels for oil and other bulk commodities to the west of China's borders remain open. . . . The second implication is that we should increase economic and trade cooperation with, and economic aid to, "all West Asian nations" [in this article, "West Asian nations" refers to all countries in South Asia, Central Asia, the Middle East and the Caspian Sea region] and establish a cooperation and development fund. . . . This, in turn, will widen China's room for strategic maneuver.[111]

Southeast Asia, though unmentioned by Wang, fits into this approach.

The alternative strategy has been articulated by Remin University's Professor Wu Zhengyu, who argues that a vigorous PRC continental strategy would turn Russia into a strategic antagonist and produce a defensive reaction among the relatively smaller powers on the PRC's periphery to the south and west. In Wu's view, the continentalist approach also ignores the defining feature of the US challenge to China, indeed the core of American power—US dominance at sea. Wu sums up his argument succinctly: "China must establish on the basis of the land/sea balance its dominant direction of development. Modern historical experience has shown that land/sea hybrid powers [such as China], once achieving stability of their land borders, principally thereafter focus their energy on sea-oriented development."[112]

If you consider these two broad strategic orientations as organizing rationales for two nascent political coalitions, the continentalist approach is intrinsically attractive to the builders of land infrastructure and landlocked provinces. More attuned to the maritime approach are China's coastal provinces, where the bulk of China's GDP, China's export-oriented enterprises, and institutional forces such as the People's Liberation Army Navy (PLAN) are located. Southeast Asia has a role to play in both strategies, if one thinks about building rail, pipeline, and highway connectivity to coastal ports and maritime routes, which appeals to a broad number of PRC localities and interests.

Stepping back and considering how politicians might address this debate as to whether to give priority to land or sea domains, one way through the political thicket is for decision makers to assert they will do *both*. Build maritime zone capacity and increase connectivity by land simultaneously—avoid a dichotomous choice. This is precisely what "One Belt, One Road" (OBOR, later rebranded BRI) represents politically. The "Belt" is backed by the continentalists and the "Road" by the maritime constituents. It is a policy that meets the needs of both coastal and landlocked areas and has something to offer both strategic approaches. As one informant in the national-level planning bureaucracy put it, "Coastal provinces play a role in both the roads and belts."[113] Most of Southeast Asia is maritime, but the region also has substantial isolated inland areas and land corridors that help avoid maritime vulnerabilities.

This is an analogous position to that in which US Defense Secretary Ash Carter found himself in February 2016 when discussing whether Washington should focus on Russia, China, Iran, North Korea, *or* terrorism as the principal security challenge. His answer was "We don't have the luxury of just one opponent, or the choice between current fights and future fights. We have to do both."[114] This "do everything" answer makes sense as a desire and political move, but it may not be feasible.

To govern is to choose. BRI represents a political decision not to choose—do it all. Build up China's maritime and continental power simultaneously. As China's economic growth slows, its population ages, and the defensive reactions of China's neighbors mount, it may well become progressively more difficult to do it all. On the other hand, if Beijing can pull off this feat, it will be a very much more capable power in the decades ahead.

Another, less-understood institutional aspect of the BRI is the balance in projects serving military interests versus the number of projects in which the PLA has little or no interest. The degree to which BRI is largely an economic initiative is the degree to which the military can feel left behind. This is a subject worthy of deeper exploration; one well-placed observer in Beijing tantalizingly observed: "The PLA is 'very worried about its position [lack of role] in OBOR. There are no words about a military element. The PLA thinks that it is being marginalized in the central government policy-making process—this is the most important foreign policy subject, so they are unhappy [to be left out]. They are thinking about their real position. So, it is not an issue of military [role in BRI]. OBOR is a business/economic initiative.'"[115] One could predict, but currently we have no evidence for, rivalry among PLA services when the issue arises of what military-relevant projects to undertake.

A final security debate arises from the fact that for the PRC's neighbors to feel comfortable with increasing connectivity with China, they must simultaneously feel reassured about Beijing's security behavior. Several Southeast Asian states do not feel entirely secure, whether it be due to competing maritime claims, frontier frictions, or fears of economic and cultural dominance. A PRC security and foreign policy strategy that creates anxiety will impede the economic cooperation BRI requires. In China, as in other big powers, there is open debate about what emphasis to give in overall policy between the frowning mask of the military and the smiling mask of economics and diplomacy. Beyond the obvious naval, commercial, and nationalistic interests involved, there are other considerations as well. Hainan Province, which has been given administrative control over the growing domain in the South China Sea by Beijing, sees consolidation of its writ in Nanyang (the Southern Seas) to be critically important, even if other countries in the region do not like it.

CONCLUSION

To start, as debate about rail development abroad has unfolded in China, there is recognition that in poorer, less-developed countries it is generally wise for China not to push for true HSR of 250 kmph and up. Slower-speed trains in the 160 kmph range are less expensive to build and more flexible with respect to passenger and freight utilization. China's encounter with realities elsewhere in the world has brought more realism over time into PRC ambitions and proposals.

At first glance China's effort to promote HSR (and conventional-speed rail) in Southeast Asia appears to be a well-orchestrated, cohesive, logical, and methodically promoted campaign. In many respects it is. This appearance, however, hides a messier reality. The reality is that different bureaucracies, localities, and groups in the PRC pursue their own interests, couched in language that fits under the broad central policy umbrella. This bottom-up dynamic means that China's efforts in the domain of rail infrastructure, like so many others, lack uniformity and discipline on the ground. This system can often be rapacious.

In a related vein, this interest group quality to policy making contributes to an over-commitment bias with respect to infrastructure—the champions of infrastructure in China are very strong and varied. The railroad companies, for example, have 2 million employees.[116] As long as Beijing has its commitment to industrial policy, strongly backs what it sees as industries of the future through budgetary and other financing mechanisms (including local government finance), and creates incentives for excess infrastructure activity, and as long as the construction industry has such enormous excess capacity, the Chinese system will remain prone to pushing these kinds of projects all over the world, often with insufficient deference to the fragile economic, financial, and political circumstances in partner countries. Moreover, this infrastructure compulsion/bias will continue to generate conflict with competitor industrial countries that see this sort of industrial policy as unfair competition.

These important problems aside, however, the undergirding vision of growth through urbanization, increased domestic and foreign connectivity, and the idea that infrastructure produces growth and therefore is the leading edge of development, all these are worthy, perhaps even visionary, ideas. The United States and others should find ways to not only give credit to these general ideas but advance them in appropriate circumstances, with China or with others. For its part, China needs to reinvigorate market-oriented economic reform, get its security behavior in greater alignment with its foreign economic policy, and improve implementation, as we will see in chapter 6.

Many Chinese see these problems. As a senior Ministry of Commerce official concluded:

> "Some scholars in China say China should be careful about BRI, be careful. Do they [the host countries] need high-speed railway, how long will it take to recover investment, how many customers will they have? . . . Railways could go one hundred thirty to one hundred sixty kilometers per hour. All this is debated, including environmental impact. Do locals feel happy? They have been undisturbed for hundreds of years. Even if we would recommend [doing these projects], you also need to understand what people will support. So we need people-to-people interaction. No single concept will apply; we need more sophisticated help from the United States and the developed world, like on environmental impact. China cannot accomplish this itself."[117]

We turn now to the domestic politics of HSR and conventional rail development in the host countries to China's south.

CHAPTER 4

Diverse Southeast Asian Responses

When I was still in school, the British [the rulers of then British Malaya] built railways from Kedah [Mahathir's home state] to the Thai border. That brought development. In my view, railroads will bring economic growth to neighboring countries. . . . China was poor when we first proposed [the Singapore-Kunming Rail Link]. But now, the Chinese have money. So for this time it will be a Chinese railroad, for a time. But there are problems of land. When you build a railroad you get faster development. They build houses, towns, villages; all bring goods into towns. I was thinking that railroads stimulate growth.

—Mahathir Mohamad, June 2016[1]

China has been successful in its own rail projects, given its technological and financial power. . . . My preferred approach [in forging a rail partnership with China] is to engage them in a joint venture, not just in construction but also in the management and maintenance of the railways [so that China has a long-term stake in ensuring the HSR is well-built and well-run]. The HSR should be a joint venture.

—Abhisit Vejjajiva, May 2017[2]

This chapter examines the role of domestic factors in shaping Southeast Asian nations' outlooks and policies toward China's railroad diplomacy. These factors account for the wide variations in the smaller states' responses to Beijing's rail initiatives. In this chapter we chose to focus on a few variations that particularly demonstrate key patterns of small state response to big power economic inducement: "receptive embrace" (Laos), "selective and flexible engagement" (Thailand), "recalibrated partnership" (Malaysia), and "limited involvement" (Vietnam and some other member countries of the Association of Southeast Asian Nations [ASEAN]).[3]

A recurring theme found across the Southeast Asian responses to Beijing's overtures is that although the policy discussion surrounding the construction of high- and conventional-speed rail and infrastructure connectivity is a developmental matter (with much technocratic content), such projects encompass much more than technocratic issues decided by developmental logic alone. A broad array of systemwide sociopolitical and economic considerations shape the responses of each of Beijing's potential and actual partners. An example of a key consideration is the domestic political narrative that state leaders use to legitimize their governance. Huge differences in political institutions, along with patterns of elite politics, distinguish the responses of one country from another. The degree to which law and institutions govern behavior, and the extent to which a system is highly centralized or decentralized, also shape responses to Beijing. Apart from the degree of pluralization, another critical factor in shaping responses is the level of development and, thus, the economic imperatives and resources in each of these societies.

The interplay of *legitimacy narratives, internal sociopolitical structures*, and *developmental needs* shapes reactions to Beijing's potential rail partnership in various ways. To start, how a potential Southeast Asian partner regime legitimizes its own rule is critical, because it determines the *relative space for a foreign power to initiate and push for connectivity* in the first place. In a regime whose main aim is the preservation of national autonomy and national security in a hostile context (with the PRC being a part of that threatening environment), fostering connectivity cooperation with Beijing is a harder sell. Conversely, in a country where the regime's raison d'être is economic development, with fewer security concerns (about Beijing), there is likely to be greater receptivity to what the PRC has to offer. It is notable that both of these scenarios are found in China's own experience. When Mao Zedong saw his regime as besieged by a hostile West, "self-reliance" became his mantra. When Deng Xiaoping took over at a time when security tension (with the West) was lower, he sought to prop up frayed party legitimacy by adopting economic development and enhanced citizen welfare as the new national narrative, accordingly launching his policy of "Reform and Opening." Deng adopted policies fostering interdependence and global connectivity. In short, the centrality of a more nationalistic and security-focused legitimation may compel a governing elite to place more insular politics before development—prompting these nations to delay or distance themselves from foreign-supported projects, despite potential benefits.

Moreover, polities have diverse institutional structures with varied patterns of elite and socioeconomic fragmentation. More authoritarian/centralized states often make faster decisions than states that are more federal/decentralized in character. Societies marked by wide economic disparities and social imbalances find moving ahead with big infrastructure projects challenging. This is particularly evident when social communities have their "rights" embedded in law or there is ethnic division, particularly in Southeast Asia where the role of local Chinese communities is often a rather delicate matter.

Prospects for connectivity cooperation between Beijing and its partners to the south reflect the character of each potential partner's legitimating narrative and its politico-socioeconomic milieu. There is no single generalizable pattern of negotiation and implementation processes for all seven potential partners for Beijing as the rail interconnectivity vision incrementally unfolds. In fact, each step toward realizing the vision requires building a unique coalition in each country. Each project is a *sui generis* negotiation with each individual negotiation influencing the prospects for subsequent states' engagements with China's rail diplomacy—variously helping, hindering, or potentially halting the component parts of Beijing's rail push in Southeast Asia.

This chapter includes five sections, starting with a framework discussion of the factors shaping weaker states' responses to infrastructure-based inducement. While the next three sections focus on the principal types of state responses in three specific countries, the last one compares the approaches and draws conclusions about how domestic politics shape weaker states' engagements with big powers and connectivity diplomacy.

STATE RESPONSES TO INFRASTRUCTURE-BASED INDUCEMENT

Although this study focuses on railroad infrastructure–related partnership, the observations here are also germane to the broader issue of *weaker-state response to big power economic statecraft*, i.e., the use of economic tools for political ends. China's various railroad projects in Southeast Asia have been promoted under its BRI (Belt and Road Initiative) signboard, a tool of economic statecraft involving connectivity development across Asia, indeed the rest of the world. As outlined in chapter 3, BRI involves infrastructure development assistance and partnership in the form of loans, investments, technical support, construction, and capacity enhancement. Here we focus on why some states are more responsive to partnership with the PRC than others, particularly in the project initiation and adoption stages.[4] This focus helps fill a gap in the literature on economic statecraft, which generally concerns itself with the *use, motives, and effects* of economic tools in foreign policy, rather than partner *responsiveness*.[5] Even fewer studies have concentrated on responses to infrastructure-related inducements.[6] We address *why* partners who are the targets of big-power economic diplomacy respond as they do.

The underlying assertion of this chapter is that the varied degrees of receptivity among the Southeast Asian states to China's rail infrastructure diplomacy are chiefly a function of *domestic* factors. That is, states' diverse politico-socioeconomic characteristics produce distinctive and varied patterns of engagement with the PRC (e.g., compare Laos's enthusiastic embrace with Malaysia's cautious recalibration or Thailand's selective involvement). The variation among state responses is best understood by reference to their individual national narratives (mode of political legitimation), economic circumstances, structure of their governing systems, and their state-society relations. It is also true, however, that Beijing's regional and bilateral foreign policy behavior can create a more or less receptive environment for PRC infrastructure initiatives.

Why states respond to infrastructure inducement differently: The legitimation and pluralization matrix. Two spectra of internal attributes help differentiate potential partner states' responsiveness to China's involvement in infrastructure development. One dimension of differentiation is *how ruling political elites legitimize their domestic rule*, the national narratives that governing elites advance to justify their right to rule and to generate support for policies. A second spectrum of state attributes concerns pluralization: *how political power is distributed across the ruling class and different segments of the society*. How diffused is power in a society? It often is easier to reach a definitive outcome with a state in which power is concentrated and more centralized than a polity in which power is diffuse and diverse interest groups deeply embedded.

Legitimation lies at the core of politics. All governing elites claim a "right" to rule by summoning the support of certain ideals, inherited practices, past events, or lineage. Plato, the Greek political philosopher, discussed the essential role that founding and authoritative myths play in governance.[7] Effective myths justify, enhance, and help consolidate the elite's domestic authority vis-à-vis contesting or aspiring elites.[8] The legitimation ideals and pathways run along a broad spectrum, from *procedural* virtues (e.g., democratic values, practices, and social justice), through *particularistic* narratives (identity politics, including nationalist sentiments, autonomous urge, ethnic and religious appeals, personal charisma), and on to *performance*-related rationales (such as ensuring economic growth and delivering development gains, to overcoming national vulnerabilities or reestablishing lost glories). No ruler relies on a single pathway to legitimacy but rather on some combination. Nonetheless, balance among rationales matters, because it is the *tradeoffs* among the alternative pathways that determine the direction and prioritization of major state undertakings. This balance differentiates one regime from another.

Given that the focus of this chapter is on weaker states' responses to big-power economic inducement, here we concentrate on a state's *relative* emphasis on *development performance legitimation* as distinct from *identity-nationalist* and *other inner justifications*. These pathways are not mutually exclusive. Nonetheless, among the Southeast Asian countries with whom Beijing is trying to partner, their emphases vary on economic performance versus a more nationalistic preoccupation with defense of physical stakes, identity, and sovereignty. Cambodian, Lao, Malaysian, and Singaporean ruling elites emphasize development performance as their *primary* legitimation rationale. This, in turn, drives their leaders to embrace external assistance or partnership that could boost their own development and economic performance; hence their inclination to see Beijing's BRI as an opportunity. In contrast, Vietnam's governing elites have a different emphasis, attaching relatively greater importance to nationalist legitimation and defense of identity and territorial sovereignty. This nationalist legitimation pathway is in part related to Vietnam's unhappy modern history with China, not to mention Hanoi's experiences with French colonialism and US intervention. More recently, land border and maritime conflicts with the PRC have arisen. The centrality of nationalist legitimation colors elite and popular perceptions of Chinese power, inclining Vietnamese leaders and citizens alike to view Beijing-backed infrastructure projects with skepticism. In short, the more central economic performance is to regime legitimation, the greater a country's receptivity to external connectivity partnership. Conversely, the more salient nationalistic legitimation is, the lower the proclivity to cooperate on connectivity projects (see diagram 1).

However, this variable alone does not explain why policy reviews or recalibrations might occur among originally enthusiastic countries (e.g., Malaysia under Mahathir in his second period of leadership). Nor does it explain why some negotiations are more protracted than others, or why some connectivity partnerships are more limited than anticipated, despite their developmental benefits and bilateral cordiality (Thailand). This is where the second domestic attribute comes in: the degree of *power pluralization* within state elites and society.

While the legitimation *driver* motivates ruling elites to pursue and prioritize "national" goals in distinctive ways (e.g., development legitimation prioritizes prosperity, whereas identity-nationalist legitimation prioritizes autonomy, security, and sovereignty), the pace and direction of such pursuits are facilitated or constrained by the degree of pluralization and power diffusion across state and society structures, as well as by the degree of decentralization.[9] Diffusion is distinct from decentralization. Decentralization is about *vertical* distribution: it concerns how political and administrative powers are distributed across various levels of the state apparatus.[10] Diffusion is a broader concept, encompassing both the *vertical and horizontal* distribution of power across the state elites, between the state and society, and within society itself.

The degree of power pluralization is a function of three considerations—regime type (democratic vs. authoritarian), inter-elite dynamics (elite contestation vs. collaboration), and societal activism (strong vs. weak society).[11] Although democracy is associated with high levels of power diffusion, this pattern can vary. For example, though Singapore has elections, its political system concentrates power (thanks to the People's Action Party's strategies of co-option and control). Conversely, a country can be an illiberal polity but, nonetheless, possess considerable power diffusion. A case in point is Thailand under military rule. The current military government came to power in 2014 through a coup, not the ballot box, and has invoked special executive powers over legislative and judicial functions several times. These authoritarian traits notwithstanding, the Thai political system displays considerable power diffusion, on-and-off again elections, intense inter-elite contestation, high societal activism, and strong pockets of civil society (including labor unions).

In one-party states such as Laos and Vietnam (and to some extent, polities with a single dominant political actor such as Cambodia), the ruling elite's authority and decisions are rarely openly contested. In these cases, because the state is strong and society weak, debate and struggle usually take place within, rather than outside, the establishment, and policy changes are rarely precipitated by bottom-up societal pressure. This is a contrast to other Southeast Asian countries, notably Indonesia, Philippines, Thailand, and Malaysia, where bottom-up forces are of considerable importance. This power diffusion originates in their respective constitutional systems, heterogeneous sociodemographic structures, fragmented elites, pluralized economies and societies, and active civil organizations. A good example of how political contestation can affect receptivity to China's infrastructure initiatives is the Indonesian election of 2019. President Jokowi, running as the incumbent for an additional five-year term, emphasized infrastructure and improved life for his people while his opponent, Prabowo Subianto, sought support through a more sectarian appeal to Muslims, an authoritarian vision, and less dependence on China. Jokowi won the election, but had his opponent prevailed, the impact upon the HSR rail from Jakarta to Bandung might have been quite different.[12]

This is significant because the degree of power diffusion determines the *political space* in which China's potential railroad partners have to operate and thereby critically shapes the processes of project negotiation and implementation. The higher the power diffusion (quadrants 2 and 3 in diagram 1), the greater the political constraint on the PRC's interlocutors.

When the power pluralization spectrum intersects the legitimation continuum, there is a fourfold table of possible circumstances, as illustrated in diagram 1. In countries in which the ruling elite relies more heavily on development performance legitimation than other pathways, there is generally a higher degree of receptivity to foreign-supported connectivity partnership (quadrants 1 and 2). This receptivity is likely to be sustained in a circumstance where power diffusion is modest (power is concentrated) (quadrant 1), because under that condition there is an absence of constraining forces that could deny or derail the elite's decision. Interconnectivity politics in Laos (and Cambodia) falls into this quadrant. Conversely, elite receptivity is likely subject to more opposition, cyclical recalibrations, or adjustments if power diffusion is high (quadrant 3), because the pluralized nature of the power structure means that all decisions are continuously scrutinized by contending elites and diversely motivated societal actors. This scenario played out in Malaysia under Mahathir 2.0, after the May 2018 elections. In countries where nationalist and other identity-based particularistic legitimation trumps developmental justification (quadrants 3 and 4), states are likely to respond to foreign economic inducement by limited involve-

Relative Degree of Development-
based Legitimation

(vs. Identity-based Legitimation)

		Low	High
		Quadrant 3	Quadrant 2
	High	Selective and flexible engagement	Receptive, with cyclical recalibration
Degree of Power Pluralization		• Thailand	• Malaysia
(vs. Power Concentration)		Quadrant 4	Quadrant 1
	Low	Limited involvement	Enthusiastic embrace
		• Vietnam	• Laos

DIAGRAM 1. The legitimation-pluralization matrix and state response to external inducement.

ment if power diffusion is low (quadrant 4), or partial engagement if power diffusion is high (quadrant 3). When the power structure is diffused, the plurality of players and interests tends to compel the ruling elites to engage in connectivity development projects in a more selective manner, taking part actively only in circumstances that benefit their core internal constituencies and external alignment positions. Thailand under military government since 2014 is an important case in point.

With this comparative framework for analysis, we can analyze the tangible realities that the PRC encounters in its dealings with potential partners in rail connectivity in Southeast Asia. China is encountering very messy realities in the diverse states in which it is trying to build its Pan-Asia Railway. These distinctive and divergent circumstances require nuance, subtlety, flexibility, and the ability to learn from mistakes— qualities not always associated with the PRC way of doing business. Nonetheless, progress has occurred.

LAOS: GRADUAL, RECEPTIVE EMBRACE

Laos's engagement with and response to China's HSR diplomacy is a case of a gradual but receptive embrace. Three features characterize Laos-China HSR engagement. To start, within the context of China-Southeast

Asia HSR interaction, the Laos railroad was the first China-related HSR project to progress to all three stages of initiation-negotiation-implementation, with large-scale construction work underway on the ground since late 2016.[13] By mid-2018, about 40 percent of phase-one work was complete, with the entire 414 kilometer-long rail project on schedule to be finished by the end of 2021.[14]

In comparison, after dozens of rounds of negotiation over years, the China-backed Thailand-China HSR project has thus far proceeded only as far as a 3.5 km section of the planned 253 km project between Bangkok and Nakhon Ratchasima.[15] No firm date has been set for the completion of the first stretch or the second leg (the 350 km stretch between Nakhon Ratchasima and Nong Khai, on the Thai-Lao border), where it would link in to the rail line coming through Laos from China. As for Malaysian (and Singaporean) rail engagement with the PRC, it has been a bumpy ride, with two rail projects being suspended by Malaysia pending renegotiation of cost and terms after the change of federal government in Putrajaya in May 2018.[16] In Indonesia, progress of the China-funded 142 km long HSR project from Jakarta to Bandung has been slow, with serious construction postponed for a protracted period due to licensing, financing, and most particularly land acquisition issues (see chapter 6).[17]

The second feature of the Laos-China railroad is that, once fully completed, it will be the first and only *modern* cross-border rail line directly linking China to Southeast Asia. The estimated US$7 billion Laos railroad, using Chinese rail standards and equipment, will directly connect Southeast Asia to the PRC's HSR system via the Yuxi-Mohan line. The 1.435 m standard-gauge railroad, linking the Lao capital of Vientiane with its northern border town of Boten, will connect directly into the line to Kunming, the provincial capital of China's southwestern province of Yunnan, which in turn connects China's southwest to the rest of the huge country. Once the Laos line extends southward to the border with Thailand and connects with the China-backed Bangkok–Nong Khai HSR line, the resulting Central Line will be the first ever cross-border railroad running through the heart of Southeast Asia to Bangkok. For China, Laos, and Thailand, Bangkok is the economic prize. Thailand views this development as solidifying its hopes of becoming the logistical hub for both east-west and north-south transport in Southeast, East, and South Asia— playing a role analogous to that played by Chicago in the North American experience.

The significance of the Laos-China rail project, therefore, goes beyond national development and bilateral ties. It is a crucial link in the wider *regional* rail network, the Pan-Asia Railway. Without this stretch, it would be extremely difficult for China to pursue its vision of building an HSR network in Southeast Asia. Beijing would be forced to try to go west from Kunming through Myanmar (to Bangkok) or east through Vietnam. Each of these alternative routes is geographically longer and politically more arduous for the reasons implied by the comparative framework discussed previously and elsewhere in this volume. The Sino-Lao project, hence, serves as an essential foundation for China's rail diplomacy in Southeast Asia.

The third characteristic of the Lao-Chinese HSR agreement is that, in terms of pace and patterns of response, the Lao embrace of Chinese rail diplomacy has been a gradual, top-down process stretching over a decade. Although talks about the concept of Laos-China rail partnership go back to the early 2000s, actual construction did not begin until December 2016. Laos's embrace is described as a *top-down* process, because Vientiane's decision was party-centered, despite widespread popular concerns about debt burdens, fiscal sustainability, economic viability, and environmental protection.

This is not to say that there has been no publicly visible political contestation surrounding Vientiane's HSR decision. Contestation has taken place (some in the National Assembly, for instance, want to play a bigger oversight role in debt management), but it unfolds primarily *within* the power establishment.[18] This is in sharp contrast to Thailand, Malaysia, and several other Southeast Asian countries, in which open challenges and criticisms from contending elites and social groups constrain, delay, or derail the governing elites' desired outcomes. In Laos, once the HSR decision was made by the party, debate concluded, for the most part, and questions since have revolved around implementation challenges, overseeing the budget, and spending issues.

What explains Vientiane's gradual embrace of rail interconnectivity with the PRC? Beyond the country's Leninist one-party political system, the ruling elite's gradual but receptive embrace of Beijing's HSR partnership in the face of its own deep concerns about dependence, debt, and other socioeconomic risks requires some explanation. The governing elite's decision reflects the interplay between its foundation of performance legitimacy (escaping poverty and isolation) and the freedom of maneuver that a system with a low level of power diffusion confers upon leaders.

Need for development, as understood by the governing Lao People's Revolutionary Party (LPRP), has been the key factor driving its grand vision of transforming Laos from a "land-locked into a land-linked country." Constructing a north-south railroad linking its capital Vientiane to China to the north and Bangkok to the south (and to other ASEAN economies) is central to this aspiration. Lao leaders view the railroad as an "iron river" that could transform the economic future of Laos, one of the poorest and least developed countries in the region, thereby securing the party-state's political survival. Just as Deng Xiaoping saw post–Cultural Revolution China's legitimacy hanging by a thread in 1977–78, and therefore radically shifted goals toward economic modernization, in Laos today, the LPRP sees its future viability depending on economic gains and interregional connectivity. The availability of Chinese resources, technology, and Beijing's aggressive commercial and political negotiating tactics have given Vientiane the sense that there is only a limited window of opportunity. Their centralized political order permits them to try to seize the opportunity. As one diplomatic official in Vientiane put it: "When you want something, you have to sacrifice something else. Yes, it will be a big burden for next generations, but we have no choice."[19]

At the project's December 2016 groundbreaking ceremony in Luang Prabang, the old royal capital, Lao Minister of Public Works and Transport Bounchanh Sinthavong remarked: "Once completed, the railway will benefit Lao people of all ethnic groups, facilitate and reduce costs of transportation, stimulate the development of agricultural and industrial sectors, tourism, investment and trade, as well as generate income for Lao people and the country."[20] His deputy minister and chairman of the Laos-China Railway Project Management Committee, Lattanamany Khounnivong, stressed that the LPRP's Central Committee and the government have "prioritized railway development as an essential solution in transforming Laos from a landlocked country into a land-linked country."

Vientiane's statements highlight three types of developmental benefits of the railroad. First, better physical infrastructure connectivity means greater market access, connecting Laos directly to huge markets in China and neighboring Southeast Asian economies. Second, increased trade and investment flows from neighboring countries mean greater opportunities to diversify the Lao production base and transform its economic structure. Third, increased people-to-people connectivity will likely boost the country's tourism and related sectors, which, given its virtually untouched heritage sites, could be a huge economic and cultural boon. Laos's leading think tank, the National Economic Research Institute (NERI), emphasized the country's role as a gateway in the expanding regional integration: "Laos's strategic location, being centrally positioned among giant economies and as a gateway connecting China with the 10-member ASEAN regional bloc, gives the country outstanding advantages."[21] A Lao business leader observed that shipping goods from coastal ports in Thailand to Chinese ports currently takes at least one month. However, once the Laos-China railroad is completed, goods from Thailand could go through Laos to China's Yunnan Province and cities and vice versa within a day. In addition, large numbers of Chinese tourists could take this route, and Laos could benefit as a transit point.[22] One senior Lao development official conveyed the image of Laos as a kind of tollbooth making great gains if it merely raked in a surcharge on everything passing through its jurisdiction. However, the vision goes beyond that of a tollbooth to include aspirations to build Laos into regional supply chains. As one Lao trade official explained, "We don't want to be just a transit corridor, but we want to be part of the value chain. We hope we can extract more investment; 'big ones in China, to set up manufacturing here, even if it is small parts, [we want] to grab something from this.'"[23]

Such development benefits are central to the party's legitimacy quest, where the "Lao party-state (*phak lat*)" essentially relies on continuous economic growth and growing prosperity.[24] Mega infrastructure projects are key to transforming the isolated, mountainous country. Laos's plan to tap its vast hydropower potential (to become "the battery of Southeast Asia") through a cascade of Chinese (and other foreign-built) hydro dams is another example of the kind of large-scale development that appeals to regimes with big infrastructure needs and legitimacy deficits. The Eighth Five-Year National Socio-Economic Development Plan (2016–20), a national strategy to facilitate Laos graduating from the status of being a lesser-developed country (LDC), envisions constructing large-scale infrastructure projects.[25]

As a small country of seven million, ruled by a communist government, the Lao political system has relatively little diffusion of political power or voice. The government's key policy decisions are seldom openly contested. This does not mean that there is no policy disagreement among party elites and government officials, nor does it mean there is no bottom-up resentment from the people. Rather, policy disagreements among party elites and officials usually are resolved behind closed doors. Bottom-up sentiments and views are typically contained and at times suppressed, with individual interests usually sacrificed in the name of social stability and the greater good. Nonetheless, Lao officials do hint at the challenges simmering below the surface. As one senior official explained: "'Many owners of land and properties will be affected. Many hospitals, many schools will have to be relocated. Government will pay compensation to those who are affected. You see, 50 meters on each side of the railway will be allocated for rail construction. This will be a painful process.' Government will have to address many issues in the process."[26]

A few examples of such bubbling-up phenomena being managed behind the screen can be found. A recent work by Lao scholar Vatthana Pholsena describes "hiccups in the decision-making process" that took place behind closed doors concerning a party decision in 2011 to halt the initiation of the HSR project. The project was suddenly postponed, allegedly because of concerns at the highest levels of the ruling party "over the terms of the contract, which included the hiring of a massive number of Chinese laborers."[27]

Another indicator of the low degree of power diffusion is the dearth of open and organized channels to express demands for compensation for those affected by the railroad project, particularly land acquisition (see chapter 6 for more). In a Radio Free Asia report in 2017, Brooks Boliek wrote that many residents who would lose land and other property to the rail project reacted adversely to the lack of information concerning "how their homes and property would be affected by the planned construction, when they would be forced to move, and how they would be compensated." Reportedly, when the villagers wanted to ask questions at meetings, "the authorities would not allow them to do so."[28]

THAILAND: PROTRACTED NEGOTIATIONS, SELECTIVE ENGAGEMENT

Thailand, like Laos, is a crucial link in Beijing's ambitious plan to build a China-centered regional HSR network in Southeast Asia. It will be an *indispensable hub* for the envisaged Kunming-Singapore Central Line and the wider Pan-Asia Railway network. To begin with, the planned Sino-Thai railroad from Nong Khai (on the Thai-Lao border) to Bangkok is the rail line connecting to the Sino-Lao railroad discussed above. Bangkok is the governmental, commercial, and logistical heart of the kingdom, and it is the designated meeting point for all three envisioned rail lines, as the western, central, and eastern routes all would converge there before rolling southward to Kuala Lumpur and terminating in Singapore, should the entire vision be completed. Geography, thus, makes Thailand the central spot on the map for pan-Asian rail connectivity, whether it be north-south or east-west.

Intersecting political and development imperatives are key determinants shaping Thai elites' policy choices on the direction, degree, and pace of the country's participation in Southeast Asian rail connectivity development. The pattern of Thailand's responses to Beijing's HSR diplomacy has included three characteristics: *protracted talks, selective and flexible engagement,* and *a broadly shared inclination* to avoid overdependence on any single power. Balance is a key word in the Thai political lexicon.

Thailand-China HSR interactions have been protracted, on-again, off-again, with delayed implementation (see chapters 5 and 6). As in the Laos case, Thailand took a long time to contemplate a rail connectivity partnership with the PRC. But unlike Laos where the one-party centralized government's decision making eventually led to breaking ground on large-scale construction of the 414 km Vientiane-Boten line in December 2016, Thailand-China HSR cooperation has traveled a bumpier route. As of the summer of 2019, large-scale construction on the Thai HSR had not yet begun, beyond the 3.5 km stretch already mentioned. Bilateral talks on the project started under the Abhisit administration (2008–11), progressed through the Yingluck (2011–14) period, and accelerated then stalled under the current coup-installed Prayut government (2014–present).[29] Each time there was a change of government in Bangkok, key elements of previously negotiated arrangements had to be significantly reworked.

For instance, the Abhisit administration's 2010 framework for Thailand-China HSR cooperation called for three routes: one connecting Nong Khai to Bangkok, the second from Bangkok eastward to the industrialized Thai eastern seaboard, and a third from the capital southward to the Thai-Malaysian border at Padang Besar.[30] Under the present military junta, the first route was retained, the second adapted, and the third ignored. The military regime similarly dismissed Yingluck's "rice for high-speed rail" program.[31] In short, throughout this entire period of more than a decade, routes and financing were under debate within Thailand and between Bangkok and Beijing.

Under General Prayut Chan-o-cha, the army head who launched a coup d'état and seized power in May 2014, Thailand has continued talking with China to move their HSR partnership forward. In fact, in December 2014, the kingdom's National Legislative Assembly approved a draft memorandum of understanding (MOU) with Beijing to construct the $10.64 billion rail project. However, after a government meeting in February 2015, the then Deputy Transport Minister Arkhom Termpittayapaisith announced the terms of agreement would "have to be renegotiated."[32] As of early 2019, the two countries had engaged in twenty-six rounds of negotiations over four years. The negotiations, co-chaired by

Thai Transport Minister and deputy head of China's National Development and Reform Commission (NDRC), dragged on over several sticking points: interest rates, costs, method of financing, seizure of assets if loans were not repaid, control, and development rights.[33] Thailand rejected PRC proposals to develop land along the planned route due to concerns about infringing on Thai sovereignty and because the State Railway of Thailand and the associated labor union did not want to lose development revenues. In the Laos case, Vientiane conceded much more with respect to right-of-way development and contemplating mine asset seizures if loans went unpaid.[34] Bangkok also rejected Chinese firms' proposals to manage the proposed line. China offered a loan with 2.5 percent interest, but Bangkok wanted 2 percent, referring to the lower rate the PRC already had offered Indonesia for the Jakarta-Bandung line. China put the total cost of the railroad at 468 billion baht, but Thailand estimated it should cost only 369 billion baht ($10.31 billion).[35]

In March 2016, Prayut announced that Thailand would solely finance the entire 250 km Bangkok to Nakhon Ratchasima section of the railroad using domestic loans, but would use Chinese technology, equipment, and construction firms.[36] This decision muted the sovereignty issue but left many other topics on the table such as employment, cost, technological quality, and so forth. Moreover, Thailand was already committed to double-tracking its existent single-track, one-meter-gauge line, so there was the issue of how the old refurbished system would relate to a new higher-speed, 1.435 m standard-gauge line slated to run parallel to it.

Many observers believe the long, drawn-out process irritated China, leading to the exclusion of the Thai Prime Minister (Prayut) from the BRI Summit in Beijing in May 2017, a move described by one Thai scholar as China's "shame offensive."[37] Perhaps it worked, as the following month, Prayut exercised his executive power, invoking Article 44 of the Interim Constitution to push though the rail project by waiving legal restrictions to allow the employment of Chinese engineers for the project, while bypassing normal procurement procedures to hire a Chinese state firm to do design work and construction consulting.[38] Chinese Foreign Minister Wang Yi traveled to Bangkok in July 2017 to push things further along.[39] Both pressure and personal, leader diplomacy are key elements of Beijing's playbook. Parenthetically, Prayut was invited to the second Belt and Road Summit in April 2019, along with other leaders from ASEAN and elsewhere.

In the language of regime legitimation in Bangkok, however, the government claimed that the special treatment for Beijing was necessary to clear many legal obstacles faced by the project, in order "to deepen the bilateral relationship [with Beijing] and bring great benefit to people."[40] Developing closer ties with China is important to the junta's legitimation both internally and externally. Moving ahead with the PRC demonstrates to the domestic audience that the nation is not isolated, especially when Washington is adopting punitive measures in reaction to the coup that brought Prayut to power in the first place. Making this huge project happen also allows the military government to use robust Thailand-China ties to incentivize Washington and the EU to be more cooperative—after all, Bangkok is still one of five American treaty allies in Asia, and Washington does not wish to see Bangkok drift geopolitically too close to Beijing (see chapter 7).

Thailand is using *both* economic and social development *and* sovereignty maintenance to strengthen its legitimacy story. Consequently, compared to the case of Laos, in Thailand there is more ambivalence toward a big infrastructure project such as China's HSR. So, for instance, Thailand buys submarines from China, but simultaneously cooperates in US naval exercises. Similarly, Bangkok rejects Beijing's rail financing and right-of-way development proposals, but awards rail contracts to Beijing. This is quintessentially a hedging approach: pursuing deliberately contradictory measures aimed at underscoring a stance of not taking sides, while keeping options open and creating a space for courtship.[41] It is what Thais refer to as "complex engagement" with the big powers. As one senior leader put it to our research team, "Thailand is like a 'beautiful lady' who will wait and see."[42] Given Thailand's financial wherewithal, greater market size, and strategic location, it is in a much better position to chart its own course than is Laos.

Legitimacy is central to the Thai ruling elites' calculations and choices vis-à-vis rail connectivity projects. The search for domestic legitimacy energizes the junta's decision to pursue megaprojects and embrace the China-backed HSR venture, but simultaneously *limits* the extent and domains where the authorities are able to collaborate and make concessions to Beijing. For the coup-installed leaders who suffer from a deficit of procedural legitimation (though they eventually won the March 2019 election), they hope to generate authority and maintain power via a combination of performance and particularistic justification. This requires the junta to pursue *multiple* goals concurrently: delivering development performance, while also restoring political stability, carrying out reforms, fighting corruption, and preserving the kingdom's unique national identity and autonomy.

Initially, construction of the north-south rail line was to start in October 2017; it began just two months later. By 2018, years-long negotiations had resulted in the construction of only a 3.5 km section between Klang Dong and Pang Asok stations, a portion of the 253 km Bangkok-Nakhon Ratchasima route, the first phase of the project. One official explained this obviously marginal first step as a foot-in-the door strategy (a "uniquely Thai" way of doing things) to show project skeptics that this could work.[43] As of this writing, construction of this phase's main section is scheduled to commence in March 2019.[44] Our research team traveled the entire distance of the proposed line from Bangkok to Nong Khai by car. The State Railway of Thailand already possesses a very wide right of way, and, if it materializes, the Chinese 1.435-m standard-gauge line will run parallel to the preexistent one-meter-gauge line that was being upgraded and double-tracked as of 2017. The higher-speed "Chinese" line would be more long-distance passenger oriented and the slower, preexistent line more freight- and local-passenger oriented.

The fact that the military junta called off most of the Yingluck administration's key policies after the coup, but decided to reinstate the Thai-Chinese rail project, is indicative of converging developmental, political, and strategic logic. As observed by Thai scholar Pavin Chachavalpongpun, the military junta "is eager for the legitimacy that comes with large-scale infrastructure investment from China at a time when relations with traditional Western partners, especially the U.S., are strained."[45]

Nevertheless, the importance of infrastructure investment and China to the junta's legitimation does not mean that the military government is ready to capitulate to PRC demands. This is in part because of the high degree of power diffusion characteristic of the Thai political system; elite contestation and societal pluralization often serve to constrain policy choices, even under military rule.[46] It is also because the Thai identity-based legitimation has been a salient source of the kingdom's external conduct.[47] According to the Thai Transport Minister Arkhom in 2015, the person responsible for leading the negotiation team for the Thailand-China HSR project, "Under the previous government, the Sino-Thai railway didn't move forward because the Chinese wanted everything, just like in Laos." He added, "They wanted the right to use the land, the right to develop the station and to import the labor, but what we started with was—*this is Thailand* so we will do our part."[48]

Take, for example, Thai elites' sensitivity concerning development rights along the right-of-way and their refusal to allow the PRC to develop land along the planned route. One analyst pointed out:

Development rights to land are normally a sticking point in rail projects because they give rights to profitable ancillary development projects along the line. This was the case in Thailand, but it turned out that the Chinese had overlooked the fact that the King [Rama V] had long since given the land to the State Railway of Thailand (SRT). In a political situation involving hyper-royalist sentiments and a royalist junta, it was neither possible nor desirable for the Thai negotiators to include land rights in the negotiation.[49]

Moreover, the SRT and the State Railway Workers' Union of Thailand saw the land as their greatest asset. As one Thai official put it, "Unions, think unions and land."[50] In short, Chinese proposals offended these actors' sense of sovereignty *and* their interests.

This brings us to another feature of Thailand's interactions with Chinese HSR inducement: *selective and adaptive engagement*. While Thai governing elites are committed to the overall *direction* of realizing the HSR partnership with China, they also observe some red lines concerning sovereignty and autonomy. And finally, they are flexible in terms of the detailed arrangements with respect to *implementation*. The actual substance of specific negotiations and subsequent implementation evolves based on the ruling elites' politically based assessments and particular group interests.

This pattern is discernible when one compares the junta's protracted, reactive, and at times ambiguous approach to negotiating the Bangkok-Nong Khai line discussed above, with the regime's more concerted, decisive, and swift push in advancing the various infrastructure programs along the Eastern Economic Corridor (EEC). Notable in this respect is the planned HSR network linking the U-Tapao Airport with Bangkok's two international airports—Suvarnabhumi and Don Mueang. Although the EEC megaproject was launched in mid-2017 (later than the adoption of the China-backed Bangkok–Nong Khai line project), the Prayut cabinet and the Parliament have fast-tracked this $20 billion EEC-related infrastructure scheme, pushing through the ambitious plan before the next election in 2019.[51] Also, the EEC infrastructure project had powerful domestic corporate support (an influential champion) in Thailand.[52] Results of the tendering process were scheduled to be submitted to the cabinet in late January 2019 and the project to open for riders in 2024.[53]

Compared to this relatively swift and smooth progress in advancing the EEC high-speed inter-airport rail link, the junta's approaches in the Thailand-China HSR rail project along the Central Line are more selective and ambiguous. The Thai authorities' various statements reveal how they anticipate China's role evolving over the progression from one project phase to the next. In June 2018, Transport Minister Arkhom reportedly said, after cochairing the twenty-fourth round of the negotiation, that the second phase of the HSR project "will be implemented by Thailand with China acting as consultants in terms of feasibility study and design."[54] A few weeks later, the minister was cited as saying, "Thailand is in talks with China for a loan to fund the project and is negotiating terms such as the interest rate and a contract for rolling stock worth eight billion baht."[55] A few months later, in October 2018, the same minister said: "Thailand has assumed all financial responsibility for the project and will handle the construction side, but will eventually sign a contract with China to purchase the rolling stock and operation equipment."[56]

Taken together, these statements do not provide a clear picture of China's exact role(s) in the second phase. It is unclear if the minister's statement that Thailand "will handle the construction side" was intended to suggest that China will not play the role of builder at all, but only a partner in providing design, finance, and equipment. If true, this arrangement may signify that this is an effort to distribute work and contracts to Thai constituencies important for electoral considerations. At a minimum, such localization suggests that the Thai government wants to legitimize the overall endeavor by demonstrating that as each phase unfolds, the Thai role will become greater and bring more local benefits.

The junta's concerted and focused efforts to promote EEC as its first priority economic development program may have to do with the fact that the military government views it as low-hanging fruit, a relatively easier and faster way for the junta to project its performance legitimacy. According to a Thai logistics expert, the EEC "builds on a nice thing that already exists", i.e., Thailand's eastern seaboard. By aiming to expand connectivity to neighboring countries, the EEC is thus promoted as "a quick win for the current government."[57] The EEC—which includes the eastern provinces of Chachoengsao, Chonburi, and Rayong—already is among Thailand's most developed areas. Consequently, "building on the best" is one way to produce rapid economic results, even if at the expense of exacerbating already evident regional socioeconomic gaps. The proposed "Chinese line" through the comparatively less developed northeast of Thailand (which has one-third of the nation's 67 million population and land but only 10 percent of its GDP) will have a longer payback period because it traverses poor locales. The economic gap between the southeast and northeast of Thailand, in part, reflects the successful implementation of the Eastern Seaboard Project two decades ago.[58] Upgrading key infrastructure in the area, especially through the HSR airport rail link, will be crucial to attracting high-tech, value-added industries to the east coast. In short, the Thai government is moving slowly forward with Beijing on the north-south line, while putting emphasis on rail development in the country's southeast—where the gains are faster and the political rewards greater.

In addition, electoral interests may have added another reason for the junta to prioritize the southeast over the northeast. The northeast region of Isan is among the kingdom's poorest, where political rival Shinawatra (family) and the "red shirts" have an electoral stronghold. Conversations with the locals during our research field trip revealed expressions of strong support for former Prime Minister Thaksin Shinawatra and his sister Yingluck. Predictably, the ruling junta, which is relatively weak in these areas, tends to emphasize arrangements that best address the political needs of its core constituencies in other regions.

Finally, Thailand's rail engagement also reflects international balance-of-power politics (also see chapter 7). This feature is less prominent in the case of Laos and several other Southeast Asian countries, where a combination of poverty, isolation, proximity to China, elites' immediate interests, and human rights issues all combine to make playing off one power against the other more challenging. As one very knowledgeable Thai expert explained to our research team:

> *Interviewer*: "The Japanese are exploring building the line to Chiang Mai. How will that line articulate in terms of standards and compatibility with the line the Chinese are doing?"
>
> *Respondent*: "Actually with high-speed trains, you can have fairly discrete lines that, in this case, really don't need to be compatible. This line is going to run from Bangkok to Chiang Mai, but it will not go farther north to [merge] with the Chinese system [that will run from Bangkok to the northeast], so there is no real need to make the two different systems compatible. There are different groups behind these two lines. . . . The military tends to favor the Chinese and the [Thai] technocrats, bureaucrats tend to favor the Japanese. . . . The Japan lobby is quite strong; Thailand wants balance [between China and Japan]."[59]

Thus, when it comes to rail connectivity development, Thailand engages China as well as Japan, and at times others. While the kingdom is negotiating with Beijing over the Bangkok–Nong Khai HSR line, it has also been working with Tokyo on a prospective 672 km rail line from Bangkok to Chiang Mai using Shinkansen (Japan's "bullet train") technology, as per the quotation immediately above. By mid-2018, the initial study for half of the 490 billion baht high-speed line was complete; both governments are (as of early 2019) negotiating the investment model, with construction expected to start in 2020.[60] Japan is the primary alternative source of connectivity partnership. One of the drawbacks of cooperation with Japan is expense, with Japanese companies and development agencies wanting to undertake the entire project to assure quality (a turnkey approach), and then hand over the keys to the finished project to the purchaser. During Prayut's European tour in June 2018, the premier visited the UK and France promoting infrastructure and other investment opportunities.[61] Moreover, in 2019 the United States became somewhat more active, at least in terms of policy, with its "Build Act" (2018). From the Thai perspective, the more suitors, the better.

Unlike Laos, Thailand has resources, alternatives, and an international modus operandi of seeking balance among powers, as well as a pluralized political system that imposes genuine limits even on its military regime. As for China, Beijing has constraints too. The Chinese feel pressure, because as they get ever closer to reaching the Lao-Thai border with their ongoing and rapidly progressing work in Laos, the question arises, What will the Lao line link to in Thailand if things do not get moving there? If the line stops at the Lao border, the Central Line endeavor becomes a dead end in the minds of the international community and Chinese BRI skeptics. Thailand has leverage. Its political character, economic strength, and international options makes Bangkok a credible interlocutor with Beijing.

MALAYSIA: FROM EARLY EMBRACE TO CAUTIOUS RECALIBRATION

Within the context of Southeast Asia–China rail connectivity cooperation, Malaysia represents an active, extensive, and dramatic case. It is *active* in that as far back as the mid-1990s, well before the word *connectivity* entered into the lexicon of international relations in Asia, Malaysia already saw the PRC as an indispensable partner in developing a regional rail network. In 1996, less than a year after Prime Minister Mahathir Mohamad proposed the Singapore-Kunming Rail Link (SKRL) at the Fifth ASEAN Summit, Kuala Lumpur pushed for the creation of a Special Working Group on the SKRL (SWG-SKRL) including not only seven ASEAN countries but China as well.[62]

The Malaysian case is *extensive* in that, by 2017, its mutual courtships with China on rail engagement had evolved into a multifaceted rail partnership involving multiple planned and actual projects in different parts of the country (see the map in chapter 1). These endeavors are more extensive than rail projects and plans of other Southeast Asian countries. The projects include the East Coast Rail Link (ECRL), an electrified double-tracked railroad (from Gemas to Johor Bahru, on the southern part of Peninsular Malaysia), and potentially the Kuala Lumpur–Singapore High Speed Rail, envisioned to run along the peninsula's more developed west coast. Moreover, China Railway Rolling Stock Corp. (CRRC)'s manufacturing center (a regional hub for Southeast Asia) is in Batu Gajah (in the state of Perak), and the China Railway Engineering Corp. (CREC) has plans to establish its Asia Pacific headquarters in Kuala Lumpur. These rail projects have run in parallel with the two countries' cooperation on other forms of BRI-related infrastructure connectivity, including industrial parks, ports, and e-commerce platforms. Admittedly, some projects have worked out better than others.

This deep and broad cooperation reflects several factors: geography (the fact that all three envisioned branches of the Pan-Asia Railway are to converge in Thailand and proceed southward through Malaysia to reach Singapore); leadership (Prime Minister Mahathir's own regional connectivity vision, especially during his first administration, along with former Prime Minister Najib Razak's commitment to energize Malaysian growth using ties to the PRC and emphasizing connectivity, especially railroads); and, to some extent, the sizable ethnic Chinese population in Malaysia.[63]

Malaysia's extensive rail connectivity engagement with China, however, underwent dramatic twists and turns following Mahathir's defeat of Najib in the May 2018 election, a defeat due to Najib's 1MDB-related corruption and his unpopular goods and services tax, among other issues.[64] The new Mahathir administration ("Mahathir 2.0") announced its intention to review and renegotiate the controversial ECRL deal (alongside two pipeline projects in Sabah and Malacca). Moreover, Mahathir postponed the planned solicitation of tender offers on the HSR line to Singapore.[65] The prime minister's decisions were unsurprising to many. Since 2016, after his fallout with Najib over the 1MDB scandal and other controversies, Mahathir had openly criticized Najib on various grounds, including the leader's deals with China, warning that several of them—particularly the RM55 billion loan from China to construct the ECRL—"may end up threatening Malaysia's sovereignty."[66] His attacks intensified during the election campaign in 2018. After returning to power in May that year, Mahathir expressed his support for the concept of ECRL (which was already under construction and which our research team visited), but wanted significantly reduced costs, better financing terms, and project implementation that was more favorable to Malaysia.[67] In remarkably pointed phraseology, Mahathir also put his position in historic terms that Beijing would understand—"China had a long experience in dealing with unequal treaties and China resolved it by renegotiation. So, we feel we are entitled to study and, if necessary, renegotiate the terms."[68] It was on these same grounds that Mahathir announced in late May 2018 that his new Pakatan Harapan (PH) government "will drop" the KL-Singapore HSR project, describing the project as "not beneficial."[69] The prime minister later clarified that the project "is postponed, not scrapped."[70] After rounds of negotiation, Kuala Lumpur and Singapore finally reached an agreement in September 2018 to postpone the HSR project bidding process until 2020.[71] This postponement accordingly defers China and other potential bidders' involvement in the project.

Notwithstanding his decisions to renegotiate ECRL, suspend the pipelines, and postpone the HSR project, Mahathir allowed other China-related projects to continue (though most of the deals were started by his predecessor). These include the Gemas-Johor double-tracking project, the Malaysia-China Kuantan Industrial Park (MCKIP), the Alibaba Group's Digital Free Trade Zone (DFTZ), and the Electronic World Trade Platform (eWTP). Mahathir repeatedly stressed that Malaysia continues to support Beijing's BRI and welcomes China's investments. All this is consistent with both Mahathir and Najib seeing China as a critical partner in Malaysia's development and external interests.[72] Prime Minister Mahathir simply wanted a far better deal from Beijing, not least to meet the expectations of his domestic constituencies.

Moreover, the prime minister has considerable leverage to obtain a better deal, since work on ECRL had begun and the Pan-Asia Railway vision makes the Malaysian stretch of the HSR critical. Moreover, other countries (including Japan, the United States, the Republic of Korea, and EU companies) are waking up to the infrastructure opportunities in Southeast Asia and beginning to see that involvement is a question concerning the future economic and strategic orientation of this region (see chapter 7). China may face growing competition. Medium and even small powers sometimes exert muscle over larger powers.

What explains Malaysia's active and extensive embrace of rail engagement with China as well as its current recalibration under Mahathir 2.0? The evolving patterns reflect both developmental and political logic, which, in turn involves domestic legitimation and the diffusion of power within the system.

Pursuing development and delivering growth has been a principal pathway of legitimation for Malaysia's successive elites since the multiethnic country gained independence from the British in 1957. The pursuit of development—as *performance*-based legitimation—has been operating and expanding in parallel with an identity-based *particularistic* pathway of inner justification (i.e., protecting and privileging Malay interests) in shaping policies and allowing the ruling coalition Barisan Nasional (BN) to claim its right to rule by winning an uninterrupted mandate through elections from 1957 to May 2018. A similar combination of pathways applies to Mahathir 2.0's PH coalition government.

Development is about politics as much as economics in Malaysia. For BN and now PH governing elites, development serves domestic legitimation via three pathways: redistribution, reassurance, and reform. Each path focuses on different constituencies, respectively: (a) Bumiputera, or "sons of the soil," a politically constructed category exclusively designated for ethnic Malay Muslims and other indigenous groups (constituting about 60 percent of the 31 million population); (b) ethnic minorities (especially Chinese and Indians, about 23 percent and 7 percent, respectively); and (c) all Malaysians, particularly young and urban voters. The country's key development policies are as follows:

1. Most notable is the promajority affirmative action program for ethnic Malays, the New Economic Policy (NEP), implemented after the May 1969 Malay-Chinese sectarian riot. It is aimed at *redistributing* the wealth of the nation in ways that eradicate poverty, reduce interethnic income inequality, and increase Malay economic participation.

2. Other development programs aim to *reassure* the non-Malays—primarily ethnic Chinese and Indians—of the government's commitment, despite its pro-Malay policy, to ensure the space and opportunities for non-Malays in Malaysia.

3. Yet other development pronouncements involve projection of *reforms,* with emphasis on *restructuring* and *enlarging Malaysia's economic cake,* intended to inject hope and win support among all voters (e.g., "Vision 2020" under Mahathir 1.0 and "2050 National Transformation" under Najib).

Satisfying each of these three broad target groups necessitates stable and sustainable economic growth. This requires Malaysia—a small and developing economy that has transformed itself from commodities-dependent backwater into a middle-income country—to continue embracing an open trade and investment regime and seeking to benefit from greater regional and global integration. Hence Mahathir's long-standing regionalist activism since the 1990s in promoting ASEAN integration, East Asian community, and South-South cooperation, alongside proposing and institutionalizing regionwide connectivity initiatives such as the SKRL and the ASEAN Plus Three (APT). In our research team's interview in 2016 with then out-of-office Mahathir, it was apparent that he was a proponent of development through infrastructure and integration. He was particularly interested in, and knowledgeable about, rail development, recalling his SKRL vision and telling us how rail lines can be connected to port infrastructure and other development across national borders in the region:

> Malaysia wanted a meter-gauge rail network that is double track and electrified, from the southern tip of Peninsular Malaysia to the Malaysian-Thai border. . . . There is a great need to tie in the ports of Thailand with Malaysia. There is no big sea port in Thailand, only a river port. It can't handle big containers and, can't take big ships. Southern Thai ports can work with Malaysian ports. So we need to build the railroad system, to connect the Thai border with our ports. So there was a proposed project to build double-track and electrified trains between Ipoh and Padang Besar [the border crossing links directly to the Thai rail network]. Now it is completed. In Johor [the southernmost state of Malaysia] we have Port of Tanjung Pelepas [a container port], which is linked to the railway connecting to southern Thailand. Malaysian ports can handle big containers. . . . We have to make some inter-governmental decisions. We have to reach agreement among different countries."[73]

Each development path—redistribution, reassurance, and reform—seeks to convince respective audiences that their interests are being protected and promoted. In practice, however, achieving these goals is complicated by the degree of power diffusion. Social, economic, regional, and ethnic pluralization results in intense elite struggle, pervasive patronage (manifest in cronyism and corruption), occasional tensions in federal-state relations, as well as constant bottom-up demands and challenges by diverse social groups. This results in a process of juggling between participation (of all stakeholders) and protection (of certain privileged groups), all finding reflection in the implementation of various development programs, including rail connectivity projects. The combination of *ever-changing* political actors, nontransparent bidding and financial arrangements, weak rule of law, and the interpenetration of family politics help account for how corruption finally ignited the passions of Malaysian voters to reject the Najib administration in 2018. One PH member of Parliament asserted that up to 40 percent of yearly government expenditure went to corruption and waste.[74]

Elite-centered politics have shaped the three rail projects of concern to this study in Malaysia (double-tracking, ECRL, and HSR), with successive leaders playing different roles. To start, in the case of the double-tracking project, Mahathir was the initial decision maker and hence the target of challenge. Abdullah Badawi was first the challenger (when he decided to overrule Mahathir's decision by canceling the project), and then he became a re-shaper when he decided to revive the project, albeit in different form, involving different partnerships and benefiting different groups. Najib was not a central actor in this project. In the case of the other two mega rail projects, HSR and ECRL, Najib was the first key decision maker and arguably the main benefactor. He, thus, was the main target of challenge from various sociopolitical forces, which, along with other contested issues, culminated in his loss of power and the end of decades-long BN rule. On the other hand, Mahathir was initially the challenger in the cases of the HSR and the ECRL. However, following his return to power in May 2018, his role has evolved into that of re-shaper of both projects. This sequence of events demonstrates how political contestation at the elite level intertwines with socioeconomic forces to shape the prospects for, and pace of, rail projects in the PRC's partner countries.

The idea of constructing HSR connecting Kuala Lumpur and Singapore—two of the most economically vibrant cosmopolitan centers in Southeast Asia—originated in the late-1990s in the private sector. Initial efforts included YTL Corp Bhd, an infrastructure conglomerate in Malaysia, which teamed up with Siemens Malaysia in 1997–2002 to build, and have since operated, the Express Rail Link (ERL) linking Kuala Lumpur (KL) city and its international airport (KLIA) in Sepang. In 2006, YTL Executive Chairman Francis Yeoh revived the HSR proposal, highlighting the need for the 350 km rail link, which could shorten traveling time between KL and Singapore to ninety minutes from the current four hours by car, thereby "boosting socio-economic growth in both countries."[75] Several attempts to get things going occurred in September 2010, about eighteen months after the replacement of Abdullah as Malaysia's sixth prime minister by Najib Razak. Najib's economic plan highlighted the HSR as a high-impact program to improve economic prospects for Kuala Lumpur. He then tasked the newly created Public Land Transport Commission (SPAD) to conduct feasibility studies in 2011–12. In February 2013, Najib and his Singapore counterpart Lee Hsien Loong agreed to kick off bilateral negotiations. In April 2015, the Malaysian government set up MyHSR Corp. to oversee the HSR project.[76] In July 2016, the Malaysia and Singapore governments signed an MOU to kick off talks. In December the same year, the HSR deal was signed, only to be postponed when Mahathir took office about two years later, as explained earlier in this chapter.

Just prior to Mahathir's election in 2018, it was widely anticipated that when all was said and done with the bidding, Chinese firms would dominate. China was learning, making sure that its firms cooperated in consortia rather than allowing all PRC firms to go their own way in a cutthroat competition among themselves.[77] After his election defeat, Najib continued to argue that the underlying developmental logic for the HSR project was sound, saying: "In reality, infrastructure projects, such as HSR, bring benefits and returns in the form of increase in property values, local economic growth, technology transfer, high-income employment opportunities, more experts into the country from Singapore, and tourism."[78]

One very high-level former Malaysian official deeply involved in transport issues at this time explained what happened to produce Mahathir's seeming turnaround on HSR:

> High-speed trains are good, but they are expensive. Dr. Mahathir was positive about all rail projects in Malaysia, but he is now "more concerned about the financial situation we are in." It makes sense for him: we are already constructing the conventional double tracking of rails, connecting Gemas to JB [Johor Bahru], with a speed of one hundred sixty kilometers per hour, and it can go up to one hundred eighty kilometers per hour. HSR costs twice what a conventional rail line does . . . "If you look at it financially, it is not feasible." On HSR, people will have to take into account the issues of feasibility, generation of new growth areas, development of new cities, etc. "Sometimes it is difficult to quantify." . . . "You do not have the critical mass, but you believe the train service will create the critical mass." It will bring industries and people and residences further out. "That's how Shinkansen did it."

This informant went on to contrast Mahathir with Najib, saying: "But Najib brought everything together. 'Because of this there were a lot of whopping expenses.' He wanted the ECRL, everything. He wanted to be remembered as the father of rail infrastructure in this country. He wanted this to be his monument."[79]

The final example is ECRL, Malaysia's largest infrastructure project to date. The megaproject, underpinned by developmental logic, was well underway in 2017–18. It has long been Malaysia's own development plan (since 2007 when first proposed) to build a railroad linking its less developed states on the east coast with the more developed west coast of Peninsular Malaysia. Malaysia and China signed the ECRL deal in November 2016, as a critical project to stimulate economic growth in the east coast corridor.[80] In an interview in April 2018, the CEO of the state-owned Malaysia Rail Link Sdn Bhd revealed the government's plans to spur cargo business, attract industrial activities along the railroad, and facilitate transit-oriented development around the stations.[81] At the groundbreaking ceremony in August 2017, Prime Minister Najib described the establishment of ECRL as a "game changer" and "mindset changer," primed to be "a catalyst for economic equality between the west and east coast as it will stimulate investment, spur commercial activities, create ample jobs, facilitate quality education and boost tourism in Pahang, Terengganu and Kelantan."[82]

While many outside the government expressed concerns about the financial burdens and economic viability of the project, others emphasized the need to take a long-term perspective. They envisioned ECRL as a catalyst unleashing Malaysia's greater economic potential by providing both passenger and freight transport spanning five states. ECRL would link the existing and expanding infrastructure along the east coast facing the South China Sea (such as the Kuantan Industrial Park, Kuantan Port, Kemaman Port, and Kota Bharu near the Malaysian-Thai border) with Port Klang and other more developed areas around Greater Kuala Lumpur on the west coast facing the Strait of Malacca. Proponents of ECRL argue that it takes advantage of Malaysia's unique location and circumstances between the Pacific and Indian Oceans, suggesting that the 688 km rail link could enable Malaysia to capitalize more effectively on its geographical conditions, maximizing returns from its commercial and civilizational links with rising China, rising India, the Muslim world, and other emerging economies.[83]

This developmental logic is amplified by multiple political rationales. The perceived and projected economic benefits are politically important to BN's performance legitimacy. This is true for the United Malays National Organization (UMNO), the Malay-based dominant party of BN. It also is true for other component parties of the coalition, especially the Chinese-based Malaysian Chinese Association (MCA). The MCA President, Liow Tiong Lai, who was also the Transport Minister (June 2014–May 2018) and a member of Parliament for Bentong (one of the anticipated hubs along ECRL), described the rail link as "one of the most important projects" for Malaysia, saying the theme is very clear: "We're pushing for connecting lines and accelerating growth."[84]

The convergence of elite interests on ECRL went beyond the component parties of the ruling coalition, also reflecting federal-state relations (e.g., between the central government in Putrajaya and the state-level authorities of the four states ECRL traverses: Pahang, Terengganu, Kelantan, and Selangor). The latter two states were ruled by opposition parties. Kelantan (Malaysia's poorest state) was ruled by the Malaysian Islamic Party (PAS, or Parti Islam Se-Malaysia), and Selangor (the richest state) by Parti Keadilan Rakyat (PKR). The chief ministers of three of the states—not Selangor—attended the groundbreaking ceremony in August 2017, witnessing a rare moment of political harmony when Najib said, "The federal leadership is also grateful to the state governments of Kelantan, Terengganu, Pahang and Selangor for their full cooperation and support to this project, particularly in matters of land acquisition."[85] In federal Malaysia, state-level governments have primary responsibility for land, so their failure to cooperate can have project-ending consequences. What we see is classic log rolling.

Such convergence of elite interests demonstrates that the ECRL was not just about development-based performance legitimation for the Najib administration, but also *identity*, ethnic-based politics. A large proportion of the railroad passes through the three ethnic Malay-predominant east coast states—Kelantan, Terengganu, and Pahang (Najib's home state)—thereby making ECRL a perfect political avenue for UMNO in two ways: boosting its pro-Malay image and collaborating with PAS, an Islamist political party.[86]

Another domestic determinant, perhaps an even more important driver, was Najib's own political survival in the face of the scandal surrounding the 1MDB. In July 2015, the *Wall Street Journal* reported that nearly $700 million related to 1MDB found its way into Najib's personal bank accounts. In November and December 2015, China's state-run firms made two very large asset purchases from 1MDB, including a stake in Bandar Malaysia, the terminus for the proposed HSR line between Kuala Lumpur and Singapore. Rafizi Ramli, an opposition lawmaker from PKR, said, "We [now] have a prime minister who is indebted to the Chinese government."[87] In July 2016, the US Department of Justice filed lawsuits in a federal court seeking to seize $1 billion in assets linked to the troubled firm, revealing that a total of $3.5 billion had been misappropriated from 1MDB. The lawsuits did not name Najib, instead referring to "Malaysian Official 1."

Najib's China visit in October 2016 took place against this backdrop. The trip and its various outcomes signified Najib's inclination to move closer to China. On the economic front, fifteen business-to-business MOUs and sixteen government-to-government MOUs were signed, covering port and rail construction, e-commerce, finance, energy, manufacturing, and other sectors.[88] Two major deals surprised many observers: the initial purchase of four Littoral Mission Ships from Beijing and the award of the ECRL project to China Communications Construction Company (CCCC).

In retrospect, not many at that time paid attention to a July 26, 2016, post on the *Sarawak Report,* an independent online blog, which reported "a secret deal" between Najib and CCCC. The post claimed that the Malaysian government had agreed "to inflate the actual cost" of the ECRL project from RM30 billion to RM60 billion, and award the project to CCCC "to launder money in order to fill the loophole [the financial hole] of 1MDB."[89] The *New York Times* and other American media subsequently have added details to this story and raised questions about the propriety and ethics of US firms McKinsey[90] and Goldman Sachs.[91]

The Najib Administration soon found itself facing the realities of domestic power diffusion and pluralization—a broad range of opposition forces and sociopolitical groups stepped up their criticisms of Najib over the 1MDB scandal and other domestic issues (such as the highly unpopular goods and services tax, his party's own political baggage, and his China policy). For instance, Mahathir seized on public disquiet about China's expanding economic presence in Malaysia, criticizing Najib for "selling Malaysia out to China" by allowing the Chinese to buy land and develop high-end projects.[92] The Malay rights NGO Perkasa cautioned that China's massive investment might affect Malay Bumiputera's business opportunities.[93] Perhaps the emerging sentiment about China's growing footprint in Malaysia is best captured by Nurul Izzah Anwar of PKR, who described China's investments as "too much, too fast, too soon."[94]

These political criticisms and pressures challenged, but did not derail Najib's decisions on ECRL and other related projects. It was not until the unprecedented change of government in May 2018 that the various deals were suspended, reviewed, postponed, and/or canceled. The ECRL, arguably the most controversial BRI project in Malaysia, was first suspended and later renegotiated. After months-long protracted negotiations, on April 12, 2019, Malaysia and China declared the resumption of the project on a smaller scale (shortened from 688 km to 648 km) and much reduced costs (from RM65.5 billion to RM44 billion), as well as a realignment of its south route that involves an additional state (Negeri Sembilan) and Putrajaya Federal Territory.[95] The Malaysian government also decided to reinstate another China-backed project, Bandar Malaysia, the integrated transport hub that will house the terminus of the planned Kuala Lumpur–Singapore HSR project.

Domestic politics appears to be the main driver of Mahathir's decisions in reviving these projects. In addition to the rationale of avoiding a huge termination penalty (estimated at RM21.78 billion), the renegotiation—led by his long-time confidante Tun Daim Zainuddin rather than any of his cabinet ministers—was aimed at substantially reducing the costs and achieving more local employment and procurement benefits. The successful renegotiation of ECRL was a boost to Mahathir's new PH government.

CONCLUSIONS

This chapter makes several points, the most fundamental of which may be this. When Beijing embraces and pursues a grandiose vision of pan-Asian connectivity (or any other such ambitious concept), and when its entrepreneurial firms, bureaucracies, and provinces seek to exploit the opportunities this vision provides, they inject themselves into situations they barely understand and over which they have limited (or no) control. Beijing and its firms, bureaucracies, and localities are usually simply reacting and adapting to ever-changing conditions in their partner countries. Moreover, given that the entire Southeast Asian rail connectivity vision embraces seven countries in addition to China, the distribution of power and the economic, demographic, political, and natural conditions in each nation are extremely different from one another. Moreover, each of these partner countries is itself very heterogeneous and fragmented. This means that even *if* Beijing and its agents "learn" from prior missteps, future situations will likely have no relation to those previously encountered. After learning of the politics of Southeast Asian countries' interactions with Beijing, one should marvel more at Chinese persistence and occasional gains rather than the problems and missteps.

The unique juxtaposition, often collision, of development, power, and legitimation considerations in each country causes each potential partner country to react to China's rail proposals distinctly, by playing either up or down the projected benefits and/or perceived risks of the initiative. The governments to China's south have tried to shape Chinese proposals to maximize local gains, often to Beijing's frustration. There are limits to Beijing's capacity to produce change, even when dealing with small and medium powers. It is fair to say that China tends to rise, or sink, to the level of governance it finds in each country in which it operates.

Varied patterns of engagement with China's rail connectivity push highlight a number of factors at work.

First, a country's socioeconomic level and developmental needs matter. By virtue of being poor, Laos has had fewer choices than Thailand and Malaysia when dealing with the PRC.

Second, the character of domestic political systems has great bearing on what we might call *deal sustainability*. Beijing continually finds itself having to adapt to partner moves to modify, postpone, or cancel deals it thought (hoped) were sealed. This volatility reflects the degree of power concentration (or diffusion) in a partner state and the degree to which regime legitimacy is firmly established and rooted in developmental logic. The cases of Thailand and Malaysia, multi-party democratic systems, are more noisy and messy than Laos's one-party, authoritarian system. From Beijing's perspective, elections introduce uncertainty, indeed dangers when it comes to making and keeping a deal.

Finally, pathways of legitimation function as drivers, motivating ruling elites to pursue and prioritize certain national goals (e.g., infrastructure development). Regimes that find legitimation in nationalism and preserving sovereignty and autonomy at all costs, while placing less emphasis on economic growth as their legitimating principle, are less responsive to Beijing's calls for connectivity partnership. Though not discussed at length in this chapter, Vietnam is the best example of this phenomenon, as seen in mid-2018 demonstrations in Hanoi against proposed long-term land leases to foreigners. One line of protester attack was "No leasing land to China even for one day."[96] Vietnam's leaders know they need help on infrastructure, particularly rail, but they are reluctant to proceed.[97] It boils down to regime legitimacy in the eyes of the regime's own people.

Looking at the big regional picture, when one national leader among our interviewees was asked for his net assessment of the prospects for HSR and rail connectivity partnership with China and others, he concluded: "It will be done in stages. It is possible to see some parts to be completed. Some parts will not. Over a period of twenty years, it will become a reality."[98] In another interview, we asked a very senior former

Malaysian official: "So the issue is time, cost, technologically faster or slower. It is not about whether it will happen, but *how* and *when* it will happen. Is that a correct characterization?" The official responded, "Yes, that is an accurate description. The issue is about when. If it happens later, higher costs. HSR has just to be a question of time. Highways reach a saturation point."[99]

CHAPTER 5

The Negotiating Tables

China and Southeast Asia

China plays a role of big brother—without a heart.
—Thai professor, July 2018[1]

Small and medium powers are not putty in the hands of Beijing. They have leverage and options in the bargaining process. Although China has the power and the tools to push forward the concept of connectivity cooperation, its smaller neighbors in Southeast Asia do not always embrace Beijing's initiatives in the ways that the PRC expects or hopes. Some follow Beijing's initiatives selectively; others have pushed back, pulled other parties into their negotiations with China, or simply stayed away. Expatriate lawyer Eric Rose in Myanmar said, when speaking of Chinese efforts to have BRI dispute resolution conducted in PRC venues, "The BRI recipients, however, always have the option of saying NO!"[2]

In the first two decades of the 2000s, history and economic and social development brought Southeast Asia and the PRC to a point that made HSR and conventional rail connectivity a feasible aspiration. Before China could be a prospective partner to other countries, it first had to develop the financial and technological resources and construct its own internal transport systems. The PRC also had to develop all the capacities essential to a new, high-tech, globally competitive export industry. For their part, China's neighbors had to progressively urbanize and develop the economic and institutional strengths that could make the vision of high-speed and conventional rail feasible. Once this moment arrives, it falls upon China and its neighbors to negotiate the arrangements that would bind them increasingly closer together—all the technical, economic, social, and political problems lying ahead notwithstanding.

Whether and how the broad Pan-Asia Railway vision takes shape through negotiations is this chapter's topic.

Given that this massive project involves eight countries and innumerable localities, the sequence of negotiations is indeterminate, with each prior round setting the context for the ones coming after. There was never the prospect for one "grand bargain" among all the parties to create one total system. Rather, each prior agreement creates a new context in which the next takes shape, incrementally moving the whole vision forward. Prior arrangements enlarge or limit future possibilities. Positive and negative experiences arising from past agreements directly shape future rounds of bargaining. The region is moving toward connectivity, but along uncertain pathways at variable speeds. Nonetheless, the direction is clear. The building of the Pan-Asia Railway system in Southeast Asia has echoes of America's construction of the Transcontinental Railroad. That project started from the two opposite ends of the line, with no initially agreed upon meeting point. The project had an objective to span the continent, but the route, specific company responsibilities, and financing all unfolded as construction proceeded. Promontory Point, Utah emerged as the meeting point only one month before the last spike was driven home in 1869. Building the famed rail line was a process, never a precise plan.

In the current case of binding the PRC and its neighbors more closely together by rail, the process is even more complex. Unlike the construction of the US Transcontinental Railroad that took place within one country and involved only internal players, the Pan-Asia Railway undertaking involves a myriad of diverse players from many countries. In addition, many of the current rail projects in Southeast Asia will, at some point, involve cross-border processes (e.g., Vientiane-Nongkhai, Bangkok–Kuala Lumpur, Kuala Lumpur–Singapore, and China-Laos). The one common salient consideration for all of these countries is the China factor—whether and how to work with China is something that each will have to reckon with in their domestic and cross-border railroad construction.

DO SMALL AND LARGE STATES HAVE LEVERAGE WHEN NEGOTIATING WITH CHINA?

With the involvement of China as a stronger external actor in Southeast Asian rail connectivity development, negotiations occur within the context of asymmetric power relations.[3] Although negotiations vary from

country to country, they all reflect three enduring realities of power asymmetry. To start, asymmetry matters even outside of security domains, such as in connectivity cooperation, because the stronger partner is a key supply source. In this case, China supplies capital and technological know-how needed for infrastructure development, resources the weaker partner does not have. The more the PRC becomes indispensable, the lower the junior partner's bargaining power. Second, connectivity cooperation may not necessarily be all about big-power "push"—it also involves smaller-state "pull." This pull may result from the junior partner having no alternatives, elite interest, and/or substate dynamics (chapter 4). Finally, power asymmetry is simultaneously a source of attraction and apprehension for weaker actors—China has the ability to either help or harm their weaker partners to a higher degree than many others.[4]

These themes help clarify the nuances and variations across Southeast Asian states' engagement with the various China-related rail projects. A critical aspect for understanding China's power is to examine how its smaller Southeast Asian neighbors respond to its initiatives and overtures, and conversely how flexible Beijing is in responding to their needs, worries, and demands. "Ultimately, major powers cannot simply decide to lead; others must also desire or be persuaded to follow."[5] Powerful states seek to ensure that less powerful ones follow by coercion or benevolence, using trade, aid, diplomacy, military means, or alliances, among other means.[6] Yet, secondary states can choose to support, follow, resist, or challenge great powers. This chapter demonstrates that secondary states are far from helpless. They do not always acquiesce, and sometimes they are able to secure their own objectives. Such an understanding of secondary states ascribes agency to them, a consideration often missing in realist international relations theory.

Realists, from Thucydides to Morgenthau and Mearsheimer, have given pride of place conceptually to the material capacities of states. Thucydides famously wrote, "You know as well as we do that, as the world goes, right is only in question between equals in power. Meanwhile, the strong do what they can and the weak suffer what they must."[7] Hans Morgenthau similarly relegated small and middle powers to dependent roles. Kenneth Waltz also argues that,

> In international politics, as in any self-help system, the units of greater capability set the scene of action for others as well as for themselves. . . . It would be as ridiculous to construct a theory of international politics based on Malaysia and Costa Rica as it would be to construct an economic theory of oligopolistic competition based on the minor firms in a sector of an

economy. The fates of all the states and of all the firms in a system are affected much more by the acts and interactions of the major ones than of the minor ones. . . . The theory once written also applies to lesser states that interact insofar as their interactions are insulated from the intervention of the great powers of a system. . . .[8]

Realism thus relegates secondary states to "either pawns on the geostrategic chessboard or actors with extremely limited policy options."[9] They must either hop on the bandwagon or seek to balance. Waltz argues that secondary states are likely to balance by flocking to the weaker side. In contrast, Stephen Walt argues that secondary states often will choose to balance against the biggest threat (which is not necessarily the most powerful state).[10] There also is the possibility that weaker states will simply bandwagon with the stronger state, hoping to get along. In any event, secondary states have limited means by which to secure their security. In seeking to ally or associate with others for protection, small states end up losing their own freedom of action: "where the quest for protection and insurance is successful a price must normally be paid in terms of sacrifice of autonomy in the control of natural resources and loss of freedom of political maneuver and choice."[11]

More recent international relations literature, however, suggests that the balance-bandwagon dichotomy is oversimplified. Secondary states do not always have to choose between the two. There are alternatives.[12] Some scholars have argued that, under the conditions of high stakes and great uncertainties amidst growing big power competition, secondary states pursue alternatives such as limited alignment and hedging.[13]

The "hedging" literature is particularly pertinent to our study of smaller powers' responses to China's rail diplomacy, for three main reasons. First, the responses to China's BRI-related economic statecraft by potential Southeast Asian partners, thus far, reflect hedging: a pragmatic approach to maximize benefits while minimizing risks; a tendency to diversify partnerships; and an insistence on keeping options open.[14] Second, the hedging literature includes nonmilitary options that capture the policy preferences of weaker Southeast Asian states, especially in the realm of connectivity cooperation negotiation. Third, the literature's wider view of risks and returns—prosperity and autonomy, in addition to security—highlights the issue of policy tradeoffs, which helps explain variations in state responses to China's rail diplomacy, as discussed in chapter 4.[15]

These theoretical underpinnings help address a long-standing problem in the literature of smaller states and weaker states.[16] Because survival is assumed to be the overriding imperative of states considered weak, their domestic politics is relegated to a secondary consideration. However, this case study of HSR development in China/Southeast Asia demonstrates that the domestic politics of secondary states is critical in promoting or hindering great power ambitions and fostering or frustrating cooperation (see chapter 4). Plans made by big powers are frequently thwarted (or advanced) by the internal politics of smaller surrounding states. This is the same intellectual observation that Pressman and Wildavsky made in the subtitle of their classic book: *Policy Implementation: How Great Expectations in Washington are Dashed in Oakland.*[17] Sometimes middle powers can just outwait the big powers. As one very senior Thai official put it: "The Thai style is to wait and see; there is no need to rush. Thailand is like a 'beautiful lady' who will wait and see [which suitor she likes]. In the meantime, it will dress nicely and get its house in order. . . . There is no need for Thailand to commit to any massive plans in the meantime. Thailand is not rich like Singapore or powerful like the US—'the groom is too powerful.' It therefore has to wait and see."[18]

Another problem with traditional international relations theory is the absence of differentiation among secondary states. The lumping together of all states that are not great powers ignores the fact that some states are more equal than others, have more autonomy and greater capacity for influencing international politics than do others. Of the 190-plus sovereign states, those generally acknowledged as great powers are the United States, China, the United Kingdom, France, Germany, Russia, Japan, and India. Non-great powers analytically fall into the categories of middle powers and small states. Middle powers occupy the tenth to thirtieth positions.[19] One definition of middle powers is that they are "states that are weaker than the great powers in the system but significantly stronger than the minor powers and small states with which they normally interact."[20] Middle powers are influential at the regional or subsystemic level.[21] Traditional middle powers include Canada, Australia, and the Scandinavian countries, among others. The great majority of states below this range are small states and even microstates.[22]

In this book, Laos, Cambodia, and Myanmar are small states. Indonesia, Thailand, Vietnam, and Malaysia are all emerging middle powers, usually characterized as developing economies, sometimes recently democratized, and having substantive regional influence.[23] Singapore is a complicated case—it is a small state in terms of population, area, and natural resource endowment, and yet its economic wealth, human development index, strategic location, and influence on the world stage make it much closer to that of a middle power.[24] Singapore "punches above its weight." In 2009, Stephen Walt named Singapore an overachieving state because of its economic success, role in promoting regional integration, and its leaders' views on international issues.[25] One should note that although in terms of World Bank "effective governance" indicators Singapore receives a top score, in terms of its "liberal democracy score" the city-state receives only middling marks from Freedom House.[26] Liberal governance and effectiveness are not the same thing.

CHINA'S NEGOTIATING PRACTICES WITH SMALL AND MIDDLE STATES

Studies on Chinese negotiation strategies range from those focusing on political negotiations, such as Richard H. Solomon's *Chinese Political Negotiating Behavior, 1967–1984*,[27] to books covering business negotiations, China's Confucian foreign policy tradition, and Sun Tzu's *Art of War*.[28] As the United States began to open up to China in the late 1960s and early 1970s, the US Congress became particularly interested in learning about negotiation with the Chinese communists.[29] It is useful to identify Chinese negotiation tactics and strategies emphasized in the prior literature and to glean new understandings from Chinese negotiations with Southeast Asian countries in the domain of HSR and conventional rail projects. For instance, a key aspect of China's HSR negotiations with Southeast Asian countries that has not been emphasized in the earlier literature is that the PRC has, on occasion, exercised great power restraint. Neither has prior literature examined Chinese negotiating behavior in an open-ended sequence of interconnected negotiations.

Cultivating "Old Friends" and "Guanxi (connections)." Solomon argues that although Chinese negotiating style is generally in line with the strategies of most countries, it is nevertheless distinctive, particularly in the efforts made to develop and manipulate interpersonal relationships (*guanxi*) with foreign officials[30]—a subset of efforts often referred to in the West as "Chinese influence operations." This is the result of Chinese political culture and tradition, which emphasizes the cultivation and maintenance of relationships to establish a favorable context for bargaining. Detached or legalistic practice has shallow roots in China. In negotiations the Chinese will work with a sympathetic counterpart to cultivate friendship that comes with reciprocal obligations.[31] Based on these obligations, Chinese officials manipulate feelings of goodwill, guilt, or dependence in order to achieve their objectives by frequent references and appeals to "old friends" (*lao pengyou*). Great attention is devoted to finding the most sympathetic member of the opposing bargaining group.

The significance of *guanxi* is highlighted by one of the most significant works in PRC international relations theory today—Qin Yaqing's *A Relational Theory of World Politics*. In Qin's view, relations are ties between entities that interact and are dynamic, creative, and transformative. Human relations and human agency are indispensable.[32] Relations are interdependent, mutually influencing, and inclusive—"persons are never seen as isolated beings with distinct properties and attributes."[33] An individual's identity is his or her personal relationship with others. Therefore, in this worldview, social relations or *guanxi* becomes the fundamental unit of analysis.[34]

As David M. Lampton noted with respect to US President Donald Trump's 2016 announcement of former Iowa Governor Terry Branstad as prospective US ambassador to the PRC, being a "friend of China" is a "fraught status."[35] The implication is that the "friend" will be solicitous of Chinese interests, understand and explain Chinese problems and constraints to American audiences, and be willing to bargain to reach mutual accommodation. An effective "old friend" provides an unobstructed channel of direct communication and access for Beijing to US leaders. The Chinese approach is comprehensive, targeting both the elite and societal levels, although the emphasis is on political and business elites, and overseas Chinese.

Elite-level Cultivation. A comprehensive report on Chinese public diplomacy jointly released by AidData, the Center for Strategic and International Studies, and the Asia Society Policy Institute in June 2018 found that the PRC favors and is particularly effective in implementing a policy of cultivating the political, military, and business elites of countries in East Asia and the Pacific.[36] To potential partners, the PRC emphasizes the win-win nature of closer ties to Beijing, especially China's declarative policy of noninterference in domestic affairs, unlike many Western states.[37] Beijing uses high-level visits to cultivate these leaders, such as Xi Jinping's April 2017 visit to see Donald Trump early in the new president's term, and the lavish hospitality Xi rained on Trump during his reciprocal visit to China in November of the same year. Beijing's leaders maintain a heavy travel schedule throughout Southeast Asia; their visits are often major events in destination countries.

With respect to the BRI, and specifically HSR projects, most agreements occur during high-level visits. Premier Li Keqiang, whom the Chinese media nicknamed China's "high-speed rail salesman," is the top promoter of overseas HSR projects.[38] In Malacca, Malaysia, for instance, billboards with Li's image regaled visitors long after his promotional tour had concluded. During his visits to countries in Latin America, Eastern Europe, Southeast Asia, and Africa, Li has signed numerous memoranda of understanding (MOUs) and agreements with top leaders to construct rail lines. In addition to supplying capital to finance priority projects, Beijing frequently attempts to enhance the standing of local elites by supporting their policies. For instance, during general elections in May 2018, China's Ambassador to Malaysia Bai Tian reportedly campaigned for the president of the Malaysian Chinese Association (which is part of the ruling coalition) in his constituency in Bentong, Pahang.[39]

Beijing is opportunistic when, where, and how it engages with leaders of other countries. It avails itself of "policy windows" created by domestic political transitions or the weakening of ties with other powers, in particular the United States, to cultivate these elites.[40] China's cultivation of former Malaysian Prime Minister Najib Razak and current Thai Prime Minister General Prayut Chan-o-cha are two such examples.

Although Malaysian-Chinese economic engagement preceded Najib becoming prime minister, it was during his period in office (2009–18) that economic ties strengthened significantly. Especially in 2015 and thereafter, China's interest in Malaysia and its cultivation of Najib rose to singular heights when Chinese state-linked firms stepped in to buy assets from the troubled 1Malaysia Development Berhad (1MDB), a semi-sovereign wealth fund owned entirely by the Malaysian Ministry of Finance, after its high debt levels and alleged involvement in wide-ranging graft were publicized.[41] This was happening against the background of deteriorating ties between Najib and the United States, particularly from July 2016, when the US Department of Justice opened an investigation into alleged money laundering at 1MDB, behavior linked to Najib and his family (see chapter 4).

The weakening of ties between Najib and Washington provided an opportunity for China to step up its cultivation of Malaysian interests. In 2016, Najib visited China and signed fourteen deals worth at least US$34 billion, including the East Coast Rail Link (ECRL) and the purchase of Chinese coastal patrol ships.[42] Prior to the trip, Najib called himself a "true friend" of China and promised to bring bilateral relations to new heights, while simultaneously criticizing the West, saying that former colonial powers should not lecture those nations they had once enslaved on how to deal with their internal affairs.[43] Najib visited China again in May 2017, signing another nine MOUs with Chinese companies. In addition to China's cultivation of Najib and agreement to fund Malaysian infrastructure projects, the China Railway Engineering Corporation (CREC) teamed up with a local Malaysian firm to acquire 60 percent of the shares of Bandar Malaysia, where the terminus of the HSR in Kuala Lumpur was to be located.[44] CREC's move added to the already-rife speculation that the KL-SIN HSR [the Kuala Lumpur to Singapore Line] was in China's pocket.

Another example of China seizing opportunities to cultivate relationships with Southeast Asian leaders is Thailand. In the aftermath of the military coup led by Prime Minister Prayut in 2014, when political/diplomatic relations between Bangkok and Washington deteriorated, China saw a good opportunity to cultivate stronger ties with Thai leaders. Even though Thailand was an American ally, the United States and other Western countries suspended or reduced their engagement with Thailand following the coup. In 2015, the United States suspended one-third of its military assistance, worth $3.5 million, to Thailand. Military cooperation was canceled, and the long-standing US-Thai joint military exercise, Cobra Gold, shrunk. Consequently, Prayut and other military leaders had few options but to lean toward Beijing for investments, trade, and military purchases. Sino-Thai relations thereafter continued to strengthen.

In November 2014, Xi Jinping and Prayut met during the APEC summit; one month later Prayut made his first official visit to China. In 2015, the two countries held their first joint air force exercise. In 2017, Thailand bought the first of three submarines from China in a deal worth $393 million. As one very senior Thai official put it,

> The US likes to tell its allies that they are wrong. It has made it difficult for Thailand to reconnect with it. Thailand cannot afford to buy US arms because of insufficient funds. The US needs to offer good packages like the Chinese who are willing to provide no restrictions on sales because of Thailand's domestic issues.[45]

When Beijing negotiates, all aspects of the relationship are on the table. For the United States, law limits the available trade-offs.

Overseas Chinese. When Deng Xiaoping opened up China in 1978, a new wave of Chinese emigration to Southeast Asia began. The new migrants (*xin yimin*) are different from the pre-1949 Chinese migrants to the region—they are better educated and wealthier, but they have not quickly integrated into their new countries. This new generation of migrants maintains strong links to the PRC, because technological development has made communication and transportation easier, and capital moves across borders faster than ever. These overseas Chinese are plugged into discussions and debates within China and remain aware of Beijing's desires despite living abroad.

The Overseas Chinese Affairs Office (OCAO) is the government department in Beijing responsible for cultivating support among overseas Chinese communities. Since the launch of the BRI in 2013, OCAO's mandate has strengthened. In March 2018, the OCAO, which was originally under the State Council, moved under the umbrella of the Chinese Communist Party (CCP) United Front Work Department—an indication of its elevated role in the CCP leadership's strategy to involve overseas Chinese in national rejuvenation. Predictably, this is not necessarily reassuring to Southeast Asian governments. Sometimes Beijing's efforts in this regard amount to putting a target on the backs of overseas Chinese.

In recent years, Beijing has encouraged and invited overseas Chinese entrepreneurs to visit the PRC to be a part of its growth and transformation. In 2014, at the second session of the Twelfth Chinese People's Political Consultative Conference, for example, some of these new migrant entrepreneurs attended as observers.[46] In July 2015, China held its first World Overseas Chinese Entrepreneurs Conference in Beijing. From Beijing's perspective, the wealth of this latest wave of Chinese emigrants and the role they play in local economies in Southeast Asia are valuable assets. As noted in chapter 3, the Thirteenth Five-Year Plan (2016–20) explicitly mentioned the importance of Chinese living abroad in relation to the BRI's success.

In 2013, when Xi Jinping launched his vision of the "Chinese Dream" and first articulated the BRI, he included only the Chinese and various ethnic groups living within the PRC. However, in 2014 he defined the "sons and daughters of China" (*zhonghua er nu*) to mean both the Chinese on the mainland and ethnic Chinese living overseas (*haiwai qiaobao*).[47] This broader definition signals Beijing's intent to utilize the Chinese overseas to work for China's national interest. China has adopted this phraseology to blur the distinction between Chinese citizens abroad and foreign citizens of Chinese descent living abroad.[48] That Beijing now considers all Chinese overseas a part of the greater

Chinese nation was underscored by Li Keqiang during the World Overseas Chinese Entrepreneurs Conference:

> Six million overseas compatriots (*haiwai qiaobao*) are important members
> of the large Chinese nation (*zhonghua minzu*). Generation after generation
> of *huaqiao* and *huaren*, their feelings are still linked to the homeland, their
> hearts are tied to *Zhonghua* [cultural China], . . . they have made special and
> important contributions to the independence and liberation of the Chinese
> nation, the reform, the opening and the modernization of China.[49]

In the 1950s and 1960s, this kind of declaratory policy often compromised people of Chinese ethnicity living abroad in Southeast Asia,
sometimes to tragic effect. Even today, with China's globalized economic and political reach, the antagonisms such appeals generate in
other societies can boomerang, bringing harm to long-standing, loyal
citizens of other countries who are of Chinese descent. Prior to Xi Jinping taking the helm, for example, Beijing had essentially adopted a
noninterventionist, hands-off policy during the May 1998 anti-Chinese
riots in Indonesia, much to the consternation of many PRC citizens.
This hands-off approach was due to China's opening up and comparatively moderate foreign policy instituted by Deng Xiaoping in the 1980s
and 1990s. Xi Jinping's formulations represent a sea change. Beijing's
hands-off approach to the May 1998 riots in Indonesia contrasts with
former Chinese Ambassador to Malaysia Huang Huikang's statements
when ethnic tensions rose in Malaysia. Huang visited Chinatown during the Mid-Autumn Festival in September that year and delivered a
prepared speech that was widely reported in the press, stating that

> . . . we will not stand idly by as others violate the national interests of China,
> infringe upon the legal rights of Chinese citizens and companies, undertake
> illegal behavior that impedes the friendly relations between China and the
> local countries in question. . . . The government of China opposes any kind
> of terrorism, opposes any form of racism or extremism that focuses on a
> certain race and ethnic group, opposes violent behavior which would destroy
> public order and social stability.[50]

Huang's speech caused an uproar in Malaysia and was seen by the political establishment to represent interference in domestic affairs.

As Stephen Fitzgerald wrote decades ago,[51] China has a long and
checkered history with its policies toward people of Chinese ethnicity
living abroad, particularly in Southeast Asia. The pattern has been that
when foreign governments and societies vigorously react to Beijing's
efforts to utilize overseas Chinese, the PRC pulls back, often with some

lag, creating a cyclical character to policy. Chinese living abroad are the first to suffer when Beijing becomes more assertive. Beijing's efforts to utilize Chinese abroad in its BRI policy and other domains are a mistake, from this perspective.

Pressure Tactics. Apart from cultivating elites and overseas Chinese, the Chinese government and PRC entities more loosely connected to the government have adopted a number of pressure tactics on Southeast Asian countries designed to bolster Chinese companies' efforts to secure infrastructure projects. These efforts come in many forms—some entirely legitimate—ranging from appeals to top leaders of Southeast Asian countries to more coercive means, issue linkages, and material inducements or even bribery.

In the case of the KL-SIN HSR, using quite conventional and legitimate means, Chinese leaders have appealed to Singaporean and Malaysian leaders and government agencies to look favorably upon Chinese companies. During Singapore Prime Minister Lee Hsien Loong's visit to China in September 2017, China's Premier Li Keqiang told Lee that he hoped Singapore would support the PRC's bid for the KL-SIN HSR Project.[52] In November of that year, the Chinese once again made a strong pitch for the HSR project at a symposium organized by China's National Development and Reform Commission (NDRC) and attended by Singapore Transport Minister Khaw Boon Wan.[53] They highlighted China's strong safety record, advanced HSR technology, and top speeds. In particular, they pointed to their experience and technological expertise in operating an HSR network in tropical climates.

Beijing has also employed issue-linkage techniques and more coercive tactics in pushing its HSR agenda. China-Singapore ties took a nosedive in 2016 and the first half of 2017 over South China Sea issues and the impounding in Hong Kong of Singapore's Terrex Infantry Carrier Vehicles *en route* to Singapore from Kaohsiung, Taiwan.[54] While most analysts see both the diplomatic spat over the South China Sea and the Terrex incident as PRC pressure to change Singapore's stance on the South China Sea and its relations with Taiwan, one high-ranking Singapore official also pointed to the possibility that China was using issue linkage to pressure Singapore into favoring Chinese bids for the KL-SIN HSR project.[55]

There also have been unconfirmed reports that Beijing pressured Malaysia to let China bag the contract for the HSR project.[56] Sheng Guangzu, the General Manager of China Railway Corporation (CRC), visited Malaysia in May 2016 to lobby for the HSR project. A high-level source in Malaysia has also said that PRC pressures related to the HSR project have come from multiple sources—targeting the Foreign Affairs Ministry, the Transport Ministry, and even Najib himself.[57]

Beijing has also used tactical pressure on Bangkok. It excluded Thai Prime Minister Prayut Chan-o-cha from the Belt and Road Summit in May 2017, a move that presumably expressed Beijing's displeasure over the delay in the Sino-Thai HSR project.[58] In response, the Thais began to take measures to push through the project. In July 2017, the Thai cabinet approved the first phase of the project. Then, in September 2017, Prayut invoked Article 44 of the Constitution to exercise his absolute power to streamline the construction of the HSR project, including exempting Chinese engineers from taking the engineering qualifying examination (as required by Thai law).

Win-Win Outcomes. Another feature of Chinese negotiating strategy is the emphasis on "win-win outcomes." In the Chinese relational view of the world, human interaction is not always a zero-sum game—shared interests exist.[59] Mutual obligations envelop the individual in a web of relationships that limit maneuverability. The principle behind the dominant strategy in game theory, self-interest, is not fully effective in this context. While recognizing that the self has interests, Confucianism also stresses shared interests and that joint efforts are required to achieve the common interest, or the self-interest of both parties. Chinese negotiations are therefore infused with emphases that the deals offered are "win-win." In negotiating BRI projects, the Chinese have placed emphasis on reciprocity and win-win outcomes. Chinese State Councilor Yang Jiechi, in a *China Daily* interview, said

> The Belt and Road Initiative was proposed by China. *Yet it is not going to be China's solo show.* A better analogy would be that of a symphony performed by an orchestra composed of all participating countries. *This Initiative is meant to be a major international public good benefiting all countries....* We are committed to the principles of extensive consultation, *joint contribution, and shared benefits.* We stress practical cooperation, *win-win outcomes* and step-by-step progress. We are looking to align China's development with that of other countries and encourage greater synergy between their respective development strategies and cooperation under the Belt and Road Initiative. This will be conducive to expanded regional investment and domestic demand, job creation and poverty reduction and to a higher level of development of the entire region.[60]

China's rise and the unease with which the region has reacted to it in the security sphere have combined to provide the Chinese incentives to stress the benefits of its economic growth and the win-win deals it can offer the entire region. In chapter 3, we saw how China's emerging concept of its own development success calls for success among neighbors.

While the region's uneasiness is primarily due to the uncertainty that surrounds China's rise and what kind of hegemon it might become, the region's concerns are also rooted in history. China shares borders with Myanmar, Vietnam, and Laos. Southeast Asian states have troubled histories with China, stemming in part from domestic discomfort with the large overseas Chinese populations, along with episodic struggles against communist insurgencies during the Cold War. These historical frictions, in addition to unresolved maritime boundary disputes in the South China Sea, fuel a sense of disquiet on the part of the smaller Southeast Asian countries. All this leads Beijing to try to reassure its neighbors when it can.

Nonetheless, Beijing sends decidedly mixed messages; its foreign and security policies do not always comport with its economic objectives. When Beijing occupied and began to develop rocks and reefs in the South China Sea, constructing installations there (e.g., Mischief Reef in early 2015), tensions between China and Southeast Asian maritime states increased. In 2013, China announced BRI in Indonesia and Kazakhstan, portraying it as China's effort to be a "responsible stakeholder" by providing public goods to the international system. In short, assertive sovereignty claims while promoting connectivity policies requiring more interdependence, trust, and cooperation work at cross-purposes.

Win-Win and HSR. HSR and conventional rail projects in Southeast Asia are described as win-win projects. Li Keqiang, in a December 2017 congratulatory letter upon the start of construction on the Bangkok–Nakhon Ratchasima line in Thailand (the first phase of the Bangkok–Nong Khai line) said that the China-Thailand HSR is a new platform for bilateral cooperation and will further "promote pragmatic cooperation of win-win and mutual benefit between the two countries. . . ."[61]

However, it is important not to overstate the benign and win-win characteristics of Chinese dealings with foreigners now, or in the past. Zhang Feng, in his study of early Ming Dynasty diplomacy with states along China's periphery, found that the Chinese practice instrumental hierarchy/rationality, that is, the maximization of self-interest by exploiting hierarchical relationships with foreign rulers.[62] Simultaneously, Zhang acknowledges that China also practices a strategy of expressive hierarchy/rationality in accordance with Confucian traditions, by establishing ethical relationships that embody Confucian relational affection and obligation.[63] He identifies two key conditions under which expressive hierarchy is employed—when the degree of conflict of interest with the other party is low and when the other actor identifies with Chinese ideas, values, and beliefs.[64]

In negotiating HSR and other rail deals with Thailand, Laos, and Indonesia, the Chinese have adopted expressive hierarchy, emphasizing Confucian traditions of relational affection and obligation, to reach win-win outcomes. This is because the two conditions that Zhang specifies currently exist in the negotiations between China and these parties. First, Thailand, Laos, and Indonesia's interest in developing their infrastructure is in line with the Chinese objective of exporting it. Second, the leaders and officials of said countries have signed on to the Chinese belief that "if you want to get rich, first build roads."

Leaders of all three countries have prioritized the development of infrastructure in their economic planning (chapter 4). The Jakarta-Bandung HSR is a flagship project under Indonesian President Joko Widodo ("Jokowi")'s ambitious plans to upgrade Indonesia's decrepit infrastructure. It is one of Jokowi's twelve national strategic projects under Presidential Regulation No. 3/2016, which calls upon Indonesian government agencies to prioritize the Jakarta-Bandung HSR through measures, including accelerating the issuance of permits.[65] In an interview, a key regional official described their opposition to the high-speed line, explaining that it was inappropriate technology—it moved so fast it was unable to stop within the city limits.[66] Nonetheless, the interviewee said that this was a strategic decision by Jokowi (in part to improve relations between Jakarta and Beijing) and that they had no desire to get crosswise with the president.[67]

Similarly, Prime Minister Prayut has prioritized large-scale infrastructure projects in his ambitious plan to position Thailand to become a regional center of connectivity. All three envisioned rail lines to Singapore from Kunming (the West, Central, and East) would go through Bangkok on their way to Singapore. In March 2018, the Thai Transport Ministry revealed that Thailand planned to build 2,506 kilometers of HSR in three phases by 2036.[68] In an indication of the significance he places on Chinese support for Thailand's connectivity plans, as noted earlier Prayut used his executive powers to overcome obstacles to the construction of the first phase from Bangkok to Nakon Ratchasima. He invoked Article 44 not only to waive the legal restrictions preventing Chinese engineers from working on the HSR project in Thailand, but also to allow the Thai rail authority to bypass normal procurement and tendering procedures in order to hire Chinese companies to design the railroad and install HSR technology, including signal systems.[69]

Likewise, in Laos, officials view infrastructure development as key to lifting their country out of poverty (chapter 4). They have agreed to the Vientiane-Boten line, even though this means deep and long-standing debt. In 2015, the Deputy Prime Minister of Laos proclaimed that Laos would be transformed from a landlocked country to a "land-linked" country.[70] The goal is to make Laos the transport hub connecting neighboring countries and facilitating the cross-border movement of goods and people, thus gaining access to the domestic markets of its bigger neighbors, to stimulate economic growth.

Great Power Restraint. Within the idea of expressive hierarchy is embedded the notion of restraint. In negotiations on the HSR projects, China has occasionally displayed restraint that does not align with realist assumptions of hegemonic behavior that "the strong do what they can, while the weak suffer what they must." David A. Lake argues that in a contractual relationship between a dominant state and subordinate state, the dominant one may restrain itself:

> Dominant states must credibly commit to limit their authority and power. In a wholly anarchic world, self-restraint is an oxymoron. . . . Yet, in a world of hierarchies, dominant states must demonstrate that they cannot or will not abuse the authority that subordinates have entrusted to them. Subordinates will not enter or remain within a social contract unless they are assured that the authority they grant to the dominant state will not be used against them. . . . This requires that dominant states tie their hands, giving up policies or options that they would otherwise have enjoyed, or send costly signals of their benign intent or willingness to act only within the bounds of what their subordinates regard as legitimate.[71]

Lake divides constraints into those that are exogenous—namely, great power competition and democratic political institutions, and endogenous—those that dominant states impose on themselves, such as by abiding by multilateral rules. If a dominant state wishes to build and sustain authority, it cannot always act as a bully. Given the economic and military strength that great powers possess, they may wish to win friends and cultivate a benign public image. For Chinese foreign policy, "soft power" became a slogan in the first decade of the 2000s.[72]

China has virtually no effective constitutional constraints upon leaders or a legal system that might give outsiders confidence. Nonetheless, in HSR projects, Beijing's chief rivals are Japan, South Korea, France, Canada, and Germany. In both a big power competition sense and commercially, this rivalry forces Beijing to constrain itself when dealing with smaller Southeast Asian nations.

A *Global Times* article categorizes infrastructure projects into three types: strategic, policy, and commercial. Only commercial projects are profit-driven, while the first two "are not necessarily profitable as they need to serve the bigger picture."[73] Although the projects in Southeast Asia have long-term commercial and economic development rationales, in the shorter term these projects have a strategic rationale. In the HSR deals signed between China and Indonesia, Thailand, and Laos, the sticker price of the projects was kept lower than strictly commercial terms would suggest. For Beijing, economic considerations took a backseat to political and strategic objectives. HSR projects are high-risk, and returns may accrue only after several decades. For instance, the Jakarta-Bandung HSR may take forty years to become profitable.[74] The Chinese acknowledged the risks when Li Ruogu, former chairperson and president of the China Exim Bank, warned of the dangers of investing in some BRI projects with high debts and low credit ratings.[75] As seen in chapter 3, there is intense debate within China over how long the PRC can tolerate long-term deals premised on protracted losses. There is also debate over the priority given to development versus strategic or commercial projects.

During the negotiations on the HSR projects, both Thailand and Indonesia gained concessions from China suggesting that Beijing restrained itself and was willing to suffer current losses for presumed long-term advantages. According to Dragan Pavlićević and Agatha Kratz,

> Thailand and Indonesia in particular have displayed a strong capacity to influence negotiations, and impose their own specifications (both technical and financial) on China. Thailand made clear it would not start the construction of the line until satisfactory conditions are [were] obtained from Beijing, and Indonesia persuaded China to set up a "business-to-business" model involving Chinese and Indonesian SOEs, rather than a government-to-government agreement that Beijing tends to favor. Overall, a review of the negotiation processes related to the projects in Indonesia and Thailand shows that both ended with significant concessions on China's side on the issues of the highest importance to both countries, namely financial and ownership structures of these projects.[76]

Among the countries examined here, Indonesia has shown some aptitude in getting China to agree to its demands. Thailand, Malaysia, and Singapore have demonstrated that they are able to resist Chinese demands and maintain autonomous positions. Laos, by contrast, seemed unable to resist many Chinese terms and instead accepted asymmetrical disadvantages vis-à-vis China that could compromise its sovereignty. Beijing's at least theoretical capacity to build around Laos (through either Vietnam or Myanmar) gave the PRC advantage.[77] For Vientiane, to be outflanked was a worse prospect than excessive debt.

Beyond each bilateral negotiating relationship, however, lies a consequential point. Even though a transboundary, interdependent rail system would benefit from multilateral, synoptic negotiations among all the parties simultaneously, Beijing prefers to deal sequentially with each partner. ASEAN and other regional organizations do not yet have the capacity to organize regional states to engage the PRC cohesively. As one very senior Thai political figure explained to our research team:

> This is a chicken and egg problem. ASEAN would be tighter if there is greater connectivity, but connectivity could only happen if ASEAN countries work more tightly together. Each ASEAN country is concerned about its own domestic connectivity problems. Connectivity projects are often carried out bilaterally, making it difficult for regional connectivity. For instance, China, Thailand, and Laos did not sit down together to discuss connectivity projects. The projects are discussed on a bilateral basis, and hence each country is waiting for the other country to construct these projects. ASEAN countries only see the projects as domestic ones, and not regional ones. Because projects undertaken by one country have spillovers for neighbors, the World Bank noted in 2019 that "Cross-border cooperation can further enhance the value of a country's investments—by adopting harmonized standards for infrastructure."[78] Furthermore, countries need to also increase engagement of international institutions. The ADB [Asian Development Bank] has the connectivity master plan, but there has been no discussion on how the priority should be worked out and how projects should be financed. If the Chinese are more proactive, the AIIB [Asian Infrastructure Investment Bank] could step in and that could open up the possibility of speeding up the projects. [The respondent stressed that] ASEAN leaders need to make joint decisions. This lack of making joint decisions reflects a much deeper problem within ASEAN, which is that ASEAN countries' sense of belonging to one community is lacking.[79]

CASE: BANGKOK–NONG KHAI HSR (THAILAND)

Thailand is an emerging and increasingly influential middle power, particularly in regional organizations. Thailand is one of the founding members of ASEAN and the leading power, next to Vietnam, in the Greater Mekong Subregion. Politically, it is a constitutional monarchy with a vibrant civil society, albeit with a political system that has gone through several upheavals and twelve military coups since 1932. The Thai military, which sees itself as the guardian of political order and of the Thai monarchy, intervenes in politics when infighting, corruption, and large-scale violent protests threaten domestic stability. Since 2014, Thailand has been ruled by Prime Minister Prayut and the junta of which he is part.

During the past decade of negotiations with Thailand on the HSR project, the Chinese encountered significant difficulties. Negotiations have been episodic, given frequent Thai government shifts. Since the beginning of HSR project discussions, China has negotiated with three different governments in Bangkok, talks that first began in 2009 under the Democrat Party–led Abhisit Vejjajiva government.

Thailand was chair of ASEAN that year, and the organization adopted a new charter to tighten ASEAN economic integration. Abhisit and his advisers became interested in the idea of an HSR line that would run through Laos to the Thai-Malaysia border, and accordingly began negotiations with China. However, when the Abhisit government lost power in the 2011 election, negotiations had not yet concluded. The Pheu Thai Party won a landslide victory in that election, leading to the formation of the Yingluck Shinawatra Government. The Yingluck government was also interested in connectivity and continued HSR negotiations with the PRC. However, negotiations were interrupted when Yingluck fell from power over allegations of corruption and abuse of power. When the current Thai military government took control in the 2014 coup, HSR discussions proceeded, but slowly.

The thorniest issues in the Sino-Thai negotiations are land acquisition, land use, and the interest rate on prospective loans. The Thai government was dissatisfied with the 2.5 percent interest rate that Beijing offered compared to the 2 percent that the Indonesians received.[80] Chinese companies also typically want development rights on the land around the railroad stations, demands that raise territorial and sovereignty concerns in Thailand. By way of context, Chinese buyers now make up between 10 and 20 percent of all real estate sales in Chiang Mai, Pattaya, and Phuket, and 5 percent of sales in Bangkok.[81] Thais are anxious about the Chinese acquisition of banana plantations in northern Thailand. The example of the banana plantations was frequently invoked when the Thai experts and people our research team spoke with expressed concerns about PRC companies possibly acquiring development rights in the areas around the HSR or conventional rail stations.

Thais are also worried about the social, economic, and political impacts of the railroad. There are concerns that this development will spur an influx of Chinese developers and tourists with all their attendant economic and cultural impacts. Thai small businesses fear competition from cheap Chinese goods pouring into the country on the rail line. Ordinary people also worry about an even larger influx of Chinese tourists into their country; the number of such tourists coming to Thailand has tripled since 2012, reaching 8.8 million (in 2016), accounting for more than a quarter of all foreign tourists.[82] These tourists, mostly from less-developed areas in the PRC, are not necessarily welcome in Thailand, because they are seen as cheap and unruly, without adding much value to the Thai economy.

During HSR negotiations, the Thai government demonstrated the ability to resist Chinese demands and forged an agreement reducing dependency on Chinese funds. When Li Keqiang visited Bangkok in December 2014, Prayut inked an MOU on the $5.5 billion project. However, the project did not go ahead until the Thai side was satisfied with all of the terms. Unhappy with the 2.5 percent interest rate that the Chinese side offered on their proposed loans, in June 2017 Prayut signed an executive order pushing forward the first phase of construction of the HSR without Chinese funds. Bangkok decided that it would fully fund the project itself using loans and issuing government bonds—there would be Thai ownership of the HSR. Thailand also retained the right to manage the project and all the stations, to better assure Thailand's sovereignty. Although Chinese engineers and workers will be involved in the design of the HSR and will be responsible for railroad technology and signal systems, Thai materials will be utilized and Thai firms and workers will be responsible for the basic construction.[83] To get to a point that Thais can eventually operate the HSR themselves, the first wave of stationmasters and engineers is undergoing technical training in China.[84]

Apart from Bangkok effectively negotiating the HSR deal with China, it has also initiated multilateral alternatives to Chinese funding for some infrastructure projects. In June 2018, during the Eighth Ayeyewady–Chao Phraya–Mekong Economic Cooperation Strategy Summit (ACMECS), Prayut proposed a financing mechanism for joint projects under the ACMECS 2019–23 master plan that focuses on enhancing connectivity among the five member countries of Cambodia, Laos, Myanmar, Vietnam, and Thailand (CLMVT). These countries represent East-West connectivity to balance the prospect of an ever-greater North-South dependence on the PRC, "to lessen reliance on Chinese investment."[85] Thai officials said that Thailand will contribute millions of dollars of seed money to kick-start this fund, which was to be up and running in 2019. The fund will rely on member-state contributions, other countries, and financial institutions, and will raise capital through the stock and bond markets.

Thailand's move to create a regional fund with its neighbors aims to reassert Thai leadership over the region and reduce overreliance on Chinese investments and loans, a desire shared by others in the CLMVT cluster. Thailand plays a natural leadership role in this region due to its relatively strong economic performance and strategic location. At the same time that Bangkok strives to have positive relations with Beijing, it also seeks to catalyze the formation of institutions that can act as a counterweight to the PRC.

CASE: THE VIENTIANE-BOTEN LINE (LAOS)

Laos, a small landlocked country of nearly 6.9 million surrounded by much larger neighbors, does have some natural resources, such as the potential for hydropower and minerals. Nonetheless, it is poor and underdeveloped, ranking 118th among nations in terms of per capita GDP (PPP) in 2018.[86] Laos is, therefore, vulnerable to manipulation by larger neighbors. Historically, the Thai court dominated Laos until it became a French protectorate in 1893. Early Lao anticolonial activities were coordinated with the Indochina Communist Party (ICP), led by Ho Chi Minh. In 1951, the Lao communists broke away from the ICP and formed the Lao People's Party, which in 1972 became the Lao People's Revolutionary Party (LPRP). The LPRP has governed Laos since 1975, making the mountainous state one of the few remaining communist regimes in the world.

The Lao People's Democratic Republic's (PDR) top priority is lifting its people out of poverty through economic development (see chapter 4). A high-ranking Lao official told our research team that "The Lao people blame the government for the lack of development."[87] Vientiane's strategy focuses on exporting its abundant hydropower to neighbors, namely Thailand, China, and Vietnam, and overcoming its landlocked status by linking up to them via railroads and highways. Vientiane hopes to balance its dependencies on China with strong ties to other neighbors.

Prior to the start of construction of the HSR project in Laos in 2016, the only stretch of railroad that existed was a 3.5 km long line between Nong Khai, in northeastern Thailand, and Thanaleng Station just outside Vientiane on the Lao side of the Mekong River. To achieve the goal of a "land-linked" country, the first step is to connect Vientiane, in the country's midsection along the Mekong River, to Boten, the border town in the north where trucks, cargo, and people cross into Laos from the PRC. For Vientiane, the ultimate goal of railroad construction is to generate an influx of trade, investment, and jobs—to transform Laos from being a "transport corridor" to an "economic corridor" full of economic activities.[88]

Apart from China, Laos has no offers from other countries to build the HSR (or much else), due to the high risks involved—Laos's underdeveloped economy, low population density, rugged terrain, and unexploded land mines and other ordnance remaining from America's "secret war" against the Vietnamese and the Pathet Lao in the 1960s and 1970s. Some feasibility studies undertaken by the Lao Ministry of Public Works and Transportation pointed to the heavy environmental and displaced persons costs that needed consideration. All this has become a topic of debate in the National Assembly of Lao PDR. One multilateral lending agency official explained that "from a cost-benefit perspective for Laos itself, it is not beneficial to build *now.*"[89]

Chinese interest in building the HSR in Laos was a major breakthrough in Vientiane's hopes for connectivity. In order to realize its pan-Asian ambition, the most logical first step for Beijing is the China-Laos "Central Line" segment, if for no other reason than it is the shortest way to Bangkok and on to Singapore via Malaysia. Moreover, the Lao segment is politically most feasible, given the strains in Beijing's relations with Vietnam and Myanmar (alternative routes), and because Laos has no alternative funders. The one-party communist regime and the low level of political and civil engagement in Laos also make the Central Line the path of least resistance.

Even so, negotiations between the PRC and Laos were not smooth sailing. Despite the fact that an understanding for a joint venture and joint management of the Lao railroad was reached in April 2010, and the Lao National Assembly approved it in 2012, construction of the HSR did not actually commence until December 2016. In the six-year gap, the two sides were negotiating terms, with interest rates and land issues being the thorniest. Another snag in the negotiations was the speed of the railroad. Because about 80 percent of the terrain that the railroad will traverse is mountainous and sparsely populated, Chinese rail experts recommended a speed reduction from 200 kmph to 160 kmph (with freight trains traveling at a maximum of 120 kmph).[90] In fact, slowing down the speed of the Lao section of the Central Line (genuine HSR is considered 250 kmph and up) was a good idea for many reasons, including initial construction costs, operating and maintenance standards and costs, and more balanced freight and passenger utilization.

Then the bidding process took nine additional months. Chinese contractors won bids for all six sectors of the railroad, meaning that the entire line was to be built with Chinese technology and equipment. Following the bidding process, land procurement and demolition came next—4,411 households were to be affected by the construction.[91] As of 2019, the project is well underway, but the task is enormous—60 percent of the railroad will be across bridges and through tunnels.[92] A total of 170 bridges and 72 tunnels will be constructed.[93] The plan is to open the HSR to traffic by 2021, after the extension from an initial 2020 deadline.

For Laos, the $7 billion cost of the Central Line constitutes more than half of its 2015 GDP.[94] The joint venture that was set up for construction of the HSR is 70 percent China-owned, 30 percent Lao-owned. For the Lao share, Vientiane will have to borrow $500 million from China. The remaining is to be repaid through land concessions. The joint venture will get development rights to the land surrounding the stations. Laos might be compelled to accept repaying the loan it owes the Chinese by granting land rights, selling commodities such as potassium and bauxite,[95] and/or selling railroad assets, which further impinges on sovereignty. Such dependence on China and acceptance of these terms gives Beijing considerable political and economic sway over Vientiane. Given the lack of alternatives and Laos's low level of economic development, however, there are few options to the agreed-upon arrangement. Of course, there are risks for China as well. Given all the pitfalls, many Chinese ask whether this is a wise investment for the PRC itself (as noted in chapter 3).

Laos is willing to accept these asymmetrical disadvantages primarily because it sees connectivity as the only way forward for its own development. As one senior Lao PDR official explained:

> China wants to develop Yunnan. So the question Laos asked itself—why don't we also benefit from it and be part of it? The logistics plan in this region is from Singapore to China. China also has to use land transportation from east to west. If Laos can be part of this logistics plan, and secure just 5 percent of this movement of goods, Laos can benefit tremendously. Five

percent for Laos will be a huge amount—its population is low, and the 5 percent share will create jobs and other development opportunities for Laos. Laos can tie itself to this regional system to be part of this logistical system. Laos can also provide peaceful conditions to promote development in the region.[96]

CASE: THE KUALA LUMPUR–SINGAPORE HSR

Malaysia and Thailand have recently moved into the ranks of middle powers, as measured by aggregate GDP.[97] Although both countries are near the bottom of the middle power cohort, they nevertheless play critical roles within ASEAN and other regional forums. Malaysia was the first ASEAN country to establish formal diplomatic relations with Beijing after the PRC assumed the "China seat" in the UN in 1971. This quick recognition reflected Malaysia's hopes that by normalizing relations with China, Beijing might cease support for the Malaysian Communist Party. This did not happen immediately, and relations were cool until 1985. Even today, Kuala Lumpur remains sensitive to the links between China and the significant ethnic Chinese minority in Malaysia. Only in the 1980s, under then Prime Minister Mahathir bin Mohamad, did bilateral relations improve. In his memoirs written in 2011, Mahathir recalled, "We had problems at first with China's support of the mainly Chinese communist insurgents in Malaysia, but as China gradually withdrew its backing, relations between us improved."[98] By 1989, with the fall of communism in Eastern Europe, the communist threat receded, and the Malaysian Communist Party disbanded the same year. Malaysia's strategic aim, first under Mahathir, then Abdullah Badawi, and then Najib Razak, has been to maximize economic benefits from China. Mahathir put it plainly: "I became convinced China was going to be a great economic power and that Malaysia must develop good relations with it, ideological differences notwithstanding."[99] Though Malaysia's pragmatic policy began under Mahathir, Najib brought engagement with Beijing to a new level.

The idea of HSR linking Kuala Lumpur to Singapore was first advanced by Malaysia at the 2013 annual leaders' retreat between Najib and Lee Hsien Loong in Singapore. After several rounds of discussion focusing on station location, the alignment of the right-of-way, and the project's financing and management, an MOU to build the line and a legally binding agreement were inked in December 2016, with the 350 km track scheduled to begin service in December 2026. Construction was to start in 2019 after open bidding to award contracts. The Chinese and Japanese were frontrunners to win the project. The HSR was to have seven stations running along the west coast of Malaysia, connecting Kuala Lumpur and Singapore, and reducing travel time to ninety minutes from up to seven hours. The plan was for Malaysia to pay most of the cost (SGD 24 billion), because 335 km of the 350 km long railroad (96 percent) was to run through Malaysia.

In 2018, when Mahathir returned to power following the victory of a coalition of opposition forces (the Pakatan Harapan), his immediate priority was reducing Malaysia's large federal debt of RM 1 trillion and dealing with the corruption scandals involving Najib and his family, some of which implicated Chinese entities. On June 12, 2018, Mahathir said that the KL-SIN HSR project would be postponed rather than scrapped (he had announced canceling the project almost immediately after being appointed prime minister). According to Mahathir, his new Pakatan Harapan government needed time to study the HSR project, like other large-scale infrastructure projects, and revisit these undertakings once the country's financial position improved. On September 5, 2018, Malaysia and Singapore agreed to suspend the construction of the HSR until May 2020. The Economic Affairs Minister Azmin Ali said, "Malaysia is committed to continue with the project after May 2020," with the HSR service expected to start by January 2031.[100] Almost immediately, the PRC sent signals to Kuala Lumpur that it would be flexible in discussions and helpful in financing.[101]

For its part, Singapore agreed to Malaysia's proposal to build the HSR in the first place as a way of integrating the two countries' economies, bringing the peoples of the two countries closer, and transforming how the two countries interact. Singapore had also hoped to leverage the HSR to develop its second central business district, known as the Jurong Lake District, where the HSR terminus would be located. The HSR terminus presumably would enhance the Jurong Lake District's commercial potential. Singapore decided that the economic value of the HSR would outweigh security concerns about a porous border and immigration issues that could emerge if the HSR eventually reached southern Thailand—where a separatist movement linked to Islamic terrorist forces boiled.[102]

With respect to the bidding process, Singapore's chief concern was that it be clean and open.[103] Singapore's image as an open economy with clear rule of law and international business standards is a key reason for its success. Singapore's usual caution increased as Najib's scandals multiplied. Some projects in Malaysia financed by the Chinese have ignored good governance practices, such as transparency and competitive bidding for tenders.[104]

Nonetheless, Malaysia-China economic ties were already strongly developed since Mahathir's first stint as prime minister and his initial policy of leveraging Chinese economic growth as key to developing Malaysia's economy during the 1990s and the following decade. The CREC has plans to make Kuala Lumpur its regional hub. The China Rolling Stock Company has established a significant presence in the state of Perak. This places Chinese companies in an advantageous position to secure the bid on the KL-SIN HSR. Apart from putting itself in a good spot to win the bid, China has also used political pressure tactics on the Malaysian and Singaporean governments (discussed earlier).

Throughout the HSR process to date, however, both Malaysia and Singapore have succeeded to a significant extent in resisting Chinese pressure. The Singapore government stood firm on policies concerning international law and made it clear to Beijing that Singapore's actions and policies were motivated by its national interest. In a keynote address during a workshop on Chinese public diplomacy held in Singapore in June 2018, retired Singapore diplomat Bilahari Kausikan, who was instrumental in charting Singapore's foreign policy before his retirement, acknowledged that "China is always going to enjoy significant influence in this region, but significant influence is not dominant or exclusive influence."[105] Such thinking exemplifies Singapore's foreign policy mindset.

As for the HSR, Singapore did not bow to Chinese pressure to favor Chinese companies in the bidding process. Instead, it insisted on transparent and open bidding in its agreement with Malaysia. During negotiations for the MOU on the HSR in 2016 and 2017, both Lee Hsien Loong and Najib consistently stressed that bidding would be conducted in a fair and transparent manner; in the joint news release to announce the tender in December 2017, both sides promised an "open, fair and transparent procurement process."[106]

Kuala Lumpur has shown similar fortitude despite the Najib government coming under heavy criticism for having compromised Malaysian interests to China. Najib's cancelation of the Bandar Malaysia deal with China, where CREC and its Malaysian partner, Iskandar Waterfront Holdings, failed to meet payment obligations as stipulated in the contract, is a potent example of Malaysia's resistance to Chinese pressure, as are Mahathir's subsequent moves to renegotiate projects his predecessor had agreed upon. In an indication of Malaysia's success in negotiating these deals, Mahathir announced in April 2019 the revival of the Bandar Malaysia project, but with a new plan that will emphasize local content and local labor.[107]

CASE: INDONESIA'S JAKARTA-BANDUNG HSR

Although the Jakarta-Bandung HSR in Indonesia is obviously not part of the continental Pan-Asia Railway vision, it is appropriate to include here inasmuch as it has provided a negotiating reference point for parties involved in the railroad projects that are the focus of this book. Being the first Chinese HSR project in the region, the Indonesian undertaking flags developments to watch for. The negotiations between Beijing and Jakarta are an interesting study in the ability of a middle power to secure advantage with the biggest power in Asia.

Indonesia has the fourth largest population in the world and is ASEAN's de facto leader. Economically, it is the world's sixteenth largest state, placing it squarely in the middle power category. It has the potential to become the seventh-largest economy by 2030.[108] However, Jakarta has limited military capability, with small armed forces and modest military spending to spread across an archipelago of more than 17,000 islands.

China's rise poses some challenges to Indonesia's regional position and arouses anxieties. Historically, like other Southeast Asian states, Indonesia has a legacy of fighting communism, in this case the Indonesian Communist Party, or PKI, which had close ties with Mao Zedong's Cultural Revolution–era China. Following an abortive coup allegedly led by the PKI in 1965, brutal measures (by both the military and mob actions) savaged both the PKI and the ethnic Chinese population, tragically conflating the two. For years thereafter, the Chinese communities in Indonesia suffered: the use of Chinese language and the establishment of Chinese schools were prohibited. Convinced that the PRC was complicit in the coup attempt, Jakarta froze relations with Beijing in 1967, reestablishing them only in 1990.

The reestablishment of bilateral relations between Jakarta and Beijing was a pragmatic calculation. Then President Suharto believed that China's strong economic growth and open policy, combined with Indonesia's own development, made communism less of a threat. Moreover, Jakarta's desire to become chair of the nonaligned movement necessitated improved relations with Beijing, given the latter's influence in the movement. Despite the passage of time, Indonesians remain suspicious of PRC links to the Chinese ethnic population in their own country as well as Beijing's assertiveness in the South China Sea—the two countries have overlapping claims in Indonesia's Exclusive Economic Zone, but not conflicting territorial claims. Following the 1997–98 Asian financial crisis and the fall of President Suharto, Indonesia's relations with China improved as its relations with the West deteriorated, primarily due to the stringent IMF and World Bank conditions attached to financial assistance for Jakarta. With its growing financial and trade strength, Beijing moved into the vacuum.[109] Although Chinese loans do not come with economic conditions such as those imposed by the World Bank and IMF, Beijing often attaches stipulations that Chinese companies and workers be hired. At present, Chinese workers top the ranks of foreign workers in Indonesia.[110] This has generated concerns in Indonesia, with its large pool of unemployed and underemployed citizens, and has triggered criticisms that technology transfer and skill upgrading is inadequate. Beijing's increasingly vociferous statements of its intention to be guardian of overseas Chinese on a global basis arouse additional anxieties.

Elected to his first term as Indonesia's president in October 2014, one of Jokowi's main goals has been to leave a legacy of mega infrastructure projects (chapter 4). Consequently, Chinese and Japanese investments in Indonesia play a significant role in his economic ambitions, and he has had the opportunity to play Tokyo and Beijing off against each other to secure advantages. With respect to the Jakarta-Bandung HSR project, Japan was the initial front-runner for securing the contracts. However, in March 2015, Jokowi discussed the Jakarta-Bandung HSR project during his visit to Beijing, with the result being that two MOUs were reached. These events took Japan by surprise, which had until then been confident that it would secure the Indonesian HSR project. Japan was interested in the initial Jakarta-to-Bandung line because of the potential to win rights to build the anticipated Bandung-to-Surabaya line along the spine of Java—the real prize.

A key reason why Japan lost out to China in the bidding process for the Jakarta-Bandung HSR project was that Beijing offered not to ask for sovereign guarantees from the Indonesian government for the project. This was in contrast to Japan's lending practice, which then required high-risk projects (such as HSRs) to be backed by the host government's sovereign guarantees. Moreover, the Japanese take longer to construct projects, and their schedule did not comport with Jokowi's desire to have a project to show off during his anticipated reelection campaign in 2019 (he was reelected). Finally, while our team has no evidence to prove or disprove this statement, one senior foreign government official posted in Jakarta told our research team that during the bidding process PRC entities engaged in "massive corruption."[111]

In dealing with major powers in the region, Indonesia plays one power against the other. In July 2015, then Coordinating Minister for Economy, Sofyan Djalil, said that to obtain the best deal for the construction of the Jakarta-Bandung HSR, the Indonesian government would hold a "beauty contest" among the parties interested in the project, and would award the contract to its winner.[112] The Indonesian government was fully cognizant of its substantial bargaining power owing to the strategic and economic competition between Japan and China. All parties knew that a successful bid in Indonesia would confer advantages in future competitions for HSR projects elsewhere, particularly those in the region. By leveraging Japan's competitive interest in the project, Jokowi managed to wring better terms from China, which included a 2 percent interest rate for the loan, dropping the requirement for sovereign Indonesian government guarantees for the project, and treating the undertaking as a business-to-business relationship. A groundbreaking ceremony was held for the project in January 2016, but problems with land acquisition immediately sprang up (detailed in chapter 6).

This negotiation on the Indonesian HSR deal directly affected the subsequent negotiations with Thailand; Bangkok used the 2 percent loan figure Jakarta had obtained to negotiate with Beijing. This deal also affected Tokyo; it eased up on its financing requirements somewhat after losing this bid. In short, the outcomes of prior HSR negotiations affect subsequent negotiations.

CONDITIONS AFFECTING THE BARGAINING POWER OF SMALL AND MIDDLE STATES

From the HSR and conventional-speed rail cases just discussed, it is possible to specify conditions affecting the bargaining power of Southeast Asian states vis-à-vis China. As we see in the following chapter, the negotiating and implementation phases are not necessarily discrete. As projects encounter challenges, they may require renegotiation amid ongoing implementation, sometimes leaving Beijing with the uncomfortable choice of making further concessions or eating the sunk costs. While Beijing has strength, it is notable how attenuated its bargaining power can become.

Size, Wealth, and Location Matter. Size does matter in international politics. Middle powers have greater leverage than smaller ones. In his 2012 speech to the International Institute for Strategic Studies Shangri-La Dialogue, then Indonesian President Bambang Yudhoyono (2004–14) said, "The relations of major powers are not entirely up to them, ... [M]iddle and small powers can help lock these powers into a durable architecture through a variety of instruments."[113] Bruce Gilley and Andrew O'Neil define middle powers as "countries with capabilities immediately below those of great powers, but still far above most secondary states in the international system."[114] Middle powers have the ability to resist Chinese demands, as seen in the cases of Indonesia, Malaysia, and Thailand, as well as Singapore. Middle powers are able to band together with others to deal with great powers, as well as act bilaterally and bargain with them to set terms that are in their interests.

What influence do Indonesia and Thailand have when bargaining with the PRC? Indonesia, in particular, occupies a special place within Southeast Asia. Beijing's willingness to go all out to prevail over Tokyo and secure the Jakarta-Bandung HSR contract was energized by the first mover advantages that the PRC would enjoy if it overcame Japan in their first head-to-head HSR contest in the region. China knew that winning that contract would help persuade others to follow suit. Xi Jinping chose to launch the BRI in Indonesia in 2013 because of its regional leading role. A successful first HSR with Southeast Asia's *de facto* leader, Beijing hoped, would persuade others to jump onto the Chinese BRI and HSR bandwagons.

Every country has its assets and liabilities in dealing with bigger powers. Geography gives Thailand a major advantage. Any Pan-Asia Railway would have to go through Bangkok, given the city's central location. While geography is an asset for Thailand, for Laos it could be a liability—the Lao PDR could be bypassed (at least theoretically) to its east (Vietnam) or west (Myanmar) if Vientiane's negotiations with Beijing foundered. However, despite its strategic location, Thailand was unable to secure as good a deal from the PRC as Indonesia (in terms of interest rate), which was a major reason for the long, drawn-out HSR negotiation process between Beijing and Bangkok. In the end, Thailand chose to self-finance the operation, thereby avoiding relinquishing land development rights to PRC entities. This option does not exist for poorer Laos, Cambodia, and Myanmar. As a Royal University of Phnom Penh report put it in about 2017, "The best choice for a small and developing country like Cambodia is to fly with the dragon. . . ."[115] Moreover, Bangkok is able to take a leadership role in the Greater Mekong region by setting up a regional fund to help finance projects within the ACMECS master plan, thereby reducing the region's reliance on Chinese loans and aid. By initiating the ACMECS fund, Thailand demonstrates middle power activism.[116]

The earlier discussion on the KL-SIN HSR highlighted Malaysia's and Singapore's ability to resist Chinese muscle in ways that slightly differ from Thailand's. Both countries have pushed for greater economic links with the PRC while maintaining greater independence in foreign and defense policy. To outside observers, Kuala Lumpur seems to have jumped on the Chinese bandwagon.[117] The reality is, however, that Malaysia is not close to uncritically bandwagoning with China in its endeavors. It may be vigorously strengthening its economic ties with China, but it is concurrently updating and modernizing its military and forging stronger US ties.[118] Najib's shelving of the Bandar Malaysia Project with China suggests that despite the PRC's deep roots in the Malaysian economy, Kuala Lumpur will maintain an independent policy. Prime Minister Mahathir's intention to renegotiate "unfair" deals with China during his visit there in August 2018 is evidence of this, as well as being a shrewd attempt to get Beijing to improve terms for its projects.

Even during Najib's reign, the China-friendly prime minister sought to maintain a fine balance between the United States and China. Despite relations with Washington dipping to a low point following the US decision to investigate the 1MDB case in 2016, Najib visited the White House in 2017. Two key areas of American-Malaysian cooperation have weathered all difficulties—counterterrorism and military-to-military ties.[119]

In the case of Laos, its size and interior location severely circumscribe its maneuvering space. It nevertheless strives to maintain autonomy. Over time, Lao leaders have swung between those leaning closer to Hanoi and those with an affinity for Beijing. In February 2016, for instance, Beijing-leaning Lao political leaders, such as Choummaly Sayasone and Somsavat Lengsavad, did not seek reelection to the Communist Party's Central Committee.[120] Their successors, many of whom were educated in Vietnam, such as Prime Minister Thongloun Sisoulith, are more inclined toward Hanoi.[121] Hence, leadership factions in Vientiane have carefully balanced their foreign policy between China and Vietnam. Laos and its neighbors also welcome international institutions such as the ADB and World Bank to ensure that they at least have some choices. Nonetheless, for some projects Beijing is the only game in town.

Then, Vientiane must consider trading its land and minerals for the infrastructure it hopes will be its salvation.

State Capacity. Secondary states have more options when they have greater capacity: robust government and civic institutions, administrative structures, rule of law, abundant human resources, and regulative and monitoring abilities.[122] Having skilled and knowledgeable interlocutors who can deal with Beijing is critical.

Singapore, despite its size, clearly has state capacity. It is not overly dependent on Beijing economically. China accounts for 13 percent of Singapore's total trade, whereas 70 percent of Laos's trade is with the PRC. Even though in 2014 China became Singapore's largest trade partner, the year before, Singapore became China's largest foreign investor.[123] China needs Singapore as much as Singapore needs China, "at least from an economics perspective."[124] Singapore tries to maintain a delicate balance in its dealings with Beijing and Washington: it is "economically pro-China and militarily pro-U.S., while remaining politically independent and culturally diverse."[125] Singapore is able to withstand pressure to favor PRC companies because it has able bureaucrats and diplomats, rule of law, and well-developed and transparent institutions and business standards. Its strong anticorruption laws are a deterrent.

However, low levels of state capacity in other Southeast Asian states constrain their abilities to bargain with China. For example, the feasibility report for the construction and financing of the China-Laos railroad was drafted by China Railway Corporation and the Provincial Government of Yunnan. Thereafter, the report was approved by China's NDRC.[126] China likely played such a decisive role because Laos lacks skilled technicians, workers, and professionals capable of independently conducting the studies.[127] To some extent, similar conditions exist in Thailand, which is somewhere between Singapore and Laos in many of these capacities. In the case of the Bangkok–Nong Khai HSR, there was a lack of ability to conduct indigenous feasibility studies.[128] Neither does Thailand yet have sufficient skills in railroad construction to do the job itself without Chinese (or outside) assistance. In Indonesia, Japan completed the feasibility report for the Jakarta-Bandung HSR from 2012 to 2014. Subsequently, when the final contract went to China, the Japanese criticized the Chinese proposal as "unrealistic, especially without government funding and likely to end up making losses as it has to deal with a complex and corrupt bureaucracy in Indonesia."[129]

Domestic Politics and Public Opinion. Robert Putnam's two-level game framework emphasizes the importance of domestic politics in negotiations among countries.[130] The first level takes place in the international arena. The second occurs domestically in each country where separate discussions are going on to ratify the international agreements struck at level 1. To varying degrees, public opinion in Southeast Asian countries has expressed concern about the impact of Chinese investments and presence in their countries. Both Najib and Jokowi have come under attack from opposition parties for compromising their respective countries' interests to secure deals with Beijing. Although Malaysians tend to take an overall positive view of Chinese investments (for example, 70 percent of Malaysians feel that Chinese investments are a net positive, according to a 2017 Merdeka Center Survey),[131] there are, nevertheless, concerns about whether locals will benefit.

Chinese companies in host countries often procure everything from China, sidelining local small and medium enterprises (SMEs).[132] This is a major concern for Malaysians, because 97 percent of Malaysian businesses are SMEs, and these SMEs employ 65 percent of the population.[133] Moreover, Chinese investments in Malaysia have focused on high-profile rail and port projects, which Malaysians see as ominous signals of Kuala Lumpur's growing indebtedness to Beijing.[134] Malaysians have questioned whether these projects are necessary or merely to serve Beijing's strategic interests.[135] Projects such as the Melaka Gateway Deep Sea Port and the Kuantan Port Expansion (both of which our research team visited) are suspect, because even Malaysia's existing ports are not operating at full capacity. Other projects, such as Forest City in Johor Bahru, which is a private community investment project, have come under heavy criticism. In the Forest City case, opposition arises because the plan is to house mostly mainland Chinese buyers. Such criticisms reflect public concerns that Malaysia will be overrun by mainland Chinese, which will infringe on Malaysia's national and cultural sovereignty.[136]

Public opinion in Vietnam is problematic as well, inasmuch as anti-Chinese sentiments infuse Vietnamese nationalism. PRC construction projects in Vietnam have come under heavy criticism from the Vietnamese public—the Hanoi light rail system in particular. Issues have ranged from complaints of poor standards, haphazard design, and safety to fears of an agglomeration of Chinese enclaves on Vietnamese soil as large numbers of Chinese workers enter Vietnam. Anti-China protests have erupted several times in recent years, including large-scale demonstrations that ignited in June 2018. These civic actions were against new land leasing and cyber security laws. Protesters targeted the law that allows the government to extend land leases to foreign investors to ninety-nine years, fearing such legislation would permit Chinese companies to occupy Vietnamese land for generations. Earlier, in 2014, disturbances in Vietnam exploded protesting Beijing's oil-rig activities in what Hanoi claimed as its waters. In reaction, "Beijing responded by freezing its financing for power projects in Vietnam."[137] The takeaway for Hanoi, and perhaps others in the region, was that the PRC would use the leverage provided by broad interdependence to achieve its goals.

These domestic concerns among Southeast Asian peoples about Chinese-connected investments mean that the theoretical "win-sets" for Southeast Asian politicians will often be small. Leaders are hovering in a danger zone between failing to win economic gains for their people and selling out national sovereignty. Ironically, this very dilemma gives Southeast Asian leaders bargaining power with Beijing. Putnam has shown that smaller win-sets can give one party leverage in negotiations with the other,[138] because some issues demonstrably cannot be conceded. If the PRC wants its projects to succeed in the region, it needs to consider public opinion in host countries.

In examining some of the negotiations between China and HSR host countries in Southeast Asia, this chapter demonstrates that secondary states have agency and are able, to varying degrees, to negotiate better terms for themselves than might be expected. For its part, China has also demonstrated great power restraint in some cases, especially when the projects serve larger strategic purposes.

Overall, both China and its current and prospective HSR infrastructure partners face dangers in their negotiations. For Beijing's would-be partners, the dangers include requirements to procure from the PRC, an overall lack of transparency, and lack of venue for unbiased dispute resolution. The risks to China include permanently damaging "brand China" and saddling the Chinese taxpayer with bad debts. The reverse also is true. If China learns and performs, the results will be economically and strategically transformational.

CHAPTER 6

Project Implementation

"The Devil Is in the Details"

I think the implementation has been slower than what had
been expected in the beginning.
—Gregory Enjalbert, Bombardier Transportation vice president,
  April 2019[1]

Negotiations on high- and conventional-speed rail projects are protracted, complex affairs, as demonstrated in the preceding chapter.
However long or short the negotiating process may be, initial agreement on these undertakings only sets the stage for an even more arduous and costly process of implementation. At this stage, high-speed rail
(HSR) projects may be delayed, postponed, renegotiated, or canceled
entirely for myriad reasons, three of which we will focus on here.

One reason for these implementation challenges is that memoranda
of understanding (MOUs) and written agreements on HSR projects are
often struck between the Chinese national government and Southeast
Asian national governments, without input from lower levels of government and the people affected by these projects. As Merilee S. Grindle
explains, because interest-aggregating structures are weak in developing
countries, "a large portion of individual and collective demand making,
the representation of interests, and the emergence and resolution of
conflict occurs at the output [implementation] stage."[2] Bargaining does
not stop with initial agreement; it continues during implementation,
providing a chance for previously ignored parties to shape outcomes.
Implementation is an ongoing process of decision making and bargaining that involves a variety of actors beyond the subset of players who
were involved in negotiating the initial agreement. The implementation
stage of rail and other infrastructure projects is thus significant, because
it is where subnational governments, local groups, and others excluded

from the initial negotiations lobby, resist, modify, and challenge projects, often leading to alteration, delay, and sometimes cancellation.[3]

A second reason HSR projects may stall is the universal problem of what Jeffrey Pressman and Aaron Wildavsky call "the complexity of joint action."[4] This phenomenon arises from the fact that any sizable government (or private) undertaking involves multiple stakeholders, each of whom can delay, modify, or sometimes abort projects. The more stakeholders ("clearance points" or veto actors) involved in an undertaking, the less likely the project will move forward without major issues. It does not take many clearance points to create a circumstance in which the probability of success drops dramatically. Pressman and Wildavsky demonstrate this tyranny of probability in a study of how an undertaking with a 99 percent probability of agreement at each of seventy clearance points still has less than a 50 percent probability of avoiding major problems after moving past the sixty-eighth clearance point.[5] In actuality, of course, stakeholders are not cooperative 99 percent of the time, and often there are many more than seventy clearance points.

There are many reasons why various "clearance points" or stakeholders may be uncooperative.[6] For one, different bureaucracies have contradictory missions, or they may generally agree about a project, but one organization is less committed than the other to that particular project. Another reason could be that agencies, companies, or others may support an undertaking but have insufficient resources to do much to further the common objective. Stakeholders may also fight over who plays the lead role and who controls the budget. The mere prospect of a project may catalyze the formation of new groups that did not exist until they found their raison d'être in opposing or modifying the initiative at stake.

The third major hurdle in implementation is state capacity. Francis Fukuyama defines governance as "a government's ability to make and enforce rules, and to deliver services, regardless of whether that government is democratic or not."[7] He names four approaches to evaluating the quality of governance: procedural measures, input measures, output measures, and measures of bureaucratic autonomy.[8] By output measures, he means state capacity. A measure of capacity is the level of education and professionalization of government officials.[9] Financial and technical capacities are also critical to the proper functioning of the government. The human development index (HDI) developed by the United Nations provides a good indicator of the capacity of states to provide public goods and regulate economic and other behaviors. It measures life expectancy and education levels, among other indicators. Among the four countries examined in this chapter—Indonesia, Thailand, Malaysia, and Laos—in 2017 Malaysia's HDI was highest, ranking 57 out of 188 countries, followed by Thailand at 83, Indonesia at 116, and Laos at 139. By way of contrast, Singapore was at 9 in 2017.[10]

Laos's construction of the 414-kilometer Boten-Vientiane HSR line, which we examine later in this chapter, provides the clearest illustration of how the lack of financial and human capacity can lead to delays in implementation. Yet relatively speaking, the Boten-Vientiane HSR line has proceeded much faster than either Indonesia's Jakarta-Bandung line or Thailand's Bangkok–Nong Khai line. It may be that Laos's relative capacity/development constraints have allowed China to assume a larger role, pushing the project faster. Moreover, the lack of capacity means there are relatively fewer veto actors in Vientiane. As one Lao planner put it to us: "We ask them not to forget Laos. . . . We lack the know-how and physical infrastructures. We have nothing but ideas. We don't want to be left behind."[11] Laos's one-party system also makes it easier for the Lao government to push through projects.

It is unsurprising, therefore, that all major infrastructure projects have problems, delays, and cost escalations. Moreover, building a rail line in a single country is less complex than building one crossing multiple international boundaries and scores of local jurisdictions, particularly if one seeks seamless interconnection. When building in just one country, language and culture, legal and administrative practices, the political system, and overall local conditions stay relatively constant; thus, implementers can rely on a degree of predictability. Lessons once learned can continue to be applied. Once implementation of a big project moves across national boundaries, everything changes, as is especially the case with this HSR project involving seven Southeast Asian nations and the PRC. With this diverse and complex set of actors, the prospect of having smooth implementation is very low, while the prospect for major problems is a virtual certainty. Moreover, policies and practices that work in China may be inappropriate or counterproductive in circumstances abroad. As one scholar in Singapore put it, "In China, major variables are controlled [by the government], but going abroad, major variables are not controlled."[12]

In short, the implementation process is messy and characterized by fits and starts, overlap among stages, and potentially long periods during which nothing happens. In the first of implementation's three stages, once a successful bidder for a project has been selected (an often protracted, conflict-laden battle of commercial wills and financial chi-canery), land needs to be acquired and cleared. Local spatial plans require updating to include the rail lines, and government permits are needed for land clearance to proceed. This first stage is the most chal-lenging and poses the greatest obstacle to the implementation process; domestic politics is most impactful here, because land acquisition requires the cooperation of a larger number of veto actors and stake-holders. Without land acquisition, the next two stages cannot proceed. This is the highest-risk stage.

The second stage of the HSR implementation process involves the disbursement of loans to construction companies so building can com-mence. However, loan disbursement from Chinese banks (e.g., China Development Bank or China Exim Bank) is often conditional on land acquisition: in some contracts, the majority of the land must be acquired before the banks will disburse the initial tranche of loans. Any delay in land acquisition in turn delays loan disbursement. Further, land acquisi-tion is the responsibility of the partner government, not the Chinese parties, so if for whatever reason (often contentious local and/or national politics) the partner government is slow in acquiring land, the project stalls. Adding further complexity, depending on the contract, host country governments must come up with their share of the capital in tandem with the different phases of construction. Governments fac-ing budgetary constraints often have difficulties meeting these obliga-tions, thereby causing further delay. Of course, the Chinese side may also encounter financial difficulties such as volatility in the PRC and firm-level economic and budgetary circumstances.

The third and final stage is the construction of the HSR or conven-tional rail line itself. At this stage, new obstacles inevitably arise, includ-ing challenging terrain, worker actions and safety-related accidents, insufficient or subpar construction materials, dearth of skilled labor, supplier issues, popular opposition to citizen displacement, controversy over cultural heritage sites, unanticipated environmental impacts and challenges, and technology and/or design flaws. Any one of these con-siderations (let alone several at once) can force changes and impose delays that increase costs, precipitating the painful process of finding additional money. Then there is Mother Nature—seismic events or other "acts of God." Finally, once a project is "finished," never-before-contemplated design flaws can crop up. A good example of just such a flaw is Boston's 2002 Central Artery/Tunnel project, the "Big Dig." After nominal completion, this US$14 billion-plus project had four faulty ceiling slabs fall, each weighing three tons, crushing a vehicle and killing a passenger going through the tunnel. This collapse required project closure for one year while costly but obviously essential repairs were completed. Similarly, in China, the 2011 Wenzhou HSR train collision required systemwide signal redesigns and forced nationwide speed reductions on HSR lines—all post completion.

Each of these broad stages represents a point in the implementation process at which disaffected people, interest groups, and subnational governments are able to exert pressure and alter project trajectory. The land acquisition and clearance stage is particularly perilous, and sometimes the military will even play a role, since it has considerable land and political clout. Moreover, in some countries it cannot be assumed that the military will not seize opportunities to make money in the process.[13] Finally, upon the completion of construction, all of the regulatory and ancillary support structures (such as customs, immigration, operational standards, and so forth) must be designed, agreed upon, and implemented. This constitutes a policy formulation and implementation problem set of its own. One Thai expert explained, "The weakest point in the system is 'border crossing' between states, 'I call it a chokehold.' The hardware issues can be solved by financial means. . . . 'There is a difference between physical connectivity and institutional connectivity.'"[14] For example, in the case of the HSR project running from Guangzhou to Hong Kong, the project was made contentious by disputes between Hong Kong groups and the PRC authorities over where the customs/immigration function would occur and whether the PRC would have police powers in its portion of the train station in downtown Hong Kong Special Administrative Region (SAR).

Hanging over these three implementation stages is the omnipresent possibility of domestic political events adding or subtracting key parties to the initial agreement. Sometimes this occurs through regular electoral or other constitutional processes and sometimes through abrupt, unanticipated, extraconstitutional regime change. For example, the May 2018 Malaysian election led to the unanticipated defeat of Prime Minister Najib Razak, who had signed agreements with Beijing for mammoth rail and other infrastructure projects. Two big rail projects, among other deals, one actually under construction and the other close to approval, came to a halt immediately after Mahathir Mohamad unexpectedly won the election. Beijing and Kuala Lumpur thereupon entered a dramatic and protracted negotiating phase in which it was unclear whether these projects would be resurrected or abandoned. This example illustrates a reality of these undertakings—the negotiating and implementation phases of these huge projects are not discrete. Deals can be reached, implementation can commence, and then big or small obstacles can necessitate additional negotiations. Sometimes these negotiations are dramatic, and other times they are just bumps in the road. As one Chinese foreign ministry official put it in an interview, "We find that in the democratic countries we have things coming along well, then there is an election, then things, like in Malaysia, change. Very unpredictable. Big political risk. We should not overcommit."[15]

This chapter addresses issues arising in the course of the implementation of several rail projects in Southeast Asia: Indonesia's Jakarta-Bandung HSR, Malaysia's suspended East Coast Rail Link (ECRL), the postponed Kuala Lumpur–Singapore HSR, Thailand's Bangkok to Nong Khai HSR, and the Lao HSR project (running from Boten at the Laos-China border to Thanaleng near Vientiane). Each of these cases illustrate to different degrees the challenges of implementation. The Jakarta-Bandung line and the Bangkok–Nong Khai line are most illustrative of the role of veto actors and bureaucratic resistance. Both undertakings are still in the early stages of implementation.[16] Malaysia's case demonstrates how changes in the political context can affect implementation of rail projects. Although construction of Laos's Boten-Vientiane line has progressed the most, it is not without problems, with a lack of state capacity being the key issue.

Prior to examining these projects, however, it is useful to consider the implementation challenges Chinese authorities and companies have confronted at home before ever venturing abroad. China's domestic implementation experience directly affects the way in which Chinese officials and companies operate in other countries. The domestic PRC toolbox does not always provide the right instruments to be effective abroad—adaptation is essential.

IMPLEMENTATION OF HSR PROJECTS IN CHINA

As Chinese rail companies and other actors move out of the PRC's domestic environment into the world beyond, they encounter many challenges similar to those confronted at home—financing, bureaucratic fragmentation, difficult terrain, land acquisition, and resettling displaced people. However, China's one-party authoritarian system makes clearing some hurdles much easier at home than abroad. The implication of centralization and authoritarianism in the PRC is that there are fewer clearance points and politically relevant resources are concentrated at upper levels. Strong central government support for the development of HSR projects within China means that land acquisition and clearance has tended to be quick, bank loans for HSR projects are given priority, and senior leadership can often compel recalcitrant bureaucracies and bureaucrats, localities, and societal groups to cooperate. By way of contrast, more negotiation and less compulsion is intrinsic in many projects abroad.

Domestically, the Chinese state is powerful, having the ability to penetrate deeply into and extract from society—"infrastructural power," as Michael Mann has discussed.[17] Taxation policy is one example of a muscular Chinese state: "financial repression" is strong in the PRC, a process whereby the state channels low-cost, forced savings to party authorities. At the same time, however, the PRC is a fragmented state, with layers of authority and multiple agencies distorting policy formulation and implementation.[18] The center alone cannot always compel recalcitrant "clearance points" to cooperate. In her study of Beijing's attempts to get local enterprises to be more innovative, for example, Ling Chen explains that national authorities often confront immovable local leaders determined to respond to local political coalitions and local bureaucrats vested in the preexistent industrial structure.[19] These two faces of the Chinese policy process coexist, and one or the other dominates depending on how important the issue is, whether there is elite cohesion on the issue, and the adequacy of human and budgetary resources, among other considerations.[20] Unified top leaders attaching great importance to a project is a precondition for comparatively smooth implementation in China.

Chapter 3 clearly demonstrated that the Chinese leadership of Jiang Zemin, Hu Jintao, and Xi Jinping have all prioritized the development of a domestic HSR industry. Below that most senior level of the Chinese hierarchy, HSR also had a skillful and committed bureaucratic champion in the person of Liu Zhijun, the subsequently disgraced former minister of railways. With all this collective political muscle, by 2013 China's domestic HSR network was the world's most extensive.[21]

Given high-level political support and the priority placed on constructing an HSR network at home, Chinese state banks and the PRC government underwrote the losses incurred by domestic HSR projects. Projects received favorable financing.[22] China's domestic HSRs are also funded by a "railway construction fund," which is a tax levied on cargo shippers, which means freight revenues in effect cross-subsidize HSR passengers.[23] The former Ministry of Railways (MOR), dissolved in 2013, depended on loans from Chinese state banks for the construction of HSR lines, so much so that by 2013, the asset-liability ratio of the MOR was at 64 percent, with its debt standing at RMB 3.2 trillion.[24] The MOR initially argued that its debts could be repaid seventeen years after most of the HSR lines had been completed, but this turned out to be grossly wrong.[25] Apart from the Beijing-Shanghai Line and Wuhan-Guangzhou HSR Line, all other lines are running at a loss.[26] However, as the MOR was a government ministry at that time, it could secure funds from the central government and operate at a deficit supported by the national treasury as long as the leadership was willing to tolerate it.

Moreover, unlike Indonesia, where strong land tenure laws favor individual landowners and local governments, land acquisition in China is easier because all land belongs to the state, albeit with land use rights granted for extended periods. Ultimately, the threat to use force and the regime's control of the judicial system can compel resettlement. The use of force to evict residents and to demolish villages is a common occurrence in China. Hence, Chinese railroad state-owned enterprises (SOEs) face relatively fewer obstacles in securing land as well as getting construction permits and financing at home, compared to the challenges they frequently face in partner countries. In Malaysia, for example, constituent states of the National Federation control land use; what Kuala Lumpur says does not necessarily get implemented in each of the thirteen states. Moreover, each of China's partner countries in this HSR venture varies along this dimension. Thailand, for instance, has relatively weaker local governments with respect to land use issues than Malaysia.[27]

China's authoritarian system, with its tight control over both print and social media, also makes dealing with negative public opinion less of an issue. Although environmental impact assessments are mandatory, in reality noncompliance happens, sometimes leading to public protests. In 2008, Shanghai citizens protested against a planned maglev train line from Shanghai to Hangzhou due to noise and feared health effects of electromagnetic radiation.[28] After a tortured negotiating process, the proposed line was shelved in favor of a slightly slower, more affordable train traveling an alternative route, which reduced public outcry. In December 2009, Chengdu residents opposed the planned Chengdu-Chongqing HSR due to noise pollution and other environmental impacts—a survey showed that 99.8 percent of the locals objected to the construction of the HSR route.[29] Construction was delayed, only starting in October 2010 after route adjustments occurred.[30] The construction of the Beijing-Shenyang HSR, which was set to begin in 2010, also encountered fierce public debate, also on noise and safety issues, which resulted in significant delays in construction.[31] Since 2009, tens of thousands of Beijing residents have conducted four sizable protests that delayed construction of the HSR route—one such protest in December 2012 involved approximately three hundred protesting citizens who were angry about a fraudulent environmental impact assessment report posted online, calling on authorities to change the proposed rail route.[32] More generally, many Chinese citizens question the necessity of HSR lines. Most respondents to a survey conducted by Guizhen He and colleagues were of the opinion that the central government and construction companies, not the local residents, would benefit most from HSR projects.[33] It is important to keep in mind, however, that while these public protests and opinions may have forced modifications in some projects, for the most part even protested lines were eventually constructed.

The Chinese government and railroad-related SOEs are able to clear these implementation hurdles with fewer difficulties than they encounter abroad, given the levers of power that the Chinese state possesses. Beijing is able to finance the debts incurred by domestic railroad SOEs, obtain land clearance and construction permits relatively quickly, and more effectively resist (and sometimes accommodate) public unhappiness about HSR projects at home. All criticism and challenges aside, in the final analysis Beijing has created a national, high-functioning rail grid with a speed and degree of thoroughness that is nearly unimaginable in many other national settings.

As Chinese railroad SOEs and other related actors expand their activities to other parts of Asia, Latin America, and Africa (not to mention the European Union, which has a deeply embedded rule of law framework and complex regulatory bureaucracy), they face a steep learning curve as they encounter varied operational contexts. A high-level Thai government source shared with our research team that the Chinese told the Thais that their (Thailand's) system is "complicated."[34] The experiences of Chinese railroad SOEs within China have not prepared them fully for the external complexities and challenges. Although the Chinese government has been able to overcome obstacles to its own domestic HSR projects, the central governments of partner countries do not necessarily possess the same level of authority to overcome or ignore domestic opposition.

Obstacles have proven so great that some PRC projects abroad (not just rail lines) have been abandoned. In other cases, Chinese interests have had to take over projects entirely for long lease periods to attempt to recoup their investments, a topic to which we will return in more detail in chapter 7. For instance, the construction of the first HSR in Latin America, the 468 km Tinaco-Anaco line in Venezuela, estimated to cost $7.5 billion, began in 2009 but was quietly abandoned in 2015, when Caracas was unable to pay for the project.[35] In Libya, the China Railway Group suspended three railroad projects worth $4.24 billion when the 2011 civil war broke out. In 2014, Mexico canceled a $3.7 billion HSR line originally awarded to the PRC and called for a fresh round of bidding after criticism from opposition parties and the public over the lack of transparency in the original bidding process. In Southeast Asia, the deal between China and Myanmar to build a 1,215 km HSR line between Kunming and the Bay of Bengal lapsed in 2014. Popular opposition, financial feasibility, distribution of gains, and national security were among the challenges that at least temporarily derailed the project.[36]

One senior researcher in China's Central Committee apparatus summed up the problems China was experiencing in its overall BRI drive:

We have problems. Among those problems are

- Fiscal work, constraints [paying for all this];
- Political risk [in the countries we work];
- How to deal with the inevitable frictions with so many countries we are in. How can we make things more predictable?
- How do we guarantee the safety and security of workers?

It is hard to secure workers. We are bringing GE [General Electric] into Pakistan and in the Silk Road Fund. "We have even thought of buying American security services from firms like Blackwater."[37]

Project implementation at home in China is not simple, but in relative terms, implementing abroad is a much harder game. These intrinsic challenges multiply when seven other nations have to cooperate, at least to the extent that the final rail system needs to have interoperability. As negotiations take place, China becomes hostage to the internal politics of host countries (see chapters 4 and 5). Some undertakings fail, others succeed, and all are a challenge. A subset of these will have transformative impact. Nonetheless, as one senior Thai official put it, "It is hard [to sustain direction] in an electoral system."[38] How does a predecessor regime bind its successor to its dreams, aspirations, commitments, and projects? In the following section, we address the key implementation challenges China faces abroad in several specific projects.

OBSTACLES TO PROJECT IMPLEMENTATION IN SOUTHEAST ASIA

Indonesia

The Jakarta-Bandung HSR deal was inked with the Chinese in October 2015. The preceding month, Jakarta had unexpectedly rejected Tokyo's bid to build the line, a decision that one well-placed foreign diplomat in Indonesia said involved sizable corruption.[39] The 142 km HSR connecting Jakarta and Bandung would reduce travel time from a three-hour drive to a forty-minute train ride. The joint agreement was signed between the government of Indonesia and PT Kereta Cepat Indonesia-China (KCIC), a joint venture formed between a consortium of four Indonesian state-owned companies, and China Railway Group (CRG), which is a subsidiary of China Railway Engineering Corporation, to build the high-speed railroad. The four Indonesian SOEs own 60 percent of the joint venture, with the remaining 40 percent owned by the CRG. In October 2015 as well, President Joko Widodo (Jokowi) signed Presidential Regulation no. 107/2015, stipulating that the project was a high priority. The HSR is a build-operate-transfer (BOT) greenfield project. The agreement between the Indonesian government and KCIC is a business-to-business arrangement that the Indonesian government prefers rather than a government-to-government deal that would have come with sovereign debt guarantees extended by Jakarta. In March 2016, the Indonesian government granted a fixed-concession period of fifty years to KCIC to operate the project starting from May 31, 2019. In July 2016, the minister of transportation approved the construction permit for the project.

Nonetheless, one year after the groundbreaking ceremony in January 2016, construction of the $5.5 billion HSR had not yet begun. The cost of the project has now ballooned to $6.1 billion. This delay alone would probably defer project completion beyond 2019, with some Indonesian officials and experts estimating that the trains will only start running in the 2021–24 period.[40] Originally, Jokowi had wanted the project completed or well underway as a centerpiece for his anticipated reelection campaign of 2019.

Altogether, four stations and thirteen tunnels are to be built. Some of the tunnels, namely the Walini Tunnel (West Bandung) and No.1 Tunnel (Halim area of East Jakarta), are under construction.[41] However, more than two years later, as of October 2018 not a single meter of track had been laid since the groundbreaking ceremony in January 2016.[42] Under the original schedule, land acquisition was to be finished by April 2018. This was delayed by a year, with 92 percent of the land acquired by March 2019 and expected to be concluded by April 2019.[43] That date, however, was pushed back further, with the last 7.7 percent of land acquisition to be completed "as soon as possible."[44] Decentralization and bureaucratic politics play a critical role in explaining the delays in implementation, particularly at the land acquisition stage (stage 1).

Decentralization

Decentralization of power results in an increase in the number of veto players, or clearance points. These players are often institutions, organizations, and groups providing structural checks and balances in a political system.[45] Public opinion can also be a veto gate, more so in a democratic system than an authoritarian one. Chinese rail companies and other PRC entities operating abroad have pursued projects in emerging democracies where a veritable panoply of actors have precipitated delays. One of the problems with the concept of China "learning" from past setbacks and failures is that as the Chinese move from country to country, veto actors change, and the nature of the rules governing decision making vary dramatically from system to system. In addition, sometimes there are dramatic changes within systems.

The democratization and decentralization process in Indonesia in the late 1990s produced an array of veto actors who have now come to pose significant obstacles to the Jakarta-Bandung HSR project. Suharto's fall from power in May 1998 during the Asian financial crisis dramatically transformed Indonesian politics:

> Old uncertainties have been overturned or contested in almost every sphere: restrictions on political parties have been lifted and democratic elections held, the army has been forced to make a significant withdrawal from political life, cultural expression has flowered . . . One area where change has been very rapid has been in *relations between Jakarta and the regions.*"[46]

Extensive powers suddenly changed hands to regional governments and grassroots civil society. Decentralization was enshrined in two laws of this new era—Laws 22 and 25 of 1999.[47] Under these acts, the central government was required to cede authority to regional governments in all fields except foreign policy, defense and security, monetary policy, the legal system, and religious affairs. The central government in Jakarta remains in charge of national planning and the setting and supervision of technical standards. Local-level parliaments were empowered to elect and dismiss district heads of government (*bupati* and mayors) and determine budgets.[48]

With greater power placed in the hands of the provinces and localities, the number of veto actors in the Indonesian system increased dramatically, thereby strengthening the capacity of lower administrative levels and interest groups to resist national priorities. In 2014, when President Jokowi committed his administration to infrastructure development, this decentralization had notable impact. Infrastructure development projects as a necessity cross domestic administrative boundaries (regencies).[49]

The tussle between the central government and the localities is most significant at the land acquisition and spatial planning phases (stage 1). Although the HSR deal was struck by national-level parties, local regencies did not feel that they had been adequately consulted. One of our team members spoke with a very senior local leader who said he opposed the project but was reluctant to take on President Jokowi.[50] Instead, this individual said that he or she would wait for other bureaucratic actors (e.g., the Ministry of Transportation [MOT]) to lead the opposition to the undertaking.

Regencies are also resistant to the construction when it takes place on their land. Even though Jokowi had revised the national spatial plan in April 2017 to incorporate HSR, revisions to region-level spatial plans were also required. Jakarta's view is that since Presidential Regulation no. 107/2015 stipulates that regional administrations must prioritize the rail project in their respective spatial plans, regions must accordingly adjust their plans to conform to those made at the national level.[51] Predictably, this has not happened. The Bandung Legislative Council in West Java, for example, expressed concern that the project had not been formally recognized in the Bandung regency spatial plan for 2007 to 2027. Local officials in West Java complained that the regency did not receive any documents detailing land clearance even when the MOT had gone ahead to approve land clearance.[52] The Greater Bandung area, which includes Bandung Municipality, Bandung Regency, West Bandung Regency, and Cimahi Municipality, will be affected: 1,224 houses are located in the project's construction zone.[53]

In total, twenty-nine districts and ninety-five villages in West Java will be directly impacted by HSR construction. The 6,800 plots of affected land (including 728 farming households) are owned by 5,580 individuals, SOEs, or private companies.[54] The project would also mean the eviction of residents from more than 2,300 houses and other buildings across nine regions in Jakarta and West Java.[55] Indonesia has strong land tenure laws giving significant rights to landowners. Consequently, negotiations with each affected household and unit must take place in order to acquire the land.

Residents who reside along the HSR route have opposed HSR construction because they are unhappy with the lack of transparency in the eviction process and feel that the offered compensation is inadequate. Residents of two villages in West Bandung, which is along the existing rail right-of-way, were offered IDR 200,000 ($15) to IDR 250,000 ($18) per square meter as compensation, but many felt shortchanged, because they were not informed in advance and were basically forced to accept the offered compensation. Forums and associations, such as the "Indonesia-China High-Speed Train Victim Struggle Forum," have been formed to seek justice.[56] However, KCIC's view is that offering any compensation is acting in good faith, as KCIC owns land right-of-way twelve meters out from the line, according to the 2007 Railway Law.[57]

With democratization, public opinion became more salient in Indonesian politics. Most Indonesians doubt that they will benefit from the HSR project. The belief is that the four Indonesian SOEs in the consortium set up to develop the project will eventually have to bear the cost of the project, since they hold a 60 percent share of the consortium. Questions have also arisen over the project's return on investment (ROI), given what many analysts fear are unrealistic projections of expected passenger numbers. Studies have shown that Indonesia has neither the population density near the rail stations nor the land use regulations necessary to support the development of HSR. In the absence of large urban populations clustered around the city center's rail terminals and extensive public transport systems that allow passengers easily to reach their ultimate destinations via feeder lines, HSR requires massive and unending subsidies.[58]

The large and sudden influx of Chinese laborers into Indonesia further turned public sentiment against HSR. Indonesia has a long history of racial tensions, which peaked during the Cold War when Mao Zedong exported communism to Southeast Asian countries. Indonesian Chinese had lived under a cloud of suspicion as a result of Mao's policies. They are the targets of racial riots during times of turbulence, as exemplified by the anti-Chinese violence in 1998. As Indonesia's economic ties with China increase and there are more Chinese investments in infrastructure projects in Indonesia, the number of Chinese workers has increased—data from Indonesia's manpower ministry showed that the number of Chinese work permit holders had jumped 30 percent in the two years 2015 and 2016 (to 21,271).[59] This has a destabilizing effect on the social fabric of Indonesian society. Fear of a large influx of Chinese laborers as a result of the HSR project must be understood against this background. For instance, rumors about the arrival of "10 million illegal Chinese workers" spread on Indonesian social media accounts.[60] Chinese staff working on the railroad made headlines in April 2016 when they were arrested for entering the Halim Air Force Base without permits.[61] Moreover, when Beijing's "overseas Chinese policy" takes an expansive view of PRC responsibilities for ethnic Chinese (*huaren*) in Southeast Asia and beyond, as has been the case under Xi Jinping, this further exacerbates communal tensions. That all this is a genuine issue is evidenced by Beijing emphasizing how good relations between Chinese and local Indonesian workers are: "Cultural difference is no longer an issue in the project."[62]

Bureaucratic politics

Bureaucratic infighting at the national level has also contributed to delays in construction. The Ministry of State-Owned Enterprises is the key proponent of the project. Its minister, Rini Soemarno, is responsible for advancing HSR, and she originally lobbied for the project to go to China. Jokowi also put Soemarno in charge of leading the implementation of HSR.[63] However, Soemarno faced opposition from the MOT. Minister of Transport Ignasius Jonan was concerned about the feasibility and impact of the project, and the fact that due diligence had not been properly conducted. As a result, he delayed the issuance of the permits for the project. In July 2016, Jonan ostensibly was replaced in order to ease permit issuance.[64]

Soemarno also came into conflict with Public Works and Housing Minister Basuki Hadimuljono on safety concerns. This dispute became public when Basuki warned the ministers involved in the project to pay attention to the route's geological conditions, particularly with respect to bridges and tunnels, since areas being traversed are prone to landslides and earthquakes.[65] Soemarno played down Basuki's warnings, saying that "It has surely been checked technically. They [project developers from China] are experienced in developing high-speed railway. We do not need to doubt."[66]

The Indonesian Air Force is another powerful entity that has expressed concerns about the project. It objected to building Halim Station, one of the designated HSR stops, on land bordering the Halim Perdanakusuma International Airport, which serves both military and civilian purposes. This is because building the station would require the air force to give up its land, the Halim Perdanakusuma Air Base in East Jakarta, a move that would impinge upon Indonesia's defense and security. Indonesian lawmakers supported the air force in resisting giving up its land; one senior lawmaker said, "A military airbase is a vital facility and part of our defense system for Jakarta. It has a jet fighter squadron, military Airbus and the presidential airplane. The base is also part of an integrated defense system . . . so it would be a cause for concern if the land should be given up."[67] The lawmaker also warned that commercial facilities around the railroad station would pose a threat to the military's strategic assets.[68] Despite these criticisms and resistance, however, a portion of the Halim Perdanakusuma Air Base eventually was carved out for the construction of the project in July 2018. The air force agreed to give up the land in exchange for KCIC building more than four hundred residences for the air force.[69]

Opposition aside, the existence of a powerful actor willing to invest resources to champion a policy or project can overcome opposition and bureaucratic infighting to drive implementation forward. Stephen Krasner argues that ultimately it is not the bureaucracies, but the highest-elected official in the form of the president who is accountable for policy outcomes.[70] Indeed, in Indonesia's case, President Jokowi has played a significant role in championing the Jakarta-Bandung HSR project. He has fought back by using the power and tools at his disposal, including presidential decrees. Jokowi appointed Soemarno minister of state-owned enterprises and, in addition, put her in charge of the HSR project. With the president's backing, Soemarno overcame resistance from other ministries and cleared the legal hurdles to begin HSR construction.

In spring 2019, Jokowi was facing reelection. In the final analysis he won, but had his opponent prevailed it was possible that the HSR project might have been stalled, modified, or canceled (as happened in the wake of Malaysia's May 2018 election). President Jokowi's main contender in the 2019 election was former General Prabowo Subianto, leader of the main opposition party, who campaigned on welfare issues and criticized what he argued was overreliance on Chinese investment.[71] Had he won, he likely would have cut back on investment in infrastructure and given more emphasis to human development and social welfare, with possibly adverse consequences for HSR.

Decentralization and bureaucratic infighting have led to significant delays in the Jakarta-Bandung HSR project. KCIC and its subcontractors encountered resistance from regencies, cities, the MOT, and individuals affected by the line. This all adds up to delays in land acquisition (stage 1) and this, in turn, affects loan disbursement (stage 2). Seventy-five percent of the funding for the project is supposed to come from the China Development Bank (CDB) loan granted to KCIC; the remaining 25 percent comes from KCIC shareholders' paid-up capital.[72] CDB initially required the acquisition of all project land before the loan agreement was signed and money transferred. The CDB also requires legal frameworks be in place in order to disburse the loan. One requirement is for the HSR project to be included in the national spatial plan and the rail route to be specified. This became a legal obstacle for land procurement, as local authorities could not act outside the conditions set in the national spatial plan.[73] The CDB has since shown some flexibility by allowing two installments, $170 million and $274.8 million, to be disbursed in April and September 2018, respectively.[74]

Thailand

The case of Thailand's efforts to modernize its existing one-meter-gauge rail system (which is its top priority)[75] and build a parallel north-south 1.435-meter-gauge HSR line (higher-speed system) demonstrates how veto actors can delay project implementation, and how a powerful champion can overcome veto actors.[76] Just to give a sense of both the policy formulation and implementation processes in Thailand, one expert explained: "These negotiations are organized chaos. What we have is compromise. Find a decision that is best at the moment. There are trade-offs. You can't move radically. You must compromise."[77]

Because Thailand has been ruled by a military junta since 2014, it would seem axiomatic that any major infrastructure decision would be carried out in a quick and orderly fashion. However, even with military rule, there are sufficient veto actors within the existing political machine to delay the construction of the HSR project—namely the State

Railway Workers' Union of Thailand, legal safeguards, and civil society. Some aspects of this process are easy in comparison to the Indonesian case: while land acquisition is an enormous problem in Indonesia, "Land access is not a problem for Thailand" [relatively speaking].[78] The State Railway of Thailand (SRT) already owns a very extensive right-of-way all the way from the border with Laos to Bangkok and beyond.

The timeline of the project is as follows: in December 2014, an MOU was signed between the Chinese and Thai governments to build an HSR [or more accurately a 1.435 m standard-gauge medium-speed rail] from Bangkok to Nong Khai in northeastern Thailand, bordering Laos, and Kaeng Khoi to Map Ta Phut in the south. By March 2016, the Thai government announced full investment in the first phase of the HSR project, from Bangkok to Nakhon Ratchasima, which is the first phase of the Bangkok to Nong Khai rail line. In December 2016, an agreement was signed to start building the first phase of the line from Bangkok to Nakhon Ratchasima, to be followed by the second phase, extending the line to Nong Khai on the border with Laos. Under the joint project contract terms, Thailand is the Bangkok-Nong Khai HSR project owner and China is responsible for engineering works and procuring track, systems, and equipment. In the agreement, there are plans for an eventual technology transfer—from China to Thailand—of design and civil works, system management, quality control, monitoring, and maintenance systems.[79] In June 2017, Prime Minister Prayut exercised Article 44 of the constitution to overrule normal laws and regulations to get the delayed project started. Then, in December 2017, the construction of the first 3.5 km stretch of the first phase of the project finally began, with a groundbreaking ceremony in Nakhon Ratchasima. The entire project connecting Bangkok to Nong Khai is tentatively scheduled for completion by 2023.[80] Hence, even though the MOU for the HSR project was signed in December 2014, actual construction of the first section of the first phase of the HSR line (from Bangkok and Nakhon Ratchasima) only commenced in December 2017.

Legal obstacles and bureaucratic resistance

There have been significant legal hurdles to the construction of the Bangkok–Nong Khai HSR. Prime Minister Prayut's invocation of Article 44 overcame legal barriers that had delayed project implementation.[81] Preexisting legal safeguards such as laws on labor protection, procurement standards, land usage, and environmental protection were impediments to the project achieving lift-off.

For example, under Thailand's current labor protection laws, Chinese architects and engineers could not work in Thailand unless they passed an examination to obtain a Thai license.[82] Prayut's executive order did away with this requirement. However, Thai engineers have expressed unhappiness that now no Thai engineers will be a part of the project. One well-informed Thai analyst said, "Thai engineers don't trust Chinese quality."[83] Another issue is that Thailand's procurement laws require careful scrutiny by a procurement committee of projects costing more than THB 5 million before construction starts. Article 44 also did away with this requirement.[84]

The biggest obstacle, however, appears to be that the HSR line will be built on designated farmland that cannot legally be used for any other purpose.[85] In addition, despite the rollback in democracy by the military, environmental NGOs continue to be an important force in Thai politics and society.[86] They are concerned that large infrastructure projects, such as dams and high-speed railroads, would lead to severe ecological and social harm. According to Thai media reports, the six-month delay between Prayut invoking Article 44 in July 2017 and the beginning of construction of the project occurred because of incomplete (required) environmental impact studies.[87]

Resistance from government bodies has also produced delays in project implementation. According to a high-level Thai government source, development of land around train stations has been a key source of contention for the State Railway Workers' Union.[88] The State Railway of Thailand (SRT), which is under the Ministry of Transportation, is composed of three groups: managers of the land, track, and operations. The Railway Union structure mirrors these three functions. The key reason for the Union's resistance to the HSR project is that the SRT makes money by selling land but loses money on rail operations. A high-level source described the SRT as "a real estate firm, it makes money from land sales."[89] Hence, compensation for the loss of land is a key issue in their negotiations with the Chinese. Moreover, historically, the SRT traces its organization back to King Rama V, the great modernizing nineteenth-century Thai king and patron of railroads. As one Thai business leader put it, "The dignity of the State Railways is very strong. . . . They embody nationalism, they are nationalistic. . . . The State Railway people all oppose the HSR—they support the dual track [one-meter gauge]"[90] expansion.

In explaining the negotiation and implementation problems thus far encountered and those expected in the future, one high-level Thai informant painted a panoramic picture:

> From our view, there are technical requirements and legal requirements. How can Chinese engineers be licensed in Thailand? How can we reclaim areas for construction [development of stations, though the Thai Rail Authority has a lot of land for rights-of-way]? How to get environmental impact studies? How to get waivers? We are experiencing a third overall slowdown in negotiations on the Korat Line—interest rates. Development around stations. There are negotiations among ministries; the public is less involved. However, a problem is that we have to negotiate with the Thai Railway Union—there are demonstrations, they block proposals, fear reforms. The Thai Rail Authority [SRT] is divided into three groups: Managers of the land, track, and operations of the system. There is only one union, but three parts of the union. They make money on the land, NOT trains [operations]. Therefore, they negotiate with the Chinese on how to get compensated for the land. So the unions and the Thai Rail Authority [SRT] all negotiate with the Chinese. The Thai Rail Authority is like McDonald's—it is a real estate firm, it makes money from land sales.[91]

Looking ahead, even when the HSR line reaches Bangkok from the Lao border in the north, then the saga of building the next line south of the capital to the border with Malaysia will open up a completely new set of challenges, especially given the political instability fueled by separatist groups in southern Thailand.

Role of champions

However, that the project has been able to move ahead in spite of these obstacles is also due to the fact that it has champions in the Thai bureaucracy. Apart from Prime Minister Prayut (like Indonesian President Jokowi) making infrastructure development a key priority and source of legitimacy for the Thai military government (see chapter 4), the backing of the Ministry of Transport (MOT) of Thailand is another important reason why the project has advanced. The MOT, the ministry in charge of implementing the HSR project, works closely with the Chinese to discuss the bidding process and design issues.[92] Transport Minister Arkhom Termpittayapaisith cochairs the Joint Committee on Railway Cooperation between Thailand and China, with Ning Jizhe, deputy head of China's National Development and Reform Commission (NDRC).[93] The MOT has five main strategies for the next twenty years, one of which is to rely less on roads and depend more on railroads and

inland water transport.[94] A high-level Thai government source said—
"We will connect to every [neighboring] country."[95] His words echo
those of Prayut, who said during a ceremony launching construction of
the first 3.5 km of the HSR project that "Thailand is developing in every
aspect to become the center of connectivity . . . and this route is to connect to Cambodia, Laos, Myanmar, and Vietnam to China, India, and
further to other countries."[96] Looking at a map (such as the one in chapter 1), Bangkok is perfectly located to play this role, being located strategically for rail lines running on both north-south and east-west axes.

Malaysia

Malaysia's East Coast Rail Link and the proposed Kuala Lumpur–Singapore HSR are two projects that illustrate well how domestic political
events and changes in government can throw monkey wrenches into
China's plans to construct railroads abroad.

East Coast Rail Link (ECRL)

When Prime Minister Najib Razak unexpectedly lost power in the May
2018 general elections, the ECRL lost a powerful patron. The economic
wisdom of a rail line along the relatively underdeveloped eastern coast-
line of Peninsular Malaysia had been debated fiercely long before the
project even began.[97] Nonetheless, China was awarded the contract in
late 2016,[98] construction commenced on August 9, 2017, and completion was estimated sometime in 2024, until the 2018 elections indefi-
nitely halted the project. Undertaken by China Communications Construction Company (CCCC), from the beginning the project was riddled
with corruption scandals involving the Najib regime. For example, the
media reported that Chinese leaders offered to help derail investigations
into 1MDB in return for approval of Chinese infrastructure projects in
Malaysia.[99] In May 2018, when the Pakatan Harapan [a political coalition, "Alliance of Hope"] unexpectedly won the Malaysian general
election, new Prime Minister Mahathir Mohamad (who also had served
as prime minister from 1981 to 2003) called for a review of all big government infrastructure projects in order to reduce Malaysia's high level
of national debt. He accused his predecessor of borrowing too much
and of padding the cost of projects. The Mahathir government's esti-
mate was that the ECRL project would cost $20 billion after taking into
account land acquisition, interest, fees, and other operational costs,

nearly 50 percent higher than estimates of the Najib regime.[100] One local leader commented: "Is it really mutually beneficial? ECRL is totally financed [by China], they have inflated costs, sell all the equipment. This is dependence. 'Bad project.' Very high price. Mahathir commented the project has a very strange financing arrangement."[101]

The incoming administration also questioned the contract and method of payment for the ECRL. According to Mahathir, "That contract [referring to the ECRL contract] is strange. The contractor must be from China and the lending is from China. And the money is not supposed to come here but [be kept abroad] to pay the contractor in China."[102] On July 4, 2018, the Pakatan Harapan (Mahathir) government instructed the CCCC to halt work on the ECRL. At the point of suspension, about 15 percent of the project had been completed, and nearly 20 percent of the loan from Exim Bank had been disbursed to the Chinese contractor in China.[103] During Mahathir's postelection visit to China in August 2018, he expressed the hope that Beijing would understand Kuala Lumpur's fiscal problems, saying, "I believe China itself does not want to see Malaysia become a bankrupt country."[104] He listed the Kuala Lumpur–Singapore HSR and the ECRL as the main projects that were "funded extensively through debt."[105]

By August 21, 2018, Prime Minister Mahathir announced the cancelation of the ECRL and two other Chinese-invested projects "until Malaysia could afford them."[106] Perhaps Mahathir was inviting Beijing to give Kuala Lumpur far better terms than the original agreement, or risk a complete loss. One week later, on August 28, 2018, he said that some companies offered to build the ECRL for as little as MYR 10 billion. The prime minister went on to say that his government was still studying whether the canceled projects could be postponed or made cheaper, even though they have been canceled "in principle."[107] In another setting, Mahathir said, "The ROI is nothing. It will take forty, fifty years for us to repay the loan."[108] He seemed to be executing a strategy of creating maximum anxiety in Beijing, presumably to wring further concessions from the Chinese government and companies.

A senior official in another Southeast Asian country's Chamber of Commerce looked at this unfolding situation and speculated: "China will not let Malaysia fall. Malaysia is important to China, so China must agree to accept Mahathir's conditions."[109] As for the bottom line position of the Mahathir Government, a senior foreign policy system person in Kuala Lumpur explained, "We want to review, renegotiate, not to scrap those projects."[110] And remember, as described in chapter 2,

Mahathir has a personal commitment to railroad development extending back to his boyhood. Predictably, after renegotiation in the first part of 2019, Beijing and Kuala Lumpur agreed to about a one-third price reduction, shortening the line by 40 km (to avoid having to dig an 18 km tunnel), with the new route going through an additional state to bring Malaysians more benefit and coverage.[111] In political terms, by renegotiating Beijing enlarged the size of the pro-project coalition in Malaysia. Mahathir had China over a barrel, with the project underway with huge sunk costs. This demonstrates that smaller states have leverage with bigger ones and that the implementation and negotiating stages are neither conceptually nor practically separate.

Kuala Lumpur–Singapore (KL-SIN) HSR

Another project that came under review immediately after the 2018 election was the Kuala Lumpur–Singapore HSR. Then Prime Minister Najib and Singapore Prime Minister Lee Hsien Loong signed an MOU in July 2016 and the joint tender process began in December 2017. However, shortly thereafter Mahathir came to power and immediately seemed inclined to scuttle the project. Following negotiations between Malaysia and Singapore in September 2018, the two countries announced that the entire matter of the KL-SIN HSR would be deferred for two years, until May 31, 2020. A joint statement released by the two countries said that the HSR line was now anticipated to commence operation by January 1, 2031, four years later than the original estimated start date of December 31, 2026. Obviously, uncertainties remain as to whether the project will be operational in January 2031 or will even be pursued. Under the new agreement between Malaysia and Singapore, if the project fails to resume by May 31, 2020, Kuala Lumpur will be in breach of the agreement, with Malaysia having to bear the costs incurred by Singapore in fulfilling its part of the HSR Bilateral Agreement.[112]

There is one additional aspect of the Malaysia-Singapore HSR that calls for comment. Broadly speaking, on the overall government level (as distinct from the views of various bureaus), Singapore is broadly favorable to the project, hoping it will stimulate growth once the project is functioning. Nonetheless, Singapore is in the odd position of being the southern terminus of the "Central Line" but having only about 4 percent of the track mileage of the entire route to Kuala Lumpur within its boundaries. Consequently, arriving at an agreed-upon Singapore cost-sharing formula with Malaysia was not easy. Moreover, security conscious as Singapore is, there are those concerned with national and internal security who are anxious about what a more porous border to the north might mean for the city-state, given that the proposed tracks north of Kuala Lumpur run through parts of separatist locales in southern Thailand. In fact, the political instability and terrorist threat in southern Thailand will become a major issue when attention turns to building rail infrastructure south of Bangkok. Finally, Singapore wants to keep its tendering process separate from Malaysia's process in order to keep the tenders "clean."[113]

The KL-SIN HSR forms the southern anchor of the Pan-Asia Railway; the northern anchor is Kunming. As with the US Transcontinental Railroad, the idea was to build it from the two ends—Singapore and Kunming. Delays in the implementation of the KL-Singapore project would delay full realization of the Pan-Asia Railway vision. This fact further multiplies Mahathir's leverage on Beijing as he seeks renegotiation of these projects. The other stretch of the Central Line that remains to be negotiated consists of the Thai-Malaysia border areas.

Laos

Of the many HSR and conventional rail projects discussed in this chapter, construction of the 414 km Boten-Vientiane line in Laos has proceeded the fastest, a seemingly odd development given Laos's low system capacity (mentioned earlier in this chapter and in chapters 4 and 5). Construction began in late December 2016, involving six Chinese contractors, subsidiaries of the state-owned China Railway Group (CRG), each of which is responsible for one section of track, and scheduled for completion by December 2021. This project is a key component of the BRI, touted by the PRC as a showcase of the enhanced cooperation between China and Southeast Asian countries.[114] By March 2019, almost half of the 414 km of track had been laid.[115] This line, running at 160–200 kmph (for passenger trains, and at 120 kmph for freight) can more accurately be described as medium-speed rather than high-speed rail. The expected number of rail passengers is projected at 3.98 million per year and could reach 8.62 million passengers per year in the future.[116] Once the train is up and running, the expectation is that more of Laos's agricultural products, such as organic rice, coffee, and bananas, can be exported to increasingly distant locations given the reduction of travel time.[117] Laos also expects the train line to make its cultural sites in Luang Prabang, Champasak Province, and the Plain of Jars more accessible to Thai and Chinese tourists, essentially creating a new tourist industry.[118]

Terrain and Geography

The processes of land acquisition and clearance were more rapidly accomplished in Laos than in Indonesia—as of late 2018, 94 percent of the land required for the railroad had been acquired.[119] Nevertheless, there have been delays in construction. Some problems are specific to Laos, such as especially difficult, hilly terrain and the enormous volume of unexploded ordnance remaining from the decades of Indochina wars. For instance, a Chinese construction company suspended construction temporarily to clear unexploded ordnance in a village in Luang Namtha Province.[120] One Chinese rail engineer working on the project said, "We should have the US demine the area."[121] Construction companies also have had to deal with extremely difficult terrain, since most of the rail line cuts through dense jungles and mountains, which means that supporting roads and electrical supplies must be constructed from the ground up. Our research team, for example, had to travel a few miles off the main road to simply get to the site of the railroad's construction. We traveled on an entirely new concrete road that cut through the jungle and was built to bear the weight of the heavy railroad construction machinery needed. Another issue is that the soil in some of regions provides poor footing for tracks and bridges—the red mud gums up everything. The transportation of building materials is also slow given the lack of existing roads and the terrain. Newly installed concrete plants dot the railroad's surveyed route, and entire sets of blue-and-white dormitory facilities for construction labor huddle in the hot, humid, often mud-encrusted jungle. When not working on the rail line, great numbers of young male workers on their motorcycles flock into the nearest inhabited places, seeking pleasure and diversion.

Financial Capacity

Beyond natural and geographical features, the lack of capacity of the Lao state is a large obstacle to the smooth completion of the HSR project. One significant delay has involved the need to compensate villagers and provide for relocation packages, not easy given the poor financial condition of the country. While construction on state land has begun, workers cannot clear land where people remain; these residents have not left since they have yet to receive compensation from the government.[122] There have been disagreements over compensation levels between the Lao government and the affected villagers. Initially, the government took into account only the cost of very basic building structures when determining how much to compensate the residents, but villagers felt that was inadequate. Eventually, the government undertook studies to evaluate the compensation levels.[123] The final decision was to compensate evicted villagers for the loss of all property, including land, buildings, fences, crops, and trees.[124] This entire process creates delay and drives up costs. As one Lao official put it to our research team, "This will be [is] a painful process."[125]

According to some media reports, there was discontent from the outset of the project in October 2016, when affected villagers were prevented from speaking out at public meetings held to promote the project.[126] Complaints have been vented at various local community meetings.[127] More than four thousand families, approximately four thousand hectares of farmland, and three thousand three hundred buildings will be affected by this rail project. When our team visited Laos in July 2017 and spoke to residents of a village around Oudomxay, which is near Boten, villagers explained how they had been informed that they would need to leave their land, but they remained in the dark about where they would go, and how and when they would be compensated. In January 2018, the Lao government revealed that a compensation law had been drafted for compulsory evictions related to infrastructure projects.[128] That the law was drafted a year after construction had already commenced suggests that the Lao state had not expected the widespread discontent from those forced to relocate and compensation was a last-minute initiative to appease those facing eviction. It is worth noting that compensation and land acquisition disputes, even in the Mao period, have slowed infrastructure projects, sometimes for a decade, even in that comparatively authoritarian setting.[129]

Reportedly, the Provincial People's Councils in Luang Namtha, Oudomxay, Luang Prabang, and Vientiane had approved the compensation rates but still needed approval by their respective local governments.[130] The total compensation package was estimated to cost more than 2,492 billion kip ($297.73 million).[131] At a time when the government is already fiscally strapped, adding more debt will further impede its capacity to solve its financial problems, and if compensation and acquisition of farmlands is a protracted process, delays will occur.[132] One senior legislator in Vientiane put it as follows:

> We cannot meet our plan when there is a financial issue. Government has been issuing instructions how to economize, to tighten our belt, not spend extra budget, to ensure everything is under control, and to fulfill regulations. Before this there were overspends. We have to understand why there was overspending, because if each province wants to develop, each allocation is limited, based on budget, overspend, then deficit, then big problem. Government wants to control each project, needs to decide either to cancel or postpone. Everything needs to go according to plan. For that reason, our role is not only to listen, but also to oversee what they said and what they do.[133]

As of late 2018, the first tranche of compensation was given out to residents in Vientiane, Luang Namtha, and Oudomxay Provinces.[134]

The Lao government's weak financial standing has also produced delays in the disbursement of funds for construction. In chapter 5, Laos's huge debt to GDP ratio in financing HSR—the approximately $7 billion cost of the HSR line constitutes more than half of Laos's 2015 GDP—was discussed. Vientiane finds it hard to come up with sufficient funds for its financial contribution to the project. In March 2018, the *Vientiane Times* reported that the deputy minister of public works and transport, who is also chairman of the Laos-China Railway Construction Project Management Committee, Lattanamany Khounnivong, urgently requested approval of a budget of LAK 510 billion ($60 million) for Laos's 2018 contribution to the project.[135]

To compound the issue of insufficient funds, Chinese banks have also begun to exercise greater prudence in the disbursement of loans. In 2014, the China Exim Bank announced that it would curb its loans to Laos for most infrastructure projects, which is a sign of its concern about the country's future ability to repay its debts.[136] The lack of funding has forced some Chinese developers to postpone the planned construction of hydropower dams on some of the tributaries of the Mekong River,[137] though our team visited one that that was under construction in the area near Luang Prabang. In the past, Laos has used its natural resources to repay debts. For instance, when the Lao government could not repay an $80 million loan to China for building a stadium for the 2009 Southeast Asian Games, Vientiane paid the contracted Chinese company with a three hundred hectare land concession.[138] As for the terms of repaying the loan for HSR construction to Exim Bank, it is widely believed that the loan was collateralized by the railroad's future income and two mining concessions.[139] There may well be other deals on the side (such as using plantation lands as collateral) about which outside observers are not fully aware.[140] A senior Lao official told our research team that

> A Special Purpose Vehicle [SPV] in the form of a joint venture will be created. China will have a 70 percent share while Laos takes the remaining 30 percent. For the Laos share, Lao will have to borrow from China US$500 million. The rest will be paid through land concessions, etc., which is part of Laos's investment costs. The SPV company gets development rights.[141]

Once financing depends on commodities as a repayment stream, this immediately raises the thorny issue of what prices can be attached to those commodities at a future date, and in which international currency will this be calculated and repaid? This is another huge source of controversy and lack of transparency surrounding the project.

Human capital and technical capacity

Lack of human capital and construction materials are capacity issues posing genuine challenges as well. Lao workers need training. Low levels of education and lack of engineering expertise and knowledge of railroad technology mean that the Chinese side needs time to train local workers, otherwise laborers need to be brought in from elsewhere (including China). While Chinese companies are responsible for 90 percent of the total construction work, the remaining 10 percent is supposed to be done by Lao labor in order to generate local employment.[142] In order for even this to happen, support needs to be in place for training and mentoring. A center in Yunnan Province trains Lao workers in railroad management.[143] Chinese technicians will also accompany and mentor Lao workers to enable them to operate the railroad once it is completed.[144]

In both Laos and Thailand, the dearth of high-quality construction materials has also caused delays. In Laos, cement supplies could not keep up with construction speed and quality demands, and eventually the parties agreed that Chinese companies would supply cement by setting up cement factories in Laos.[145] In the case of Thailand, there was initial disagreement over cement and metals because the locally manufactured materials did not meet Chinese quality standards.[146] However, this was resolved when the Thais changed their products' composition to conform to Chinese standards. Thailand's capacities to modify inputs are greater than Laos's. Overall, Thailand is managing to keep much more control over the process due to its greater civil, technical, and governance capacities than is the case in Laos, but it also means that things will move more slowly than would otherwise be the case.

In the long run, for the line through Lao PDR to make economic sense, it will have to smoothly connect with the Thai HSR, because having a line that runs only from southern China to Laos will never generate sufficient revenue. However, this could prove to be a challenge. Just one example of how complex this process can be is the planned extension of the rail line between Laos and Thailand at Thanaleng Station— very near Vientiane and the crossing point of the Mekong River into Thailand. This project was slated to begin in late 2010 but was scrapped by the Lao authorities, because they wanted to study in detail how the currently existing one-meter-gauge Laos-Thailand track could be joined to the 1.435 m standard-gauge track width of the planned Laos-China HSR Railway.[147] The extension at the Mekong only resumed in 2017, a delay of six years, after it was decided that one of the stations planned for Vientiane as part of the Laos-China line would be built in Thanaleng village so that the two lines can be integrated and in close proximity.[148]

Once the hardware of the HSR system is built, there remains the issue of system "software": customs, immigration, and other operational and regulatory issues. The World Bank finds that regulatory measures to reduce border-crossing times can dramatically increase income gains from infrastructure projects.[149] Beijing has faced issues in this regard dealing with its own Hong Kong SAR, where locals resent China's extension of its police powers to the station in Hong Kong's city center, seeing it as an infringement on local autonomy. As one Lao senior official summed up: "It is easy to produce all these beautiful plans on paper, but having to implement them is the hard part."[150]

CHINESE "IMPLEMENTATION STYLE" MEETS
LOCAL POLITICS

In this chapter, the "complexity of joint action" is seen at every turn, at every stage. Smoothly achieving policy implementation is hard enough within a single system, as China's own experience makes clear. However, implementation challenges are geometrically compounded when eight distinct sovereignties require some degree of coordination for one common purpose. Even if each country considers each project as just one more "bilateral" undertaking (China and a partner country alone),[151] smooth policy implementation across even two differing cultural and political systems, at different levels of socioeconomic development, with distinct interests, makes policy implementation extremely challenging. As one Chinese lending institution official put it, "In some areas [the problems] are not entirely financial problems but also governance problems."[152] Considering this, it is impressive that progress has been as rapid as it has.

Although China is "learning" in all its encounters abroad, the fact is that the implementation environment outside of the PRC is new in each setting. The veto players ("clearance points") vary by system. State capacity varies among systems—the obstacle course changes in each country, and relative capacities differ across national systems. In short, every undertaking in which the PRC is involved is essentially a *sui generis* exercise.

The decentralization of power and institutionalization in emerging democracies, the role of bureaucracies and public opinion, and checks and balances in the form of laws and regulations increase the number of veto actors in the implementation stage, as we have clearly seen in the Indonesian and Thai cases. This, in turn, leads to delays and modifications of plans. The Jakarta-Bandung HSR, the Bangkok–Nong Khai HSR, the ECRL in Malaysia, and the Kuala Lumpur–Singapore HSR all illustrate the various roles that domestic actors can play in stalling or aborting plans entirely. One senior local leader in Malaysia with whom our team spoke made it clear that local residents were concerned about local effects: "I want to assure employment, that local people get employed. I read that in Africa, equipment, workers, and everything is from China, and this breeds resentment."[153] In the case of the Boten-Vientiane HSR, the weak capacity of the Lao state is a considerable challenge, even in an authoritarian political setting.

The Chinese "implementation style" when it comes to dealing with the inevitable frictions that arise in the course of building infrastructure, especially across cultures, is one recurring issue across many Southeast Asian systems. As one Thai expert put it, "China, however, does things differently. In construction, it will use its own labor. It does not follow rules."[154] There is an attitude among more than a few Chinese who interface with their neighbors that is reminiscent of other countries' colonial attitudes. One PRC researcher expressed this, saying, "I also mean the culture of the people. In Southeast Asia, people are not efficiency-minded. 'Chinese pursue efficiency—time is money. Southeast Asians want to enjoy life. . . .'"[155] This Chinese worldview can be off-putting in other societies, or as one Thai businessperson put it, "Anything about China we fear."[156] Even in Cambodia, which is probably the closest Southeast Asian country to China in political and diplomatic terms, one Cambodian informant revealed, "The perception of the Cambodian public is in fact quite negative. The reason is that the PRC Embassy here has not gotten out of its comfort zone and does not engage the public by clarifying media reports, for instance—radio silence from the Chinese. The Embassy here is just completely silent on negative media reports about the Chinese presence here."[157]

This chapter and separate work by Daniel Russell and his colleagues at the Asia Society,[158] have highlighted China's implementation problems in the course of building HSR and other BRI projects (see chapter 8 for more extensive coverage of the topic). Among these are inadequate transparency in project design and procurement; failure to undertake adequate financial and political risk analysis; a lack of rigorous environmental and human impact analysis; insufficient local resourcing, both human and material; and considerable corruption associated with many of these projects. Ultimately, project implementation of early projects will affect the climate of negotiation for later projects, not only in Southeast Asia but globally as well.[159]

Having said this, however, the comprehensive vision of a Pan-Asia Railway described in chapters 2, 3, and 7 has only entered the early stages of implementation. To date it has been a disjointed, incremental, and uncertain process. In the future, observers will see the kinds of phenomena documented in this chapter unfold in many permutations as the new rail system gradually emerges. Beijing is trying to learn from its implementation challenges, with this inclination clearly on display at the April 2019 Second Belt and Road Forum in Beijing, where Chinese officials at the conclave acknowledged many of the problems and promised adjustments would be made. Whether these lessons will shape future PRC practice on the ground and in future negotiations remains to be seen.

Nonetheless, decades from now individual projects, including those described here, probably will aggregate into a regionwide system of some kind. This will take time, almost certainly two decades or so. Such a system will likely transform Asia, and its progress and impact should not be underestimated. Still, it is, and will remain, a messy process. The precise form this broad vision will ultimately assume, much less when it will arrive at its imprecise destination, is not easily predicted today. All this notwithstanding, this network of high-speed and conventional-speed rail projects is likely to be revolutionary. It will connect both China and Southeast Asia, and Southeast Asians themselves, in new and unexpected ways.

CHAPTER 7

Geopolitics and Geoeconomics

I see this epic story of regional connectivity as overlapping circles. The first circle contains individual countries' own domestic plans. The second circle involves projects being implemented under various subregional cooperative frameworks such as the GMS (Greater Mekong Subregion), which is coordinated by the ADB (Asian Development Bank) and partly funded with Japanese loans. The third circle is ASEAN's work on the issue under its own Master Plan, adopted in 2010 at the ASEAN Summit in Hanoi. All these circles are connected to the fourth circle of China's One Belt—One Road (OBOR), now the Belt and Road Initiative (BRI).

—Former Thai diplomat, July 2016[1]

Remember, in the 1980s and the 1990s, China built ports in its own underdeveloped coastal cities. Look at them today! You must look at thirty years from now, not today.

—Chinese diplomat, April 2019[2]

This chapter delves into the geopolitical and geoeconomic factors shaping rail connectivity development in Southeast Asia.[3] In the 1990s and 2000s, geoeconomics drove developments, but now, at the end of the second decade of the new millennium, geopolitics and security concerns have become increasingly salient considerations for Southeast Asia and surrounding powers, including the United States and Japan.

In chapter 3, we addressed the strategic considerations undergirding Beijing's pursuit of connectivity with Southeast Asia and some of the debates to which these ideas give rise in the PRC. The drive for rail and other forms of connectivity manifests Beijing's desire to change the regional economic geography to sustain PRC growth, the leadership's commitment to achieve big power aspirations, and the PRC's belief in industrial policy as an essential tool in global economic competition. One of the most central strategic debates occurring in Beijing concerns the definition and operationalization of China's interests, with maritime interests facing off against the "continentalists." These Chinese objectives, commitments, and debates have ignited both anxiety and a sense of opportunity among Southeast Asian nations, powers in Asia and Europe, not to mention the United States.

Southeast Asian countries also have their own strategic concerns with respect to each other and with respect to *other powers*. Moreover, *other powers*, including the United States, have their own singular considerations with respect to both the security and economic issues implicit in China's growing connectivity with its periphery. These outsider considerations provide *options, opportunities,* and *obstacles* to both China and the Southeast Asian countries as they negotiate increasing connectivity. Beyond the PRC, there is an entire universe of strategically important interactions between Southeast Asian nations and *other powers*. These are the animating concerns of this chapter.

Japan, and to a lesser degree the Republic of Korea (ROK, or South Korea), India, Canada, European countries, and others perceive themselves to have important stakes in the Pan-Asia Railway vision and other similar-scale undertakings. The concerns, capabilities, and behaviors of these powers are important features of the overall political, economic, and strategic landscape. These other powers have history and also contemporary interactions with Southeast Asia that bear on today's regional rail development. Their roles range from having been pioneer railroad developers (France, Britain, and Japan) during the region's colonial period (chapter 2) to being competitors with China for contracts today, and from being potential partners in China's high-speed and conventional rail projects regionally and globally, to providing a strategic alternative for Southeast Asian nations in their respective attempts to balance PRC power.

A core question is, therefore, why, and to what extent, do individual Southeast Asian states view other powers and players as *credible alternatives or supplements to Beijing* in their own railroad construction? How do other powers view unfolding developments, how are they seeking to become involved, and how do Southeast Asian states engage with them? How does China react to the competition they may represent?

This chapter proceeds in three parts. The first traces how geoeconomic and domestic imperatives drove Southeast Asian countries' own railroad developments in the pre-BRI (Belt and Road Initiative) period, with an initial focus on their own regionwide railroad network—the Singapore-Kunming Rail Link (SKRL) project discussed in chapter 4. This was a period when geoeconomics overrode geopolitics in driving rail infrastructure planning and construction. This section also traces the roles played by multinational actors, including the Association of Southeast Asian Nations (ASEAN), the Asian Development Bank (ADB), and the United Nations Economic and Social Committee for Asia and the Pacific (ESCAP), in Southeast Asian railroad development throughout the post–Cold War era.

The second and third parts focus on developments after 2013, when geopolitics (power balancing) became a mounting consideration in infrastructure connectivity cooperation in Southeast Asia. Specifically, this chapter illuminates how a desire to limit China's regional influence and offset BRI has driven Japan and other powers to pursue their own versions of railroad statecraft. Most notably, under Prime Minister Shinzo Abe, Tokyo has actively promoted the Partnership for Quality Infrastructure (PQI) since May 2015 as an alternative to BRI, by exploring transparent connectivity projects in Southeast Asia and beyond. Tokyo has sought to project Japan as a trustworthy development player in Asia, while encouraging and working with fellow Quadrilateral Security Dialogue (Quad) members (India, the United States, and Australia) and other like-minded nations (e.g., the EU) to put forward various forms of connectivity schemes as alternatives, or supplements, to Beijing's initiatives.

Geopolitical imperative—the competition among powerful players vying for regional influence—has become an increasingly weighty consideration alongside the geoeconomic rationale of optimizing cross-border production chains, resources, and markets through integration. As security considerations have gained prominence, Southeast Asia and other powers increasingly interact to achieve comprehensive regional strategic balance, as well as economic objectives. This trend has given rise to growing prospects for Southeast Asian rail and other infrastructure cooperation with China, on the one hand, and with Japan and more distant powers on the other hand. This creates more space—and leverage—for the smaller regional states to explore, negotiate, and advance their respective HSR and conventional rail partnerships.

This chapter's concluding section illuminates *how* and *why* the intersecting geopolitical and geoeconomic dynamics have given rise to some degree of power-balancing behavior in several weaker states' rail infra-structure partnerships. The argument is that while economic and geoeconomic rationales are necessary conditions to unleash the quest for connectivity, they alone do not determine the specific shape of the connectivity that eventually emerges. The form of connectivity that emerges from the negotiating and implementing activities described in the two preceding chapters also reflects the geostrategic calculations and fears of Southeast Asian states and other powers. What emerges on the ground represents a dynamic equilibrium between economic hopes and strategic fears, filtered through the eyes of Southeast Asian states, surrounding middle powers, and more distant big powers.

GEOECONOMICS REIGNS (1996–2013)
The SKRL Project

This section examines Southeast Asia's rail development before the BRI by focusing on the Singapore-Kunming Rail Link (SKRL) project—the multination, regional rail network that forms part of what we have referred to loosely as today's Pan-Asia Railway undertaking. SKRL was conceived in the 1990s, a period when geoeconomics was the ascendant consideration rather than security and geopolitics—it was the kinder and gentler era of the immediate post-Cold War era, the "peace divi-dend," and Beijing had a low-profile foreign policy and preoccupation with domestic concerns. In this context, several questions arise: What is the significance of the SKRL project? What were the origins of the SKRL idea in 1995 and how was it institutionalized? Finally, this section takes stock of the scope, scale, and speed of the ensuing SKRL-related rail construction in selected Southeast Asian countries, while identifying unfinished business, remaining gaps, and ongoing challenges.

Those gaps and challenges are important, because *they are the very reasons* why the SKRL project has remained a work in progress after nearly a quarter century, and why Southeast Asian countries still require external assistance and support in pursuing their railroad visions. The ongoing gaps provide the space for China's BRI push, Japan's "Shinkansen diplomacy," and the competition for contracts among other actors. Basi-cally, under the signboard of BRI, China is seeking to complete and expand the SKRL vision and become the principal outside commercial and strategic power bringing an updated version of the original vision to fruition. Other powers are competing as best they can.

Significance of SKRL. The Singapore-Kunming Rail Link (SKRL) project is *not* about building a new, single railroad linking southern China and Singapore, as many have mistakenly assumed. Rather, the project is about *connecting* all currently existing railroads in the region by building physical links within and between seven ASEAN member countries and China.[4] Specifically, it aims at upgrading existing sections of rail line by double-tracking and electrifying railroads (including rehabilitating national rail tracks), constructing missing links, and building *spur lines* in and across the related ASEAN countries, namely Cambodia, Laos, Malaysia, Myanmar, Singapore, Thailand, and Vietnam.[5]

The SKRL is significant in three ways: First, it was the first regionwide rail network plan developed and institutionalized by the countries themselves in postcolonial Asia—although, as noted in chapter 2, the colonial powers each had their own visions during their eras of control, the imprints of which are still visible. The 1995 SKRL proposal sought to promote regional cooperation on rail connectivity in Southeast Asia well before the word *connectivity* entered the lexicon of Asian international relations. In terms of institutionalization, the special working group (SWG-SKRL) as an international cooperative mechanism came into being in June 1996, a milestone in Asian rail cooperation. The SWG-SKRL emerged when ministers from the respective countries gathered in Kuala Lumpur for the inaugural meeting of the ASEAN-Mekong Basin Development Cooperation (AMBDC) organization.[6] Six months after the formation of the SWG-SKRL, the host, Malaysia, pledged MYR 2 million for the feasibility study of the proposed Asia rail link to connect Kunming with Singapore. The second SWG-SKRL meeting took place in September 1997, again in Malaysia's capital.[7] The feasibility study began in March 1997 and concluded in August 1999, as the region was struggling to recover from the Asian financial crisis (1997–98). The SWG-SKRL resumed activities only after 2002, when financial conditions had stabilized. The other member countries—Cambodia, Laos, Myanmar, Singapore, Thailand, Vietnam, and China—have since been taking turns hosting annual meetings. Malaysia, which hosted the SKRL Regional Secretariat from 2004 to 2006, was appointed permanent chair of the rail cooperative mechanism at the Ninth SWG-SKRL in Singapore in 2007.[8] Indonesia participated and hosted the SWG-SKRL meeting in 2015.

Second, SKRL in retrospect is significant because by inviting China as a member of the SWG alongside the seven ASEAN countries, it has allowed the PRC to take part directly in *regionwide rail connectivity cooperation* from the start. Beijing's direct involvement during this earliest phase, from 1996 to the first decade of the 2000s, planted the seeds for its growing role thereafter, when the PRC's mounting capabilities and its own domestic demand for deepening regional integration energized its HSR diplomacy.

Third, the SKRL project—the flagship project under the AMBDC framework and the Master Plan of ASEAN Connectivity—also provides unique avenues for ASEAN countries to engage and cooperate with other partners, including the northeastern Asian economic powerhouses (Japan and South Korea) and international multilateral organizations.[9] ADB also attends the SWG-SKRL meetings as an observer, along with representatives from the ASEAN Secretariat and ESCAP.[10] The Bangkok-based ESCAP Secretariat is the agency responsible for promoting the development of the regionwide rail network.[11] The annual SWG-SKRL meeting provides a platform for the transport ministries of all member countries to discuss—in the presence of all institutional partners—the progress and problems of the implementation of the SKRL project. Each country briefs the others about its previous year's work on construction, double tracking, filling in missing links, and laying spur lines in their jurisdiction, alongside other significant developments.[12]

Driving and Enabling Factors. When Malaysian Prime Minister Mahathir Mohamad put forward the SKRL proposal at the Fifth ASEAN Summit in 1995, the move represented much more than personal or national aspirations. Rather, it was one of the Southeast Asian responses to the changing geoeconomic conditions of the post–Cold War era. Small- and medium-size ASEAN countries started to see *regional integration* as the indispensable means by which they could cope with the common challenges of globalization in the face of economic regionalism elsewhere, most notably the North American Free Trade Area (NAFTA) and the European Union (EU). They also saw it as a means by which they could benefit from both engaging and working with rising China. The guiding belief was that better policy and physical connectivity would facilitate regional economic integration, serving as a catalyst for growth, competitiveness, and prosperity.[13]

The SKRL vision represented one of several regional multilateral endeavors aimed at promoting greater integration and closer interconnectivity across Asia by expanding institutionalized arrangements. These efforts ranged from regional institutions like the Asia-Pacific Economic Cooperation (APEC, 1989), to regional agreements such as the ASEAN Free Trade Area (AFTA, 1992), and subregional initiatives such as the Greater Mekong Subregion (GMS, 1992).[14] Some of these arrangements were promoted by outside powers, others decided upon by ASEAN as a group, and still others were advanced by individual ASEAN countries with participation by other members. All this had its origins in the commonly felt need to promote integration and forge connectivity as a way to gain competitiveness and protect themselves against globalization and global economic volatility.

None of these regional initiatives and institutions would have been possible absent the benign geopolitical regional and global environment during most of the 1990s. The collapse of the Soviet Union and the final resolution of the Third Indochina conflict in 1991 enabled old, noncommunist ASEAN members to engage former foes (China, Russia, and Vietnam). In due course, this created the opportunity to expand ASEAN-6 to ASEAN-10, while simultaneously drawing big powers into the ASEAN-based solar system and exploring new regional and multilateral economic and security institutions.[15] Simultaneously, Deng Xiaoping and his heirs in the PRC focused on domestic economic growth and fostered a relatively reassuring, economically oriented foreign policy. In short, while geoeconomic imperatives were the drivers of regional initiatives like the SKRL project, improved geopolitical conditions were the enabling factors permitting and motivating regional countries to move in these directions.

Ultimately, ASEAN countries' drive to take advantage of the post–Cold War geopolitical/strategic relaxation to pursue geoeconomic initiatives is rooted in their respective domestic politics (see chapter 4). The various external initiatives aimed at enhancing regional integration were motivated by the desire to boost development and increase welfare, all in the service of enhancing elites' performance legitimacy. This internal imperative underpins the SKRL and its associated institutional platform, the AMBDC.[16] Physical connectivity, including rail connectivity, is central to it all.

In our research team's interview in 2016 with then retired former Prime Minister Mahathir, we asked him about his thoughts and rationale in proposing the SKRL project in 1995. He said:

> "I thought shipping, oil demand, was up and maritime shipping is cheapest, but then trains are the next cheapest mode of transport for bulk goods. Also, originally I was not thinking high-speed trains, I was thinking of slower trains for bulk goods, not passengers. But, as you know, "trains were [at that time] out of favor. I went to Japan in 1961 and I was very interested in Japanese trains. I was in Tokyo Station, there were endless trains moving in and

out, twenty-four hours a day, so I began to think about trains more than others. Trains in Japan were very efficient, one minute in a station, not an hour, so I began to think of a train from Singapore to Bangkok, but it was a meter-gauge train, not a fast or heavy train. Malaysia, Singapore, Thailand, and also Vietnam all used meter-gauge trains. *We already have trains, but not the link, the connectivity.* There are breaks in Thailand, Cambodia. Cambodia is not linked to Thailand and there is no train in Laos. So I thought, *"if we can fill in the missing links"* then we could go all the way (Singapore to Kunming). Also, there were some east-west lines, Cambodia to Vietnam. So all this wouldn't cost too much [to knit all the pieces together and fill in the gaps]. *"All we need to do is to have the decisions."*[17]

Progress and Gaps. Today, a quarter century after the ASEAN leaders decided to launch the SKRL, progress across individual countries has been positive, but slow. While all member countries have made progress in at least one of the main tasks of the project scope (double tracking and electrification, building missing links, and laying spur lines), their scale and speed have been uneven; many problems persist.

In a 2010 report, the Development Centre of the OECD noted that since 2000 the SKRL member countries had rehabilitated national rail tracks, built new rails, and undertaken feasibility studies for missing sections as well as spur lines.[18] Subsequent studies have provided updates on developments in individual countries; some do so on a comparative basis. In a study of selected ASEAN countries' participation in the SKRL project, Wong Yau Duenn reports that thus far Malaysia and Thailand have made the greatest and fastest progress on upgrading to double-track and electrified railroads—completing a total of 606 km and 586 km of lines, respectively. In comparison, Vietnam's three double-track rail projects (i.e., Hanoi–Ho Chi Minh City, Hanoi–Hai Phong, and Hanoi–Lao Cai) are all still in the planning stages.[19] A similar pattern exists with respect to the development of missing links and spur lines. Thailand completed both the Aranyaprathet-Klong Luk missing link project and the Htiki–Ban Phu Nam Ron–Kanchanaburi spur line project in August 2015, whereas Vietnam's missing link and spur-line undertakings remain in preconstruction phases.[20]

Several types of challenges have prevented, delayed, or complicated the implementation of rail projects in Southeast Asia (see chapter 6 for more). Chief among these issues is funding and land acquisition. Indeed, funding is among the main factors contributing to the postponement of construction on some 1,780 km (or about 27 percent of the entire alignment of the SKRL project).[21]

There are other problems. Tauch Chankosal, the Secretary of State of the Cambodian Ministry of Public Works and Transport, observes, "So far, the SKRL has concentrated on removing the physical barriers to regional rail connectivity rather than on institutional issues. But the SKRL now needs to establish the framework for a streamlined regulatory environment and to harmonize cross-border processing and define standards for the interoperability of the region's railway network."[22] Institutional incompatibilities among involved nations and lack of coordination within them are both problems.

Having described why and how China's southern neighbors have sought to push forward rail connectivity, and the problems dogging this effort, it is obvious why foreign nations and their firms see a commercial opportunity. Foreign strategists see openings for influence and profit. This, in turn, energizes strategic and economic competition among outsiders. No competition is more intense or long-standing than that between China and Japan.

GEOPOLITICS IN THE ASCENDANCY (2014-PRESENT)
Japan's Rail Diplomacy in Southeast Asia

Why has Japan—and to a lesser extent other powers—promoted their own infrastructure-based economic statecraft to compete with, push back, and limit China's rail diplomacy and expanding influence in Southeast Asia, particularly since 2014? To answer this we first examine the stages, sources, and strategies of Japan's rail ambitions in Southeast Asia, before discussing the involvement of other powers in the region in the next section.

Stages and Sources of Japanese Rail Diplomacy. Japan's involvement in Southeast Asian rail and other infrastructure development goes back at least to the World War II era, as explained in chapter 2. Indeed, the full story of Japan's involvement in Asian infrastructure development would also have to address Tokyo's role in Taiwan and on the Korean Peninsula in the colonial period, and its large official development assistance (ODA) efforts in the modern period. Considering only recent decades, however, there are differences in terms of Tokyo's primary motives and roles before and after 2014. In the pre-2014 period, economic development and commerce were the primary considerations motivating Japan's infrastructure involvement (often ODA) in Southeast and East Asia (including in China).[23] After Xi Jinping announced BRI in late 2013, however, the geopolitical and strategic inclination of limiting China's regional influence became a more potent driver of Japan's rail statecraft.[24] China had passed Japan to become the country with the second-largest global GDP in 2010; by World Bank reckoning of purchasing power parity for 2013, the PRC had just surpassed the United States. Militarily, Beijing's behavior in the East and South China Seas had become worrisome to maritime Japan. From 2014 on, Japan's rail diplomacy has aimed at exporting its Shinkansen system as an alternative to China's HSR projects in the region and to maintain the preeminence of Japanese manufacturing in a world where major powers are competing to move up the value chain. Balancing China's economic and military power has become an animating concern in Tokyo.

The visible signs of this new phase of global industrial competition first appeared in 2014–15. In addition to competing with China for Indonesia's 142 km Jakarta-Bandung HSR project, Japan has also talked with Thailand about three major rail projects and made its interest in bidding for the Kuala Lumpur–Singapore HSR project clear.[25] In September 2015, a Japanese consortium lost a US$5 billion contract to build the Jakarta-Bandung rail line, Southeast Asia's first HSR project, to China Railway International. Indonesia's announcement came after its decision to abruptly scrap the entire project and drop *both* Chinese and Japanese rail proposals earlier that month, because of high financial costs. Jakarta's later decision to then award the project to Beijing was apparently in response to a later offer by China that proposed to construct the line "without Indonesian fiscal spending or debt guarantee."[26] At the time Japan had a requirement for sovereign debt guarantees on such projects, a restriction Tokyo soon dropped in the face of competition from Beijing. Moreover, China pledged to complete the construction in three years, compared to Japan's five years. This latter consideration was important to Indonesian President Jokowi, who anticipated running for reelection in 2019 (which he did and won) and wanted to have an achievement with which he could anchor his anticipated campaign. According to an Indonesia specialist:

> Jokowi wanted it finished by the election and he didn't want the Indonesian government to have to provide a guarantee. "The Chinese agreed to Indonesian terms on almost everything." In terms of financing and costs, they are cheaper than the Japanese. The project was also changed from government-to-government to business-to-business. Jokowi suddenly changed. The Japanese do not have state companies, hence there is a mismatch between the Indonesian SOEs and the Japanese side. There is a better match with the Chinese—state company to state company. The Chinese also promised to

finish the project earlier, which is normal Chinese practice to "sign first, and solve problems later."[27]

This view was echoed by a Japan expert, who adds:

> There is a clear link between the Japanese failure to win the bid and Japanese fiscal prudence. The Chinese agreed to do away with state guarantees. Jokowi does not want the debt to be on the government's debt sheet. The Japanese saw Rini [Mrs. Rini Soemarno, minister of state-owned enterprises of Indonesia] and Luhut [Mr. Luhut Binsar Pandjaitan, coordinating minister for maritime affairs] close to China. As a result of their loss, the Japanese have changed this practice—Prime Minister Abe has allowed sovereign debt guarantees based on a case-by-case approach. "This is a big change for Japan."[28]

One observer opined that Beijing's come-from-behind victory and Tokyo's setback would "undermine a pillar of the Abe government's Asian regional diplomatic strategy."[29] Scholar Chietigj Bajpaee describes the two countries' emerging HSR rail competition "as a microcosm of a broader Sino-Japanese rivalry for industrial supremacy in Asia, with power generation, nuclear power, telecoms, and port and road infrastructure also emerging as areas of potential competition."[30]

Motivated by *both* geoeconomic and geopolitical considerations, Japan's Shinkansen activism is a notable component of its efforts to boost its global competitiveness. Nevertheless, evidence discussed next reveals that while economic aims underpin Tokyo's rail diplomacy in Southeast Asia, an urgent consideration has become geopolitics, i.e., Tokyo's determination to challenge and limit the PRC's expanding influence in Asia.

Southeast Asia's expanding populations and rapid economic growth have fueled demands for railroad construction, which provide room for the involvement of Japan and other external players. Tokyo's targeting of lucrative railroad projects around Southeast Asia and beyond (e.g., India) is attributable to Prime Minister Shinzo Abe's overall strategy: selling infrastructure to fast-growing Asian economies as one of Japan's national growth drivers.[31] In June 2013, the Abe administration released its Japan Revitalization Strategy, vowing to triple its infrastructure exports from the then JPY 10 trillion to JPY 30 trillion by 2020.[32] On May 21, 2015, the administration announced the "Partnership for Quality Infrastructure" (PQI), under which the Japanese government will collaborate with a strengthened ADB in providing approximately $110 billion for "quality infrastructure development" in Asia over the next five years.[33] This occurred concurrently with the establishment of the Asian Infrastructure Investment Bank (AIIB).[34] Tokyo's rail activism also is part of Japanese corporations' quest for profitable business opportunities abroad in the face of Japan's anemic domestic economy. According to an assessment by Stratfor, a private global intelligence firm, regional rail projects promise considerable economic benefits because infrastructure construction deals "typically include public-private partnerships of broad consortiums, providing opportunities to an array of companies," while creating opportunities for Japanese firms in other sectors.[35]

Tokyo prioritizes Southeast Asia for its infrastructure exports due to geographic proximity and the region's long-standing economic importance to Japan.[36] A Singapore-based analyst observes that Japan has been playing the long game: "Japanese developers and financial institutions (including its export credit agency) have, cautiously and over time, built up extensive networks and experience around infrastructure development across Southeast Asia and beyond, mainly to shore up soft growth at home."[37] Australian analyst Amelia Long shares a similar view, adding that

> . . . strong economic growth and development in Southeast Asia could have positive trickle-down effects for the Japanese economy, which has suffered at the hands of structural weaknesses, stagnant incomes and China's slowdown. Southeast Asia's rapidly growing middle class, with a projected membership of 400 million by 2020, is an attractive market to both Japanese exporters and private sector—which already has a competitive edge in ASEAN—who stand to gain plenty from engaging Southeast Asia on infrastructure and development projects. A heightened Japanese presence could also have the added effect of diluting China's economic penetration of the region.[38]

Southeast Asia is a crucial region where Japan's economic and geopolitical interests converge. This has been evident in Japan's annual *White Paper on Development Cooperation* (or the "ODA White Paper") in recent years. Japan expert Purnendra Jain observes that the 2016 ODA White Paper highlights the importance of Southeast Asian nations as "partners" against the backdrop of the changing security landscape in East Asia. In light of the Japan-China standoff in the East China Sea and Beijing's increasingly assertive claims in the South China Sea, Tokyo has actively promoted the notion of freedom of navigation. It also seeks to develop a network of like-minded nations in the region, including the ASEAN states, as part of its wider pursuit of the rule of law, maritime security, cyber security, and peace-building measures.[39] These are all aspirations shared with the United States, whether during the Obama or the Trump administrations. Jain notes that although national interest had implicitly guided Japan's aid policy in the past, this is "the first time that it has been explicitly stated in a government document and defended by the Ministry of Foreign Affairs and the Japan International Cooperation Agency."[40] The 2017 ODA White Paper reiterated all of these points, placing emphasis on promoting "quality infrastructure" development and connectivity under the "Free and Open Indo-Pacific Strategy."[41]

Japan's "rediscovery" of Southeast Asia geopolitically reflects Tokyo's judgment that there is a convergence of interest between Japan and ASEAN states in the face of China's growing influence and assertiveness. To quote Amelia Long, "[in] Japan's ideal Asia, Southeast Asian states would effectively counterbalance China's increasing regional influence. While Tokyo can't match China's economic muscle, it expects Southeast Asian nations to shoulder some of the burden by hedging against China's growing weight."[42] Continuing, Long adds that for Tokyo, nurturing Japan's links with Southeast Asian partners and pursuing their shared interests in maritime security and rules-based regional architecture would be "a good outcome" and far preferable to "a Southeast Asia that bandwagons with China."[43] For all these reasons, rail and other infrastructure development in Southeast Asia has become a battleground of sorts for Tokyo and Beijing.

An additional indicator of the ascendancy of geopolitics in driving Japan's Shinkansen diplomacy is Tokyo's widening scope of infrastructure partnerships. Japan's connectivity strategy started with Abe's PQI. Over time, however, this has been pursued together with additional layers of bilateral, trilateral, and coalition partnerships between and among its fellow members of the Quad—India, Australia, and the United States.

In September 2017, during Abe's visit to India, the prime minister of Japan and his Indian counterpart Narendra Modi issued a joint statement declaring their bilateral relationship as a "Special Strategic and Global Partnership," a values-based "partnership for prosperity." The two leaders further pledged to align Japan's Free and Open Indo-Pacific Strategy with India's Act East Policy, through "improving connectivity in the wider Indo-Pacific region," "strengthening cooperation with ASEAN," etc. They also reaffirmed the importance of "quality infrastructure," while emphasizing that all countries should ensure "development and use of connectivity infrastructure in an open, transparent and non-exclusive manner based on international standards and responsible debt financing practices"[44]—a scarcely disguised slap at Beijing. During Modi's visit to Japan in October 2018, the two leaders renewed their commitments, again emphasizing their cooperation on connectivity development through quality infrastructure.[45]

Japan has worked with Australia and the United States on connectivity partnerships too. On July 31, 2018, the three countries announced a trilateral partnership to invest in projects that would build infrastructure, address development challenges, increase connectivity, and promote economic growth in the Indo-Pacific region. A statement on the website of the Australian Department of Foreign Affairs and Trade notes that the trilateral partnership "is in recognition that *more support* is needed to enhance *peace and prosperity in the Indo-Pacific region.*"[46] This partnership is seen by observers worldwide as "an apparent attempt to counter the growing influence of China" in the region.[47] Other bilateral and trilateral partnerships between and among Quad members have similarly pledged to strengthen their multi-dimensional partnerships, including collaboration to promote connectivity in the Indo-Pacific region.[48] Around 2018, more voices emerged calling for the Quad—as a group—to forge connectivity cooperation, in effect making infrastructure and economic partnership a second domain of cooperation for the coalition, alongside the security dialogue (the Quad's primary domain since its inception in 2007).[49] Infrastructure connectivity cooperation is emerging as a new chessboard for Asian geopolitics, playing balance-of-power politics using multiple means.

Thus far, these Quad-related bilateral, trilateral, and group partnerships in the connectivity domain remain as statements of intention. None have become actual rail or other infrastructure projects in Southeast Asia (as of 2019), except undertakings involving Japan. Several Japanese projects are still in the stage of initiation and negotiation, including an HSR project in Thailand (to run from Bangkok to Chiang Mai). Other Japan-related projects include an urban rail line in Bangkok, urban railroad networks in Hanoi and Ho Chi Minh City (discussed later in this chapter), and an HSR line running from Mumbai to Ahmedabad in western India that began construction in 2017.

Strategies of Japan's Rail Diplomacy. Since China's rail statecraft enjoys advantages in terms of cost and speed of construction, Japan has promoted its rail diplomacy using several means, including three main ones: (a) promoting an international discourse on "quality infrastructure," (b) emphasizing Japan's commitment to strengthening the local economy (providing jobs and sourcing materials in the client country), and (c) offering attractive financing packages through investment, low-interest loans, and other financial assistance. This last point was adopted after Tokyo lost the Jakarta-Bandung HSR line to Beijing, as noted earlier.

First and more specifically, Japan has been promoting a *new discourse on "quality infrastructure"* that highlights what Japan sees as the merits of its products and associated services, ranging from higher safety standards, better technology, and more environmental sustainability, to more transparent administrative procedures, more reliable operational support, and very competitive life-cycle costs (total costs over the project's lifetime). All are features associated with Japan's Shinkansen system. Each aspect of Japan's case aims to offset China's low cost and short construction period advantages. At a railroad conference and exhibition held in Kuala Lumpur in September 2014, Vice Chairman of East Japan Railway Co. Masaki Ogata touted the superiority of Japanese technology as well as the safety and reliability of its system design: "Japan's Shinkansen is not only safe, but the starting point of its strengths also lies in its on-time operations."[50] One very senior former Malaysian official explained how he compared Chinese and Japanese systems:

> "A lot of people say [the Japanese rail system] is expensive. In my view, when you look at costs, you shouldn't look at the cost up front; you should look at life-cycle costs." We find the life-cycle costs in terms of Japanese technology [to be] lighter, there is saving not just on maintenance but also energy costs. In a life cycle of 25–30 years, Japan is cheaper. In Japanese philosophy, a crash is to be avoided entirely. They take a long time to put out trains; lots of meticulous parts. "China tends to pay attention to speed. They want to finish things fast; they are more customer driven." At one of the HSR fairs here, we asked how fast they could do it and the Chinese asked me: "How fast do you want to build?"[51]

As the first country in the world to build an HSR system when it started its Shinkansen passenger service bullet train running between Tokyo and Osaka in 1964, Japan has a head start to tout. Japan has advantages in terms of its advanced technology, a zero fatality rate during "normal operations" in Japan,[52] and superior system design. It must be said, however, that by any fair judgment, China's relatively new HSR system still has a very admirable safety record, despite the July 2011 Wenzhou crash. Outside the realm of rail, Japan has also enjoyed a decades-long reputation as a pioneering development player in Asia due to its early involvement in regional infrastructure development. These considerations, in combination, constitute Japan's notion of "quality" infrastructure.

Japanese companies tend to further strengthen their proposals with comprehensive services that cover operations support, maintenance, and inspection, as well as other technical assistance. Such comprehensive offers are possible because Japanese rail operators often join with heavy-industry manufacturers and trading houses, backed by aid. As observed by Jain, "aid money is now increasingly linked to Japanese technology, design, and construction."[53] In November 2013, a Japanese consortium composed of East Japan Railway, the trading house Marubeni, and electronics conglomerate Toshiba secured a deal to construct a new 23 km urban rail line in Bangkok. The deal covered supplying train cars, building the power grid, signals, rail yards, and stations, as well as providing maintenance services and operational expertise.[54]

A second means Japan uses to promote its rail expertise is by highlighting its commitment to strengthening the local economy in its connectivity partnership with host countries. This is done through promoting local employment, conducting training and initiating capacity-building efforts, as well as providing technical assistance and sharing technological know-how with the locals. According to a 2016 study of Japan-China rail rivalry, Japanese projects provide "more benefits to local economies through hiring and training local workers, as opposed to the common Chinese practice of importing labor for Chinese-funded infrastructure projects."[55]

Japan is adept in adapting and tailoring its unique Shinkansen system to the local context and national needs. A member of our research team attended a Shinkansen symposium and exhibition in Kuala Lumpur in April 2016, co-organized by the East Japan Railway Company, Japan Overseas Railway System Association, and Japan Railway Technical Service. The event, sponsored by Japanese government agencies (including Land, Infrastructure, Transport, and the Tourism Ministry, along with the Foreign Affairs Ministry and the Economy, Trade and Industry Ministry), was part of Japan's ongoing efforts to compete with China over the planned Kuala Lumpur–Singapore HSR project. Speech after speech at the pavilion, packed with standing room only, focused on a message that was also featured in the exhibition banners and attractions: Japan is here to share its fifty-one years of HSR experience and Shinkansen features *to benefit Malaysia*. For example, one slide illustrated contributions to Malaysia-Singapore HSR in terms of technology transfer, human resource development, and education and training.

Through other exhibition features, the Japanese organizers also high-lighted the multifunction role of the Shinkansen station as a hub for social, commercial shopping, office space, and transport, in an apparent effort to relate to and echo Malaysian officials' emphasis on integrated development, as well as the needs to connect and develop rural areas. The Japanese exhibitors also touted Taiwan's "success testimonial" as an overseas Shinkansen, and showcased the relevance of the Shinkansen system for bringing socioeconomic benefits to Malaysia in terms of enhancing integration, revitalizing communities, and minimizing "total life-cycle costs" in maintaining the infrastructure. Unfortunately, just after this exhibition in October 2018, the Japanese high-speed system installed in Taiwan had a fatal accident, killing 18 persons and injuring 187.[56]

A third way Japan promotes its rail diplomacy is by offering sustainable financing arrangements, on the basis of careful feasibility studies. These include providing low-interest loans and other financial assistance, depending on the client's circumstances. A case in point is the planned Bangkok-Chiang Mai HSR project. Japan reportedly offered soft loans to aid the construction, rather than the joint investment arrangement suggested by the Thai military government.[57] Another example, also in Thailand, is the proposed Eastern HSR Line linking the three main airports in the Eastern Economic Corridor (EEC). In March 2019, the Japan Bank for International Cooperation (JBIC) confirmed its plan to provide soft loans to finance the THB 224 billion HSR project. The Thai authorities described JBIC's support to the HSR as "an example project of investment cooperation between the private sectors of Japan and China in a third country."[58]

Other Players

Japan and China are not the only players on the field of Southeast Asian railroad competition. Other countries, such as South Korea, India, Canada, and European nations, have also played periodic roles in the region's rail connectivity development. Their varied involvements take multiple forms such as: (a) donors and expertise providers to multilateral organizations, including ASEAN, ADB, and ESCAP; (b) partners providing technical and training services to individual Southeast Asian nations; (c) investors or developers in bidding and/or constructing rail projects in individual Southeast Asian countries; and (d) promoters and (potential) exporters of HSR and other systems and/or subsystems.

South Korea. The ROK has been a donor country to the ESCAP's Trans-Asian Railway (TAR) program through the Korea-ESCAP Cooperation Fund. Through this program, the Korean Ministry of Land, Transport, and Maritime Affairs has provided expert services to TAR projects.[59] South Korea is a latecomer in ODA. Nonetheless, since becoming a member of the OECD Development Assistance Committee in 2010, Seoul has increased its ODA funds and expanded its development partnerships. The bulk of its ODA funds are allocated to Asian countries, with a focus on infrastructure in ASEAN developing countries.[60] Southeast Asian countries are the major beneficiaries of Korea's ODA because of geographical proximity, cultural familiarity, and Korea's own pragmatic needs.[61] Like Tokyo, Seoul hopes to augment its own national growth by tapping overseas commercial opportunities.

The state-owned Korea Rail Network Authority (KR), which established its overseas business office in 2004, has made progress in securing dozens of conventional rail projects in emerging global markets.[62] It has collaborated with the Korea International Cooperation Agency (KOICA) in undertaking training programs for railroad officials from emerging countries, particularly those with long-term growth potential, including Indonesia and Vietnam.[63] Over the past decade or so, KR has provided technical services and management consultancy assistance for rail development in various Southeast Asian countries, including the Philippines, Vietnam, Indonesia, Cambodia, Thailand, Malaysia, and Laos.[64]

Thus far, South Korea's involvement in Southeast Asia's rail landscape has been limited to providing technical support and supervision for project development, rather than undertaking project construction. ROK involvement has also been confined to conventional train rather than HSR projects. Since 2015, however, South Korea—alongside Germany, France, and Canada—have expressed interest in bidding for the proposed $15 billion Kuala Lumpur–Singapore HSR project. KR's director of overseas projects reportedly said, "We're zeroing in on the deal, which will hopefully become our first overseas venture for high-speed trains."[65] South Korea adopted French systems for its own first-generation HSR in 2004 and rolled out its first made-in-Korea bullet trains in 2010.[66]

Similarly to Japan, the ROK seeks to export its HSR technology and systems to foreign markets, in part to stimulate a struggling construction industry and energize domestic economic growth. Like the Japanese railroad-industrial complex, KR seeks to become a globally competitive HSR builder and services provider. It wants to form a Korean consortium by teaming up with construction companies and other private firms to secure HSR deals in global markets. Unlike Japan, whose Shinkansen technology and system was exported to Taiwan in 2007 (followed by India in 2017), South Korea's HSR has yet to leave home.[67]

Most importantly, unlike Japan, whose post-2014 rail activism has important geopolitical objectives, South Korea's rail ambitions are largely economic. Counter-balancing Beijing is not the reason behind Seoul's growing regional rail aspirations. Despite Korea's clear memory of Chinese domination under the Sino-centric tributary order, this has not translated into a contemporary geopolitical desire to challenge the PRC regionally. Rather, South Korea's long-term geoeconomic calculations put a premium on regional integration and infrastructure connectivity, including rail connectivity. Since coming to power in 2017, current ROK President Moon Jae-in has promoted a vision of connecting South Korea with the Trans-China and Trans-Siberian railroads, a plan potentially transforming Korea "from a geostrategic island into an integral part of the mainland of continental Asia."[68] In March 2018, the South Korean firm CJ Logistics announced future plans to expand its rail freight transport services by opening fifty-two routes from China to Europe and seventy-four routes from Europe to China. Using the Trans-China Railway "will cost one-fifth of air transport and is three times faster than sea transport."[69]

These considerations help explain why Seoul has pursued a distinctive China policy compared to most other US regional allies and partners. South Korea did not take long to decide to join the Beijing-initiated AIIB (unlike Japan) against Washington's preferences.[70] Korea has also kept a low profile over the South China Sea disputes and underlying contest for maritime dominance, keeping its distance from US Freedom of Navigation Operations (FONOPs) and distancing itself from the Quad's "Indo-Pacific" strategy. Although Seoul competes in connectivity cooperation, it does so for economic, not strategic reasons. The ROK resists using infrastructure partnerships for balance-of-power purposes (unlike Japan, Australia, India, and several European countries).

India. Beyond Sino-Indian border disputes, the baseline for thinking about New Delhi's attitudes toward China's BRI is Beijing's very heavy involvement in infrastructure construction with Pakistan, one of the six BRI corridors. Islamabad–New Delhi strategic hostility and border issues color Indian attitudes and limit cooperation on rail and other connectivity development with the PRC.[71]

Despite its relatively underdeveloped rail capacity as compared with its neighbors in eastern and northeastern Asia, India has been a quiet player in Southeast Asian rail development. With over one hundred fifty years of history, Indian Railways is the oldest rail network in Asia, running twenty thousand passenger trains and nine thousand two hundred freight trains daily, with passenger trains averaging 50 kmph. New Delhi struggles to upgrade its colonial-era rail system in a number of ways. Internally, it is developing its own locally made express train (with a rated top speed of 180 kmph, 20 percent faster than the next fastest train in service on the subcontinent). Bilaterally, India is enlisting Japan's technical and financial assistance to develop its HSR system, though it is encountering land acquisition problems.[72] And regionally, New Delhi is forging rail cooperation with selected Southeast Asian countries.[73] Due to geographic proximity, India's efforts in Southeast Asia have thus far concentrated on Myanmar. Myanmar is the route through which the proposed Western Line of China's three-pronged pan-Asian network would be built, setting up an implicit geopolitical competition between New Delhi and Beijing in terms of which is to prevail—east-west connectivity or north-south?

As the only Southeast Asian country bordering India, Myanmar is an indispensable link for New Delhi's possible rail expansion into Vietnam, Thailand, and other economically vibrant parts of Asia, especially China. In other words, India, Myanmar, Thailand, Cambodia, and Vietnam are the east-west path that could make "balanced connectivity" possible against the background of China's north-south thrust. India plans to build a 212 km railroad to connect Imphal (the capital of its Manipur State) with Kalay (also Kale) in Myanmar via the Indian border town of Moreh, with an eye to connect India with the 81,000 km Trans-Asian Railway network. Undertaken by the Rail India Technical and Economic Service (RITES), a public enterprise under the Indian Ministry of Railways, survey work for the India-Myanmar rail link was completed in March 2019.[74] With this planned rail link, as well as the India-Myanmar-Thailand Trilateral Highway, Manipur is being positioned as India's gateway to Southeast Asia.

India's current rail diplomacy includes enhancing Myanmar's rail networks and standardizing tracks. For example, the Indian government offered a $56 million credit line to Myanmar (for the 2004–9 period) for upgrading the 640 km rail system between Mandalay and Yangon.[75] In addition, in 2017–18 the Indian authorities also supported Myanmar's rail development by delivering eighteen Indian YDM-4 diesel electric locomotives to be used on several Myanmar rail lines.[76]

The enhancements of Myanmar's rail network, alongside the updating and construction of tracks in India's northeastern region, are central to New Delhi's rail ambition of eventually connecting with Vietnam and other parts of Southeast and East Asia. India has plans to build the Delhi-Hanoi Railway Link (DHRL). A preliminary study conducted by the RITES in 2006 envisaged developing the DHRL through two possible routes, both of which require the construction of missing links in Myanmar.[77]

India's rail ambitions in Myanmar and Vietnam are both central to New Delhi's hope to strengthen the India-ASEAN connectivity partnership. The DHRL was among the major connectivity projects highlighted at the ASEAN-India Connectivity Summit hosted by India in December 2017. Another flagship project featured at the summit was the Mekong-India Economic Corridor (MIEC), which promotes India's integration with four Mekong countries (Cambodia, Myanmar, Thailand, and Vietnam). After Japan and China, India is the third country to initiate an institutionalized meeting with the ASEAN Connectivity Coordinating Committee (ACCC).[78] In short, India and China both have plans in which Myanmar and Vietnam figure prominently, and herein lie key elements of the competition between the two.

India's rail ambitions, however, are not limited to mainland Southeast Asia. They also involve rail development in maritime Southeast Asia, where India's activities take the form of developer and builder. A subsidiary of Indian Railway, Ircon International Limited (formerly Indian Railway Construction Company Limited, IRCON) has clients and projects in Indonesia, the Philippines, and Malaysia.[79] Malaysia has long remained IRCON's principal market in Southeast Asia. The Indian state-run firm has been the developer of multiple rail projects in the country since the 1990s, some financed through barter trade arrangements (where Malaysia paid in palm oil instead of cash). These projects include the construction of a 30 km rail line linking the Port of Tanjung Pelepas in Johor with the Malaysian main line (1999–2002), electrified double-tracking of the KL–Port Klang line (1991–94), the Rawang-Seremban line (1990–94), the 97 km Seremban-Gemas double-tracking project worth $1 billion (2008–13), and several track rehabilitation projects in Paloh-Singapore, Slim River–Seremban, Sungai Siput–Ipoh, and other lines.[80] Recently, there has been some two-way rail development cooperation between the two countries. In June 2017, the Indian government announced a project worth more than $1.5 billion, where it would seek Malaysian expertise in modernizing twenty railroad stations located in tier-two cities in India.[81]

India's role in Asian regional rail and infrastructure development also takes other forms. A founding member of UN ESCAP, India has been among the top ten donors to the agency.[82] With plans to link its northeast region to the emerging network in Southeast Asia, New Delhi's interests in regionwide connectivity are genuine, both strategic and economic in purpose. Unlike South Korea, New Delhi has clear interests in counterbalancing China strategically, in addition to its economic and development goals. In this sense, New Delhi's objectives align with those of fellow Quad countries.

Of note is the fact that while today New Delhi is an advocate of regional connectivity, this has not always been the case. In the 1960s, geopolitical considerations led India to avoid developing infrastructure in its northeast, in order to create a buffer against China in the aftermath of the 1962 border war. In recent years, however, geopolitics have pushed India in the *opposite* direction. New Delhi now seeks security through integration, not isolation of its own periphery. According to Suyash Desai, a scholar based at Jawaharlal Nehru University:

> After the 1962 war against China, Indian leadership choose not to develop infrastructure in the northeast as a defence against Chinese penetration. However, the lack of infrastructure development has cost India on both the domestic and foreign policy fronts. Domestically, the disconnect of the northeast from the mainland was one of the many reasons for the rise of insurgencies in this region. On the foreign policy front, India missed out on opportunities to diversify its energy needs to Myanmar and enhance its economic relations with Southeast Asia due to modest connectivity infrastructure.[83]

He adds:

> Giving substance to ASEAN-India relations through connectivity will gradually change the geopolitical landscape of this region. Exploring opportunities through connectivity projects will not only curb existing insurgencies, but also help India's north-eastern states to develop their economic potential and integrate with mainland India. These projects will also help India to remove physical impediments to trade with ASEAN countries and further integrate the two regions for better economic and security relations.[84]

Western Powers. The Western colonial authorities of the nineteenth and early twentieth centuries were the pioneers of rail and other infrastructure in Southeast Asia for economic and other reasons, as detailed in chapter 2. In the postwar, postcolonial era, however, Western powers have not played notable roles in Asian regional rail construction. Nonetheless, over recent decades, EU countries have been involved in rail development indirectly. Individually and collectively, EU nations have contributed to multilateral organizations such as the ADB and ESCAP. Commercially, EU countries and others (e.g., Canada) have been involved through their national champion firms, such as Germany's Siemens, France's Alstom, the UK's Fenix Rail Systems, and Canada's Bombardier. Until recently, this involvement has focused chiefly on conventional rail systems (including light rail and metro services). It is only recently that Western players—primarily European and Canadian firms—have shown greater interest in becoming involved with the HSR sector.

The HSR sector in Southeast Asia is a new frontier for the Western rail companies. Following the announcements of the Kuala Lumpur—Singapore HSR project (suspended in mid-2018 pending a decision in mid-2020) and the airport-linked HSR project in Thailand's EEC, several Western firms expressed interest and teamed up with local enterprises in bidding for the projects. Alstom and Siemens, for instance, have joined hands with Italy's Ferrovie dello Stato Italiane and the Austrian construction firm PORR in forming a consortium alongside the Malaysian engineering firm George Kent to bid for the KL-Singapore HSR project.[85] As the consortium put it: "This partnership shall result in a powerful team combining European technology and project experience with the best local expertise."[86]

It will not be easy for the European players to outmaneuver Asian competitors from China and Japan in their own backyard. As observed by Agatha Kratz, an adviser to the New York–based consultancy Rhodium Group: "In Asia, particularly in Southeast Asia, where governments have much more intense and long-lasting ties with Japan and China" and their companies, it would be a challenging task for European players who are "less important diplomatic actors in the region" to win these big-ticket contracts. However, Kratz remains optimistic: "But this situation might also represent an opportunity for the European consortium," if it "can play the 'neither China nor Japan' card, by presenting itself as a non-politicized choice and spare the regional governments the trouble of having to pick between the region's two prominent players."[87] It remains uncertain whether or not the European consortium actually can play such a card in light of the September 2018 decision by Malaysia's new Pakatan Harapan government and

Singapore to defer decision on the KL-Singapore HSR project until May 2020, due to "Malaysia's financial health."[88]

Another project, Thailand's Eastern Line to connect the three main airports (Suvarnabhumi, Don Mueang, and U-Tapao in Rayong) also attracted interest from Western rail players Siemens, Bombardier, and SNCF of France.[89] As of late December 2018, however, it became clear that none of these firms would emerge as the final contenders, when the State Railway of Thailand (SRT) revealed that only two groups were qualified to contest the contract: a consortium led by the Charoen Pokphand Group (CP) and the BSR Joint Venture.[90] The CP-led consortium is composed of CP, China Railway Construction Corporation Ltd (CRCC), Bangkok Expressway and Metro Plc (BEM), CH Karnchang Plc (CK), and Italian-Thai Development Plc (ITD). BSR is composed of Bangkok Mass Transit System Plc (BTSC, which operates the Skytrain in Bangkok), Sino-Thai Engineering and Construction Plc (STEC), and Ratchaburi Electricity Generating Holding Plc (RATCH). The CP consortium, which offered the lowest bid, was reportedly close to winning the bid for the project.[91] On April 27, 2019, the SRT decided to grant the concession for the THB 220 billion HSR project to the CP consortium.[92] In these consortia, one sees Chinese firms beginning to join with others—this is a significant development.[93]

Interestingly, while the European companies' involvement in Southeast Asian rail business is motivated by commercial interests, EU governments also increasingly have geopolitical considerations in the region, concerns shared by the Quad powers. In September 2018, the European Commission released a joint communication titled "Connecting Europe and Asia: Building Blocks for an EU Strategy," a document that is widely known as the "EU-Asia Connectivity Strategy."[94] The document emphasizes the principles of "sustainable, comprehensive, and international connectivity."[95] Some analysts have described this new strategy as "Europe's answer to China's Belt and Road."[96] Others view it as the EU's "alternative plan for Asia," as doubts grow over Beijing's way of promoting infrastructure projects.[97] In 2018, twenty-seven of the twenty-eight EU ambassadors to Beijing criticized the PRC's BRI initiatives in Europe, complaining that the initiative was nontransparent, tilting the competitive field toward Chinese firms, and designed to split EU members apart (in particular Hungary and Greece).[98] More recently, China has signed a BRI agreement with Italy, much to the consternation of other EU members and Washington.

The new EU-Asia Connectivity strategy comes after European Commission President Jean-Claude Juncker's call for "a more muscular EU foreign policy" corresponding to the bloc's economic clout.[99] Fraser Cameron, a former EC adviser, observes that, against the backdrop of increasing geopolitical competition, the EU strategy "has set down a marker that the EU is part of the game."[100]

CONCLUSIONS

This chapter has described why Southeast Asian states, and bigger powers at greater distances, have sought to diversify their partnerships and become involved in rail development in Southeast Asia. While China's position is strong, at the same time geopolitics is a growing consideration, with everyone watching the PRC warily. Strategic concerns provide reasons for Southeast Asians to hedge, to diversify dependencies, and to keep options open. They also provide incentives to outside powers to become more involved. Geopolitics can provide incentives to act where economic incentives may be insufficient. China's assertive foreign policy is stimulating reactions within the region, and far beyond, as we explain at greater length in the next and final chapter.

There are three key conclusions of this chapter concerning the geopolitical and geoeconomic dimensions of the high- and conventional-speed rail build-out race in Southeast Asia.

1. The slow pace of the Southeast Asian states' progress on SKRL (Singapore-Kunming Rail Line) since the mid-1990s reflects a basic fact. Many of the region's states lack the financing, technology, and human resources necessary to bring the full rail connectivity vision into being. Consequently, they look favorably upon external partnerships in pursuing their national rail construction and regional rail network aspirations and plans. Coupled with the region's strategic location, abundant resources, and huge economic potential, this circumstance creates space for external powers such as China and Japan to promote both their commercial and strategic ambitions throughout the region. This, in turn, sets off both commercial and strategic rivalries. These conflicts create dangers for the nations to China's south, yet also provide them opportunities to gain resources and cooperation they might not otherwise obtain. They can use the commercial and strategic ambitions of one as leverage against the other.

2. Japan—a long time development partner to all Southeast Asian nations—has become an important force in the current, emerging geopo-

litical dynamic. Determined to limit China's regional influence by competing with Beijing's rail and other infrastructure projects across the region, Tokyo has pursued a multipronged strategy. It has promoted its own Partnership for Quality Infrastructure, while working with fellow Quad members (India, Australia, and the United States) in launching multiple connectivity partnership schemes at bilateral, trilateral, and group levels, all with an eye to presenting alternatives to China's BRI. These nations partnering with Japan seek east-west connectivity to offset Beijing's desire for north-south economic and human flows. It remains to be seen what they actually can, and will, do. As more players involve themselves in Southeast Asian rail development, infrastructure connectivity cooperation is becoming an important avenue for geopolitics in Asia. Economics are a foundational consideration, but geopolitics have become a progressively more important factor in Southeast Asia and beyond, in part because of the deterioration in US-China ties. It is worth noting that the Republic of Korea alone has a different, less conflicted vision of the role rail connectivity with China might play in its national economic future—at least under the Moon Jae-in administration.

3. Finally, whether, and to what extent, individual Southeast Asian states can utilize the leverage they theoretically possess depends on several considerations: (a) What practical alternatives to the PRC does each country have? (b) Can other potential partners match or exceed the PRC in terms of project costs and speed of construction? While economists might say these countries should consider life-cycle costs, in fact the initial cost is what is foremost in the minds of political leaders (since most politicians' own life cycles can be brief). (c) To what extent is China willing and able to learn from past missteps, adapt, and offer a better deal that conforms to international norms? The Chinese people and their desires to spend at home and avoid excessive risk with national investments may place limits on Beijing's largesse abroad. Reciprocally, to what extent are Japan and others capable (financially and politically) of adapting to an ever-more nimble PRC, if that is the face China turns to the world?

CHAPTER 8

Implications for China, Asia, and the World

Rail projects take time. It is like growing trees: if you want trees, you plant trees, and then wait for thirty to forty years. China is a communist country; they can wait. They are planting trees [building the rails] now.

—Thai businessperson, June 2017[1]

We are concerned about security, but we don't want the gravy train to stop [from China]. Let's show some displeasure, but keep the economic thing going.

—Malaysian researcher, June 2016[2]

The development of high-speed and conventional-speed railroads (along with other infrastructure such as roads, ports, airports, electrical and communications grids, and cyber pathways) holds out the prospect of transforming the East and Southeast Asian regional economies and societies over the coming decades, faster than many outside observers have appreciated. This undertaking contributes to the ongoing integration of the East and Southeast Asian economies and therefore carries with it security and economic challenges and opportunities. How should America and its partners respond to this development?

The United States and allies should participate in this growing connectivity, not stand apart from it. *Participate* does not mean signing on to the Belt and Road Initiative (BRI) but rather adopting the concept of what we call *balanced connectivity* development—a connectivity that multiplies points of interdependence rather than simply focuses on links to the PRC. In the memorable words of the scholar of the Middle East

Professor Fouad Ajami, America and the West should not be "A dog baying as the camel caravan departs the oasis."

If progress in developing the HSR and conventional-speed network continues—which we assess is likely—growing connectivity will make China the hub of the regional system, which will have wide-reaching global effects economically, socially, and strategically. By undertaking this multiobjective effort, the PRC seeks to lay the foundation for future decades of domestic growth by increasing its own centrality to supply chains and improving its neighborhood. Building the pathways for the projection of power in all its forms (coercive, economic, and normative) is the essence of China's "great national rejuvenation." Beijing's emphasis on infrastructure in its foreign policy is core to its efforts to elevate its own status as a great power.

Underlying this broad set of economic and strategic purposes lie two central facts. First, strategically, as China's relations with the United States (and the West more broadly) become increasingly problematic under Xi Jinping, Beijing is motivated to diversify its dependencies and widen the divisions between Washington and its historic allies. Second, in 2017 ASEAN countries had almost the same share (12.5%) of China's total international trade as the EU (15%) and the United States (14.2%).[3] ASEAN is a growing region close to China with logistical alternatives to the PRC's maritime vulnerabilities. The region is already of immense importance to China economically. Diversification of China's value-added chain southward will make Southeast Asia even more valuable. Already, as David Bulman reports, "the US, EU, and Japan account for less than 30% of East Asian exports, down from 50% in the 1990s, and East Asian intraregional trade grew to 57.3% in 2016.[4] As China's civil and military maritime fleets grow, the region's many ports and attendant production zones will become increasingly important. Building infrastructure and connectivity between China and Southeast Asia is not a harebrained scheme, although significant questions remain, including what types of connectivity to construct, where to build, and at what pace. What about negative externalities? What type of financing? What are the political risks inherent in many of these projects? Will China become more transparent in its negotiating and financing arrangements, becoming a better citizen in terms of multilateral norms such as the Santiago Principles[5] and those of the Paris Group?[6] We also must keep in mind that what makes sense for China's future may not jibe with its neighbors' aspirations or unforeseen developments (e.g., COVID-19).

China's *lead with infrastructure approach* to development (despite the backlash that such efforts often produce) contrasts with a US approach grounded in *political institution, human resource, and norm building.* Some observers, including this book's three coauthors, would argue that America has forgotten the role infrastructure played in its own national development and foreign policy history. For example, with respect to foreign policy, consider the long-term consequences of the Panama Canal for US economic and military reach. Just as the Panama Canal affected all maritime nations, the impact of China's huge infrastructure efforts will spill out globally in ever wider concentric circles. Thinking strategically, the United States and others should find ways to participate in the development of this increasingly interconnected system. America and its allies should seek to contribute to *balanced connectivity,* not the old-world pursuit of dominance while remaining disconnected from the process of building connectivity in Asia.

In the preceding chapters, beyond relating the unfolding story of constructing new infrastructure and pathways of power in East Asia, we have addressed three groups of questions:

1. *Does China have the power and political dexterity to engineer the realization of regionwide connectivity?* Will Beijing be able to bring the complex, ongoing, and future negotiations involved in this overall project to a productive and mutually satisfactory conclusion? And why are some of China's neighbors more receptive to Beijing's entreaties than others? These questions speak more to the PRC's political power and influence than to its civil engineering acumen. China clearly has the engineering talent, considerable financial wherewithal, and the capacity to plan long term. The underlying question is, Does Beijing have the sophistication and political sensitivity/flexibility to adapt to ever-changing circumstances and draw adaptive conclusions from the inevitable setbacks as negotiations move from one country to another? Moreover, will the Chinese people support a long-term commitment that requires current investment abroad when so many domestic needs remain unmet in China itself? Were Chinese domestic economic growth to severely falter, Beijing's capacity to sustain its outward push would correspondingly decline. Thus far, progress has exceeded reasonable expectations on the way to creating this huge system, but uncertainties abound, and there is a long way to go. Some component projects of the grand vision likely will flounder.

2. *What ability do China's neighbors have to shape their own fates in the face of the exertions and ambitions of the colossus to their north?* Are they destined to be the blank canvas upon which Beijing writes its own calligraphy? The answer to this question varies somewhat by country, but the capacity of China's smaller neighbors to shape unfolding development is considerable. They do so individually, together through multilateral organizations, and by enlisting the help of bigger powers in a variety of ways. Domestic political and economic changes in some partner countries (e.g., Malaysia, Myanmar, and Pakistan) provided some countries the opportunity to renegotiate deals made by preceding governments with Beijing. In the case of Thailand, its strategic DNA of power balancing, the pluralistic and divisive electoral system, the country's financial wherewithal, and powerful domestic interest groups enabled Thai leaders to make better deals with Beijing.[7]

3. *What are the difficulties encountered in the implementation of massive projects in a globalized, increasingly interdependent international system?* The implementation of China's domestic HSR system in just over a decade was a staggering accomplishment viewed from almost any perspective—economic, political, technological, or engineering. However, the complexity of that domestic challenge pales in comparison to the difficulty of consecutively implementing a group of projects that would potentially connect seven sovereign countries to the PRC. Each of these seven countries, in turn, is embedded in a different set of linkages with a distinct constellation of its own neighbors, as well as each having distinct domestic constraints. To date we have seen limited but meaningful progress on the Pan-Asia Railway, with construction ongoing in two countries and serious negotiations with three others underway as of 2019.

There are several pathways along which development of the overall Pan-Asia Railway project in Southeast Asia could move. Some observers look at the scope of the project and presume failure. Leaving aside what would constitute "failure," after years of grassroots research we believe this is unlikely. Much attention has focused on the elections in Malaysia in mid-2018 and the subsequent process of renegotiation of major Sino-Malaysian projects. These renegotiations could end in project failure, but they also very well could result in modifications and mutual concessions that make the overall endeavor more viable and sustainable. Not every hiccup along the way spells total failure, though failure is, of course, a possibility.[8]

The incremental, protracted, and indeterminate process of realizing the broad vision is a marathon, not a sprint. Each prior agreement, each problem solved, indeed each failure that occurs shapes how the next stage of implementation unfolds. When implementation prospects appeared problematic (e.g., the cases of Malaysia's ECRL and the Kuala Lumpur–Singapore HSR) we have sometimes seen renegotiation. This demonstrates that implementation and negotiation are not two hermetically separated phases of the policy-making process. Overall, there has been movement toward the broad goal of interconnectivity, along an ever-shifting, still indeterminate, pathway. The process is a bit like pinball: one knows the goal (reach the bottom with the most possible points scored), but each round is sui generis, with the ball following a path that could not have been predicted, and in which no two iterations are the same.

Examining implementation, one almost by definition is looking with a magnifying glass at problems, though sometimes undertakings are so successful that the success itself calls for explanation. By focusing exclusively on the problems of implementation, are we losing sight of the overall direction and progress of this huge project? What will be the costs to powers that decide not to become involved? Do all of the implementation challenges blind us to a larger transformation that is occurring? Our suspicion is that decades from now, foreign policy analysts and intelligence agencies will come to see that they underestimated the importance of what is underway with the creation of the Pan-Asia Railway. Indeed, such a reassessment is already underway. After the United States initially opposed creation of the Asian Infrastructure Investment Bank (AIIB) in the mid-2010s (a decision for which no one in the Obama administration, including the then Treasury Secretary,[9] would take responsibility), in its initial years the Trump administration began exploring ways to contribute to building what the authors of this volume call "balanced connectivity" in the region. In 2018, the United States government appropriated modest funds for US Overseas Private Investment Corporation (OPIC) activities in the development of infrastructure, including in Asia.[10] US Secretary of State Mike Pompeo called this "a down payment on a new era of U.S. economic commitment to the region [emerging Asia]."[11] Prior to this move by Washington, in May 2015 Tokyo responded meaningfully to China's infrastructure moves with its Partnership for Quality Infrastructure. This is a meaningful move, but insufficient to compete with China's connectivity statecraft. Washington and its allies should work together and do more. At the same time, they should engage with China on infrastructure development in third countries, not least to shape Beijing's practices in connectivity development.

Against the background of these broad questions and concerns, this chapter brings together principal conclusions of our research.

THE *RIVERS OF IRON* STORY FUNDAMENTALS

The Big Picture: What Makes Development Go? Sometimes it seems as though Western countries have forgotten how it was that they themselves modernized. They fail to recall the role that infrastructure played in their own growth, or the role that central governments played in supporting infrastructure and the development of key technologies. The United States, along with other developed countries, is beginning to reconsider its own history and development nostrums, partly because China has been promoting an alternative approach, and partly because other developing nations are calling for adjusted efforts.

While much divides China's elite from the leaders and citizens of Southeast Asian nations, one assumption conceptually unites them—that developing states need activist governments when it comes to building the prerequisites for economic growth and social change. They almost all believe that infrastructure is key. The PRC and its neighbors believe, to one degree or another, in the Chinese aphorism "If you want to get rich, build a road." Another maxim that captures the spirit of rail connectivity is "When the train whistle blows, prosperity will follow." Indeed, China's southern neighbors embraced this modern vision even before Beijing. This is one reason that China's neighbors gravitate toward the rail connectivity vision, even though they are leery about the PRC as a polity, a power, and as a neighbor. On a March 2019 trip to the Philippines, for instance, Prime Minister Mahathir of Malaysia saw fit to warn President Duterte and others in Manila that although there were upsides to cooperation with the PRC, there were also downsides. A few downsides he highlighted were excessive debt, large numbers of migrants and workers coming from China, and Beijing's goals in the South China Sea.[12]

Despite the pitfalls, our research team saw variations on this theme of growth through connectivity in our conversations throughout Southeast Asia—whether it was in Indonesia with then Governor of Jakarta Ahok, then former Prime Minister Mahathir in Malaysia, planners in Laos, or the military junta in Thailand. Indeed, more than a century ago, Thailand's King Rama V (1853–1910) was a proponent of rail development. So Bangkok's attraction to rail connectivity clearly antedates the existence of the PRC. Vietnam's communist leaders also believe in connectivity and fear that their country will lag as neighbors build out railroads and other infrastructure with Chinese involvement. However, Hanoi is simultaneously apprehensive about an increasingly Sino-centric system. The basic orientation of all of these Southeast Asian leaders is that creating pathways for connectivity catalyzes economic growth and modernization. They believe that countries in their circumstances cannot wait for growth to come and then build the pathways. There is a predisposition in all of these countries to see growth and development as a spontaneous combustion process ignited by infrastructure.

For much of the past two hundred years, as the United States experienced intense periods of modernization, this is exactly the same mindset Americans had. In the second half of the nineteenth century, the US government, in intimate partnership with the private sector, built its own rivers of iron, the Transcontinental Railroad, and other connectivity pathways.[13] In the mid-twentieth century, Washington built concrete pathways [the Eisenhower Interstate Highway System] using both economic growth and national security as the rationale. In the second half of the twentieth century, the US Department of Defense built cyber pathways—the internet. This infrastructure development was transformative for America. All involved a heavy government hand, along with partnership with the private sector to varying degrees. Each of these undertakings ignited periods of enormous growth and social change with positive consequences for US global power. And in each of these cases there were many initial apprehensions, fierce debates, and often corruption as is the case with the Pan-Asia Railway. In a sense, China and its like-minded neighbors are not carving a new path through the jungles of poverty and development theory, they are trying to follow the trail that the United States already blazed. For Washington to now argue that strategic aspects of development should be left entirely to the private sector and await more solid economic footing strikes many in Asia as not only inconsistent with East Asia's own experience but also inconsistent with America's. With respect to US rail development, William Greever recalls, "As explicit quid-pro-quos for building designated routes, railroads were *given* land amounting in the aggregate to more than 9 percent of the entire continental United States."[14]

In the 1990s, with the collapse of the Soviet Union and the Third Wave of democracies about which Samuel Huntington[15] and Francis

Fukuyama[16] powerfully wrote, developmental concerns in the United States and elsewhere in the West focused on fashioning governing institutions, systemic capacities, legal and regulatory frameworks, and institutions of interest articulation, as well as fostering transparency and accountability.[17] As Fukuyama put it in later work, "Political development has three components: the state, rule of law, and accountability."[18] Moreover, in terms of accountability, the parallel rise of the environmental and human rights movements simultaneously put a spotlight on the human costs (displacement and environmental impacts) of large-scale infrastructure projects. In turn, starting in the 1990s there were ever more demands for environmental and human impact statements as a precondition for starting big projects. While political development and impact assessments are important, economic growth needs infrastructure. The focus on political development (norms and institutions), along with the preoccupation with a range of negative externalities, had the cumulative effect of making large-scale infrastructure undertakings appear risky, politically costly, and unacceptable given the human costs.

Consequently, the resources for big infrastructure became tougher to find in the 1990s and the following decade, whether from multilateral lending institutions or the US government. Fukuyama and his colleagues had this to say about the World Bank's activities prior to 2010 when, once again, the Bank and others began to reconsider the role of infrastructure in development:

> Throughout the 1990s the [World] Bank markedly shifted away from infrastructure project lending into social sectors and further underwent an "institutional culture shift" from a focus on the "business of lending" to an institution that functions as a "knowledge bank." While there were several factors that contributed to this trend, one was clearly "excessively rigorous and demanding fiduciary and social/environmental safeguards attached to Bank Projects" which "slowed down Bank lending and increased its effective cost to borrowers. . . . By 2010 . . . the world's largest infrastructure lending institution had largely exited the business of infrastructure lending."[19]

A similar conclusion emerges if one looks at American patterns of foreign assistance. Total US government requests for various categories of foreign assistance in fiscal year 2019 reveal the priorities: the category "Economic Development" came in at a request of US$2 billion and "Democracy, Human Rights, and Governance" came in at $1.4 billion. Much larger categories in the FY 2019 request were "Peace and Security" ($7.7 billion), "Health" ($7.1 billion), and "Humanitarian Assistance" ($6.4 billion).[20] Granting that these categories each include expenditures that could be multifunctional in nature, funds devoted to economic development are relatively small, governance and environmental concerns are significant, and there is not much room for pure infrastructure projects. In contrast, through its policy banks, grants, and other mechanisms, Beijing is spending vastly more on infrastructure in the developing world than its competitors. As of 2017, Beijing was spending (pledging) $150 billion per annum on infrastructure in sixty-eight nations.[21] In FY 2018, the World Bank lent "only" $64 billion.[22] To put it crudely, where Westerners skeptically see "aid," the Chinese see "business opportunity." While China's commitments on such a scale may prove to have been (and be) unwise, unsustainable, and/or unachievable, its Belt and Road Initiative in 2013 and AIIB in 2016 signaled China's arrival on the international development stage as a real player placing emphasis on infrastructure, particularly in Asia. Beijing's emphasis on infrastructure is precipitating reassessment in the broader global development community. This is one measure of PRC impact.

Beyond development theory and practice, this book has examined many other domains, including the character of the PRC polity and policy making. We have explored the dual character of the sociopolitical system in the politics of rail development in China and abroad. This system is a unique mix of top-down and bottom-up processes, defying easy categorization. It is messy. These are subjects to which we now turn.

Chinese Politics. BRI is a big umbrella concept ("slogan," or *kouhao* in Chinese), under which PRC companies (state-owned and not), provinces,[23] and ministries all promote their pet projects, aligning their parochial priorities with "the Great Leader's" general policy thrust. These companies, provinces, and ministries fight to get their projects listed as a "BRI project" in order to gain access to cheap loans and other preferential treatment from Beijing, even if these projects are high risk and their profitability questionable.[24] This is a policy process that begins with a vague, broad central strategic direction. Then lower levels of the political and economic system fill in the specifics, deflecting all choices in the direction of their own interests—what Barry Naughton long ago labeled the "implementation bias."[25] There is indeterminacy as to where this goes—sometimes China's center embraces projects while trying to contain, redirect, or stop others. China's policy process is a distinctive mix of strategic direction and authoritarian vision combined with an extremely entrepreneurial system that keeps generating things to do— some are visionary, others unwise. There is broad vision from the top and spontaneous "jumping in" by the bottom. Once this jumping-in process proceeds for a time, then central organizations in Beijing, such as the National Development and Reform Commission (NDRC) or the Ministry of Finance, try to discern what is working and guide resources in preferred directions. One member of the Chinese think-tank community put it as follows: "[There is a] certain disorganization in BRI. Some units/programs just want to get money, so there is over-hype."[26]

The story, however, is not simply what is happening in Beijing, China's localities, and among PRC firms. There are also the demands of China's would-be and actual partners abroad. Outside observers are used to thinking of the Chinese domestic political system as hermetically sealed, impenetrable to participation or even influence by outsiders. This is not entirely accurate. As Raffaello Pantucci observes, "in many cases the countries in question are developing countries needing investment. . . . For China's neighbors, there is a natural logic in them trying to tap the Chinese economic boom . . ."[27] These potential partners turn into lobbyists in Beijing (and multilateral agencies) trying to wring as many resources out of Beijing as possible. They build alliances with Chinese ministries and firms that share their objective (making money), project by project. The dynamics among China's Guangdong Province and Guangxi Zhuang Autonomous Region and local authorities in Malaysia (e.g., Malacca and Pahang States) are emblematic of the kind of locality-to-locality initiatives designed to enmesh Beijing in the schemes and dreams of localities in China and abroad.

Moreover, the more experience Chinese firms and agencies gain on the ground in potential partner countries, and the more they establish their alliances with political and economic forces in these nations, the more they learn what kinds of projects tend to be most profitable; namely, projects having reliable revenue flows, quickly generated.[28] This is one reason that Chinese multinational SOEs emphasize hydro- and coal-fired power projects. Commercially minded firms and banks in China tend to look for reliable revenue streams, leaving the less profitable or longer-term projects, of which rail is one, to the more policy-oriented (development) banks and long-term planners. The Chinese taxpayer is subsidizing development-oriented growth abroad with more commercially minded firms looking for profit whether through market mechanisms or guaranteed government subsidies. This in turn raises a profound question for Chinese politicians: How long will Chinese taxpayers wish to subsidize the build-out of other countries when they see significant unmet needs at home? This is a great, often unarticulated, vulnerability of the Xi Jinping administration. As this book went to press, for instance, the COVID-19 virus was sickening much of China and spreading abroad. Chinese citizens were asking Beijing why the nation had inadequate public health preparedness and why hospital capacity was widely inadequate.

Beyond Chinese politics and the underlying character of the PRC system, *Rivers of Iron* explains the consequences of rolling negotiations. We have documented a cross-border process in which the outcomes of prior rounds of bargaining and implementation set the context for subsequent rounds—resulting in a blur of deals and negotiations heading in diverse directions (at times backward) without a precise destination or time of arrival.

Incremental versus Synoptic Change. The construction of regional rail connectivity between China and its southern neighbors is an incremental process. The final shape of the system is indeterminate as to precise routes, technology adopted, and configuration. Also uncertain is which global companies will build various parts of the overall system, although, in the final analysis, China is likely to be the dominant player both in terms of construction and procurement. Many planners and politicians in Southeast Asian states realize that they could gain bargaining advantage over Beijing and system coherence if they cooperate with one another and with regional organizations to present more of a united front to the PRC. Such an effort occurred in the mid-1990s and into the following decade, but the subsequent momentum behind the Chinese outward push after 2010 made an overall regional solution increasingly infeasible. Such added coordination among China's neighbors could involve regional organizations (e.g., ASEAN, the Greater Mekong Subregion, multilateral organizations such as ADB, the United Nations Development Program, or ad hoc regional groups of countries. Indeed, Thailand took the lead in working with Vietnam, Myanmar, and Laos to pool funds for more systematic, less dependent infrastructure development (as seen in chapter 5).

Laos, another example, clearly understands the benefits of looking at the HSR system in larger, regional terms. When dealing with Beijing on its own, Vientiane has been obliged to assume unfair burdens. From the Lao point of view, the Central Line must simply traverse their country to reach Bangkok and beyond. Laos is geographically central to the overall project, but its own gains might be limited. Thus, the huge financing burden may be excessive. Vientiane thinks, therefore, that others who more clearly benefit should help offset some of its disproportionate burdens. Nonetheless, despite some discussion of creating larger negotiating arenas involving more parties, for the most part this has been a bilateral process between China and each individual country. An awe-inspiring, comprehensive agreement on a total pan-Asian rail system is not likely. Incrementalism rules.[29] As one Thai professor put it, this is "a building-block-like process, not a megaproject all done at once, either in Southeast Asia or even Thailand."[30]

Again, we return to the central question that has animated this volume from the start—"What have we learned about Chinese power? Can Beijing do it?"

Does China Have the Power to Succeed? In addressing this question, we must remember a fundamental uncertainty: "Will China have continuity of leadership, will, and domestic stability?" As one Malaysian informant put it, much "depends on development in China. In twenty years, if China can sustain direction and a new emperor [in Beijing] doesn't change [policy] and not want trains, there will be a train in twenty years [in Southeast Asia]."[31] Ironically, as analysts focus on China's dynamism abroad, they run the risk of underestimating the domestic problems and weaknesses that can and will hobble Beijing to an indeterminate extent.

Nonetheless, China has considerable power to shape the contours of the region and induce cooperation among its neighbors, one by one. This power stems from the PRC's sheer heft, its growing economic and technological resources, central location, and the magnetic pull of its growing (even if slowing) domestic economy—giving it choices that its smaller neighbors do not have. *Rivers of Iron* started with a Lao transportation planner explaining that his country's choice about participating in the rail project essentially amounted to a national decision about whether or not Laos wanted to be included in the new Sino-centric economic world and become more connected to its ASEAN neighbors. If Vientiane declined, Beijing could, at least in theory, bypass Laos entirely by taking the railroad to the west through Myanmar or the east through Vietnam. In effect, Lao leaders felt obliged to decide whether their country would remain eternally isolated and poor, or not.

Although in somewhat analogous circumstances to Laos, Myanmar and Cambodia have size, geopolitical choices, and maritime options that are important and give them some maneuverability with Beijing. Vietnam has size, other geopolitical suitors (Japan and the United

States), and far greater capacity to resist Chinese blandishments than do Vientiane, Naypyitaw, and Phnom Penh. Nonetheless, despite other options and historically bad relations, even Hanoi is enticed by Beijing's overtures. When asked about whether Vietnam would participate in BRI, one senior policy official in Hanoi explained, "With respect to BRI, my attitude is that 'we have to be part of it, no choice, otherwise it goes around us.'"[32] One planner in Hanoi put Vietnam and Myanmar in the same vulnerable position as Laos: "China's ties with Laos and Cambodia may mean it can bypass Vietnam and Myanmar and connect directly with Laos and Cambodia."[33] In short, many Southeast Asian neighbors provide Beijing with the ability to say, "If you don't cooperate, we have options."

China's power comes from another source as well: until recently, China was nearly the only provider of infrastructure investment in many developing countries, particularly the poorest ASEAN members. This was in part due to notions in the Western development community, as explained previously. Very recently, there is some hint of change in this regard with Tokyo's Partnership for Quality Infrastructure initiative[34] and America's Build Act (2018) and the appropriation of limited funds for Asian infrastructure. The World Bank also is warming up to infrastructure. As one Cambodian senior ruling party (Cambodian People's Party) member put it to our research team, "We are open to any country and any bank; the railroads that we want to build can be [built] by different countries [doesn't all have to be Chinese]."[35] In the final analysis, however, China's system—fragmented and disorganized as it is in many respects—can make decisions relatively quickly. As one Vietnamese official put it: "Japan cannot order its firms to put in money [to these projects] but China can do so—can decide in a flick."[36] Washington's decision process is not fast either. As one very senior US Department of Transportation official put it in an interview (in close paraphrase), "Even in infrastructure [building in the US], everyone wants it until you try to begin to specify what actually to build. . . ." The respondent went on to say that some people want bicycle paths and others highways.[37]

Beijing's strengths notwithstanding, China's neighbors vary significantly in their capacities to resist, shape, or promote PRC initiatives. Relatively high-capacity polities such as Singapore, Thailand, and Malaysia (see chapters 4, 5, and 6) are able to effectively push back when negotiating with China, in part because they have more financing options available (including self-funding in the case of Thailand and Singapore). These states also possess more institutionalized governmental, administrative, and civic society systems constraining both the PRC and their own domestic actors. Consequently, as chapters 4 and 5 showed, in rail negotiations Thailand was able to extract somewhat favorable terms from Beijing (though not all it wanted), eschew Chinese loans, and whittle back Chinese preferences on train speed and development rights along the right-of-way. Thailand also is a more attractive site for foreign investment in general compared to Myanmar, Cambodia, or Laos and can therefore lure Japanese projects. Strategically, Tokyo wants a flow of goods and people going from west to east (to the Pacific and up to Japan); it does not prefer north-south flows making the PRC central. In order to create regional equilibrium, Thailand is considering a proposal for a Japanese-constructed HSR line (built to Japanese standards) running between Chiang Mai and Bangkok while having PRC companies build the line from Bangkok to Laos via Nong Khai. Thailand does not seem concerned that the two lines would not seamlessly connect, given their differing standards. Indeed, Bangkok seems to see this lack of connectivity to be strategically desirable.

Singapore, with its developed infrastructure, does not require Chinese financing. Instead, it has carved out a unique partnership role for itself in China's BRI. During a visit to China in July 2018, then Singapore Deputy Prime Minister Teo Chee Hean said, "As globally connected countries, Singapore and China are natural partners for the long-term development of the BRI."[38] Singapore will partner with China in four areas: infrastructure connectivity, financial connectivity, cooperation in third countries, and professional services, such as architectural, engineering, legal, and auditing services to support BRI projects.

Turning to countries with less developed political and economic systems (e.g., Cambodia, Myanmar, and Laos), these states appear more accepting of Chinese resources and plans, which at first glance would suggest PRC strength. However, within this seeming strength resides danger—when there are fewer checks and balances imposed by partners on Beijing, the PRC assumes a lead role and thereby more political and financial risk, and at times acts in ways not consistent with its own long-term interests. China can appear powerful, but this strength sometimes permits it to act in ways not in its own medium- and long-term interests. The PRC's less-developed partners frequently do not have the internal checks and balances that force prudence upon either themselves or Beijing. This means that the PRC and its agents can stumble into unstable political circumstances and risky economic ventures. For example, Beijing can end up with a 99-year lease on a very underutilized port, as happened in Sri Lanka's Hambantota Port. Similarly, Beijing can win a contract in Indonesia for a high-speed train that travels so fast it cannot make more than one stop within Jakarta's city limits.

Lastly, with reference to Beijing's political dexterity, or the absence thereof, there is always the distinctive character of the PRC's political, economic, and foreign policy systems to consider. Politically, China's center generates an idea, slogan, or opportunity, and the entire Chinese economic system and territorial hierarchy kicks into overdrive. Eventually, Beijing must try to rein in the inevitable excesses. Moreover, given China's "stovepiped," very hierarchical system, its foreign and external security policy bureaucracies often send one set of hard-line messages to neighboring governments while Beijing's economic apparatus is simultaneously trying to persuade said countries to join China in an ever closer economic embrace.

In addition, the PRC's domestic bureaucracies and internal policies also create anxieties among potential partners. For example, several Southeast Asian states—most notably Malaysia and Indonesia—have significant percentages of Muslim citizens. China's systematic crackdown on very large numbers of its own Muslim citizens in Xinjiang can create additional resistance to cooperation among some nations in Southeast Asia.[39] This behavior makes it difficult for China to reassure its neighbors. As one former Southeast Asian foreign ministry official put it:

> "The Chinese have taken the initiative and they are seeing how we are responding. ASEAN is slow to respond, either individually or together as a group, because we are not sure what China's agenda is, and the situation in the South China Sea doesn't help." Cooperation initiatives have been clouded by all these developments. Also, what has become worse is that "Chinese have reacted too strongly to what ASEAN is trying to do [in terms of connectivity]. Seems like they are spiraling out of control."[40]

In short, to the degree that China does not act reassuringly as a great power to its neighbors and others, those parties will hedge not only their security strategies, but also their embrace of connectivity with the PRC.

The question concerning how to assess Chinese power segues to twin reciprocal questions. What have we learned about the power of smaller states dealing with larger ones? Why are some states more receptive to connectivity cooperation with Beijing than are others?

China's Neighbors—Who is Strong? Who is Most Receptive to Beijing's Entreaties? What influence do China's smaller, weaker neighbors have over the outcomes of their interactions with a country the size and strength of the PRC? Do the findings of this book support the image of the Southeast Asian tail wagging the Chinese dog or instead reveal a circumstance in which China does what it may, and neighbors suffer what they must?

The general answer is that China's neighbors are not passive bystanders; they have more capacity to achieve favorable outcomes in bilateral negotiations than is often assumed. These neighbors sometimes use their strength in numbers, and they always have strength in their knowledge and understanding of local circumstances and dynamics compared with Beijing. At times, these smaller countries can also draw upon regional and global multilateral organizations for support, and they can enlist the support of distant powers to create space for their own maneuvers—if distant powers choose to play that role. When necessary, small countries on the PRC's periphery can drag their feet. As one foreign diplomat in Laos explained to our research team: "In the future [with respect to HSR], if the Lao are unhappy they have ways to throw sand in the gears of the whole operation in ways to get the Chinese to reduce cost—passive aggression is the style here in Laos." The Lao view is, "The Chinese will do what the Chinese do, and we need a railroad."[41] In speaking of the Laotian style, another senior foreign diplomat observed, "They can slow things down very effectively."[42]

Perhaps the single most important piece of evidence concerning the capacity of China's southern neighbors to shape outcomes has been the transformation of Beijing's initial vision of regional railroad development in the course of negotiations. In 2013 and shortly thereafter, Beijing came to the table with a vision that built upon, but far exceeded, the preexistent colonial, postcolonial, and regional multilateral organizations' visions of rail connectivity between China and its Southeast Asian neighbors. Beijing's initial vision was for genuine high-speed rail lines [250 kmph and up] along three routes, running from Kunming to Singapore. In effect, it would be a southern, international extension of China's domestic HSR system. Currently, however, little of what is under construction, nor what may be built in the medium-term future, will be truly high speed.[43] As one very senior Vietnamese economic adviser put it: "Yes the (HSR) train would be too fast, no freight, too costly. . . . We need a train in the range of one hundred sixty to two hundred kilometers per hour, with some freight, not just passengers."[44] Moreover, it is not preordained that all projects will be Chinese-built; Southeast Asian states (e.g., Thailand) have sought and may seek in the future to balance their dependencies, as long as the outside powers (e.g.,

Japan and the United States) are willing to be actively involved. Finally, not all projects will go forward. Some deals will collapse. Others will be renegotiated along the way (e.g., Malaysia). Many times Beijing will simply have to "eat bitterness" and do the best it can under competitive and difficult circumstances, at times facing criticism at home for devoting resources abroad rather than meeting the needs of China's own people. Also, to improve its odds at winning bids, China shows a willingness to join with other foreign firms in consortia.

One of the important contributions of this study is the systematic and comparative examination of why some of China's neighbors are more receptive to Beijing's blandishments than are others (see chapter 4). Three types of state attributes help differentiate the various degrees of receptivity to China's connectivity push. One dimension of differentiation is how each state legitimizes itself: What is the national narrative and set of objectives that each nation's elite promotes to legitimize its right to rule in the eyes of its own people?[45] These narratives run along a spectrum from an identity-based "security-autonomy" legitimating rationale, to a development-based "economic performance" narrative. A second spectrum of state attributes concerns where the state and its political and social institutions fall on the "authoritarian/centralized" to "pluralized/decentralized" spectrum. It often is easier to reach a definitive outcome with a centralized and authoritarian state than a pluralized and decentralized polity. The final set of attributes concerns economic and human resources, from "bountiful" to "impoverished." States with higher incomes and more resources have more choices than those that do not. Singapore has great capacity to choose; Laos does not.

Taking into consideration these admittedly simplified continua, and accepting the fact that all states fall into an imprecise mix across them, the "hardest" state for China to negotiate with (theoretically and practically) has been Vietnam. China's envisioned set of rail connectivity projects in Vietnam have made little discernible progress, except for the problem-plagued Hanoi light rail system.[46] Vietnam is authoritarian and has a tight central negotiating group. Hanoi legitimizes itself in terms of nationalistic and security consciousness born of its turbulent and often unhappy history with China (particularly in the post-1949 period), and its resources, while not abundant, allow it to go its own way if necessary. Moreover, other powers (e.g., Japan and the United States) find their strategic interests aligned with Hanoi in the Xi Jinping era. These outside powers can provide Hanoi with strategic and development alternatives they would not provide to smaller, less strategically located states.

Laos—the other extreme of capacity to resist Beijing's entreaties—is a country with legitimation primarily by economic growth. The Lao PDR elite seeks domestic support by producing growth and reducing isolation, not by adopting a more assertive posture of assuring autonomy at all costs with respect to its neighbors. Vientiane has very few deployable economic and human resources, or strategic alternatives to dependence on the PRC, though Vientiane does try to balance between Hanoi and Beijing to give itself some minimal maneuverability. Moreover, Laos's authoritarian government gives it the ability to make decisions, free of many constraints that a more pluralized and differentiated society would impose. It is, therefore, unsurprising that China has been able to advance fastest in its rail efforts in the Lao PDR, and has had far less success in Vietnam. Interestingly, both Laos and Vietnam border China directly, so proximity to the PRC does not necessarily mean plasticity in the face of Beijing's demands. It is instructive that the two communist regimes in Southeast Asia involved in this vision represent the two ends of the cooperation continuum with Beijing—ideology is not everything.

In the middle range in terms of presenting negotiating challenges to Beijing are Thailand and Malaysia. Thailand has a mixed legitimating rationale: development and autonomy/security are proportionately balanced. Moreover, Thailand has resources that permit it to choose among financing strategies and alternative terms. Additionally, Thai society and the Thai elite do not generally perceive Beijing as a serious security threat and, hence, reasonable interdependence with Beijing is not overly controversial, though the farther north you go in Thailand the more guarded attitudes become. Finally, while Thailand is an increasingly pluralized society, its military government can impose a solution as we have seen in its invocation of Constitutional Article 44 to kick-start phase one of the rail line from Bangkok to Nong Khai. Also falling into the midrange, Malaysia is a mixed case somewhat similar to Thailand, but its vibrant electoral system means that electorally imposed government change can produce dramatic policy change. The May 2018 election of Mahathir as prime minister and his immediate call to renegotiate two large rail projects with which Beijing is involved or highly interested is emblematic.

Finally, this then, brings the story to the last question: Once an arrangement has been reached, what are the kinds of problems encountered in moving from plan to realizing actual projects on the ground?

CROSS-BORDER POLICY IMPLEMENTATION
CHALLENGES

The challenges of implementation across national boundaries stem from the intrinsic challenge of "the complexity of joint action" and the fact that no two countries in which China works teach it the same lessons. Circumstances within and among countries keep changing. Sometimes these changes are abrupt and unanticipated. This is even before the geographic, engineering, and economic challenges confronting all such massive and protracted projects are considered. As societies develop and become increasingly urbanized, specialized, and globally connected, they inevitably pluralize, with new groups seeking to express their diverse interests and values. Speaking of his own society, one Thai academic explained, "As we get more democratic, it gets harder to do deals, it is harder to deal with domestic politics and foreign policy."[47]

The projects we examined in earlier chapters amply demonstrate that massive projects often requiring decades of negotiating and construction efforts are destined to encounter unsettling domestic changes along the way in the partner country, in China itself, or both. Projects requiring long completion times must try to maintain a continuity of domestic support and leadership attention, even as both domestic and foreign conditions continually fluctuate. The case of Malaysia suddenly stopping rail projects and seeking renegotiation with Beijing in mid-2018 is just one conspicuous example of what can happen. Myanmar's abrupt movement to distance itself from the PRC and move toward the United States in 2011 is another example, as is its later limited rapprochement with the PRC.[48] Part of Myanmar's move away from China in the 2011 period was a result of controversy over a massive PRC-sponsored water project (the Myitsone Dam). The PRC had already invested substantial money that Beijing may well seek to recoup from Myanmar's government to the tune of possibly $800 million.[49] To avoid this, Myanmar and China are looking for substitute projects. In October 2018, the two sides signed a memorandum of understanding to examine the feasibility of a railroad linking Muse on the border with China to Mandalay.[50] The link from Kunming to the Myanmar border has been under construction since 2015 and is scheduled to be completed in 2020. The point is, international politics, negotiation, and implementation are a rolling game, often with no clearly defined endpoint.

Chapter 6 dealt at length with the multitude of specific problems encountered in the implementation phase of the several rail projects under discussion in *Rivers of Iron*. Just one example will serve here to illustrate the kinds of implementation challenges faced, in this case by the China Railway No. 6 Bureau Group Company's greatly delayed construction of the Cat Linh–Ha Dong Railway project in Vietnam. The project started in 2011; it was originally scheduled to be completed by 2013, but was delayed until December 2019. A Vietnam Institute for Economic and Policy Research (VEPR) analysis of the implementation process on this rail line gives us insight into the kinds of problems encountered, in this case ongoing safety issues during construction. Year upon year, the Chinese company made no progress in project accident reduction. The report concluded in 2014, "No improvement made"; in 2015, "Follow-up actions have not been known to the public"; and in 2016, "No progress, no systematic changes made."[51]

What calls for more explanation here is why, despite the myriad problems encountered in this array of undertakings, there has been as much progress on rail connectivity development as there has. Variable degrees of construction are underway (as of 2020) in Indonesia, Laos, Malaysia, and Thailand, and there is a reasonable prospect that Malaysia and Singapore will move forward with the KL-Singapore HSR in the not-too-distant future. Among the reasons for this forward movement are the following.

To start, in each case where there has been forward movement, there are national leaders in both China and its partner countries who generally subscribe to the theory that infrastructure construction must precede growth. Second, we find national leaders (President Jokowi in Jakarta, Prime Minister Prayut in Bangkok, Prime Minister Najib [and Mahathir] in Kuala Lumpur, and certainly Xi Jinping in Beijing) who have sought to anchor regime legitimacy in economic growth and development, joining regional and global value chains, and infrastructure development. Third, to be successful, below the supreme leader level there must be an energetic bureaucratic champion fighting the day-to-day skirmishes in order to keep things moving forward. As one Thai transportation researcher put it, "Organization is important, you need a champion. 'If no proper, regular institutions, things can be stalled easily.'"[52] Former Chinese Minister of Railways Liu Zhijun is almost a caricature of a champion. Without his "damn the torpedoes" leadership style, it is almost certain China would not have the domestic HSR network and domestic industry that it today possesses.

Lastly, in all cases of forward movement, China has been willing to scale back its initial hopes, expectations, and demands, whether they be interest rates and financing terms, travel speeds in different segments of the overall system, level of technology sold, right-of-way width, accompanying development concessions, or the project construction timetable, to name a few examples. Of course, Beijing's ability to sustain these outlays and remain adaptable depends on the ability of the Chinese economy to underwrite flexibility, the continued willingness of the Chinese people to defer the satisfaction of many domestic needs and wants, and sustained leader commitment at the top. It is quite possible that China's people will one day awake and reject such vigorous external involvement when there is so much to do at home, or its workers may fall prey to domestic instability elsewhere, or Chinese assets may simply be expropriated. Future leaders also may choose to focus on other dreams.

Two important studies presented at an ADB workshop in 2018, one by VEPR[53] and the other by China's Center for International Knowledge on Development, part of the Development and Reform Commission,[54] highlight the core implementation problems encountered to date for such projects. Key challenges have been poor governance (lack of legal institutionalization) in project countries, financing, economic viability, continual policy change, transparency of information, environmental externalities, engagement with local communities, and security threats.

STRATEGIC CONSEQUENCES FOR ALL PLAYERS

Growth in China has ignited strategically significant economic and security competition in Asia (see chapter 7) and beyond in two ways. To start, the PRC's increasing economic wherewithal and rising per capita income creates new Chinese capabilities of all kinds (economic, coercive, and intellectual/diplomatic); it incubates new ambitions and creates new interests to protect. These developments excite economic and security competition in the region and beyond. Second, as China's own domestic economy slows, the PRC must move up the value chain, export excess domestic production, and secure reliable resource flows. These needs, in turn, drive China's urge to connect to its growing periphery.

With respect to China's neighbors, they are highly ambivalent about interdependence, because it can easily morph into dependence. China's neighbors are anxious to reap the economic rewards of growing closer to the PRC and simultaneously anxious about Beijing's smothering embrace. As to bigger powers at greater distance (Japan, the United States, the EU, and others), they see the trend toward connectivity, perceive its advantages and its inevitability, and nonetheless are unreconciled to it. To them, these developments look like an emerging PRC sphere of influence from which they fear exclusion or, worse yet, an economic juggernaut that inevitably will encroach on their home turf.[55] They want to participate in the development of Southeast Asia but are unsure how to do so, also fearing that their resources are insufficient or better spent elsewhere.

Neither China's neighbors nor the big powers can escape the need to respond both economically and in traditional security terms. What are the issues and what is the nature of the gathering response? This study of China's push for rail connectivity offers insight into these much larger questions. As chapter 7 emphasizes, we are moving from a multidecade period in which geoeconomics was the ascendant preoccupation to one in which geopolitics and security, big power rivalry, are increasingly important drivers of state behavior.

China's broad concept of infrastructure as a driver for growth, and its creation of the AIIB and other organizations to help implement this vision abroad (as well as cooperating with the international multilaterals such as the World Bank and the ADB), have motivated others to reassess their allergies to infrastructure. In the case of the United States, Washington has positioned its newfound commitment to infrastructure as, in part, a reaction to China's BRI, and what the Trump administration has come to call "debt-trap diplomacy."[56] On October 4, 2018, in a major speech on China policy, US Vice President Mike Pence said, "China uses so-called 'debt diplomacy' to expand its influence. Today, that country is offering hundreds of billions of dollars in infrastructure loans to governments from Asia to Africa to Europe to even Latin America. Yet the terms of those loans are opaque at best, and the benefits flow overwhelmingly to Beijing." In 2018, Washington tried to up its game by allocating "$113 million in technology, energy, and infrastructure in emerging Asia."[57]

There is still a long way to go, but the US government now sees merit in cooperating with other transportation and infrastructure actors to emphasize what the authors call "balanced connectivity." Balanced connectivity is north-south connectivity (oriented toward China) complemented by east-west connectivity (oriented toward the area from India to Vietnam). This drive toward balanced connectivity could help provide some substance to the broader Indo-Pacific strategy to which Washington and its allies have been increasingly committing themselves. A balanced connectivity approach fosters diversified growth and is consistent with the PRC's overriding notion that when its neighbors prosper, it also prospers.

Most of China's neighbors to the south also would welcome an injection of infrastructure balance into the geopolitical equation. As one very senior policy adviser in Vietnam put it to one of our team, "We would prefer the US, Japan, the ROK, and other Westerners get involved in helping us build infrastructure so we are not reliant on China."[58] This preference for a diversity of sources for infrastructure investment in the region comes from more than just Vietnam. Even countries more closely identified with Beijing (Myanmar,[59] Cambodia, and Laos) have a similar desire not to be vassals of the PRC. However, they often find the West, particularly the United States, reluctant to engage with them due to human rights and political system considerations, limited economic interest among American firms, a sense that these states already are firmly in the Chinese "camp," and long-running strategic commitments in the Middle East and Central Asia. Not least, many Americans would ask themselves why help build railroads in Laos when getting between New York and Washington by rail is often an exercise in frustration.

It is not simply the smaller governments to China's south that are attracted to the notion of "balanced connectivity," private firms throughout Southeast Asia would also welcome not being overly dependent upon the PRC. One major multinational firm in the region expressed the idea as follows:

> "The private [sector] and ASEAN would like dialogue with Trump on private business here. We should go to the White House and take it up with Trump, on this topic, to invite the US to participate in development. . . . This is an opportunity for the US to respond and to not have China dominate everything." . . . "You need to balance this." If the Americans started to get interested in ASEAN, 600 million people, "China would have a reaction and it would help rebalance." . . . The east-west corridor—Japanese would love this. "ADB proposed it long ago. Western-oriented ADB. Only China wanted AIIB. . . . In the old times there was only China. Now, we don't want to go back to the old times."[60]

The political ecology of China's periphery, particularly Southeast Asia, is an interlocking and competitive set of small and medium powers, each of which has one eye cast warily on China and the other fixed on its neighbors, all the while looking out of the corner of both eyes at more distant big powers. It is easy for outside observers to see a uniformity of interest among China's neighbors with respect to the PRC without fully appreciating how competitive China's Southeast Asian neighbors are among themselves. There is hedging by China's neighbors directed at Beijing-related risks, as well as hedging by all of China's neighbors directed at one another and wider regional uncertainties. The Vietnamese want to preserve a dominant position in mainland Southeast Asia to the degree they can, and Cambodia sees both Thailand and Vietnam as security problems for which Phnom Penh sometimes turns to Beijing to achieve local balance. China can take advantage of this mutual distrust and intraregional competition among its neighbors. One Vietnamese strategist said:

> Vietnam will be affected negatively, because if China is directly connected to Laos and Cambodia, "Vietnam's role as the bridge between China and ASEAN will be diminished." . . . Vietnam's role was important, but with this increased connection between China and Laos and Cambodia, Vietnam's role as bridge has decreased. "An increase in China's connectivity weakens Vietnam's role."[61]

When our research team was in Cambodia, it was striking the degree to which Phnom Penh viewed Bangkok and Hanoi as security and sovereignty challenges and sought a PRC presence in key strategic locations to assuage their anxieties. Phnom Penh's foreign policy strategy and the degree to which it sides with China in regional affairs is energized by the perceived need to secure Cambodia's borders against its historical enemies, Thailand and Vietnam.

Strategic Economic Competition. HSR and conventional-speed rail provide a clear panoramic window on cooperation and competition, indeed conflict, between China, its neighbors, and the United States. Industrial policy is one such area of contention; the setting of global standards is another.[62] If Beijing wins the early contracts in a protracted construction competition, subsequent projects will have to bend toward Chinese standards. Chinese intellectual property and designs will then be compensated, giving rise to long-term revenue streams, as explained earlier. Moreover, successful early projects increase the likelihood that the Chinese will prevail in later competitions for contracts. Inversely, if prior Chinese projects are problem-plagued, possible future clients will seek alternative suppliers. PRC project implementation, thus far, has not been uniformly smooth, and potential clients in Southeast Asia would like to diversify (e.g., Thailand). The Japanese are one option, but their high-cost, turnkey approach to construction and longer construction times work against Tokyo. An additional consideration is the PRC's relatively liberal funding approach, though Japan is trying to become more competitive by, for instance, not always requiring sovereign guarantees to obtain Japanese financing.

The PRC has built a globally competitive, transformative domestic and export HSR industry in less than twenty years. This competitive global industry has emerged from literally nothing at the turn of the millennium. These days, for example, European rail competitors feel they must promote mergers and acquisitions among their own firms in order to compete with Beijing (e.g., Alstom in France and Siemens in Germany in 2019 were seeking to merge rail assets).[63] For its part, Beijing has learned many lessons from its feat of building a competitive industry from the ground up rapidly, and those lessons are inconsistent with the more *laissez-faire* approach that industrial competitors in the West claim they support in principle, though sometimes ignore in practice.

In telling its HSR story, the PRC sees the coordinated action of banks, research institutes, national champion firms, and intelligence collection organizations in pursuit of moving up valued-added production chains as essential and successful. Beijing also believes that America's own development experience was successful precisely because at key points the US government (often mobilizing the private sector) drove the construction of critical infrastructure, went to space, and developed the internet. Washington's calls now for a relatively hands-off approach to the government's role in the economy strike many objective observers as unreflective of America's own experience.

More recently, the combination of the Asian financial crisis (1997–98) and the global financial crisis (2008–9) taught Beijing (at least under Xi Jinping) that unfettered markets and hands-off government are formulae for volatility, instability, and on occasion dangerous breakdown. Beijing underscores that its own robust government intervention early in these crises produced at least short- and medium-term stability (albeit at the cost of worrisome long-term debt accumulation, inefficient use of capital, and dramatically declining return on investment in state firms during 2006–16).[64] In short, Beijing is unlikely to comply when Washington makes curtailing Chinese industrial policy programs such as "Made in China 2025" the basis for deescalating trade tensions. At the end of the second decade of the twenty-first century, this fundamental divergence over the role of government in the economy has provided fertile soil in the United States (and other large Western economies) for an emerging set of policies targeting China as a formidable and unfair economic competitor. China is seen as engaging in credit policies that create permanent and unfair dependencies that work to the disadvantage of nations that receive what seems to be largesse from the PRC. US Secretary of State Mike Pompeo said in late 2018, "We're very worried that China will put the people in many countries around the world . . . in a debt trap that will cause those countries decades of pain."[65] This ascendant view is deeply embedded not only in the Trump administration's strategic outlook, but many parts of the Democratic and Republican Parties as well, and expressed by a former very high-ranking Trump administration official, who said,

> "China is not a trusted partner economically. Better off not doing business with China. Move the [production] chains out of China, and not dependence [that] we should not encourage. It is foolish to think that they [who do business with the PRC] will get anything but fleeced by China."[66]

As of 2019, US trade, tariff, technology transfer, and educational exchange policies all increasingly reflected this analysis. Sino-American economic competition is morphing into strategic (military) rivalry, and this rivalry (some say "competition") metastasizes into economic policies, reinforcing tendencies toward closure and national security limitations on market transactions.[67] A perfect example is legislation working its way through the congressional process in the US Capitol in spring 2019, aimed at denying federal funding to the cash-strapped DC Metro system if it buys next-generation rolling stock from the China Railway Rolling Stock Corporation which, incidentally, has production facilities in several US locations. The motivation behind this move is a combination of security anxieties (China's electronic access to the rail and other systems), opposition to Beijing's subsidies of SOEs, and old-fashioned protectionism by US steel, manufacturing, and other interests.[68] Predictably, as Washington seeks to play a more intrusive role in the name of opposing China's industrial policy by invoking national security rationales, it adopts economic policies that echo those Beijing promotes—closure and control. The core issue is, therefore, will previously open economic systems adopt measures that make them similar to what they profess to oppose?

Talk of "decoupling" from the Chinese economy is a topic of more than idle conversation in the United States as China is promoting connectivity. Over the long haul it is doubtful that decoupling can work, or that America's allies and friends in Europe, Japan, Southeast Asia, and elsewhere would follow such a lead. Connectivity is the wave of the future, and in all probability progress toward connectivity will continue along a bumpy path. However, security and economic concerns among the big powers and among the countries throughout Asia will shape the process, making the resulting systems less efficient or compatible with one another than would be the case under more favorable conditions. A prime example of what is happening is the consideration by the US government of disapproving, for security reasons, an undersea communications cable from Los Angeles to Hong Kong that is already under construction. Similarly, efforts are underway by Washington to persuade allies not to procure from or provide to PRC firms high-tech electronic components and 5G telecommunication systems.

The Security Dimensions of Strategic Competition. This unfolding big power contest has implications for China's Southeast Asian neighbors that have been the focus of the HSR story told here. All China's Southeast Asian neighbors, including Vietnam, accept the inevitability of meaningful connectivity with the PRC and others. They cannot imagine a successful economic or security future that lies in trying to disconnect from the PRC. Nonetheless, each nation in Southeast Asia has security and economic anxieties regarding the PRC, particularly the maritime nations. One very senior Southeast Asian former minister, who has held several relevant portfolios germane to these points, candidly described their dilemma and concerns as follows:

> The US is worried about geostrategic implications. In ASEAN we do not want to be the theater of power rivalry. However, it is already happening. "We are getting sucked into strategic rivalry." The Chinese are playing for world leadership, in part because of Trump. We don't want problems like those we saw with Chinese investment in Africa. Not good. Here in Southeast Asia, China is building features in South China Sea. US Freedom of Navigation operations did not stop them.[69]

These nations are right to have concerns. As discussed in chapter 3, there is a debate in the PRC between "continentalists," who see China's future principally in terms of consolidating Beijing's land position in Asia, and the advocates of maritime power, who tend to look east and southeast. Of note here is that Southeast Asia is important to *both* groups. Strategically, Southeast Asia's waterways and ports are key to the maritime group for reasons of economic flows, energy lifelines, and the protection of China's major cities along the coast, where the bulk of the PRC's GDP is produced. For the continentalists, Southeast Asia is a region of high current and future economic growth, a place where the PRC will construct value chains, and the area provides the land transport routes that reduce risks from the Malacca Straits bottleneck. The region's valuable ports stretch from Haiphong-Hanoi, through Ho Chi Minh City, to Cambodia's Sihanoukville and Koh Kong, to Thailand's Bangkok, to Peninsular Malaysia's western ports such as Klang and Tanjung Pelepas and its eastern port Kuantan, on to Thailand's westward harbors, and farther on to the coast of Myanmar on the Andaman Sea at the margins of the Indian Ocean. Southeast Asia cannot escape either the problems or the opportunities that its own centrality presents. Land connectivity, of which rail is a key part, is central to both of the predominant schools of strategic thinking in China—the continentalist and the maritime interests. These forces represent both opportunities and dangers to China's neighbors and to the big powers further afield.

PITFALLS AND PROMISE

The vision of increasing rail connectivity between China and much of continental Southeast Asia is taking shape. This development will be transformative—boosting China's global position and rippling across global economic and strategic systems. One of the most thoughtful of our many informants in China and Southeast Asia made a remark that sets the whole question of connectivity and high-speed rail development in a broad, global context:

> We need to look at the world differently. Whether we like it or not, we have no choice, we have to be connected. Maybe the multipolar system is better than the unipolar system; multipolar for checks and balances in the international community. "Morgenthau, balance of power." The cost of conflict is too great. Sixty million refugees around the world and the world cannot deal with it. Too much money spent on potential war and conflict. The money should have been spent on something else. "Immigrants, conflict—we have to invest in staying put."[70]

Indeed, perhaps more efficient transport and easier interaction can provide people everywhere the benefits of interaction with other places without having to relocate permanently.

In the future, what is to be the relative weight of America and China in Asia? China's power and presence will continue to grow. Will America's continue to wane? Or, instead, will the United States remain involved? How? And to what effect? One Vietnamese official summed up the conundrum. "We have a dilemma. We didn't like the US as world policeman, but what do we do without it?"[71]

The next two decades of trying to realize the interconnectivity that is the subject of this book will not be easy for China, for its partner countries, nor for other powers. When asked about Beijing's global infrastructure initiative, one of China's most influential financial regulators said in a speech in Washington, DC:

Full of challenges and risks: political risks—bombs, bombs; . . . Part of life; inflation; economic risks; market risks, Forex risks, can wipe out your profit, erase it to nothing; lack of financing support. Lack of professionals who have knowledge of best practices and the local business environment. You cannot sit in Beijing and talk. Even the holidays are different. You must check information and do research. You need to think about Google accessibility.[72]

While connectivity is good in theory, not all of the projects initiated under the BRI signboard are economically sound or desirable. China has not yet proven to be patient or discriminating. Nor has the PRC proven able to cooperate easily with others. Can China proceed prudently? Can the government learn? Will China invite cooperation in creating balanced connectivity, and will others accept the invitation? At the same time, the West underestimates current progress and future possibilities at its own peril. The basic lesson of the last fifty years of China's change is that the outside world underestimated it, along multiple dimensions. There may not be a "China model," but there is a "China approach" that marries strategic direction, relentless entrepreneurialism and opportunism, a willingness to work with nations as Beijing finds them (not as it wishes them), and a capacity to focus resources. This approach is not to be underestimated. Sitting back and waiting for China to fail is neither productive nor wise. The train is leaving the station.

Notes

PREFACE: SETTING THE STAGE

1. Cary Huang, "How Lee Kuan Yew Crafted Singapore into a Role Model for China," *South China Morning Post,* March 24, 2015, www.scmp.com/news /china/article/1746072/how-lee-kwan-yew-crafted-singapore-role-model-china.

2. Federal Reserve Bank of St. Louis, https://fred.stlouisfed.org/tags/series?t =china%3Bgdp%3Bworld+bank.

3. See Nadege Rolland, "A Concise Guide to the Belt and Road Initiative," The National Bureau of Asian Research, April 11, 2019, www.nbr.org /publication/a-guide-to-the-belt-and-road-initiative/; see also Thomas P. Cavanna, "Unlocking the Gates of Eurasia: China's Belt and Road Initiative and Its Implications for U.S. Grand Strategy," *Texas National Security Review* 2, no. 3 (July 2019), https://tnsr.org/2019/07/unlocking-the-gates-of-eurasia-chinas-belt-and-road-initiative-and-its-implications-for-u-s-grand-strategy/.

4. Xi Jinping, "New Approach for Asian Security Cooperation" (speech, Fourth Summit of the Conference on Interaction and Confidence-Building Measures in Asia, Shanghai, May 21, 2014) in Xi Jinping, *The Governance of China* (Beijing: Foreign Languages Press, 2014), 392.

5. See Rolland, "Concise Guide."

6. Zhang Ye, "Chinese Firms to Make $120bn-$130bn Investment Annually in Next Five Years," *People's Daily Net,* from *Global Times,* May 12, 2017, accessed September 30, 2019, http://en.people.cn/n3/2017/0512/c90000-9214616.html.

7. Nikki Sun, "China Development Bank Commits $250bn to Belt and Road," January 15, 2018, https://asia.nikkei.com/Politics-Economy/Economy /China-Development-Bank-commits-250bn-to-Belt-and-Road.

8. McKinsey has estimated that globally $57 trillion may be required for infrastructure between 2013 and 2030. See "Infrastructure Productivity: How

to Save $1 trillion a Year," McKinsey Global Institute, January 2013, cited in Cavanna, "Unlocking the Gates."

9. Enda Curran and Karl Lester M Yap, "ADB Says Emerging Asia Infrastructure Needs $26 Trillion by 2030," Bloomberg News, February 27, 2017, www.bloomberg.com/news/articles/2017–02–28/adb-says-emerging-asia-infrastructure-needs-26-trillion-by-2030-izouvxn8.

CHAPTER ONE. CHINESE POWER IS AS CHINESE POWER DOES

1. Phouphet Kyophilavong, "Laos' Response to Chinese Belt and Road Initiative," in *Asymmetry and Authority: ASEAN States' Responses to China's Belt and Road Initiative*, program document, UKM-QMUL Workshop 2, February 10–11, 2018, Le Meridien, Kuala Lumpur, Malaysia, 16; James Kynge, Michael Peel, and Ben Bland, "China's railway diplomacy hits buffers," *Financial Times*, July 17, 2017, www.ft.com/content/9a4aab54–624d-11e7–8814–0ac7eb84e5f1; "China-Laos Railway to Complete 90 pct Bridge, Tunnel Construction in 2019," Xinhua, February 14, 2019, www.xinhuanet.com/english/2019–02/14/c_137820833.htm.

2. Lao government official, interview by David M. Lampton, Selina Ho, and Cheng-Chwee Kuik, Vientiane, Laos, June 6, 2017.

3. Senior Lao official, interview by David M. Lampton, Selina Ho, and Cheng-Chwee Kuik, June 7, 2017. In the authors' field notes, close paraphrase is without quotation marks and exact quotes are in quotation marks.

4. Note that in this book we use the vocabulary of high-speed railway or HSR variably in its strict and its more lax meanings. Its strict meaning is a rail line in which the trains move at 250 km per hour and up. The more lax definition is 120 kmph, in recognition of the fact that these trains are high speed compared to what preceded them.

5. "Xi Wraps Up State Visit to Laos and Strengthened Partnership," Xinhua, www.xinhuanet.com/english/2017–11/14/c_136752151.htm.

6. Gordon H. Chang, *Ghosts of Gold Mountain: The Epic Story of the Chinese Who Built the Transcontinental Railroad* (Boston: Houghton Mifflin Harcourt, 2019).

7. John Pomfret, *The Beautiful Country and the Middle Kingdom: America and China, 1776 to the Present* (New York: Henry Holt and Company, 2016), 71–72; see also Roland De Wolk, *American Disruptor: The Scandalous Life of Leland Stanford* (Oakland: University of California Press, 2019).

8. Stephen E. Ambrose, *Nothing Like It in the World* (New York: Touchstone, 2000), 382. For a somewhat more iconoclastic view of the transcontinental effort in the United States, see Richard White, *Railroaded: The Transcontinentals and the Making of Modern America* (New York: W. W. Norton, 2011).

9. See Chu Daye, "Blueprint will boost links with neighbors," *Global Times*, July 20, 2016, www.globaltimes.cn/content/995497.shtml; Luo Wangshu, "Rail System to Grow by 4,000 km in 2018," *China Daily*, January 3, 2018. Other Chinese sources claimed the plan was to have 30,000 km of high-speed rail line by 2020 and 38,000 km by 2025. Frank Tang, "Full Speed Ahead for China's Fast Rail Network with US$112 Billion Investment," *South China Morning Post*,

January 3, 2018, www.scmp.com/news/china/economy/article/2126548/full-speed-ahead-chinas-fast-rail-network-us112-billion; see also Luo Wangshu, "China's High-Speed Railway Length to Top 30,000 in 2019," Xinhua, January 3, 2019, www.xinhuanet.com/english/2019–02/14/c_137820833.htm.

10. "Laos-China Railway Project 16% Complete," *The Laotian Times,* January 9, 2018, https://laotiantimes.com/2018/01/09/laos-china-railway-project-16-complete/.

11. "China-Thailand High-Speed Railway to Be Operational in Early 2023: Thai Minister," Xinhua, December 23, 2017, www.xinhuanet.com/english/2017–12/23/c_136847439.htm.

12. "Laos to Join High-Speed Rail Talks," *Bangkok Post,* February 11, 2018, www.bangkokpost.com/news/transport/1410474/laos-to-join-high.

13. "Thai-Chinese Rail Project Falls in Price," *Bangkok Post*, March 23, 2018, www.bangkokpost.com/news/general/1433350/thai-chinese-rail-p. See also "China-Thailand High-Speed Railway in Early 2023: Thai Minister," Xinhua, December 23, 2017, www.chinadaily.com.cn/a/201712/23/WS5a3e13f0a31008cf16da313a.html. Within this overall plan, there are subschedules for each phase of the construction.

14. "Malaysia, Singapore Sign Agreement to Defer Construction of High Speed Rail to 2020," Xinhua, September 5, 2018, www.xinhuanet.com/english/2018–09/05/c_137447028.htm.

15. Royce Tan, "Liow: Thailand Keen to Hold Talks on KL-Bangkok HSR Link," *The Star,* October 17, 2017, www.thestar.com.my/news/nation/2017/10/17/liow-on-high-speed-rail/. Earlier, in February 2017, Thai Transport Minister Arkhom Termpittayapaisith said Thailand and Malaysia "are set to begin talks" on the HSR project, adding that they "will discuss how to get foreign countries in the project, with China and Japan mooted as possible partners." See "Thailand, Malaysia to Begin Talks on HSR Linking Bangkok and Kuala Lumpur: Thai Minister," Today Online, February 8, 2017, www.todayonline.com/world/asia/thailand-malaysia-begin-talks-hsr-linking-bangkok-and-kuala-lumpur-thai-minister.

16. Both of these statistics come from Worldometers, www.worldometers.info/world-population/population-by-country/.

17. World Bank, "GDP growth (annual %) Data," accessed February 14, 2018, https://data.worldbank.org/indicator/NYGDP.MKTP.KD.ZG. While this indicator is no longer available, the website suggests a different way to get the information.

18. HRH Sultan Nazrin Shah, "ASEAN and Asia Pacific: Peace and Prosperity," speech delivered at the ASEAN-Australia Dialogue (unpublished manuscript, March 13, 2018).

19. "Countries Compared by Geography: Land Area, Square Miles: Countries," www.nationmaster.com/country-info/stats/Geography/Area/Land.

20. Nielsen, *ASEAN 2015: Seeing Around the Corner in a New Asian Landscape*, 2014, www.nielsen.com/content/dam/nielsenglobal/apac/docs/reports/2014/Nielsen-ASEAN2015.pdf.

21. Exhibit 3 in Imanol Arbulu, Vivek Lath, Matteo Mancini, Alpesh Patel, and Oliver Tonby, *Industry 4.0 Reinvigorating ASEAN Manufacturing for the Future,*

McKinsey, Digital Capability Center Singapore, 2017, https://www.mckinsey
.com/~/media/mckinsey/business%20functions/operations/our%20insights/indus-
try%204%200%20reinvigorating%20asean%20manufacturing%20for%20
the%20future/industry-4–0-reinvigorating-asean-manufacturing-for-the-future
.ashx, 10; see also "The Future of Factory Asia: A Tightening Grip," *The Economist*,March 12,2015,https://www.economist.com/briefing/2015/03/12/a-tightening-
grip.

22. Hu Angang, "From Secondary Industry to Tertiary Industry: China's
Economic Transition," in Hu Angang, *English Articles* (Beijing: Institute for
Contemporary China Studies, Tsinghua University, March 2017), 73–74.

23. "Future of Factory Asia."

24. Aaron Back, "Trade Feud Has Surprise Winners," *Wall Street Journal*,
December 14, 2018.

25. Francis Fukuyama, *State Building: Governance and World Order in the
Twenty-First Century* (Ithaca, NY: Cornell University Press, 2004).

26. Francis Fukuyama, Michael Bennon, and Bushra Bataineh, "Chinese and
Western Approaches to Infrastructure Development," working paper, February
2019.

27. Ministry of Foreign Affairs, Japan, *Partnership for Quality Infrastructure*, circa 2015, www.mofa.go.jp/files/000117998.pdf.

28. Looking at the 1,814 BRI projects underway around the world as of
2018, about 32 percent (by value) were categorized by RWR Advisory Group
as "troubled." This, of course, implies that many projects were either not troubled or successful. James Kynge, "China's Belt and Road Project Drives Overseas Debt Fears," *Financial Times,* August 8, 2018.

29. National People's Congress, "The Report on the Work of the Government," Key Points, March 5, 2018, 2. See Chris Buckley and Keith Bradsher,
"China's Leaders Meet, and See 'Critical Battles' on Economy and Pollution,"
New York Times, March 4, 2018, www.nytimes.com/2018/03/04/world/asia
/chinas-leaders-meet-xi-jinping.html.

30. Guojia Fazhan Gaigewei, Waijiaobu, Shangwubu (Jingguo Wuyuan
Shouquan Fabu) [National Development and Reform Commission, Ministry of
Foreign Affairs, and Ministry of Commerce of the PRC, with State Council
authorization], "Tuidong gongqian sichouzhilu jingji daihe 21 shiji haishang
sichouzhilu de yuanjing yu xingdong" [Vision and Proposed Actions Outlined
on Jointly Building Silk Road Economic Belt and Twenty-First-Century Maritime Silk Road], NDRC, March 30, 2015, www.ndrc.gov.cn/gzdt/201503
/t20150328_669091.html.

31. Ann Listerud, "A Tale of Two Rail Lines: China and Japan's Soft Power
Competition in Indonesia," *The Diplomat,* May 12, 2017, https://thediplomat
.com/2017/05/a-tale-of-two-rail-lines-china-and-japans-soft-power-competition-
in-indonesia/.

32. Ling Chen, *Manipulating Globalization: The Influence of Bureaucrats
on Business in China* (Stanford, CA: Stanford University Press, 2018).

33. On where China gets the capital to finance the export of big infrastructure products, see Zongyuan Liu, "Sovereign Leveraged Funds and Financial

Statecraft: A Comparative Analysis of China and Japan" (PhD diss., School of Advanced International Studies, Johns Hopkins University, April 22, 2019).

34. Scott Kennedy, "Made in China 2025," Center for Strategic and International Studies, www.csis.org/analysis/made-china-2025.

35. Bo Kong and David M. Lampton, China Nuclear Series, Reports 1–8, done for US Nuclear Regulatory Commission and National Nuclear Security Administration, 2010–12.

36. National Bureau of Statistics, National General Public Budget Expenditure, cited in Wu Xiangning, "Tackling Nontraditional Security Challenges," presented at the Pacific Community Initiative Conference, Washington, DC, November 12, 2018, 14.

37. Jonathan E. Hillman, "China's New Silk Road Conundrum," *Washington Post*, February 14, 2018, www.washingtonpost.com/news/theworldpost /wp/2018/02/14/cpec/?utm_term=.ac8a73eefb37.

38. For a discussion of what constitutes the domestic content of "The China Model" see Daniel A. Bell, *The China Model: Political Meritocracy and the Limits of Democracy* (Princeton, NJ: Princeton University Press, 2015).

39. Xi Jinping, "Secure a Decisive Victory in Building a Moderately Prosperous Society in All Respects and Strive for the Great Success of Socialism with Chinese Characteristics for a New Era," Xinhua, Full Text of Xi Jinping's Report at the 19th CPC National Congress, October 18, 2017, www.xinhuanet .com/english/special/2017–11/03/c_136725942.htm.

40. David M. Lampton, *The Three Faces of Chinese Power: Might, Money, and Minds* (Berkeley: University of California Press, 2008), 9.

41. Niccolò Machiavelli, *The Prince*, trans. W.K. Marriott (New York: E.P. Dutton, 1908).

42. Luo Kuan-chung, *Romance of the Three Kingdoms*, 2 vols. (Hong Kong: Kelly & Walsh, 1925).

43. Lee Kuan Yew, *From Third World to First: The Singapore Story: 1965–2000* (New York: HarperCollins, 2000). Dr. Mahathir, *A Doctor in the House: The Memoirs of Tun Dr. Mahathir Mohamad* (Selangor, Malaysia: MPH Group, 2011).

44. Brantly Womack, *Asymmetry and International Relationships* (London: Cambridge University Press, 2015).

45. Andrew Mertha, *Brothers in Arms: Chinese Aid to the Khmer Rouge, 1975–1979* (Ithaca, NY: Cornell University Press, 2014).

46. Kenneth N. Waltz, *Theory of International Politics* (1979; repr. Long Grove, IL: Waveland Press, 2010).

47. Cheng-Chwee Kuik, "Smaller States' Alignment Choices: A Comparative Study of Malaysia and Singapore's Hedging Behavior in the Face of a Rising China" (PhD diss., Johns Hopkins University–SAIS, June 2010).

48. Kuik, "Smaller States' Alignment Choices."

49. Cheng-Chwee Kuik and Gilbert Rozman, "Introduction to Light or Heavy Hedging: Positioning between China and the United States," in *Joint U.S.-Korea Academic Studies 2015*, vol. 26, ed. Gilbert Rozman (Washington, DC: Korean Economic Institute of America, 2015), 1–9; Jurgen Haacke, "The

Concept of Hedging and Its Application to Southeast Asia: A Critique and a Proposal for a Modified Conceptual and Methodological Framework," *International Relations of the Asia-Pacific* 19, no. 3 (September 2019): 375–417.

50. Alastair Iain Johnston, *Social States: China in International Institutions, 1980–2000* (Princeton, NJ: Princeton University Press, 2007).

51. Amitav Acharya, *Asian Regional Institutions and the Possibilities for Socializing the Behavior of States,* ADB Working Paper Series on Regional Integration, no. 82 (Manila: Asian Development Bank, 2011).

52. Alice D. Ba, "Is China Leading? China, Southeast Asia, and East Asian Integration," *Political Science* 66, no. 2 (2014): 143–65.

53. David A. Lake, *Hierarchy in International Relations* (Ithaca, NY: Cornell University Press, 2009).

54. David M. Lampton, chap. 7 in *Following the Leader: Ruling China, from Deng Xiaoping to Xi Jinping,* 2nd ed. (Oakland: University of California Press, 2019); Richard H. Solomon, *Chinese Political Negotiating Behavior* (Santa Monica, CA: RAND, 1995).

55. Kenneth T. Young, *Negotiating with the Chinese Communists: The United States Experience, 1953–1967* (New York: McGraw-Hill, 1968).

56. Ashish Dutta, "10 Things about Japan's Shinkansen Bullet Train which Is All Set to Revolutionize Indian Railways," ScoopWhoop, September 15, 2017, www.scoopwhoop.com/japan-shinkansen-bullet-train-revolutionize-indian-railways/.

57. Robert D. Putnam, "Diplomacy and Domestic Politics: The Logic of Two-Level Games," *International Organization* 42, no. 3 (Summer 1988): 427–60.

58. Kenneth G. Lieberthal and David M. Lampton, eds., *Bureaucracy, Politics, and Decision Making in Post-Mao China* (Berkeley: University of California Press, 1992), 1–91.

59. Czeslaw Tubilewicz and Kanishka Jayasuriya, "Internationalization of the Chinese Subnational State and Capital: The Case of Yunnan and the Greater Mekong Subregion," *Australian Journal of International Affairs* 69, no. 2 (2015): 185–204; Selina Ho, "River Politics: China's Policies in the Mekong and the Brahmaputra in Comparative Perspective," *Journal of Contemporary China* 23, no. 85 (2014): 1–20.

60. Tubilewicz and Jayasuriya, "Internationalization," 199.

61. Lisa Murray, "Speed Bumps in China's New Silk Road," *Australian Financial Review,* September 29, 2016, www.afr.com/news/world/asia/speed-bumps-in-chinas-new-silk-road-20160928-grqxe8.

62. Chen, *Manipulating Globalization.*

63. Pongkwan Sawasdipakdi, "Making the History: How Belt and Road Initiatives Give Thailand Its Long-Awaited High-Speed Rail," in *Asymmetry and Authority: ASEAN States' Responses to China's Belt and Road Initiative* (program document, UKM-QMUL Workshop 2, Le Meridien, Kuala Lumpur, Malaysia, February 10–11, 2018), 22.

64. Merilee S. Grindle, ed., *Politics and Policy Implementation in the Third World* (Princeton, NJ: Princeton University Press, 1980); David M. Lampton, ed., *Policy Implementation in Post-Mao China* (Berkeley: University of California Press, 1987).

65. Jeffrey L. Pressman and Aaron B. Wildavsky, *Implementation: How Great Expectations in Washington Are Dashed in Oakland* (Berkeley: University of California Press, 1973); Lampton, *Policy Implementation*.

66. Barry Naughton, "The Decline in Central Control over Investment in Post-Mao China," in Lampton, *Policy Implementation*, 51–79.

67. Kitano Naohiro, "China's External Economic Cooperation: Ties to the Mekong Region," Nippon Communications Foundation, www.nippon.com/en /in-depth/a00803.

68. For a detailed discussion of interviews and interviewing in China, see Lampton, *Following the Leader*, 233–46.

69. Christine Lagarde, "Speech: The Case for a Global Policy Upgrade by Managing Director Christine Legarde," International Monetary Fund, January 12, 2016, www.imf.org/en/News/Articles/2015/09/28/04/53/sp011216.

CHAPTER TWO. THE GRAND VISION

1. "China's 12th Five-Year Plan Achievements a Milestone for Centenary Goal," *China Daily*, October 26, 2015, www.chinadaily.com.cn/china/2015–10/26/content_22280214.htm.

2. Unpublished notes on the remarks of PRC senior academic and adviser to David M. Lampton, Shanghai, November 20, 2015, 1–2.

3. Thai officials, interview by David M. Lampton and Cheng-Chwee Kuik, Bangkok, Thailand, July 25, 2016. Because Thailand was not colonialized, it had relatively small-scale rail development in the 1890s operated by a Western private company, Paknam Railway Co., a Danish firm. Modest rail development was later funded by the Thai government.

4. Dr. Mahathir, interview by David M. Lampton, Cheng-Chwee Kuik, and Ithrana Lawrence, Putrajaya, Malaysia, June 27, 2016. In our interview, Dr. Mahathir talked about growing up in the colonial period and the role of British rail in development. "When I was still in school, the British built railways from Kedah to the Thai border. That brought development. In my view, railroads will bring economic growth to neighboring countries."

5. Brantly Womack, "Yunnan's French Connection Restored," unpublished manuscript, 1997.

6. Jean-François Rousseau, "An Imperial Railway Failure: The Indochina-Yunnan Railway, 1898–1941," *The Journal of Transport History* 35, no. 1 (June 2014): 1–4.

7. Murray Hughes, *The Second Age of Rail: A History of High-Speed Trains* (Brimscombe Port, Stroud, Gloucestershire, UK: The History Press, 2015).

8. Foreign Ministry–related official, interview by David M. Lampton, Selina Ho, and Cheng-Chwee Kuik, Vientiane, Laos, June 7, 2017.

9. Rousseau, "Imperial Railway Failure," 4.

10. Rousseau, 10.

11. Selda Altan Öztürk, "Labor and the Politics of Life along the Yunnan-Indochina Railway, 1898–1911" (PhD diss., New York University, September 2017), 85–86.

12. Rousseau, "Imperial Railway Failure," 11.

13. Rousseau, 14.

14. Jay Taylor, *The Generalissimo: Chiang Kai-shek and the Struggle for Modern China* (Cambridge, MA: Harvard University Press, 2009), 264.

15. Toru Wakabayashi, *Teikoku nihon no koutsumou* [Transportation Network of Imperial Japan]" (Tokyo: Seikyūsha). The book has the subtitle of "The Great East Asian Co-Prosperity Zone That Was Not Connected," according to correspondence from Seiichiro Takagi, April 18, 2016.

16. Frank McLynn, *The Burma Campaign: Disaster into Triumph, 1942–1945* (New Haven, CT: Yale University Press, 2010).

17. David M. Lampton, Selina Ho, and Cheng-Chwee Kuik's meeting notes with transport experts, Hanoi, Vietnam, January 5, 2017.

18. ASEAN Secretariat, chapter 2, *Master Plan on ASEAN Connectivity*, December 2010, https://www.asean.org/storage/images/ASEAN_RTK_2014/4_Master_Plan_on_ASEAN_Connectivity.pdf.

19. United Nations Economic and Social Commission for Asia and the Pacific (UNESCAP), "Existing Organizations and Initiatives to Promote Cooperation among Countries for Railway Transport," www.unescap.org/sites/default/files/pub_2681_ch3.pdf. See also "Malaysia to Propose Early Construction of Singapore-Kunming Rail Link," *Malay Mail*, October 27, 2015, www.malaymail.com/s/994603/malaysia-to-propose-early-construction-of-singapore-kunming-rail-link.

20. Tun Dr. Mahathir Mohamad, interview by David M. Lampton and Cheng-Chwee Kuik, Putrajaya, Kuala Lumpur, June 27, 2016.

21. Chinese banker, meeting with David M. Lampton and Cheng-Chwee Kuik, Beijing, July 18, 2016.

22. ASEAN Secretariat, *Master Plan*.

23. ASEAN Secretariat, "First ACCC-China Meeting on Connectivity," November 7, 2012, https://asean.org/first-accc-china-meeting-on-connectivity/.

24. Asian Development Bank Institute, *Connecting Asia: Infrastructure for Integrating South and Southeast Asia* (Northampton, MA: Edward Elgar Publishing, 2016).

25. Barry Naughton, "A Political Economy of China's Economic Transition," in *China's Great Economic Transformation*, ed. Loren Brandt and Thomas G. Rawski (Cambridge, UK: Cambridge University Press, 2008), 121.

26. World Bank, "Foreign Direct Investment, Net Inflows (Bop, Current US$)," World Development Indicators, https://data.worldbank.org/indicator/bx.klt.dinv.cd.wd; "China Foreign Exchange Reserves," Trading Economics, https://tradingeconomics.com/china/foreign-exchange-reserves.

27. "Total Length of Public Highways in China from 2006 to 2016 (in Kilometers)," Statista, https://www.statista.com/statistics/276050/total-length-of-chinas-freeways/.

28. Jonathan D. Spence, *The Search for Modern China* (New York: W. W. Norton, 1990), 249–50.

29. Spence, *Search for Modern China*, 250.

30. There is a rich history of rail development that is too extensive to be told here. However, one of the most interesting early Chinese railway leaders was Jeme Tien Yow (Zhan Tianyou), who graduated from Yale University in 1881.

Jeme returned to China and led railway development there in the late 1880s into the twentieth century.

31. Interestingly, after serving as US president, Herbert Hoover subsequently returned to Stanford University, from which he graduated, and through his philanthropy helped Stanford strengthen its international footprint. Stanford University was founded by Leland Stanford, one of the four entrepreneurs who played a key role in building and running the Central Pacific, one of the two companies (the other being the Union Pacific) that constructed the US Transcontinental Railroad in the 1860s. For Hoover's early years in China, see Ellsworth C. Carlson, *The Kaiping Mines, 1877–1912*, East Asian Monograph, 2nd ed. (Cambridge, MA: Harvard University Press, 1971).

32. Spence, *Search for Modern China*, 250–54.

33. Zongyuan (Zoe) Liu, "The Development of Chinese High-Speed Rail (HSR)—Its Development Strategy and Implementation," April 11, 2016, informal, unpublished research paper, 1–2.

34. Evan Osnos, "Boss Rail: The Disaster that Exposed the Underside of the Boom," *New Yorker,* October 22, 2012, https://www.newyorker.com/magazine /2012/10/22/boss-rail.

35. Spence, *Search for Modern China*, 249–68.

36. Association of American Railroads, "Chronology of Railroading in America," https://www.aar.org/data/chronology-railroading-america/.

37. Deng Xiaoping, "Quandang jiang daju, ba guomin jingji gao shangqu" [The Whole Party Must Consider the Overall Situation and Raise the National Economy], speech to the Central Committee of the Communist Party of China, March 5, 1975, *People's Daily,* http://zg.people.com.cn/GB/33839/34943/3494 4/34946/2617437.html.

38. National Bureau of Statistics, PRC.

39. National Bureau of Statistics, PRC.

40. "Lishi tongji: jinzhuan guojia linian tielu yingye licheng bijiao (1838– 2010)" [Historical Statistics: BRICS Countries Annual Operational Mileage of Railroads Comparison, 1838–2010], September 24, 2011, www.360doc.com /content/11/0924/16/5931940_150892508.shtml; for a slightly different number, see "Length of Transportation Routes," National Bureau of Statistics, in *China Statistical Yearbook,* www.stats.gov.cn/tjsj/ndsj/2011/indexeh.htm.

41. Selina Ho, in her book *Thirsty Cities,* argues that following the tragedy of Tiananmen, Chinese leaders, particularly Deng Xiaoping, were looking for ways to bring more benefits to the people in order to ensure stability. Ho, *Thirsty Cities: Social Contracts and Public Goods Provision in China and India* (Cambridge, UK: Cambridge University Press, 2019), 60–61.

42. The Ministry of Railways under the State Council existed until March 2013, whereupon it was abolished and its former tasks divided among three entities. The task of regulating railways (safety and rule making) was given to the Transport Ministry (*Jiaotongbu*); the task of inspection was given to the National Railway Administration (under the Transport Ministry); and China Railway Corporation (CRC) was charged with railway construction and operations. The purpose behind these changes was to separate regulation, safety, and rule making from operations and construction.

43. "Wenjiabao xuanbu jing-hu gaosu tielu quanxiankaigong bin wei tielu dianji" [Wen Jiabao Announces Start of Construction of Beijing-Shanghai High-Speed Railway and Holds Groundbreaking Ceremony], Central People's Government of the People's Republic of China, April 18, 2008, www.gov.cn /jrzg/2008–04/18/content_947868.htm. See also Zhenhua Chen and Kingsley E. Haynes, *Chinese Railways in the Era of High-Speed* (Bingley, West Yorkshire, UK: Emerald Group Publishing, 2015), 49.

44. The EMU train design requires no discrete locomotive and is composed of various numbers of self-propelled cars, with one connected to another, sometimes with nonmotorized units dispersed among EMUs. See also Hughes, *Second Age of Rail*, 123.

45. "Shoulie Guochan Gaosu Lieche 'LanJian' Hao Zai Guang-Shen Shi-YunyYing" [First Chinese-Made "Blue Arrow" High-Speed Train Conducting Trial Run on the Guangzhou-Shenzhen line], *Sina*, December 29, 2000, http:// news.sina.com.cn/c/163578.html.

46. Jamil Anderlini and Mure Dickie, "China: A Future on Track," *Financial Times*, September 23, 2010, www.ft.com/content/2b843e4c-c745–11df-aeb1–00144feab49a.

47. "Guojia 'zhongchangqi tieluwang guice' neirong jianjie" [Introduction to the National Medium- and Long-Term Railway Network Plan], Central People's Government of the People's Republic of China, September 16, 2005, www .gov.cn/ztzl/2005–09/16/content_64413.htm. The track length of 100,000 km was later adjusted to 120,000 km in the 2008 revised plan. See also Chen and Haynes, *Chinese Railways*, 49.

48. Kitano Naohiro, "China's External Economic Cooperation: Ties to the Mekong Region," Nippon Communications Foundation, www.nippon.com/en /in-depth/a00803.

49. "Hukun gaotie guiyang zhi kunming duan 12 yue 28 ri kaitong" [Guiyang-Kunming Section of the Shanghai-Kunming High-Speed Railway to Open on December 28], *Sohu*, December 24, 2016, www.sohu.com/a/122463250_114731. For a slightly different figure, see "Bullet Train Network Still Moving at Speed," *China Daily* (USA), February 2, 2017, 5.

50. Liu, "Development of Chinese High-Speed Rail," 4–5.

51. China's exports to the world went up 9.4 times in the January 2000 to January 2015 period. Organization for Economic Co-operation and Development, "Exports: Value Goods for China," Federal Reserve Bank of St. Louis, http://fred.stlouisfed.org/series/XTEXVA01CNM667S.

52. Anderlini and Dickie, "China: A Future."

53. Anderlini and Dickie.

54. Chen and Haynes, *Chinese Railways*, 80.

55. Chen and Haynes, *Chinese Railways*, 40.

56. Osnos, "Boss Rail," 2.

57. Hughes, *Second Age of Rail*, 122.

58. Hughes, 123–24.

59. Hughes, 124. CSR is Zhongguo Nan Che and CNR is Zhongguo Bei Che. Zhongguo Nan Che (China South Locomotive & Rolling Stock Corp., Ltd.) was merged with China CNR Corp., Ltd. to form CRRC Corp., Ltd.

60. *2016 Annual Report*, CRRC Corporation Limited, www.hkexnews.hk
/listedco/listconews/SEHK/2017/0427/LTN201704272466.pdf; Zhibo Qiu, "Political Centralization Drives Upcoming Industrial Consolidation," *China Brief*, April
3, 2015, https://jamestown.org/program/political-centralization-drives-upcoming-
industrial-consolidation/.

61. Hughes, *Second Age of Rail*, 138.

62. Osnos, "Boss Rail."

63. Osnos, 6.

64. Hughes, *Second Age of Rail*, 134–36.

65. "National Railway Administration," http://english.gov.cn/state_council
/2014/10/01/content_281474991089722.htm.

66. Osnos, "Boss Rail," 3. See note 42.

67. Chinese think-tank researchers, personal communication, Beijing, September 22, 2016.

68. Luo Wangshu, "Rail System to Grow by 4,000 km in 2018," *China
Daily*, www.chinadaily.com.cn/a/201801/03/WS5a4bfb27a31008cf16da4b5c
.html.

69. When considering railway safety, one should keep in mind the metric of
passenger distance traveled per passenger fatality. Using this metric, China's
high-speed train system has been remarkably safe. Massachusetts Institute of
Technology mathematician Arnold I. Barnett said, "Chinese high-speed rail has
so far established a mortality risk level that equals or exceeds that of the world's
safest airlines." Cited in Keith Bradsher, "Despite a Deadly Crash, Rail System
Has Good Safety Record," *New York Times,* September 23, 2013. See also
Salvatore Babones, "China's High-Speed Trains Are Taking On More Passengers in Chinese New Year Mass Migration," https://www.forbes.com/sites
/salvatorebabones/2018/02/13/chinas-high-speed-trains-are-taking-on-more-
passengers-in-chinese-new-year-massive-migration/#7565c5b6423f.

70. Emma G. Fitzsimmons, "Amtrak at a Junction: Invest in Improvements,
or Risk Worsening Problems," *New York Times,* April 24, 2017, www.nytimes
.com/2017/04/24/nyregion/amtrak-infrastructure-crisis.html.

71. Renminwang, "High-Speed Rail to Cover over 80% of China's Large
Cities by 2020," http://en.people.cn/n3/2018/0103/c90000–9310790.html.

72. James C. Scott, *Comparative Political Corruption* (Englewood Cliffs, NJ:
Prentice-Hall, 1972), 69.

73. Osnos, "Boss Rail," 13.

74. Didi Kirsten Tatlow, "An Investor's Guide to Buying Influence in China,"
New York Times, August 25, 2011, www.nytimes.com/2011/08/25/world
/asia/25iht-letter25.html.

75. Tatlow, "Investor's Guide."

76. See Zhang Jianping, "Building China Railway in Comprehensive Transpor-
tation System," *Journal of Transportation Systems Engineering and Information
Technology* 6, no. 1 (2006): 15–18. Cited in Liu, "Development of Chinese High-
Speed Rail," 24.

77. Bo Kong and David Lampton, under contract with the National Nuclear
Security Administration and the Nuclear Regulatory Commission in the 2010–
12 period, wrote a series of eight unpublished reports on developments germane

to the evolution and regulation of the civil nuclear power industry in China. This research included extensive field research.

78. Anderlini and Dickie, "China: A Future."

79. Hughes, *Second Age of Rail*, 138.

80. Agatha Kratz and Dragan Pavlićević, "China's High-Speed Railway Diplomacy: Riding a Gravy Train," Lau China Institute Working Paper Series, King's College London, January 1, 2016, 6, n. 32.

81. "China's High-Speed Rail Diplomacy," Global Security, last modified November 26, 2017, www.globalsecurity.org/military/world/china/hsr-diplomacy .htm. This article provides information on the scope of China's rail-building efforts globally.

82. "Kenya Opens Nairobi-Mombasa Madaraka Express Railway," BBC, May 31, 2017, www.bbc.com/news/world-africa-40092600; Kimiko De Freytas-Tamura, *New York Times*, international edition, June 10–11, 2017.

83. Istvan Tarrosy and Zoltán Vörös, "China and Ethiopia, Part 2: The Addis Ababa-Djibouti Railway," *The Diplomat*, https://thediplomat.com/2018 /02/china-and-ethiopia-part-2-the-addis-ababa-djibouti-railway/; Conor Gaffey, "Kenya Just Opened a $4 Billion Chinese-Built Railway, Its Largest Infrastructure Project in 50 Years," *Newsweek*, May 31, 2017, www.newsweek.com /kenya-railway-china-madaraka-express-618357.

84. Petaling Jaya, "Malaysia-Singapore HSR Postponed, Not Scrapped: PM Mahathir," *Straits Times*, June 12, 2018, www.straitstimes.com/asia/se-asia /malaysia-singapore-hsr-postponed-not-scrapped-pm-mahathir.

85. "China's High-Speed Rail Diplomacy."

86. Former senior Malaysian official, interview by David M. Lampton, Selina Ho, and Cheng-Chwee Kuik, Malaysia, May 31, 2018.

87. Singapore think-tank researcher, meeting with Selina Ho, Cheng-Chwee Kuik, and David M. Lampton, May 30, 2018.

88. Virginia Greiman and Roger Warburton, "Deconstructing the Big Dig: Best Practices for Mega-Project Cost Estimating," 2009, https://pmilic.org/index.php /docman-all-files/bod/conferences/global-congress-2009/adv-pm-skills/333- deconstructing-the-big-dig/file. Originally published as part of the PMI Global Congress Proceedings, Orlando, Florida.

89. Chen and Haynes, *Chinese Railways*, 233–35.

90. Chen and Haynes, 234.

91. Wayne M. Morrison, "China's Economic Rise: History, Trends, Challenges, and Implications for the United States," Congressional Research Service, Document 7–5700, February 5, 2018, especially 45–48.

92. Nicholas R. Lardy, *The State Strikes Back: The End of Economic Reform in China?* (Washington, DC: Peterson Institute for International Economics, 2019), 35.

93. Responsible Chinese rail official, interview by David M. Lampton, Beijing, July 20, 2016.

94. *Constitution of the Communist Party of China*, revised and adopted at the Nineteenth National Congress of the Communist Party of China on October 24, 2017, 8, www.china.org.cn/20171105–001.pdf.

CHAPTER THREE. CHINA'S DEBATES

1. Hu Angang, "A New Era of 'Win-winism': Reshaping Chinese Economic Geography," monograph published by Tsinghua University Institute for Contemporary China Studies, April 2016, 11.

2. Chinese banker, interview by David M. Lampton, Beijing, July 23, 2017.

3. US Chamber of Commerce, *Made in China 2025: Global Ambitions Built on Local Protections* (Washington, DC: US Chamber of Commerce, 2017).

4. Barry J. Naughton, "Grand Steerage," in *Fateful Decisions: Choices That Will Shape China's Future*, ed. Thomas Fingar and Jean C. Oi (Stanford, CA: Stanford University Press, 2020).

5. "B&R initiative benefits all, says NDRC official," *Global Times*, April 19, 2018, B2. For a delicate critique of what the IMF sees as a slowing reform effort, see the conclusions of IMF Executive Board's 2017 Article IV Consultation with the PRC, which "urged further reforms, including hardening budget constraints, accelerating restructuring of under-performing debt, and allowing exit of non-viable firms." The Fund also called for "improvement in the investment climate, including reducing barriers to entry, ensuring a level playing field, and reducing trade barriers," along with "efforts to reduce overcapacity . . . and greater reliance on market forces." International Monetary Fund, press release no. 17/326, August 15, 2017, www.imf.org/en/News/Articles/2017/08/15/pr17326-china-imf-executive-board-concludes-2017-article-iv-consultation.

6. Chinese think-tank leader and researcher, interview by David M. Lampton, Washington, DC, June 16, 2017.

7. David M. Lampton, conference meeting notes, Beijing, April 2018.

8. David P. Goldman "A Tragedy in the Making as the US Confronts China," *Asia Times*, June 24, 2018, www.asiatimes.com/2018/06/article/a-tragedy-in-the-making-as-the-us-confronts-china/.

9. Chinese university delegation, meeting with David M. Lampton, Johns Hopkins–SAIS, April 4, 2017.

10. US Chamber of Commerce, *Made in China 2025*.

11. Keegan Elmer, "EU Presents (Nearly) United Front against China's 'Unfair' Belt and Road Initiative," *South China Morning Post*, April 20, 2018, www.scmp.com/news/china/diplomacy-defence/article/2142698/eu-presents-nearly-united-front-against-chinas-unfair.

12. Hu Angang, in conversation with David M. Lampton, Washington, DC, May 2, 2017.

13. Senior Chinese IR analyst, interview by David M. Lampton, July 17, 2016.

14. Chinese analyst, conversation with David M. Lampton, Beijing, mid-2017.

15. See, for example, Li Luxi and Fran Wang, "Veteran Banker Warns of 'Belt and Road' Risks," Caixin Global, April 13, 2018.

16. Selina Ho, "Infrastructural Power and Regional Governance: China's Railway Projects in Southeast Asia," unpublished manuscript, May 2018.

17. Lawrence Lau, remarks at the China Development Forum, Diaoyutai, Beijing, September 6, 2019, notes by David M. Lampton.

18. Chinese General Chamber of Commerce, "Frederick Ma: Hong Kong Moves towards High-Speed Rail Era," *CGCC Vision* (January 2018): 12, www .cgcc.org.hk/en/temp_publication.php?cid=5&sid=65&tid=0&tabid=0&id=51 &cpid=77.

19. See Clemens Breisinger and Xinshen Diao, *Economic Transformation in Theory and Practice: What are the Messages for Africa?* discussion paper, International Food Policy Research Institute, 2008, 10, www.ifpri.org/publication /economic-transformation-theory-and-practice.

20. Senior planner, interview by David M. Lampton, Beijing, July 17, 2016.

21. World Bank, *Reshaping Economic Geography* (Washington, DC: Office of the Publisher, World Bank, 2009), xxii.

22. Zaw Zaw Aung, "China's Rise Holds Great Promise," *Myanmar Times,* February 2, 2018, www.mmtimes.com/news/chinas-rise-holds-great-promise .html.

23. Angang Hu, Yuning Gao, and Yunfeng Zheng, "From Chasing to Surpassing in All Aspects: An Empirical Study of Comprehensive National Powers of China and the US (2000–2020)," Institute of Contemporary China Studies, Tsinghua University, Working Papers, March 2017, 5–6.

24. "Market to Play 'Decisive' Role in Allocating Resources," Xinhua, www .china.org.cn/china/third_plenary_session/2013–11/12/content_30577689.htm.

25. *Adhering to the Planning, Orderly and Pragmatically Build the 'Belt and Road': The Belt and Road Progress Report*, Chongyang Institute for Financial Studies, Renmin University, September 26, 2016, 2.

26. Chinese banker, interview by David M. Lampton and Cheng-Chwee Kuik, Beijing, July 18, 2016.

27. Hu Angang, "New Era of 'Win-winism.'"

28. Hu Angang, in conversation with David M. Lampton, Washington, DC, May 2, 2017. See also World Bank, *Reshaping Economic Geography.*

29. *Adhering to the Planning*, 4.

30. *Adhering to the Planning*, 7.

31. Hu Angang, "New Era of 'Win-winism,'" 26–27. Emphasis added.

32. *Constitution of the Communist Party of China,* revised and adopted at the Nineteenth National Congress of the Communist Party of China, October 24, 2017, www.china.org.cn/20171105–001.pdf.

33. David M. Lampton, *The Three Faces of Chinese Power: Might, Money, and Minds* (Berkeley: University of California Press, 2008).

34. *The Thirteenth Five-Year Plan for Economic and Social Development of the People's Republic of China (2016–2020)* (Beijing: Central Compilation & Translation Department, Central Committee of the Communist Party of China, 2016), 146–48.

35. *Thirteenth Five-Year Plan*, 146–48.

36. Daniel Keeton-Olsen, "Flying High: As Mainland Money and Visitors Pour into Cambodia, China Backs Two New Airports," *Forbes Asia* (May 2018): 12.

37. Keeton-Olsen, "Flying High," 14.

38. Keeton-Olsen, "Flying High," 14.

39. Yuichi Nitta and Thurein Hla Htway, "Myanmar Will Ask China to Downsize Project, Minister Says," *Nikkei Asian Review*, July 4, 2018, https://

asia.nikkei.com/Politics/Myanmar-will-ask-China-to-downsize-project-minister-says.

40. Technically, as long as gauges and standards, both electrical and mechanical, are compatible, the technology could come from different suppliers.

41. *Thirteenth Five-Year Plan*, 146–48.

42. Andrew Polk, "China Is Quietly Setting Global Standards," Bloomberg, May 6, 2018, www.bloomberg.com/view/articles/2018–05–06/china-is-quietly-setting-global-standards.

43. Li Qiang, "Qinghua xiaoyou: huyu xiaozhang jiepin hu angang weihu xueshu shengyu [Tsinghua Alumni: Call for President to Dismiss Hu Angang to Maintain Academic Reputation]," *China Digital Times*, www.chinadigitaltimes .net/chinese/2018/08/%E6%Ao%A1%E5%8F%8B%E5%91%BC%E5%90% 81%E6%B8%85%E5%8D%8E%E8%A7%A3%E8%81%98%E8%83%A1 %E9%9E%8D%E9%92%A2-%E7%BB%B4%E6%8A%A4%E5%AD%A6 %E6%9C%AF%E6%B8%85%E7%99%BD%E9%AB%98%E6%Ao%A1% E5%BA%94%E5%8F%91%E5%A3%Bo/.

44. "Fairly gauging China, US strength gap," *Global Times*, August 2, 2018, www.globaltimes.cn/content/1113616.shtml.

45. William Hinton, *Hundred Day War: The Cultural Revolution at Tsinghua University* (Monthly Review Press: New York, 1972).

46. Xu Zhangrun, "Imminent Fears, Immediate Hopes—A Beijing Jeremiad," *China Heritage*, July 2018, http://chinaheritage.net/journal/imminent-fears-immediate-hopes-a-beijing-jeremiad/.

47. Think-tank expert, interview by David M. Lampton and Cheng-Chwee Kuik, Beijing, July 19, 2016.

48. Ziying Fan and Guanghua Wan, "The Fiscal Risk of Local Government Revenue in the People's Republic of China," ADB Institute, ADBI Working Paper Series, no. 567 (April 2016): 3.

49. International Monetary Fund, *People's Republic of China: Staff Report for the 2017 Article Consultation*, July 13, 2017, 27–28. This report says, "Currently, local governments in China have the highest share of national spending responsibility in the world yet very limited revenue autonomy."

50. Fan and Wan, "Fiscal Risk of Local Government," 7.

51. Fan and Wan, abstract, "Fiscal Risk of Local Government."

52. Fan and Wan, "Fiscal Risk of Local Government," 3.

53. Fan and Wan, 3.

54. Think-tank expert, Beijing, July 19, 2016.

55. Think-tank expert, interview by David M. Lampton, Beijing, March 28, 2017.

56. Think-tank expert, Beijing, March 28, 2017.

57. Note, financing of projects in China is very complex and nontransparent. The State Administration of Foreign Exchange (SAFE) has become increasingly active in investing foreign exchange accumulations in projects involving both CDB and the China Exim Bank. This opens up a whole new area of financing in which accumulations of foreign exchange are recycled to subsidize Chinese companies involved in the export of infrastructure such as high- and conventional-speed railways. See chapter 4 of Zongyuan Liu, "Sovereign Leveraged

Funds and Financial Statecraft: A Comparative Analysis of China and Japan" (PhD diss., School of Advanced International Studies, Johns Hopkins University, April 22, 2019), especially 179–217.

58. Chinese Foreign Ministry official, interview by David M. Lampton, February 6, 2018.

59. Nicholas R. Lardy, *The State Strikes Back: The End of Economic Reform in China?* (Washington, DC: Peterson Institute of International Economics, 2019), 15.

60. David M. Lampton, notes from a group meeting with very senior Chinese leader, December 1, 2017, 11.

61. Chinese think-tank researcher, conference notes by David M. Lampton, November 11, 2017, 31–32.

62. Senior Chinese rail official, interview by David M. Lampton, Beijing, July 20, 2016.

63. David M. Lampton, notes on a discussion with think-tank researchers and professors, Beijing, September 22, 2016, 4.

64. Think-tank expert, interview by David M. Lampton and Cheng-Chwee Kuik, Beijing, July 18, 2016.

65. Lampton, notes on a discussion with think-tank researchers and professors, September 22, 2016, 3–4.

66. It is worth noting that the economics of HSR are much more problematic than slower, conventional-speed systems. Hence, though China may initially push an HSR system, often in the course of negotiation and with increasing local knowledge China lowers the ambitions of its projects to slower speeds.

67. International Monetary Fund, *People's Republic of China*, 26.

68. Senior Chinese scholar, interview by David M. Lampton and Cheng-Chwee Kuik, Beijing, July 19, 2016.

69. Senior Chinese scholar, July 19, 2016.

70. Senior Chinese scholar, July 19, 2016.

71. Senior Chinese scholar, July 19, 2016.

72. Both quotations come from Keith Bradsher, "China Taps the Brakes on Its Global Push for Influence," *New York Times*, June 29, 2018, www.nytimes.com/2018/06/29/business/china-belt-and-road-slows.html.

73. Larry Elliott, "China's debt levels pose stability risk, says IMF," *Guardian*, December 7, 2017, www.theguardian.com/world/2017/dec/07/china-debt-levels-stabil. See also International Monetary Fund, *People's Republic of China*, 19.

74. Jamil Anderlini and Mure Dickie, "China: A Future on Track," *Financial Times*, www.ft.com/content/2b843e4c-c745-11df-aeb1-00144feab49a.

75. Anderlini and Dickie, "China."

76. Maria Abi-Habib, "In Hock to China, Sri Lanka Gave Up Territory: How Beijing Exploited a Wasteful Project for Strategic Gain," *New York Times*, June 26, 2018. See also how the Sri Lanka case affected willingness to assume debt in Myanmar in Nitta and Hla Htway, "Myanmar Will Ask."

77. "How China Tricked Sri Lanka to Acquire 'Hambantota' Port," *New Delhi Times*, July 9, 2018, www.newdelhitimes.com/how-china-tricked-sri-lanka-to-acquire-hambantota-port/.

78. Senior Chinese scholar, Beijing, July 19, 2016.

79. Selina Ho, Cheng-Chwee Kuik, and David M. Lampton, notes on conference, Singapore, May 28, 2018, 18, 21.

80. Senior Chinese scholar, Beijing, July 19, 2016.

81. Bradsher, "China Taps the Brakes."

82. Reuters, "Pakistan Seeks Economic Lifeline with Fresh Chinese Loans," *Straits Times* (Singapore), May 27, 2018.

83. "KL to See How to Cut S'pore Compensation If HSR Ditched," *Straits Times*, May 27, 2018.

84. Senior professor, in conversation with David M. Lampton, Cheng-Chwee Kuik, and Selina Ho, Laos, June 4, 2017; Foreign ambassador to Laos, interview by David M. Lampton, June 5, 2017,Vientiane, Laos; Western ambassador to Laos, interview by David M. Lampton, Cheng-Chwee Kuik, and Selina Ho, Vientiane, June 5, 2017.

85. Senior Chinese scholar, Beijing, July 19, 2016.

86. Anonymous PRC official, interview by David M. Lampton, July 17, 2016.

87. Senior Chinese scholar, Beijing, July 19, 2016.

88. "Market to Play 'Decisive' Role."

89. Think-tank expert, interview by David M. Lampton, Beijing, July 21, 2016.

90. PRC think-tank expert, interview by David M. Lampton, Washington, DC, September 10, 2016.

91. Naughton, "Grand Steerage," in Fingar and Oi, *Fateful Decisions*, 54.

92. Andrew Walder, "China's National Trajectory," in Fingar and Oi, *Fateful Decisions*, 351.

93. Kenneth G. Lieberthal and David M. Lampton, eds., *Bureaucracy, Politics, and Decision Making in Post-Mao China* (Berkeley: University of California Press, 1992); David M. Lampton, chap. 3 in *Following the Leader: Ruling China, from Deng Xiaoping to Xi Jinping*, 2nd ed. (Oakland: University of California Press, 2019).

94. David J. Bulman, *Incentivized Development in China: Leaders, Governance, and Growth in China's Counties* (New York: Cambridge University Press, 2016).

95. *Adhering to the Planning*, 33.

96. Senior Chinese analyst, conversation with David M. Lampton, Beijing, April 19, 2018.

97. Lee Jones, Jinghan Zeng, and Shahar Hameir, "Evidence on China's 'Belt and Road' Initiative," House of Commons, United Kingdom, December 2017, http://data.parliament.uk/writtenevidence/committeeevidence.svc/evidence document/foreign-affairs-committee/china-and-the-international-rulesbased-system/written/75536.html.

98. Chinese institute director, interview by David M. Lampton, Washington, DC, February 17, 2016.

99. Senior Chinese scholar, Beijing, July 19, 2016.

100. Think-tank expert, Beijing, March 28, 2017.

101. Western ambassador to Laos, Vientiane, June 5, 2017.

102. Western diplomat in southwestern China, interview by David M. Lampton, June 24, 2015.

103. Mo Yelin, "China Seeks to Rein In Ambitious High-Speed Rail Projects," Caixin Global, May 9, 2018, accessed May 10, 2018, www .caixinglobal.com/2018-05-09/china-seeks-to-rein-in-ambitious-high-speed-rail-projects-101246540.html.

104. David M. Lampton, notes on briefing by university group from PRC," Washington, DC, June 14, 2017, 4.

105. Mo Yelin, "China Seeks to Rein In."

106. Mo Yelin.

107. Mo Yelin.

108. For more on the emergence of continentalist thinking, see Kent E. Calder, *The New Continentalism: Energy and Twenty-First Century Eurasian Geopolitics* (New Haven, CT: Yale University Press, 2012).

109. Agatha Kratz and Dragan Pavlićević, *China's High-Speed Railway Diplomacy: Riding a Gravy Train?* Lau China Institute Working Paper Series, January 2016, doi: 10.13140/RG.2.2.31771.16163.

110. Wang Jisi, "'Marching Westwards': The Rebalancing of China's Geostrategy," Center for International and Strategic Studies, Report no. 73 (October 7, 2012).

111. Wang Jisi, "'Marching Westwards,'" 1–3.

112. Wu Zhengyu, "Toward 'Land' or Toward 'Sea'?" *Naval War College Review* 66, no. 3 (Summer 2013): 12.

113. Planning official, in conversation with David M. Lampton, Beijing, July 17, 2016.

114. US Secretary of Defense Ash Carter, "Remarks by Secretary Carter on the Budget," Economic Club of Washington, February 2, 2016, www.defense .gov/News/Transcripts/Transcript-View/Article/648901/remarks-by-secretary-carter-on-the-budget-at-the-economic-club-of-washington-dc/.

115. Institute director, interview by David M. Lampton, Washington, DC, February 17, 2016.

116. Lampton, notes on a discussion with think-tank researchers and professors, September 22, 2016, 4.

117. David M. Lampton, notes from briefing by Ministry of Commerce official, Beijing, August 7, 2017, 4–5.

CHAPTER FOUR. DIVERSE SOUTHEAST ASIAN RESPONSES

1. Tun Dr. Mahathir Mohamad, in conversation with David M. Lampton, Cheng-Chwee Kuik, and Ithrana Lawrence, Perdana Leadership Foundation, Putrajaya, Malaysia, June 27, 2016.

2. Abhisit Vejjajiva, interview by David M. Lampton, Selina Ho, and Cheng-Chwee Kuik, Democrat Party headquarters office, Bangkok, May 30, 2017. Abhisit Vejjajiva was then leader of the Democrat Party in Thailand and a former prime minister (2008–11).

3. This chapter concentrates on the cases of Laos, Thailand, and Malaysia, because they are the three countries where construction of China-related rail infrastructure projects was taking place as of 2019. Vietnam and other ASEAN countries are categorized as cases of "*limited* involvement," because the China-

related rail projects in some of these countries are still in the early stage of initiation. These include the "Lao Cai–Hai Phong" and the "Dong Dang–Hanoi–Hai Phong" HSR projects in Vietnam, as well as the "Kyaukphyu–Kunming" HSR project running from Myanmar to southern China. The Cat Linh–Ha Dong Elevated Railway in Hanoi is an exception (construction was completed in 2018 after protracted delays), but that is an urban rail and not a national-level railroad project. Indonesia's Jakarta-Bandung HSR project, on the other hand, still faces land acquisition problems (as of early 2020), although the groundbreaking ceremony was held in January 2016.

4. Regarding measurement, a state's receptivity is deemed negative if the state decides to avoid or decline a foreign power's proposal to initiate connectivity partnership (when that happens, there will be no negotiation and no implementation). The receptivity is low if the state takes a long time to consider the foreign power's initiative, high if the state responds positively and promptly to the initiative, and very high if the state is the one which initiates the partnership. The same can be said about the next two stages. Receptivity is negative or low if the state takes a relatively long time to go through the negotiation and/or implementation phases; the converse is also true. Negative receptivity is often a sign of gaps in connectivity partnership. See Cheng-Chwee Kuik, "Connectivity and Gaps: The Bridging Links and Missed Links of China's BRI in Southeast Asia," in *The Belt and Road Initiative and Global Governance*, ed. Maria A. Carrai, Jean-Christophe DeFraigne, and Jan Wouters (Cheltenham, UK: Edward Elgar, 2020).

5. For instance, David A. Balwin, *Economic Statecraft* (Princeton, NJ: Princeton University Press, 1985); Jean-Marc F. Blanchard, Edward D. Mansfield, and Norrin M. Ripsman, eds., *Power and the Purse: Economic Statecraft, Interdependence and National Security* (London: Routledge, 2000); Jean-Marc F. Blanchard and Norrin M. Ripsman, *Economic Statecraft and Foreign Policy: Sanctions, Incentives and Target State Calculations* (New York: Routledge, 2013); James Reilly, *Chinese Economic Statecraft: Turning Wealth Into Power* (Sydney, Australia: Lowy Institute for International Policy, November 27, 2013); Matt Ferchen, "How New and Crafty is China's 'New Economic Statecraft'?" (Carnegie-Tsinghua Center for Global Policy, Department of International Relations, Tsinghua University, March 8, 2016); William J. Norris, *Chinese Economic Statecraft: Commercial Actors, Grand Strategy, and State Control* (Ithaca, NY: Cornell University Press, 2016). Exceptions include Evelyn Goh, ed., *Rising China's Influence in Developing Asia* (Oxford, UK: Oxford University Press, 2016).

6. For instance, Robert D. Blackwill and Jennifer M. Harris, *War by Other Means: Geoeconomics and Statecraft* (Cambridge, MA: Belknap Press of Harvard University Press, 2016).

7. *The Republic of Plato*, 2nd ed., trans. Allan Bloom (New York: Basic Books, 1991), 340.

8. On elite legitimation, see Max Weber, "Legitimacy, Politics, and the State," in *Legitimacy and the State*, ed. William Connolly (New York: New York University Press, 1984), 32–62; David Beetham, *The Legitimation of Power* (London: MacMillan, 1991); Muthiah Alagappa, ed., *Political Legitimacy in Southeast Asia: The Quest for Moral Authority* (Stanford, CA: Stanford University Press, 1995); Bruce Gilley, *The Right to Rule: How States Win*

and *Lose Legitimacy* (New York: Columbia University Press, 2009); John Kane, Hui-Chieh Loy, and Haig Patapan, eds., *Political Legitimacy in Asia: New Leadership Challenges* (New York: Palgrave MacMillan, 2011).

9. On state-society relations, see, for instance, Joel S. Migdal, *State in Society: Studying How States and Societies Transform and Constitute One Another* (Cambridge, UK: Cambridge University Press, 2001); Joel S. Migdal, *Strong Societies and Weak States: State-Society Relations and State Capabilities in the Third World* (Princeton, NJ: Princeton University Press, 1988).

10. On decentralization, see David M. Lampton, ed., *The Making of Chinese Foreign and Security Policy in the Era of Reform, 1978–2000* (Stanford, CA: Stanford University Press, 2001), especially 19–24.

11. On the complex interplays of sociopolitical and economic forces across the state elites, competing elites, and diverse segments of societies in Southeast Asia, see, for instance, Dan Slater, *Ordering Power: Contentious Politics and Authoritarian Leviathans in Southeast Asia* (Cambridge, UK: Cambridge University Press, 2010); William Case, *Politics in Southeast Asia* (London: Routledge, 2002); Michael R. J. Vatikiotis, *Blood and Silk: Power and Conflict in Modern Southeast Asia* (London: Weidenfeld & Nicolson, 2017).

12. Richard C. Paddock and Mukitta Suhartono, "President of Indonesia Re-elected, Polls Indicate," *New York Times,* April 18, 2019.

13. See, for example, "Tender Announcement," *Vientiane Times,* June 7, 2017.

14. Jing Shuiyu and Ren Xiaojin, "Sino-Lao Railway Project Drives Full Steam Ahead," *China Daily,* July 19, 2018, www.chinadaily.com.cn/a/201807/19/WS5b4ff418a310796df4df760f.html.

15. In correspondence with a senior Thai official in July 2017, our research team was told: "My understanding is that we plan to build the whole route from Bangkok to Nong Khai eventually. But we will do it in stages. The first stage is the 3.5 km stretch. But this 3.5 km is an integral part of the 253 km Bangkok to Korat [short for Nakhon Ratchasima] route in any case."

16. Of the two projects, the ECRL was revived in April 2019. The fate of the other project, the Kuala Lumpur–Singapore HSR, however, will be determined by the Malaysian and Singapore governments only in mid-2020. Singapore and Malaysia have been in extended discussions about the terms and character of the HSR line from Singapore to Kuala Lumpur, but only a very small percentage of the length of the prospective line is in Singapore, meaning that though Singapore plays an important role in shaping the project's technical and contractual features, Malaysia's role is primary. When Kuala Lumpur suspended the project in mid-2018, Singapore simply had to agree to accommodate to that decision, one way or another.

17. "Indonesia Seeks Ways to Speed Up China High-Speed Rail Project," *Straits Times* (Singapore), May 2, 2018, www.straitstimes.com/asia/se-asia/indonesia-seeks-ways-to-speed-up-china-high-speed-rail-project.

18. As observed by a Lao analyst, "Disagreements within the Party's inner circles will be aired behind closed doors. Few people will know the details of such discussions. However, glimpses of these internal debates can come to the public's knowledge through the disgrace of high-ranking cadres." See Vatthana Pholsena, "Laos," in *Regional Outlook: Southeast Asia 2012–2013* (Singapore:

ISEAS, 2012), 62. See also Somsack Pongkhao, "Projects without Bidding Unacceptable," *Vientiane Times,* June 7, 2017; senior official, interview by David M. Lampton, Cheng-Chwee Kuik, and Selina Ho, Vientiane, June 7, 2017.

19. Lao diplomat, interview by David M. Lampton, Selina Ho, and Cheng-Chwee Kuik, June 7, 2017.

20. "Construction of China-Laos Railway Officially Commences," *People's Daily Online,* December 25, 2016, en.people.cn/n3/2016/1225/c90000–9158981.html.

21. "Lao Think Tank Suggests to Maximize Laos-China Railway," Xinhua, November 6, 2018, www.xinhuanet.com/english/2018–11/06/c_137586120.htm.

22. "Railways May Build the New ASEAN Community," *Laotian Times,* September 5, 2016, https://laotiantimes.com/2016/09/05/railways-may-build-the-new-asean-community/.

23. Lao trade official, in conversation with David M. Lampton, Vientiane, June 7, 2017.

24. Oliver Tappe, "On the Right Track? The Lao People's Democratic Republic in 2017," in *Southeast Asian Affairs 2018* (Singapore: ISEAS, 2018), 172.

25. Tappe, "On the Right Track?" 169.

26. Lao senior official, interview by David M. Lampton, Selina Ho, and Cheng-Chwee Kuik, June 7, 2017.

27. Pholsena, "Laos," 62.

28. Brooks Boliek, "Clearing for Lao-China Railway Begins, but Questions about the Project Still Remain," Radio Free Asia, January 4, 2017, www.rfa.org/english/news/laos/clearing-for-lao-china-01042017150124.html.

29. In an interview with the authors in 2017, Abhisit revealed how his government started to talk with China, which was interested in building HSR from Yunnan through Laos and Thailand, and southward to the Thai-Malaysian border. Abhisit, who met with the chairman of the CREC during his visit to China in November 2009, said the idea of linking South China to Singapore is an attractive one. His government started negotiations with the Chinese, but the talks were not completed by the time his government left office. Abhisit Vejjajiva, Democrat Party Headquarters Office, May 30, 2017.

30. "Beijing and Bangkok Agree to High-Speed Railway Linking the Two Countries," *AsiaNews,* October 22, 2010, www.asianews.it/news-en/Beijing-and-Bangkok-agree-to-high-speed-railway-linking-the-two-countries-19797.html.

31. Under the bilateral barter agreement, signed in October 2013 in Bangkok by Yingluck and her Chinese counterpart Premier Li Keqiang, China was to provide equipment and help Thailand construct HSR with Chinese technology, whereas Thailand was to pay "in part or totally" by bartering rice and rubber. See Eric Meyer, "The End of the 'Chinese Rice for Train Plan' in Thailand, Right?" *Forbes,* September 14, 2014, www.forbes.com/sites/ericrmeyer/2014/09/14/the-end-of-the-chinese-rice-for-train-plan-in-thailand-right/#2a5ea8079e1e.

32. Rod Sweet, "Thailand Demands Better Terms in Historic Chinese Rail Deal," *Global Construction Review,* February 6, 2015, www.globalconstructionreview.com/news/thailand-demands-better-terms-historic-ch8i8n8e8se/.

33. Senior officials, interview by David M. Lampton, Cheng-Chwee Kuik, and Ithrana Lawrence, Bangkok, July 25, 2016; former senior officials and researchers, interview by David M. Lampton, Cheng-Chwee Kuik, and Ithrana Lawrence, Bangkok, July 26, 2016; logistics specialist, interview by David M. Lampton, Selina Ho, and Cheng-Chwee Kuik, Bangkok, May 29, 2017; senior officials, interview by David M. Lampton, Selina Ho, and Cheng-Chwee Kuik Bangkok, August 21, 2018.

34. Wichit Chaitrong, "China's Loan Terms Rejected," *The Nation* (Thailand), August 14, 2017, www.nationthailand.com/national/30323682.

35. Pairat Temphairojana and Manunphattr Dhanananphorn, "Thailand to Sign Rail, Rice, Rubber Deal with China," Reuters, December 2, 2015, https://in.reuters.com/article/idINL3N13R3HB20151202.

36. "Thailand to Go It Alone on Thai-Sino High-Speed Rail," *Bangkok Post,* March 24, 2016, www.bangkokpost.com/news/general/908328/thailand-to-go-it-alone-on-thai-sino-high-speed-rail.

37. Pongphisoot Busbarat, "China's 'Shame Offensive': The Omission of Thailand's Prime Minister from the Belt and Road Initiative Summit 2017," *ISEAS Perspective,* July 19, 2017.

38. Logistics specialist, interview by Lampton, Ho, and Kuik, Bangkok, May 29, 2017; senior official, interview by David M. Lampton and Cheng-Chwee Kuik, Bangkok, August 21, 2018; Tan Hui Yee, "Prayut Fast-Tracks Sino-Thai Rail Project," *Straits Times,* June 17, 2017, www.straitstimes.com/asia/se-asia/prayut-fast-tracks-sino-thai-rail-project.

39. "Beijing Pushes for Immediate Start to China-Thai Railway," *South China Morning Post,* July 24, 2017, www.scmp.com/news/china/diplomacy-defence/article/2103895/beijing-charts-stability-course-trouble-rumbles-south.

40. Thammasat University professor Ruth Banomyong describes the military government's use of Article 44 as "a double-edged sword," because in Thailand "one of the reasons things take so long to execute is that we have a number of safeguards. If we use Article 44, it would mean that some of the safeguards will not be applied." Tan Hui Yee, "Prayut Fast-Tracks Sino-Thai Rail."

41. Cheng-Chwee Kuik, "How Do Weaker States Hedge? Unpacking ASEAN States' Alignment Behavior towards China," *Journal of Contemporary China* 25, no. 100 (2016): 500–14.

42. Senior official, interview by Selina Ho, David M. Lampton, and Cheng-Chwee Kuik, Bangkok, May 31, 2017.

43. Senior official, Bangkok, May 31, 2017.

44. "Construction of Thai-Chinese High-Speed Rail to Start Fully Next Year: Thai Official," *China Daily,* June 3, 2018, www.chinadaily.com.cn/a/201806/03/WS5b134181a31001b82571ddae.html.

45. "Thailand's Junta Sees 'One Belt, One Road' As Potential Source of Legitimacy," *World Politics Review,* May 18, 2017, www.worldpoliticsreview.com/trend-lines/22198/thailand-s-junta-sees-one-belt-one-road-as-potential-source-of-legitimacy.

46. An analyst observes that because the junta has to look to China for diplomatic and strategic support at a time when America and the EU have criticized the

military's suspension of democracy, Prayut "had faced politicized criticism for not driving a harder bargain vis-à-vis Beijing, a not-so-subtle insinuation that the country has grown overly dependent on Chinese succor under his military rule." See Shawn W. Crispin, "China-Thailand Railway Project Gets Untracked," *The Diplomat,* April 1, 2016, https://thediplomat.com/2016/04/china-thailand-railway-project-gets-untracked/.

47. A. Kislenko, "Bending with the Wind: The Continuity and Flexibility of Thai Foreign Policy," *International Journal* 57 (2002): 537–61; Ann Marie Murphy, "Beyond Balancing and Bandwagoning: Thailand's Response to China's Rise," *Asian Security* 6, no. 1 (2010): 1–27; Benjamin Zawacki, *Thailand: Shifting Ground between the US and a Rising China* (London: Zed Books, 2017).

48. Alan Parkhouse, "Thai Connectivity on Fast-Track under Junta," *Asia Times,* October 28, 2018, https://cms.ati.ms/2018/10/thai-connectivity-on-fast-track-under-junta/. Emphasis added.

49. Laurids S. Lauridsen, "Changing Regional Order and Railway Diplomacy in Southeast Asia with a Case Study of Thailand," in *Mapping China's 'One Belt One Road' Initiative*, ed. Li Xing (Cham: Palgrave Macmillan, 2019), 235.

50. Thai official, interview by David M. Lampton and Cheng-Chwee Kuik, Bangkok, August 21, 2018.

51. Parkhouse, "Thai Connectivity."

52. The Charoen Pokphand (CP) Group is Thailand's largest private firm and one of the world's largest conglomerates. The Bangkok-based company, known in China as Zheng Da, was the first foreign investor in China since the launch of "Reform and Opening" in 1978. Started as an agricultural commodity company, the CP Group is today a high-tech conglomerate with a diversified portfolio of investments across Asia and beyond. A CP executive told the three coauthors during an interview on May 29, 2017, that "CP's priority is the EEC," the Eastern Economic Corridor in southeastern Thailand, because this is "the most developed region in Thailand, with 60 percent of the country's GDP, 20 million people, also includes connectivity to the sea."

53. Thodsapaol Hongtong, "CP, BSR in Race for High-Speed Airport Rail Link Deal," *Bangkok Post,* November 13, 2018, www.bangkokpost.com /business/tourism-and-transport/1574706/cp-bsr-in-race-for-high-speed-airport-rail-link-deal.

54. "Construction of Thai-Chinese High-Speed Rail to Start Fully Next Year: Thai Official," *China Daily,* June 3, 2018, www.xinhuanet.com/english /2018–06/03/c_137226904.htm.

55. Natnicha Chuwiruch, "Bids Sought for $5.5 Billion Thailand to China High-Speed Rail," *Bloomberg,* June 25, 2018, www.bloomberg.com/news/articles /2018–06–24/bids-sought-for-5-5-billion-thailand-to-china-high-speed-rail.

56. Parkhouse, "Thai Connectivity."

57. Logistics specialist, Bangkok, May 29, 2017.

58. Parkhouse, "Thai Connectivity."

59. Knowledgeable Thai expert, interview by David M. Lampton and Cheng-Chwee Kuik, Bangkok, August 20, 2018.

60. Chuwiruch, "Bids Sought."

61. Jitsiree Thongnoi, "Thai PM on First EU Visit after Easing of Sanctions against Junta," *Straits Times*, June 20, 2018, www.straitstimes.com/asia/se-asia/thai-pm-on-first-eu-visit-after-easing-of-sanctions-against-junta.

62. The SWG-SKRL, chaired by Malaysia, is an institutionalized meeting among transport ministries of seven ASEAN countries (Cambodia, Laos, Malaysia, Myanmar, Singapore, Thailand, and Vietnam) and China, which has convened annually most years since 1996. This conclave discusses the development and progress of the implementation of the SKRL project.

63. In Malaysia, 22.6 percent of the population is ethnically Chinese, while in Thailand the comparable figure is 14 percent.

64. The 1Malaysia Development Berhad (1MDB) is a semi-sovereign investment fund launched in July 2009 after Najib came to power. The firm came under criminal and regulatory investigation in July 2015 over alleged money laundering, fraud, and theft.

65. "KL Calls Tender to Design, Build Malaysia's Side of Infrastructure Works for High Speed Rail," *Straits Times*, November 20, 2017, www.straitstimes.com/asia/se-asia/kl-calls-tender-to-design-build-malaysias-side-of-infrastructure-works-for-high-speed.

66. "Dr M: Najib's China Deals May Threaten Malaysia's Sovereignty," *Malaysiakini*, November 2, 2016, www.malaysiakini.com/news/361440.

67. Mahathir commented in an interview that the ECRL terms need to be renegotiated and "if we get better terms, then of course we will continue," stressing that his government hopes to reduce costs significantly. He said that the existing terms undertaken by the previous government were not good for Malaysia. For example, "payments were made without regard for the progress of the construction," and, with respect to the loan Najib borrowed from China, RM55 billion, "we don't think it should cost that much." He added, "Then there's the issue that they give the contract to a Chinese company, and they bring in workers and everything from China, so what is there for Malaysia? We must gain something for Malaysia." See Adam Aziz, "ECRL Can Proceed If Better Terms Can Be Obtained, Says PM," Edge Markets, June 25, 2018, www.theedgemarkets.com/article/ecrl-can-proceed-if-better-terms-can-be-obtained-says-pm. See also "No Go for ECRL at RM81b, unless Cost Goes Down," *Star* (Malaysia), July 3, 2018, www.thestar.com.my/business/business-news/2018/07/03/final-cost-for-ecrl-rm81b-but-costs-must-be-reduced-further/#BLrTtCOfYpm6wird.99.

68. Ben Bland, "China's South-East Asia Push Threatened by New Malaysia Regime," *Financial Times*, May 15, 2018, www.ft.com/content/94906ad4-57eb-11e8-bdb7-f6677d2e1ce8.

69. In Mahathir's own words: "It's going to cost us a huge sum of money. We'll make no money at all from this arrangement." See "Mahathir confirms Malaysia Will Scrap KL-Singapore HSR Project," *Channel News Asia*, May 28, 2018, www.channelnewsasia.com/news/singapore/mahathir-mohamad-confirms-malaysia-pulls-out-of-kl-singapore-hsr-10284144; Manirajan Ramasamy and Fairul Asmaini Mohd Pilus, "HSR to Be Scrapped: 'Not Beneficial,'" *New Straits Times* (Malaysia), May 29, 2018.

70. "HSR Project Postponed, Not Scrapped, Dr M Tells Japanese Media," *Star*, June 12, 2018, www.thestar.com.my/news/nation/2018/06/12/hsr-project-postponed-not-scrapped-dr-m-tells-japanese-media/.

71. "Malaysia, Singapore Agree to Postpone High-Speed Rail Project for Two Years: Report," *Channel News Asia*, September 3, 3018, www.channelnewsasia.com/news/asia/high-speed-rail-malaysia-singapore-agree-postpone-project-10679982.

72. Cheng-Chwee Kuik, "Making Sense of Malaysia's China Policy: Asymmetry, Proximity, and Elite's Domestic Authority," *Chinese Journal of International Politics* 6, no. 4 (2013): 429–67.

73. Tun Dr. Mahathir Mohamad, Perdana Leadership Foundation, Putrajaya, June 27, 2016.

74. Ben Bland, "Seeking a Clear Path to Reform," *Financial Times*, May 24, 2018.

75. "Another Try at Bullet Train," Edge Markets, March 16, 2009, www.theedgemarkets.com/article/another-try-bullet-train.

76. Sharon Kaur, "HSR May Begin Ops in 2027," *New Straits Times*, April 25, 2016, www.nst.com.my/news/2016/04/141321/hsr-may-begin-ops-2027.

77. "Chinese Consortium to Bid for High-Speed Rail Project Linking Singapore and Kuala Lumpur," *Straits Times*, December 27, 2017, www.straitstimes.com/asia/east-asia/chinese-consortium-to-bid-for-high-speed-rail-project-linking-singapore-and-kuala.

78. "Najib: Project's Benefit Goes beyond Ticket Sales," *New Straits Times*, May 31, 2018.

79. David M. Lampton, Cheng-Chwee Kuik, and Selina Ho, notes with former senior Malaysian official, Kuala Lumpur, May 31, 2018, 1–5. Within the excerpt, quoted material is direct quotations, whereas the rest is close paraphrasing.

80. According to a press statement in November 2016 by then minister in the Prime Minister's Department Datuk Abdul Rahman Dahlan the rail project "has been periodically discussed and at various stages of planning since 1981." See "Statement: ECRL Project Not Hastily Decided; Proposed Since 2007," *New Straits Times*, November 9, 2016, www.nst.com.my/news/2016/11/187009/statement-ecrl-project-not-hastily-decided-proposed-2007.

81. Shahrizan Salian, Nora Mahpar, and Amir Hisyam Rasid, "Long-Term Benefits," *New Straits Times*, April 30, 2018.

82. Bernama, "ECRL Project Will Be Game Changer for East Coast, Says PM," *Free Malaysia Today*, August 9, 2017, www.freemalaysiatoday.com/category/nation/2017/08/09/ecrl-project-will-be-game-changer-for-east-coast-says-pm/.

83. Personal communications with senior government officials, former diplomats, and board members of the Chinese Chamber of Commerce, Kuala Lumpur, November–December 2018.

84. See "Liow: Do not politicise the ECRL," *Star*, August 11, 2017, www.starproperty.my/index.php/articles/property-news/liow-do-not-politicise-the-ecrl/.

85. Bernama, "ECRL Project." See also Abdul Razak Raaff and Nik Sukry Ramli, "ECRL projek berteraskan rakyat: PM," *BH Online*, August 9, 2017, www.bharian.com.my/berita/nasional/2017/08/310325/ecrl-projek-berteraskan-rakyat-pm.

86. Hong Liu and Guanie Lim, "The Political Economy of a Rising China in Southeast Asia: Malaysia's Response to the Belt and Road Initiative," *Journal of Contemporary China* 28, no. 116 (2019): 216–31.

87. Rozanna Latiff, "Malaysia's 1MDB in $1.7 Bln Asset Sale, PM Says Debt Mostly Gone," Reuters, December 30, 2015, www.reuters.com/article/malaysia-1mdb-idUSL3N14K11920151231.

88. "China to Pour in Billions for Rail Project," *Star,* November 1, 2016, www.thestar.com.my/news/nation/2016/11/01/china-to-pour-in-billions-for-rail-project-engineeringandconstruction-contract-will-also-be-signed/.

89. "Outrage!—Najib's Secret Deal with China to Pay Off 1MDB (and Jho Low's) Debts! Shock Exclusive," *Sarawak Report*, July 26, 2016, www.sarawakreport.org/2016/07/outrage-najibs-secret-deal-with-china-to-pay-off-1mdb-and-jho-lows-debts-shock-exclusive/.

90. Walt Bogdanich and Michael Forsythe, "Turning Tyranny into Client: How McKinsey Helps Autocrats Rise, Countering U.S. Interests," *New York Times,* December 16, 2018.

91. Callum Burroughs, "The Bizarre Story of 1MDB, the Goldman Sachs–Backed Malaysian Fund that Turned Into One of the Biggest Scandals in Financial History," *Business Insider*, December 27, 2018, www.businessinsider.com/1mdb-timeline-the-goldman-sachs-backed-malaysian-wealth-fund-2018-12.

92. John Chalmers, "Selling the Country to China? Debate Spills into Malaysia's Election," Reuters, April 27, 2018, www.reuters.com/article/us-malaysia-election-china/selling-the-country-to-china-debate-spills-into-malaysias-election-idUSKBN1HY076.

93. "Pembatalan rahmat bagi Bumiputera, kata PERKASA," *Malaysiakini*, May 4, 2017, www.malaysiakini.com/news/381210.

94. Nurul Izzah Anwar, "China's Investment in Malaysia: Too Much, Too Fast, Too Soon," *Malaysiakini*, May 29, 2017, www.malaysiakini.com/news/383898.

95. "Daim: RM21.5 Bil Saved from Renewed ECRL Project," *Star,* April 12, 2019, www.thestar.com.my/news/nation/2019/04/12/daim-rm215bil-savings-from-ecrl-enough-to-build-two-twin-towers/#dDtVjEDDTJFo6xOp.99; see also Chun Han Wong and Yantoultra Ngui, "China Cuts Price on Malaysian Railway," *Wall Street Journal,* April 13–14, 2019.

96. "Vietnam Protesters Clash with Police over New Economic Zones," BBC, June 11, 2018, www.bbc.com/news/world-asia-44428971.

97. World Bank Group and Ministry of Planning and Investment of Vietnam, *Vietnam 2035: Toward Prosperity, Creativity, Equity, and Democracy* (Washington, DC: World Bank, 2016), 31.

98. Very senior leader, interview by David M. Lampton and Cheng-Chwee Kuik, somewhere in Southeast Asia, June 27, 2016.

99. Former senior official, interview by David M. Lampton, Cheng-Chwee Kuik, and Selina Ho, Kuala Lumpur, May 31, 2018.

CHAPTER FIVE. THE NEGOTIATING TABLES: CHINA AND
SOUTHEAST ASIA

1. Thai professor, interview by David M. Lampton, Cheng-Chwee Kuik, and Ithrana Lawrence, Thailand, July 28, 2016.

2. Su Phyo Win and Thompson Chau, "Experts divided over ramifications of Belt and Road court on Myanmar," *Myanmar Times*, February 2, 2018.

3. On negotiation and power asymmetry in historical and contemporary international relations, see Brantly Womack, *Asymmetry and International Relationships* (Cambridge, UK: Cambridge University Press, 2016); Anthony Reid and Zheng Yangwen, eds., *Negotiating Asymmetry: China's Place in Asia* (Singapore: NUS Press, 2009); Brantly Womack, *China Among Unequals: Asymmetric Foreign Relationships in Asia* (Singapore: World Scientific Publishing, 2010).

4. Alice D. Ba and Cheng-Chwee Kuik, "Southeast Asia and China: Engagement and Constrainment," in *Contemporary Southeast Asia: The Politics of Change, Contestation, and Adaptation*, 3rd ed., ed. Alice D. Ba and Mark Beeson (London: Palgrave, 2018), 229–47.

5. Alice Ba, "Is China Leading? China, Southeast Asia and East Asian Integration," *Political Science* 66, no. 2 (2015): 145–46.

6. Neal G. Jesse, Steven E. Lobell, Galia Press-Barnathan, and Kristen P. Williams, "The Leader Can't Lead When the Followers Won't Follow: The Limitations of Hegemony," in *Beyond Great Powers and Hegemons: Why Secondary States Support, Follow, or Challenge*, ed. Kristen P. Williams, Steven E. Lobell, and Neal G. Jesse (Stanford, CA: Stanford University Press, 2012), 2.

7. Thucydides, *History of the Peloponnesian War* (Harmondsworth, UK: Penguin, 1972), 402.

8. Kenneth Waltz, *Theory of International Politics* (Long Grove, IL: Waveland Press, 2010), 72.

9. James Manicom and Jeffrey Reeves, "Locating Middle Powers in International Relations Theory and Power Transitions," in *Middle Powers and the Rise of China*, ed. Bruce Gilley and Andrew O'Neil (Washington, DC: Georgetown University Press, 2014), 24.

10. Stephen Walt, "Alliance Formation and the Balance of World Power," *International Security* 9, no. 4 (1985): 3–43.

11. David Vital, "The Inequality of States: A Study of the Small Power in International Relations," in *Small States in International Relations*, ed. Christine Ingebritsen, Iver Neumann, Sieglinde Gstohl, and Jessica Beyer (Seattle: University of Washington Press, 2006), 79.

12. Alastair Iain Johnston and Robert Ross, eds., *Engaging China: The Management of an Emerging Power* (New York: Routledge, 1999); Yuen Foong Khong, "Coping with Strategic Uncertainty: The Role of Institutions and Soft Balancing in Southeast Asia's Post-Cold War Strategy," in *Rethinking Security in East Asia: Identity, Power, and Efficiency*, ed. J.J. Suh, Peter J. Katzenstein and Allen Carlson (Stanford, CA: Stanford University Press, 2004), 172–208.

13. Evan S. Medeiros, "Strategic Hedging and the Future of Asia–Pacific Stability," *Washington Quarterly* 29, no. 1 (2005): 145–67; Evelyn Goh, "Meeting the China Challenge: The US in Southeast Asian Regional Security Strategies," *Policy Studies* 16 (Washington, DC: East–West Center Washington,

2005); Cheng-Chwee Kuik, "The Essence of Hedging: Malaysia and Singapore's Response to a Rising China," *Contemporary Southeast Asia* 30, no. 2 (2008): 159–85; John D. Ciorciari, *The Limits of Alignment* (Washington, DC: Georgetown University Press, 2010).

14. See Cheng-Chwee Kuik, "How Do Weaker States Hedge? Unpacking ASEAN States' Alignment Behavior towards China," *Journal of Contemporary China* 25, no. 100 (2016): 500–514; Cheng-Chwee Kuik, "Malaysia between the United States and China: What do Weaker States Hedge Against?" *Asian Politics and Policy* 8, no. 1 (2016): 155–77.

15. Cheng-Chwee Kuik, "Connectivity and Gaps: The Bridging Links and Missed Links of China's BRI in Southeast Asia," in *The Belt and Road and Global Governance*, ed. Maria Adele Carrai, Jean-Christophe DeFraigne, and Jan Wouters (Cheltenham, UK: Edward Elgar, 2019).

16. See Annette Baker Fox, *The Power of Small States: Diplomacy in World War II* (Chicago: University of Chicago Press, 1959); Robert Keohane, "'Lilliputians' Dilemmas: Small States in International Politics," *International Organization* 23, no. 2 (1969); Michael Handel, *Weak States in the International System* (London: Frank Cass, 1981); Andrew F. Cooper and Timothy M. Shaw, eds., *The Diplomacies of Small States* (New York: Macmillan, 2009).

17. Jeffrey L. Pressman and Aaron B. Wildavsky, *Policy Implementation: How Great Expectations in Washington are Dashed in Oakland* (Berkeley: University of California Press, 1973).

18. Very senior Thai official, interview by David M. Lampton, Selina Ho, and Cheng-Chwee Kuik, Bangkok, May 31, 2017. Within the excerpt, quoted material is direct quotations, whereas the rest is close paraphrasing.

19. Bruce Gilley and Andrew O'Neil, "China's Rise through the Prism of Middle Powers," in Gilley and O'Neil, *Middle Powers*, 5.

20. Carsten Holbraad, *Middle Powers in International Politics* (London: Macmillan Press, 1984), 4.

21. Holbraad, *Middle Powers*, 5.

22. There is little consensus on the definitions of small states and middle powers—definitions have ranged from those that stress material capabilities to those that emphasize self-perception and self-identity. See David Vital, *The Inequality of States: A Study of the Small Power in International Relations* (Oxford: Clarendon Press, 1967) for a material capability definition of states. See Robert O. Keohane, "Lilliputians' Dilemmas: Small States in International Politics," in Ingrebritsen et al., *Small States*, 60, for a self-perception definition. It is not the purpose of this book to debate these definitions. In this book, we based the categorization of Southeast Asian states on two broad criteria: the set of population size, area, GDP levels, and military strength, as well as whether they generally are regarded or self-identify as middle powers or small states.

23. Amy L. Freedman, "Malaysia, Thailand, and the ASEAN Middle Power Way," in Gilley and O'Neil, *Middle Powers*, 104.

24. Tommy Koh, "Is Singapore a Small Country?" *Straits Times* (Singapore), August 5, 2017, www.straitstimes.com/opinion/is-singapore-a-small-country.

25. Stephen Walt, "Over-achievers and Under-achievers," *Foreign Policy Blogs*, April 21, 2009, cited in Yee Kuang Heng and Syed Mohammed Ad'ha

Aljunied, "Can Small States Be More than Price Takers in Global Governance?" *Global Governance* 21, no. 3 (2015): 436.

26. Donald K. Emmerson, "Minding the Gap between Democracy and Governance," *Journal of Democracy* 23, no. 2 (April 2012): 65.

27. Richard H. Solomon, *Chinese Political Negotiating Behavior, 1967–1984* (Santa Monica, CA: RAND, 1995).

28. See David M. Lampton, chap. 7 in *Following the Leader: Ruling China, from Deng Xiaoping to Xi Jinping,* 2nd ed. (Oakland: University of California Press, 2019).

29. Committee on Government Operations, Subcommittee on National Security and International Operations, US Senate, "Peking's Approach to Negotiation: Selected Writings" (Washington, DC: Government Printing Office, 1969); see also Committee on Government Operations, Subcommittee on National Security and International Operations, US Senate, "American Shortcomings in Negotiating with Communist Powers" (Washington, DC: Government Printing Office, 1970).

30. Richard H. Solomon, *Chinese Negotiating Behavior: Pursuing Interests through "Old Friends"* (Washington, DC: United States Institute of Peace, 1999), 4.

31. Solomon, *Chinese Negotiating Behavior,* 4.

32. Qin Yaqing, *A Relational Theory of World Politics* (Cambridge, UK: Cambridge University, 2018), 112.

33. Qin Yaqing, *Relational Theory,* 114.

34. Qin Yaqing, 118.

35. David M. Lampton, "The Challenge of Being an 'Old Friend' of China," *South China Morning Post,* December 12, 2016, www.scmp.com/comment/insight-opinion/article/2053922/challenge-being-old-friend-china.

36. Samantha Custer, Brooke Russell, Matthew DiLorenzo, Mengfan Cheng, Siddhartha Ghose, Harsh Desai, Jacob Sims, and Jennifer Turner, *Ties That Bind: Quantifying China's Public Diplomacy and Its "Good Neighbor" Effect* (AidData, CSIS, and Asia Society Policy Institute, June 2018), 14.

37. Custer et al., *Ties That Bind,* 14.

38. "Li Keqiang: China's High-Speed Rail Salesman," *People's Daily,* October 9, 2014, accessed June 25, 2018, http://en.people.cn/n/2014/1009/c90883-8791853.html.

39. Ho Wah Foon, "China Factor Looms ahead of Election," *Star* (Malaysia), March 25, 2018, www.thestar.com.my/news/nation/2018/03/25/china-factor-looms-ahead-of-election-the-china-card-was-flashed-in-almost-every-general-election-in/.

40. Custer et al., *Ties That Bind,* 14.

41. Bhavan Jaipragas, "Does China Have the Inside Track in Race with Japan for Singapore-Malaysia High-Speed Rail Contract?" *South China Morning Post,* October 1, 2017, www.scmp.com/week-asia/article/2113440/does-china-have-inside-track-race-japan-singapore-malaysia-high-speed-rail.

42. Sumisha Naidu, "Capital Controls, High-Speed Rail behind Collapse of Bandar Malaysia Deal?" Channel News Asia, June 23, 2017, www.channelnewsasia.com/news/asia/capital-controls-high-speed-rail-behind-collapse-of-bandar-8823716.

43. Zhang Hongri, *"Ma lai xi ya zong li fang hua qi jian pao hong xi fang guo jia. Wai mei: mei guo zai du shou chuang"* [PM Najib of Malaysia blasted Western countries during his visit to China. Foreign Media: Another blow to the US], *Guanchazhe*, November 5, 2016, www.guancha.cn/Neighbors/2016_11_05_379550.shtml.

44. The deal, which fell through in May 2017, is discussed further later in this chapter.

45. Very senior Thai official, Bangkok, May 31, 2017.

46. Leo Suryadinata, *The Rise of China and the Chinese Overseas: A Study of Beijing's Changing Policy in Southeast Asia and Beyond* (Singapore: Institute of Southeast Asian Studies Publishing, 2017), 15.

47. Suryadinata, *Rise of China*, 19.

48. Suryadinata, 33.

49. Cited in Suryadinata, *Rise of China*, 156.

50. Cited in Suryadinata, 114.

51. Stephen Fitzgerald, *China and the Overseas Chinese: A Study of Peking's Changing Policy, 1949–1970* (Cambridge, UK: Cambridge University Press, 1972).

52. Bhavan Jaipragas, "Does China Have the Inside Track."

53. Tan Weizhen, "China Eyes HSR Project, Sells Know-How on Operating Rail in Tropical Climate," *Today* (Singapore), November 17, 2017, www.todayonline.com/singapore/china-eyes-hsr-project-sells-knowhow-operating-rail-tropical-climate.

54. See Alan Chong and David Han, "Foreign Policy Lessons from the Terrex Episode," *RSIS Commentary* 22, February 2, 2017, www.rsis.edu.sg/wp-content/uploads/2017/02/CO17022.pdf, for an analysis of the Terrex incident and how Singaporean-based researchers view the event.

55. High-ranking Singapore official, interview by Selina Ho, May 12, 2017.

56. Du Jinxuan, *"'Yi dai yi lu' he yi shen xian ma lai xi ya zheng zhi ni zhao?"* [How did the BRI sink into the swamp that is Malaysian Politics?], *IFENG*, May 20, 2017, http://pit.ifeng.com/a/20170520/51128101_0.shtml.

57. High-level Malaysian source, interview by David M. Lampton, Selina Ho, and Cheng-Chwee Kuik, May 29, 2018.

58. Pongphisoot Busbarat, "Why was Thailand's Prime Minister absent in the Belt and Road Initiative Summit," *ISEAS Commentary*, June 9, 2017, www.iseas.edu.sg/medias/commentaries/item/5557-why-was-thailands-prime-minister-absent-in-the-belt-and-road-initiative-summit-by-pongphisoot-busbarat.

59. Qin Yaqing, *Relational Theory*, 138.

60. "Building the Belt and Road for Win-Win Development," *China Daily*, February 3, 2017, www.chinadaily.com.cn/opinion/2017–02/03/content_28087627.htm. Emphasis added.

61. "China, Thailand Inaugurate Construction of High-Speed Railway in Thailand," *China Daily*, December 21, 2017, www.chinadaily.com.cn/a/201712/21/WS5a3bb132a31008cf16da2b76.html.

62. Zhang Feng, *Chinese Hegemony: Grand Strategy and International Institutions in East Asian History* (Stanford, CA: Stanford University Press, 2015), 15.

63. Zhang, *Chinese Hegemony*, 15.

64. Zhang, 39.

65. Siwage Dharma Negara and Leo Suryadinata, "Jakarta-Bandung High Speed Rail Project: Little Progress, Many Challenges," *ISEAS Perspective* 2 (2018): 2, www.iseas.edu.sg/images/pdf/ISEAS_Perspective_2018_2@50.pdf.

66. Very senior regional official, interview by David M. Lampton, Indonesia, January 28, 2016.

67. Very senior regional official, Indonesia, January 28, 2016.

68. Yang Zhou and Li Xinying, *"Tai guo ji hua dao 2036 nian xiu jian yu 2500 gong li gao tie,"* [Thailand plans to build more than 2,500 km of HSR by 2036], Xinhua, March 30, 2018, www.xinhuanet.com/thailand/2018–03/30 /c_1122617845.htm.

69. Tan Hui Yee, "Prayut Fast-Tracks Sino-Thai Rail Project," *Straits Times,* June 17, 2017, www.straitstimes.com/asia/se-asia/prayut-fast-tracks-sino-thai-rail-project.

70. *"Zhong lao tie lu jie ju: wei he zhe ma nan, wei he reng yao jian?"* [Resolving the Sino-Laotian Rail: Why Is It So Difficult, Why Must We Forge On?], *Sohu,* April 19, 2018, accessed June 29, 2018, www.sohu.com/a/228822426_7310211.

71. David A. Lake, *Hierarchy in International Relations* (Ithaca, NY: Cornell University Press, 2009), 14.

72. Joshua Kurlantzick, *Charm Offensive: How China's Soft Power Is Transforming the World* (New Haven, CT: Yale University Press, 2007).

73. Wang Jiamei, "China's SOEs Can Aid B&R Route Countries in Economic Development," *Global Times,* April 13, 2017, www.globaltimes.cn /content/1042351.shtml.

74. Aleksander Purba, Fumihiko Nakamura, Chatarina Niken DWSBU, Muhammad Jafri, and Priyo Pratomo, "A Current Review of High Speed Railways Experiences in Asia and Europe," *AIP Conference Proceedings* (2017), 1.

75. Li Luxi and Fran Wang, "Veteran China Banker Warns of 'Belt and Road' Risks," Caixin Global, April 13, 2018, www.caixinglobal.com/2018–04–13/veteran-china-banker-warns-of-belt-and-road-risks-101234218.html.

76. Dragan Pavlićević and Agatha Kratz, "Testing the China Threat Paradigm: China's High-Speed Railway Diplomacy in Southeast Asia," *Pacific Review* (2017): 11–12. Epub ahead of print, June 29, 2017.

77. Senior Lao official, interview by David M. Lampton, Selina Ho, and Cheng-Chwee Kuik, Vientiane, June 6, 2017.

78. World Bank Group, *Belt and Road Economics: Opportunities and Risks of Transport Corridors* (Washington, DC: World Bank, 2019), 13.

79. Senior Thai political figure, in conversation with David M. Lampton, Selina Ho, and Cheng-Chwee Kuik, Bangkok, May 30, 2017.

80. Li Wannan and Ding Meng, *"Zhong tai tie lu mian lin de tiao zhan ji dui ce fen xi"* [An Analysis of the Challenges and Countermeasures on China-Thailand Railway Project], *Chuangxin* 2, no. 12 (2018).

81. "Chinese Are Becoming Investors First, Tourists Second in Thailand," *PropertyGuru Property Report*, February 2, 2017, www.property-report.com /detail/-/blogs/chinese-are-becoming-investors-first-tourists-second-in-thailand.

82. Natnicha Chuwiruch, "Chinese Tourists Could Cause Years of Misery for Thai Airports," *Bloomberg,* December 21, 2017, www.bloomberg.com /news/articles/2017–12–20/thai-airport-misery-may-last-years-as-chinese-over-whelm-upgrades.

83. Arno Maierbrugger, "Thailand Gives Nod to New $5.5b [Billion] High-Speed Railway Connecting with China," *Investvine,* July 11, 2017, http:// investvine.com/thailand-gives-nod-to-new-5–5b-high-speed-railway-connecting-with-china/.

84. Maierbrugger, "Thailand Gives Nod."

85. Yukako Ono, "Thailand Plans Regional Infrastructure Fund to Reduce China Dependence," *Nikkei Asian Review,* June 4, 2018, https://asia.nikkei .com/Politics/International-Relations/Thailand-plans-regional-infrastructure-fund-to-reduce-China-dependence.

86. IMF Database, Report for selected countries and subjects, www.imf.org /external/pubs/ft/weo/2019/01/weodata/weorept.aspx?pr.x=69&pr.y=14&sy=2 017&ey=2021&scsm=1&ssd=1&sort=country&ds=.&br=1&c=544&s=NGD PD%2CPPPGDP%2CNGDPDPC%2CPPPPC%2CPCPIPCH.

87. Senior Lao official, Vientiane, June 6, 2017.

88. Senior Lao official, Vientiane, June 6, 2017.

89. Senior development officer, interview by David M. Lampton, Selina Ho, and Cheng Chwee-Kuik, June 7, 2017.

90. "*Zhong lao tie lu jie ju*" [Resolving the Sino-Laotian Rail].

91. "*Zhong lao tie lu jie ju.*"

92. Senior Lao official, Vientiane, June 6, 2017.

93. "*Zhong lao tie lu jie ju.*"

94. Zhang Shu and Matthew Miller, "Behind China's Silk Road Vision: Cheap Funds, Heavy Debt, Growing Risk," Reuters, May 15, 2017, www .reuters.com/article/us-china-silkroad-finance/behind-chinas-silk-road-vision-cheap-funds-heavy-debt-growing-risk-idUSKCN18B0YS.

95. Senior multilateral institution official, interview by David M. Lampton, Selina Ho, and Cheng-Chwee Kuik, June 7, 2017.

96. Senior Lao official, Vientiane, June 6, 2017.

97. Freedman, "Malaysia, Thailand," 104.

98. Tun Dr. Mahathir Mohamad, *A Doctor in the House* (Kuala Lumpur: MPH Group Publishing, 2011), 431.

99. Mahathir, *Doctor in the House,* 431.

100. Mazwin Nik Anis, "Azmin: HSR Construction Off until May 2020," *Star* (Malaysia), September 5, 2018, www.thestar.com.my/news/nation/2018/09 /05/azmin-hsr-construction-off-until-may-2020/.

101. Rebecca Rajaendram, Sandhya Menon, Lee Chonghui, and Ashley Tang, "Maszlee: Give Us More Time," *Star,* June 1, 2018, www.thestar.com .my/news/nation/2018/06/01/maszlee-give-us-more-time-debt-situation-affected-ptptn-pledge-says-education-minister/.

102. Senior Singapore government official, interview by David M. Lampton, Selina Ho, and Cheng-Chwee Kuik, Singapore, May 28, 2018.

103. Senior Singapore government official, Singapore, May 28, 2018.

104. See the example of ECRL in Wan Saiful Wan Jan, "Malaysia's Priority Is to Manage, Not Stop, China's Investments," *ISEAS Perspective* 46 (2017): 7. The ECRL project was awarded to a Chinese company without an open tender, but through direct negotiation.

105. Charissa Yong, "Singaporeans Should Be Aware of China's 'Influence Operations' to Manipulate Them, Says Retired Diplomat Bilahari," *Straits Times*, June 28, 2018, www.straitstimes.com/singapore/singaporeans-should-be-aware-of-chinas-influence-operations-to-manipulate-them-says.

106. Mayuko Tani, "Singapore and Malaysia Open Bidding for Historical Railway Link," *Nikkei Asian Review*, December 20, 2017, https://asia.nikkei.com/Business/Singapore-and-Malaysia-open-bidding-for-historic-railway-link.

107. Clarissa Chung, "Dr M Announced Revival of Bandar Malaysia Project," *Star*, April 19, 2019, www.thestar.com.my/news/nation/2019/04/19/dr-m-announces-revival-of-bandar-malaysia-project/.

108. Cited in Ann Marie Murphy, "Indonesia Responds to China's Rise," in Gilley and O'Neil, *Middle Powers*, 126.

109. Murphy, "Indonesia Responds," 136.

110. Murphy, 136.

111. Senior foreign government official, interview by David M. Lampton, Jakarta, January 2017.

112. Ezra Sihite and Deti Mega S.P., "Indonesia Plans 'Beauty Contest' between China and Japan for High-Speed Train," *Jakarta Globe*, July 13, 2015, https://jakartaglobe.id/news/indonesia-plans-beauty-contest-china-japan-high-speed-train/.

113. Cited in Murphy, "Indonesia Responds," 143.

114. Gilley and O'Neil, "China's Rise," 2.

115. 21st Century Maritime Silk Road Research Center, Royal University of Phnom Penh, "Cambodia's IDP [Industrial Development Policy] and China's BRI," unpublished manuscript, 25. Undated, but sources cited from 2017 are in the text.

116. Gilley and O'Neil, "China's Rise," 10.

117. Max Fisher and Audrey Carlsen, "How China Is Challenging American Dominance in Asia," *New York Times*, March 9, 2018.

118. Cheng-Chwee Kuik, "Making Sense of Malaysia's China Policy: Asymmetry, Proximity, and Elite's Domestic Authority," *Chinese Journal of International Politics* 6, no. 4 (2013): 429–67; Cheng-Chwee Kuik, "Malaysia between the United States and China: What Do Weaker States Hedge Against?" *Asian Politics and Policy* 8, no. 1 (2016): 155–77; Freedman, "Malaysia, Thailand," 109; Ian Storey, *Southeast Asia and the Rise of China: The Search for Security* (London: Routledge, 2013), 223.

119. Murray Hiebert, "Trump-Najib Meeting Gives Malaysia-U.S. Relations Shot of Adrenaline," *Center for Strategic and International Studies*, September 14, 2017, www.csis.org/analysis/trump-najib-meeting-gives-malaysia-us-relations-shot-adrenaline.

120. Fanny Potkin, "Is Laos Moving Away from China with Its Leadership Transition?" *The Diplomat*, February 3, 2016, https://thediplomat.com/2016/02/is-laos-moving-away-from-china-with-its-leadership-transition/.

121. Marius Zaharia, "As Obama Heads to Laos, Signs of a Tilt away from China," Reuters, August 28, 2016, www.reuters.com/article/us-laos-china-vietnam/as-obama-heads-to-laos-signs-of-a-tilt-away-from-china-idUSKC-N11300Z.

122. Francis Fukuyama, *State-Building: Governance and World Order in the 21st Century* (Ithaca, NY: Cornell University Press, 2004).

123. Narendra Aggarwal, "S'pore is China's largest investor," *Business Times,* November 6, 2015, www.businesstimes.com.sg/hub/business-china-special/spore-is-chinas-largest-investor.

124. Tan Zhi Xin, "Singapore's Big Balancing Act: The US vs. China," *ASEAN Today,* December 24, 2016, www.aseantoday.com/2016/12/singapores-big-balancing-act-the-us-vs-china/.

125. Tan Zhi Xin, "Singapore's Big Balancing Act."

126. *"Guo jia fa zhan gei ge wei guan yu xin jian yu xi zhi mo han tie lu ke xing xing yan jiu bao gao de pi fu"* [A Reply from the NDRC on the Feasibility Report of the Railway between Yuxi and Mohan], *Notification from NDRC,* July 29, 2015, accessed February 27, 2020, www.ndrc.gov.cn/fggz/zcssfz/zdgc/201509/t20150908_1146029.html.

127. *"Lao wo ren min zhu gong he guo zhu hua da shi wan di bu da sa feng: jiao yu jiao liu shen hua zhong lao quan mian zhan lue he zuo"* [Ambassador Vandy Bouthasavong of Lao People's Democratic Republic: Education deepens comprehensive Sino-Laotian strategic cooperation], *Shijie Jiaoyu Xinxiwang,* May 5, 2016, www.wei.moe.edu.cn/index.php?m=content&c=index&a=show &catid=14&id=195.

128. Chaiyot Yongcharoenchai, "Academics Slam Lack of Details for Sino-Thai Railway Project," *Bangkok Post,* June 23, 2017, www.bangkokpost.com /news/general/1273747/academics-slam-lack-of-details-for-sino-thai-railway-project.

129. Emirza Adi Syailendra, "Indonesia's High Speed Rail: A China-Japan Scramble for Influence?" *RSIS Commentary* 269, S. Rajaratnam School of International Studies, Nanyang Technological University, Singapore, December 9, 2015, 1–2.

130. Robert D. Putnam, "Diplomacy and Domestic Politics: The Logic of Two-Level Games," *International Organization* 42, no. 3 (Summer 1988): 427–60.

131. Cited in Custer et al., *Ties That Bind,* 29; very senior local Malaysian official, interview by David M. Lampton, Selina Ho, and Cheng-Chwee Kuik, Malaysia, May 29, 2018.

132. Tham Siew Yean, "Chinese Investment in Malaysia: Five Years into the BRI," *ISEAS Perspective* 11, February 27, 2018.

133. Cited in Wan Jan, "Malaysia's Priority," 6.

134. Custer et al., *Ties That Bind,* 30.

135. Custer et al., 30.

136. Shibani Mahtani, "Fears of a New 'Colonialism,'" *Washington Post,* September 11, 2018.

137. Mitsuru Obe and Marimi Kishimoto, "High-Speed Dreams," *Nikkei Asian Review,* January 14, 2019.

138. Putnam, "Diplomacy and Domestic Politics."

CHAPTER SIX. PROJECT IMPLEMENTATION: "THE DEVIL IS IN THE DETAILS"

1. Gregory Enjalbert, vice president of Bombardier Transportation's Asia-Pacific Control Solutions, spoke of the Belt and Road Initiative (BRI) in an interview. Zach Coleman, "China's Belt and Road Impact 'Limited' So Far, Bombardier Says," *Nikkei Asian Review*, April 9, 2019, https://asia.nikkei.com/Editor-s-Picks/Interview/China-s-Belt-and-Road-impact-limited-so-far-Bombardier-says.

2. Merilee S. Grindle, ed., *Politics and Policy Implementation in the Third World* (Princeton, NJ: Princeton University Press, 1980), 15.

3. David M. Lampton, *Policy Implementation in Post-Mao China* (Berkeley: University of California Press, 1987).

4. Jeffrey L. Pressman and Aaron B. Wildavsky, chap. 5 in *Implementation: How Great Expectations in Washington Are Dashed in Oakland* (Berkeley: University of California Press, 1973).

5. Pressman and Wildavsky, *Implementation*, 107.

6. Pressman and Wildavsky, 99–102.

7. Francis Fukuyama, "What Is Governance?" *Governance: An International Journal of Policy, Administration, and Institutions* 26, no. 3 (July 2013): 350.

8. Fukuyama, "What Is Governance?" 351.

9. Fukuyama, 354.

10. United Nations Development Programme, *2018 Human Development Reports,* http://hdr.undp.org/en/composite/HDI.

11. Official, meeting with David M. Lampton, Selina Ho, and Cheng-Chwee Kuik, Vientiane, Laos, June 6, 2017.

12. Selina Ho, Cheng-Chwee Kuik, and David M. Lampton, "Interview—Roundtable," Singapore, May 30, 2018.

13. High-level Thai government source, interview by David M. Lampton, Selina Ho, and Cheng-Chwee Kuik, Bangkok, Thailand, August 21, 2018.

14. Thai transport expert, interview by David M. Lampton, Cheng-Chwee Kuik, and Ithrana Lawrence, July 28, 2016. Direct quotations are given in single quote marks, whereas the rest is close paraphrase.

15. PRC Foreign Ministry official, interview by David M. Lampton, April 11, 2019.

16. Thailand's HSR project, which will run at a maximum speed of 250 kmph, will be carried out in different phases, with phase 1, the 252.5 km track between Bangkok and Nakhon Ratchasima, starting construction in December 2017. There are four sections in this first phase; the first (pilot) section is 3.5 km, the second section 11 km, the third 119 km, and the fourth section also 119 km. As of September 2018, construction had started only for the first 3.5 km section. After the completion of the first phase, the railway project will enter the second phase, where the track from Nakhon Ratchasima will be extended to Nong Khai at the border with Laos. "Thai-China High-Speed Railway," Global Security, undated, www.globalsecurity.org/military/world/thailand/hsr.htm.

17. Michael Mann, "The Autonomous Power of the State: Its Origins, Mechanisms, and Results," *European Journal of Sociology* 25, no. 2 (1984): 185–213.

18. Lampton, *Policy Implementation*.

19. Ling Chen, *Manipulating Globalization: The Influence of Bureaucrats on Business in China* (Stanford, CA: Stanford University Press), especially 5–7.

20. See David M. Lampton, "A Plum for a Peach: Bargaining, Interest, and Bureaucratic Politics in China," in *Bureaucracy, Politics, and Decision Making in Post-Mao China*, ed. Kenneth G. Lieberthal and David M. Lampton (Berkeley: University of California Press, 1992), 33–58.

21. Yin Ming, Luca Bertolini, and Duan Jin, "The Effects of the High-Speed Railway on Urban Development: International Experience and Potential Implications for China," *Progress in Planning*, no. 98 (2015): 2.

22. Li Wannan and Ding Meng, "*Zhong tai tie lu mian lin de tiao zhan ji dui ce fen xi*" [An Analysis of the Challenges and Countermeasures of the China-Thailand Railway Project], *Chuangxin* 12, no. 2 (2018): 101–2.

23. Wu Weiping and Wu Xiaoming, "Study on Fund Raising Means for China's Railways," Economic and Planning Research Institute of the Ministry of Railways, PRC, undated manuscript, 1. See also Zhenhua Chen and Kingsley E. Haynes, *Chinese Railways in the Era of High-Speed* (London: Emerald Group Publishing, 2015), 142–49.

24. Zhao Jian, Zhao Yunyi, and Li Ying, "The Variation in the Value of Travel-Time Savings and the Dilemma of High-Speed Rail in China," *Transport Research*, Part A, no. 82 (2015): 139.

25. Zhao Jian et al., "Variation in the Value," 139.

26. Li Ping and Jia Boqun, "*Fan si zhong guo gao tie jian she de zhi dao li nian*" [Reflecting on the Guiding Doctrines of China's High-Speed Railway Constructions], *Journal of University of Science and Technology Beijing (Social Sciences Edition)* 33, no. 1 (February 2017): 61.

27. Senior former Southeast Asian official, interview by David M. Lampton and Cheng-Chwee Kuik, July 26, 2016.

28. David M. Lampton, *Following the Leader: Ruling China, from Deng Xiaoping to Xi Jinping* (Oakland: University of California Press, 2019), 92–93.

29. Guizhen He, Arthur P. J. Mol, Zhang Lei, and Lu Yonglong, "Environmental Risks of High-Speed Railway in China: Public Participation, Perception and Trust," *Environmental Development* 14 (2015): 41.

30. Guizhen He et al., "Environmental Risks," 41.

31. Guizhen He et al., 41.

32. Guizhen He et al., 41.

33. Guizhen He et al., 47.

34. High-level Thai government source, Bangkok, August 21, 2018.

35. Tyler Durden, "The Tinaco-Anaco Railway Line: A Look at How China Overextended in a Failed Venezuela," ZeroHedge, May 15, 2016, www.zerohedge.com/news/2016-05-15/tinaco-anaco-railway-line-look-how-china-overextended-failed-venezuela.

36. Debby Chan Sze Wan, "China-Myanmar High-Speed Railway Quietly Back on Track," *Myanmar Times*, July 6, 2018, www.mmtimes.com/news/china-myanmar-high-speed-railway-quietly-back-track.html. This newspaper report suggests that the National League for Democracy–led government, which took over power from the military junta in 2015, has been restarting talks on

the HSR as part of the China-Myanmar economic corridor and gradually improving relations with Beijing.

37. Senior researcher in Central Committee, meeting with David M. Lampton, China, April 20, 2018.

38. Senior Thai official, interview by David M. Lampton and Cheng-Chwee Kuik, August 21, 2018.

39. Senior foreign diplomat, interview by David M. Lampton, Jakarta, Indonesia, January 28, 2016.

40. "Indonesia Seeks Ways to Speed Up China High-Speed Rail Project," *Straits Times* (Singapore), May 2, 2018, www.straitstimes.com/asia/se-asia /indonesia-seeks-ways-to-speed-up-china-high-speed-rail-project; "Interview: Expert sees China-Built High-Speed Rail Transportation, Economic Game-Changer for Indonesia," Xinhua Silk Road Information Service, March 29, 2019.

41. "Jakarta-Bandung High Speed Railway to Begin Construction in May," PricewaterhouseCoopers Indonesia, February 9, 2018, accessed September 4, 2018, www.pwc.com/id/en/media-centre/infrastructure-news/february-2018 /jakarta-bandung-high-speed-railway.html.

42. Takehiro Masutomo and Teng Jing Xuan, "Indonesia's China-Financed High-Speed Rail Project off Track," Caixin Global, October 11, 2018, www .caixinglobal.com/2018–10–11/indonesias-china-financed-high-speed-rail-project-off-track-101333896.html.

43. "Land Acquisition for Jakarta-Bandung High-Speed Train to Conclude in April," *Jakarta Post*, March 20, 2019, www.thejakartapost.com/news/2019 /03/20/land-acquisition-process-for-jakarta-bandung-high-speed-train-to-conclude-in-april.html.

44. "WIKA Records RP2 Trillion Net Profit," ACN Newswire, April 2, 2019.

45. See Gary W. Cox and Mathew D. McCubbins, "The Institutional Determinants of Economic Policy Outcomes," in *Presidents, Parliaments, and Policy*, ed. Stephan Haggard and Mathew D. McCubbins (Cambridge, UK: Cambridge University Press, 2001), 21–63.

46. Edward Aspinall and Greg Fealy, "Introduction: Decentralisation, Democratisation and the Rise of the Local," in *Local Power and Politics in Indonesia: Decentralisation and Democratisation* (Singapore: Institute of Southeast Asian Studies, 2003), 1. Emphasis in the original.

47. Aspinall and Fealy, "Introduction," 3.

48. Aspinall and Fealy, 4.

49. Regencies are directly administered by provinces. After the 1998 democratic reforms, the number of regencies proliferated and became an increasingly powerful level of government. In precolonial times, before the Dutch abolished the monarchy in Indonesia, regents were local lords who paid tribute to the king.

50. Senior leader, interview by David M. Lampton, Indonesia, January 28, 2016.

51. Arya Dipa, "Thousands of Households to Be Evicted," *Jakarta Post*, January 25, 2016, www.thejakartapost.com/news/2016/01/25/thousands-households-be-evicted.html.

52. Arya Dipa, "Rail Project Condemned for Ignoring Spatial Plan," *Jakarta Post,* January 29, 2016, www.thejakartapost.com/news/2016/01/29/rail-project-condemned-ignoring-spatial-plan.html.

53. Dipa, "Thousands of Households."

54. Dipa, "Rail Project Condemned."

55. Dipa, "Rail Project Condemned."

56. Arya Dipa, "Locals Oppose Evictions for High-Speed Rail Project," *Jakarta Post,* May 10, 2017, www.thejakartapost.com/news/2017/05/10/locals-oppose-evictions-high-speed-rail-project.html.

57. Dipa, "Locals Oppose Evictions."

58. See, for example, Aleksander Purba, Fumihiko Nakamura, Chatarina Niken DWSBU, Muhammad Jafri, and Priyo Pratomo, "A Current Review of High Speed Railways Experiences in Asia and Europe," *Proceedings of the 3rd International Conference on Construction and Building Engineering,* November 14, 2017, https://aip.scitation.org/doi/pdf/10.1063/1.5011558.

59. Eveline Danubrata and Gayatri Suroyo, "In Indonesia, Labor Friction and Politics Fan Anti-Chinese Sentiment," Reuters, April 18, 2017, www.reuters.com/article/us-indonesia-election-china/in-indonesia-labor-friction-and-politics-fan-anti-chinese-sentiment-idUSKBN17K0YG.

60. Masutomo and Teng Jing Xuan, "Indonesia's China-Financed High-Speed Rail."

61. Masutomo and Teng Jing Xuan.

62. "Feature: Indonesian Workers Excited about China's Advanced Technology in High-Speed Railway Construction," *People's Daily Online,* March 25, 2019.

63. Aspinall and Fealy, "Introduction," 6.

64. Siwage Dharma Negara and Leo Suryadinata, "Jakarta-Bandung High Speed Rail Project Poses Big Challenge for Jokowi," *Today Online,* January 12, 2018, www.todayonline.com/commentary/jakarta-bandung-high-speed-rail-project-poses-big-challenge-jokowi.

65. See "Ministers Differ in Jakarta-Bandung High-Speed Railway Project," *Jakarta Post,* April 25, 2017, www.thejakartapost.com/news/2017/04/25/ministers-differ-in-jakarta-bandung-high-speed-railway-project.html.

66. "Ministers Differ."

67. Nani Afrida and Ina Parlina, "High-Speed Rail Plan Hits Another Snag," *Jakarta Post,* January 28, 2016, www.thejakartapost.com/news/2016/01/28/high-speed-rail-plan-hits-another-snag.html.

68. Afrida and Parlina, "High-Speed Rail Plan."

69. Masutomo and Teng Jing Xuan, "Indonesia's China-Financed High-Speed Rail."

70. Stephen D. Krasner, "Are Bureaucracies Important? (Or Allison Wonderland)," *Foreign Policy* 7 (Summer 1972): 159–79.

71. "Indonesia's Presidential Challenger Wants a Better China Trade Deal," *Business Times,* January 17, 2019, www.businesstimes.com.sg/government-economy/indonesias-presidential-challenger-wants-a-better-china-trade-deal.

72. "Jakarta-Bandung High Speed Railway."

73. Negara and Suryadinata, "Jakarta-Bandung High Speed Rail Project."

74. Riza Roidila Mufti, "High-speed Railway Project to Accelerate after Fund Disbursement," *Jakarta Post,* September 5, 2018, www.thejakartapost .com/news/2018/09/05/high-speed-railway-project-accelerate-after-fund-disbursement.html.

75. Thai professor, interview by David M. Lampton and Cheng-Chwee Kuik, Thailand, August 20, 2018.

76. Perhaps the best example of a project champion for infrastructure, beyond the case of Chinese Railway Minister Liu Zhijun discussed in chapter 2, was New York City's master builder, Robert Moses. Robert A. Caro wrote the definitive biography of Moses, *The Power Broker.* Caro discusses why Moses was so successful and powerful in his *Working: Researching, Interviewing, Writing* (New York: Alfred A. Knopf, 2019).

77. Thai professor, Thailand, August 20, 2018.

78. Thai professor, Thailand, August 20, 2018.

79. Several technician training programs have been set up involving Wuhan Railway Vocational College and Thailand, with Thai students spending time both at home and in China being trained. Yang Zhou, "Thailand, China establish Lu Ban High-Speed Railway Institute," Xinhua, April 4, 2019.

80. "Rail Progress Tracks Full Steam Ahead," *Bangkok Post,* December 2, 2018, www.bangkokpost.com/news/special-reports/1586186/rail-progress-tracks-full-steam-ahead.

81. Laura Zhou, "Engineers Put Brakes on Chinese-Thai Rail Plan," *South China Morning Post,* June 19, 2017.

82. High-level Thai government source, Bangkok, August 21, 2018.

83. Thai analyst, interview by David M. Lampton and Cheng-Chwee Kuik, Bangkok, August 20, 2018.

84. "Article 44 Exemptions for Rail Line," *The Nation* (Thailand), June 14, 2017, www.nationmultimedia.com/detail/politics/30317994.

85. "Regional Rail Boom Creating New Opportunities," *Bangkok Post,* December 18, 2017, www.bangkokpost.com/business/news/1380887/regional-rail-boom-creating-new-opportunities.

86. See Pichamon Yeophantong, "River Activism, Policy Entrepreneurship and Transboundary Water Disputes in Asia," *Water International* 42, no. 2 (February 2017): 173–76, to get a sense of the environmental NGOs in Thailand.

87. Sarah Zheng, "US$5.2 Billion First Phase of China-Thailand Railway Project Facing Further Delays, Reports Say," *South China Morning Post,* October 7, 2017, www.scmp.com/news/china/diplomacy-defence/article/2114359 /us52-billion-first-phase-china-thailand-railway-project.

88. High-level Thai government source, Bangkok, August 21, 2018.

89. High-level Thai government source, Bangkok, August 21, 2018.

90. Thai business leader, interview by David M. Lampton, Selina Ho, and Cheng-Chwee Kuik, Khon Kaen, Thailand, June 3, 2017.

91. Senior Thai official, August 21, 2018.

92. Natnicha Chuwiruch, "Bids Sought for $5.5 Billion Thailand to China High-Speed Rail," Bloomberg, June 23, 2018, www.bloomberg.com/amp/news /articles/2018-06-24/bids-sought-for-5-5-billion-thailand-to-china-high-speed-rail.

93. "Construction of Thai-Chinese High-Speed Rail to Start Fully Next Year: Thai Official," Xinhua, June 3, 2018, www.xinhuanet.com/english/2018–06/03/c_137226904.htm.

94. High-level Thai government source, personal communication, August 21, 2018.

95. High-level Thai government source, personal communication, August 21, 2018.

96. "After Delays, Ground Broken for Thailand-China Railway Project," Reuters, August 21, 2017, www.reuters.com/article/us-thailand-china-railway /after-delays-ground-broken-for-thailand-china-railway-project-idUSKB-N1EF1E6.

97. Ho, Kuik, and Lampton, "Interview—Roundtable," Singapore, May 30, 2018, unpublished manuscript, 9–10.

98. "Malaysia to Award $18.3b KL-Kelantan Rail Project to China," *Straits Times*, November 1, 2016, www.straitstimes.com/asia/malaysia-to-award-183b-kl-kelantan-rail-project-to-china (Singapore dollars).

99. Tashny Sukumaran, "Malaysia Won't Say Yes or No to Reports China Offered to Bail Out 1MDB and Spy on Journalists in Return for Infrastructure Deals," *South China Morning Post*, January 8, 2019, www.scmp.com/news /asia/southeast-asia/article/2181188/malaysia-wont-say-yes-or-no-reports-china-offered-bail-out.

100. "Malaysia's East Coast Rail Link to Cost US$20b, up 50% from Estimates: Finance Minister," *Channel News Asia*, July 3, 2019, www.channelnews asia.com/news/asia/malaysia-east-coast-rail-link cost-china-finance-minister-10494484.

101. Malaysian leader, interview by David M. Lampton, Selina Ho, and Cheng-Chwee Kuik, Malaysia, May 29, 2018.

102. Trinna Leong, "Malaysia Cancels Deal with China Company, Seeks New Contractor for East Coast Rail Link," *Straits Times*, January 22, 2019, www.straitstimes.com/asia/se-asia/malaysia-cancels-deal-with-china-company-seeks-new-contractor-for-east-coast-rail-link.

103. Melissa Goh, "Nearly 1,000 Jobs Lost As Fallout from Malaysia's Suspended East Coast Rail Link Project Digs In," Channel News Asia, July 21, 2018, www.channelnewsasia.com/news/asia/1–000-jobs-lost-fallout-malaysia-east-coast-rail-link-10551208.

104. "Malaysia's Mahathir Cancels China-Backed Rail, Pipeline Projects," Reuters, August 21, 2018, www.reuters.com/article/us-china-malaysia/malaysias-mahathir-cancels-china-backed-rail-pipeline-projects-idUSKCN1L60DQ.

105. "Dr M Says Hopes for Beijing's Sympathies for Malaysia's Fiscal Problems," *Malay Mail*, August 20, 2018, www.malaymail.com/news/malaysia /2018/08/20/pm-calls-for-chinas-help-with-fiscal-problems/1664159.

106. "Chinese-backed East Coast Rail Link, Pipeline Projects Cancelled for Now: Malaysia PM Mahathir," Channel News Asia, August 21, 2018, www .channelnewsasia.com/news/asia/mahathir-malaysia-china-east-coast-rail-link-pipeline-cancelled-10637048.

107. Justin Ong, "Report: PM Claims Some Firms Offered to Build ECRL for RM10b," *Malay Mail*, August 28, 2018, www.malaymail.com/news

/malaysia/2018/08/28/report-pm-claims-some-firms-offered-to-build-ecrl-for-rm10b/1666643.

108. Harizah Hanim Mohamed, "Finance Minister Hopes Decision on ECRL Soon," *Bernama Daily Malaysian News*, March 7, 2019, www.bernama.com/en/news.php?id=1702316.

109. Senior official, interview by David M. Lampton, Cheng-Chwee Kuik, and Selina Ho, Southeast Asia, August 23, 2018.

110. Senior foreign policy expert, interview by David M. Lampton, Selina Ho, and Cheng-Chwee Kuik, Kuala Lumpur, Malaysia, May 31, 2018.

111. Nur Aqidah Azizi and Adrian Lai, "Loke: New ECRL Route Will Benefit Five States," *New Sunday Times* (Singapore), April 14, 2019, www.nst.com.my/news/nation/2019/04/478972/loke-new-ecrl-route-avoid-titiwangsa-range.

112. "KL-Singapore High-Speed Rail Formally Postponed; Service Targeted to Start by Jan 2031," Channel News Asia, September 6, 2018, www.channelnewsasia.com/news/asia/high-speed-rail-postponed-malaysia-singapore-agreement-10686032.

113. Singapore government official, interview by David M. Lampton, Selina Ho, and Cheng-Chwee Kuik, Singapore, May 28, 2018.

114. Wu Chengliang, "China-Laos Railway Project Set to Be Complete by Late 2021," *People's Daily*, November 15, 2017, http://en.people.cn/n3/2017/1115/c90000-9293209.html.

115. Xie Yu, "China's US$7 Billion Railway Link to Laos Is Almost Half Done, on Schedule to Begin Service in 2021," *South China Morning Post*, March 21, 2019.

116. "Full Steam Ahead for Laos-China Railway," *Laotian Times*, December 26, 2016, https://laotiantimes.com/2016/12/26/laos-china-railway-begins-construction/. In 2017, Chinese tourists were one of the few markets to grow, up 17 percent to 639,185 arrivals. When the rail line is ready, the number of Chinese tourists is expected to swell. Peter Janssen, "Chinese Tourist 'Invasion' Feared as High-Speed Laos-China Railway Will Boost Visitor Numbers Dramatically," *South China Morning Post*, August 24, 2018. A caveat is essential here. Promoters of any project always make the most optimistic possible assumptions about revenue forecasts and always minimize projected costs. The Chinese system is particularly vulnerable to this human tendency.

117. "Laos-China Ties Flourish," *Laotian Times*, November 20, 2017, https://laotiantimes.com/2017/11/20/laos-china-ties-flourish/.

118. Foreign Ministry-related official, interview by David M. Lampton, Selina Ho, and Cheng-Chwee Kuik, Vientiane, June 7, 2017; stationmaster, interview by David M. Lampton, Selina Ho, and Cheng-Chwee Kuik, Northern Thailand, June 4, 2017.

119. "Laos Government to Pay Compensation to Families Displaced by Railway," *Borneo Bulletin*, November 26, 2018, https://borneobulletin.com.bn/laos-govt-to-pay-compensation-to-families-displaced-by-railway/.

120. "Laos-China Railway Awaits Landmine Clearance," *Laotian Times*, December 9, 2016, https://laotiantimes.com/2016/12/09/laos-china-railway-awaits-landmine-clearance/.

121. Railway engineer, interview by David M. Lampton, China, July 20, 2016.

122. "China's Fast Track to Influence: Building a Railway in Laos," Radio Free Asia, undated, www.rfa.org/english/news/special/laoschinarailway/.

123. "China's Fast Track."

124. Patpon Sabpaitoon, "The Great Rail Dilemma," *Bangkok Post,* July 22, 2018, www.bangkokpost.com/news/special-reports/1507722/the-great-rail-dilemma.

125. Foreign Ministry-related official, Vientiane, June 7, 2017.

126. "China's Fast Track."

127. Marwaan Macan-Markar, "China's Belt and Road Rail Project Stirs Discontent in Laos," *Nikkei Asian Review,* March 15, 2018, https://asia.nikkei.com/Politics/China-s-Belt-and-Road-rail-project-stirs-discontent-in-Laos2.

128. Macan-Markar, "China's Belt and Road."

129. Here we have in mind the Danjiangkou Dam on the Hubei-Henan border, where the dam initially could not be built to its designed height because of local opposition to land acquisition. The dam could only be heightened decades later.

130. "Budget Approval Urgently Needed for Laos-China Railway," *Vientiane Times,* March 13, 2018, www.laolandinfo.org/2018/03/13/budget-approval-urgently-needed-for-laos-china-railway/.

131. Sabpaitoon, "Great Rail Dilemma."

132. Sabpaitoon, "Great Rail Dilemma."

133. Senior legislator, interview by David M. Lampton, Cheng-Chwee Kuik, and Selina Ho, Vientiane, June 7, 2017.

134. "Laos Government to Pay Compensation."

135. "Budget Approval Urgently Needed."

136. Daniel Hutt, "Laos on a Fast Track to a China Debt Trap," *Asia Times,* March 28, 2018, https://asiatimes.com/2018/03/laos-track-china-debt-trap/.

137. Hutt, "Laos on a Fast Track."

138. Macan-Markar, "China's Belt and Road."

139. Macan-Markar.

140. Private sector foreign corporate management, interview by David M. Lampton, Selina Ho, and Cheng-Chwee Kuik, Vientiane, June 8, 2017; senior foreign diplomat, interview by David M. Lampton, Selina Ho, and Cheng-Chwee Kuik, Vientiane, June 5, 2017.

141. Lao senior official, interview by David M. Lampton, Selina Ho, and Cheng-Chwee Kuik, Vientiane, June 6, 2017.

142. Li Yan, "China-Laos Railway Project Set to Be Completed in 2021, despite Challenges," *Global Times,* November 14, 2017, accessed July 31, 2018, www.ecns.cn/business/2017/11-14/280819.shtml.

143. Nirmal Ghosh, "China's Dream of Rail Link to S-E Asia Coming True," *Straits Times,* January 21, 2016, www.straitstimes.com/asia/east-asia/chinas-dream-of-rail-link-to-s-e-asia-coming-true.

144. Ghosh, "China's Dream."

145. "Chinese-Owned Cement Factories Pollute Lao Villages," Radio Free Asia, November 30, 2018, www.rfa.org/english/news/laos/chinese-owned-cement-factories-pollute-lao-villages-11302018123954.html.

146. Om Jotikasthira, "Thai-Chinese Rail Project Falls in Price," *Bangkok Post,* March 23, 2018, www.bangkokpost.com/news/general/1433350/thai-chinese-rail-project-falls-in-price.

147. Rapeepat Mantanarat, "Laos Rethinks Rail Project," *TTR Weekly,* November 9, 2010, https://archive.is/20130205005950/http://www.ttrweekly .com/site/2010/11/laos-rethinks-rail-project/.

148. "Laos-Thailand Railway Extension Construction to Begin Shortly," Xinhua, June 28, 2017, www.xinhuanet.com//english/2017–06/28/c_136400807 .htm.

149. World Bank Group, *Belt and Road Economics: Opportunities and Risks of Transport Corridors* (Washington, DC: World Bank, 2019), 15.

150. Lao senior official, Vientiane, June 6, 2017.

151. Very senior former leader, interview by David M. Lampton, Selina Ho, and Cheng-Chwee Kuik, Bangkok, May 30, 2017. This leader explained: "Each ASEAN country is concerned about its own domestic connectivity problems. Connectivity projects are often carried out bilaterally, making it difficult for regional connectivity. For instance, China, Thailand, and Laos did not sit down together to discuss connectivity projects."

152. Chinese bank official, in conversation with David M. Lampton, Beijing, July 23, 2017.

153. Malaysian leader, interview by David M. Lampton, Selina Ho, and Cheng-Chwee Kuik, Malaysia, May 29, 2018.

154. Thai transport expert, Thailand, July 28, 2016.

155. Researcher, interview by David M. Lampton, Beijing, September 22, 2016.

156. Thai business leader, Khon Kaen, Thailand, June 3, 2017.

157. Selina Ho, David M. Lampton, and Cheng-Chwee Kuik, unpublished notes on a roundtable discussion, Phnom Penh, Cambodia, August 22, 2018.

158. Daniel Russell, "Presentation on Asia Society Study of BRI," Stanford University, June 6, 2019. Russell handed out a document titled, "BRI Matrix: Recommendations."

159. Hong Yu, "Motivation behind China's 'One Belt, One Road' Initiatives and Establishment of the Asian Infrastructure Investment Bank," *Journal of Contemporary China* 26, no. 105 (2017): 353–68, especially 367–68.

CHAPTER SEVEN. GEOPOLITICS AND GEOECONOMICS

1. David M. Lampton, Cheng-Chwee Kuik, and Ithrana Lawrence, unpublished notes on meeting with Thai former diplomats, Bangkok, July 26, 2016, 2–3.

2. Chinese diplomat, interview by David M. Lampton, April 3, 2019. This is a close paraphrase.

3. Early in the life of BRI, Hong Yu addressed the broad issue of China's geopolitical and geoeconomic motivations for BRI writ large. See "Motivation behind China's 'One Belt, One Road' Initiatives and Establishment of the Asian Infrastructure Investment Bank," *Journal of Contemporary China* 26, no. 105 (2017): 353–68.

4. Tauch Chankosal, "The Singapore Kunming Rail Link," *Infrastructure Investor* (April 2013): 11; Mate Sebok, "Connectivity in Transport and ASEAN Economic Community Building: The Case Study of the Singapore-Kunming Railway Link" (master's thesis, National Chengchi University, Taipei, September 2014). The authors thank Professor Lee Chyungly of NCCU for sharing this thesis.

5. Wong Yau Duenn, "Sambungan Rel Singapura-Kunming: Penjelasan ke atas Corak Penglibatan Malaysia, Thailand, and Vietnam, 1996–2018" [The Singapore-Kunming Rail Link: Explaining the Participation Patterns of Malaysia, Thailand, and Vietnam, 1996–2018] (PhD diss., National University of Malaysia, Bangi, Malaysia, ongoing).

6. The AMBDC was initiated by Malaysia at the 1995 ASEAN Summit, the same meeting where Mahathir proposed the SKRL. According to Vietnamese economist Nguyen Quoc Viet, the AMBDC, which consists of all ASEAN members and China, represents a broader regional mechanism than the Mekong River Commission (MRC), a mechanism set up in April 1995 between Cambodia, Laos, Vietnam, and Thailand. See Nguyen Quoc Viet, "Institutionalization of Sub-regional Cooperation: The Case of the Greater Mekong Sub-region," in *Institutionalizing East Asia: Mapping and Reconfiguring Regional Cooperation*, ed. Alice Ba, Cheng-Chwee Kuik, and Sueo Sudo (London: Routledge, 2016), 169. On AMBDC and SKRL, see ASEAN Secretariat, *ASEAN Economic Co-operation: Transition and Transformation* (Jakarta: ASEAN Secretariat, 1997), 210.

7. Hidetaka Yoshimatsu, *The Political Economy of Regionalism in East Asia: Integrative Explanation for Dynamics and Challenges* (London: Palgrave Macmillan, 2008); "Meeting on Singapore-Kunming Rail Link Ends in Myanmar," May 15, 2002, http://en.people.cn/200205/15/eng20020515_95738.shtml.

8. "Malaysia in Cross Border Rail Initiative," Economic and Social Commission for Asia and the Pacific (ESCAP), December 20, 2017, www.unescap.org/sites/default/files/Country%20presentation%20-%20Malaysia_MOT.pdf. See also "Speech by Mr Raymond Lim, Minister for Transport and Second Minister for Foreign Affairs," Opening Ceremony of the 9th Special Working Group Meeting of the Singapore-Kunming Rail-Link, Carlton Hotel, Singapore, October 19, 2007.

9. Organisation for Economic Co-operation and Development, *Southeast Asian Economic Outlook 2010* (Paris: Development Centre, OECD, 2010), 133; "Media Statement by H.E. Dato Seri Rafidah Aziz, Chairman of the 7th Ministerial Meeting on the ASEAN-Mekong Basin Development Cooperation," Kuala Lumpur, November 28, 2005.

10. UN Economic and Social Committee for Asia and the Pacific, *Evaluation of Projects on Promotion, Development and Formalization of the Trans-Asian Railway* (Bangkok: ESCAP, 2009).

11. "Our Work: Trans-Asian Railway," UN Economic and Social Committee for Asia and the Pacific, www.unescap.org/our-work/transport/trans-asian-railway.

12. "Existing Organisations and Initiatives to Promote Cooperation among Countries for Railway Transport," chap. 3 in *Consolidated Study*, UN Eco-

nomic and Social Committee for Asia and the Pacific, December 2013, www
.unescap.org/sites/default/files/pub_2681_ch3.pdf.

13. Helen Nesadurai, ed., *Globalisation and Economic Security in East Asia:
Governance and Institutions* (London: Routledge, 2006); Alice Ba, Cheng-
Chwee Kuik, and Sueo Sudo, eds., *Institutionalizing East Asia: Mapping and
Reconfiguring Regional Cooperation* (London: Routledge, 2016).

14. David Capie, "Explaining ASEAN's Resilience: Institutions, Path
Dependency and Asia's Emerging Architecture," in Ralf Emmers, ed., *ASEAN
and the Institutionalization of East Asia*, (London: Routledge, 2012), 168–79;
Alice D. Ba, *[Re]Negotiating East and Southeast Asia: Region, Regionalism and
the Association of Southeast Asian Nations* (Stanford, CA: Stanford University
Press, 2009).

15. Yuen Foong Khong, "Coping with Strategic Uncertainty: Institutions
and Soft Balancing in ASEAN's Post–Cold War Strategy," in *Rethinking Secu-
rity in East Asia*, ed. Peter Katzenstein, Allen Carlson, and J.J. Suh (Stanford,
CA: Stanford University Press, 2004), 172–208; Amitav Acharya, "Culture,
Security, Multilateralism: The 'ASEAN Way' and Regional Order," *Contempo-
rary Security Policy* 19, no. 1 (1998), 55–84; Evelyn Goh, "Great Powers and
Hierarchical Order in Southeast Asia: Analyzing Regional Security Strategies,"
International Security 32, no. 3 (2008): 113–57.

16. ASEAN Secretariat, *ASEAN Economic Co-operation: Transition and
Transformation* (Jakarta: ASEAN Secretariat, 1997), 210.

17. Tun Dr. Mahathir Mohamad, in conversation with David M. Lampton,
Cheng-Chwee Kuik, and Ithrana Lawrence, Perdana Leadership Foundation,
Putrajaya, Malaysia, June 27, 2016. Italics added.

18. OECD, *Southeast Asian Economic Outlook 2010*, 133.

19. Wong, "Sambungan Rel Singapura-Kunming."

20. Wong.

21. Nuradzimmah Daim, "Singapore-Kunming Rail Link's Delay to Be
Addressed," *New Straits Times* (Malaysia), October 27, 2015, www.nst.com
.my/news/2015/10/Singapore-kunming-rail-link's-delay-be-addressed.

22. Tauch Chankosal, "Singapore Kunming Rail Link," 11.

23. Lee Poh Ping, "A Japanese Marshall Plan for the Developing Areas?"
Australian Journal of International Affairs 42, no. 22 (1988): 91–94; Shafiqul
Islam, "Foreign Aid and Burden Sharing: Is Japan Free Riding to a Coprosperity
Sphere in Pacific Asia?" in *Regionalism and Rivalry: Japan and the United
States in Pacific Asia*, ed. Jeffrey Frankel and Miles Kahler (Chicago: The Uni-
versity of Chicago Press, 1993), 321–90; Akira Suehiro, *The Evolution of
Japan's Perspective and Policies on Asia*, Japan's Diplomacy Series (Tokyo:
Japan Institute of International Affairs, 2016).

24. Hidetaka Yoshimatsu, "New Dynamics in Sino-Japanese Rivalry: Sustaining Infrastructure Development in Asia," *Journal of Contemporary China*
27, no. 113 (2018): 719–34; Taro Kono, "Japan to Discontinue Development
Assistance Projects for China," *Japan Times*, October 23, 2018, www
.japantimes.co.jp/news/2018/10/23/national/politics-diplomacy/japan-turn-off-
oda-spigot-china-projects-sources-say/#.XKOrSaQpA2w. In 2018, in light of
China surpassing Japan in aggregate economic size, and given that Japan had

already provided total assistance totaling $32.4 billion, Japan declared it would not continue providing ODA to Beijing, expressing the hope that the two countries could cooperate instead on building infrastructure and providing assistance in third countries.

25. "Competition Heats Up between Japan, China for Railway Projects in Asia," *Japan Bullet*, September 17, 2014, www.japanbullet.com/news/competition-heats-up-between-japan-china-for-railway-projects-in-asia; Daniel Gallucci, "China and Japan Vie for Influence with Thai Rail Projects," *Financial Times*, March 3, 2015, www.ft.com/content/ef68a484–45f1–33cf-b529–28cdd8308f2d; "Muhyiddin: Japan Reiterates Keenness for High-Speed Rail Project Involvement," *Star* (Malaysia), March 25, 2015, www.thestar.com.my/news/nation/2015/03/15/dpm-japan-wants-in-high-speed-rail/; Steve Herman, "Rail Rivals China, Japan Compete for High-Speed Track in Asia," *VOA News*, April 22, 2015, www.voanews.com/a/rail-rivals-china-japan-compete-for-high-speed-track-in-asia/2730173.html.

26. "China Wins Indonesia High-Speed Rail Project as Japan Laments 'Extremely Regrettable' U-Turn," *South China Morning Post*, September 29, 2015, www.scmp.com/news/asia/southeast-asia/article/1862459/china-wins-indonesia-high-speed-rail-project-japan-laments; "And the Winner Is . . . Nobody: Indonesia Scraps High-Speed Railway Project after Fierce Bidding War between China, Japan," *South China Morning Post*, September 4, 2015, www.scmp.com/news/asia/southeast-asia/article/1855181/and-winner-isnobody-indonesia-scraps-high-speed-railway.

27. Selina Ho, David M. Lampton, and Cheng-Chwee Kuik, notes on meetings with researchers and experts, Singapore, May 30, 2018, 4–5.

28. Ho et al., notes, 5.

29. Stephen Harner, "Japan's Rail Project Loss to China: Why It Matters for Abe's Economic Diplomacy and for China's," *Forbes*, October 1, 2015, www.forbes.com/sites/stephenharner/2015/10/01/japans-rail-project-loss-to-china-why-it-matters-for-abes-economic-diplomacy-and-for-chinas/#74cc20d52fae.

30. Chietigj Bajpaee, "Japan and China: The Geo-Economic Dimension," *The Diplomat*, March 28, 2016, https://thediplomat.com/2016/03/japan-and-china-the-geo-economic-dimension/.

31. Kei Koga, "Japan's 'Strategic Coordination' in 2015: ASEAN, Southeast Asia, and Abe's Diplomatic Agenda," *Southeast Asian Affairs 2016*, 67–79; Dragan Pavlićević and Agatha Kratz, "Implications for Sino-Japanese Rivalry in High-Speed Railways for Southeast Asia," *East Asian Policy* (April 2017): 15–25.

32. "Towards Strategic Promotion of the Infrastructure Export," Keidanren (Japan Business Federation), November 17, 2015, www.keidanren.or.jp/en/policy/2015/105.html.

33. Ministry of Foreign Affairs of Japan, "Announcement of 'Partnership of Quality Infrastructure: Investment for Asia's Future,'" May 21, 2015, www.mofa.go.jp/policy/oda/page18_000076.html.

34. Natalie Lichtenstein, *A Comparative Guide to the Asian Infrastructure Investment Bank* (Oxford: Oxford University Press, 2018).

35. "China and Japan Compete for Southeast Asia's Railways," Stratfor, May 4, 2016, https://worldview.stratfor.com/article/china-and-japan-compete-southeast-asias-railways.

36. Sueo Sudo, *Japan's ASEAN Policy: In Search of Proactive Multilateralism* (Singapore: ISEAS-Yusof Ishak Institute, 2014); Malcolm Cook, Leo Suryadinata, Mustafa Izzuddin and Le Hong Hiep, "Japan Seeks Stronger Strategic Ties in Southeast Asia," *ISEAS Perspective*, January 25, 2017.

37. Ai Ai Wong, "How Asia Could Be the Winner in the US and China's Belt and Road Race," *World Economic Forum Report*, January 16, 2019, www.weforum.org/agenda/2019/01/china-the-us-and-the-great-asean-infrastructure-race/.

38. Amelia Long, "Japan's Presence and Partnerships in Southeast Asia," *Australian Strategic Policy Institute*, February 3, 2016, www.aspistrategist.org.au/japans-presence-and-partnerships-in-southeast-asia/.

39. Purnendra Jain," Japanese Foreign Aid: What's in It for Japan?," *East Asia Forum*, July 21, 2016, www.eastasiaforum.org/2016/07/21/japanese-foreign-aid-whats-in-it-for-japan/.

40. Jain, "Japanese Foreign Aid."

41. Ministry of Foreign Affairs of Japan, *Japan's International Cooperation: White Paper on Development Cooperation 2017* (Tokyo: Ministry of Foreign Affairs, February 2018).

42. Long, "Japan's Presence and Partnerships."

43. Long.

44. Ministry of External Affairs, Government of India, "India-Japan Joint Statement during Visit of Prime Minister of Japan to India," September 14, 2017, www.mea.gov.in/bilateral-documents.htm?dtl/28946/IndiaJapan.

45. Ministry of External Affairs, Government of India, "India-Japan Vision Statement," October 29, 2018, www.mea.gov.in/bilateral-documents.htm?dtl/30543/IndiaJapan_Vision_Statement.

46. "Australia, US and Japan Announce Trilateral Partnership for Infrastructure Investment in the Indo-Pacific," Department of Foreign Affairs and Trade, Australia, July 31, 2018, https://dfat.gov.au/news/news/Pages/australia-us-and-japan-announce-trilateral-partnership-for-infrastructure-investment-in-the-indo-pacific.aspx. Italics added.

47. Jonathan Pearlman, "US, Japan and Australia Sign Infrastructure Agreement to Counter China's Belt and Road," *Telegraph*, July 31, 2018, www.telegraph.co.uk/news/2018/07/31/us-japan-australia-sign-infrastructure-agreement-counter-chinas/.

48. The White House, "U.S.-Japan Joint Statement on Advancing a Free and Open Indo-Pacific Through Energy, Infrastructure and Digital Connectivity Cooperation," November 13, 2018, www.whitehouse.gov/briefings-statements/u-s-japan-joint-statement-advancing-free-open-indo-pacific-energy-infrastructure-digital-connectivity-cooperation/; "India, US, Japan Push for Cooperation for Free and Inclusive Indo-Pacific Region," *Hindustan Times*, April 4, 2018, www.hindustantimes.com/india-news/india-us-japan-push-for-cooperation-for-free-and-inclusive-indo-pacific-region/story-qtDrlFNyW6bJVdSCmiWnEP.html.

49. Yusuf T. Unjhawala, "Quad Needs Both Economic and Military Plan for Indo-Pacific," *Economic Times,* February 23, 2018, https://economictimes. indiatimes.com/news/defence/quad-needs-both-economic-military-plan-for-indo-pacific/articleshow/63049831.cms; Ankit Panda, "US, Japan, India, and Australia Hold Working-Level Quadrilateral Meeting on Regional Cooperation," The Diplomat, November 13, 2017, https://thediplomat.com/2017/11 /us-japan-india-and-australia-hold-working-level-quadrilateral-meeting-on-regional-cooperation/; "India-Australia-Japan-US Consultations," Ministry of External Affairs, Government of India, November 15, 2018, www.mea.gov.in /press-releases.htm?dtl/30593/IndiaAustraliaJapanUS_Consultations.

50. "Competition Heats Up."

51. Very senior former Malaysian official, interview by David M. Lampton, Selina Ho, and Cheng-Chwee Kuik, Kuala Lumpur, May 31, 2018.

52. "Normal operations" excludes fatalities in Japan such as those that resulted from an earthquake and an incident in which a passenger self-immolated. Also, as mentioned later in the chapter, a Japanese-made high-speed train crashed in 2018 with a tragic loss of life in Taiwan.

53. Jain, "Japanese Foreign Aid."

54. "Japan Group to Build Train System in Bangkok, Says Report," *Malay Mail,* November 3, 2013, www.malaymail.com/news/money/2013/11/03 /japan-group-to-build-train-system-in-bangkok-says-report/555165.

55. Bajpaee, "Japan and China."

56. "Japanese Maker of Train in Deadly Taiwan Crash Finds Design Flaw," Reuters, November 1, 2018, www.reuters.com/article/us-taiwan-accident-nippon-sharyo/japanese-maker-of-train-in-deadly-taiwan-crash-finds-design-flaw-idUSKCN1N702T.

57. Pavin Chachavalpongpun, "Why the Derailing of the Japan-Thailand Train Deal Makes Sense," *The Diplomat,* February 28, 2018, https://thediplomat. com/2018/02/why-the-derailing-of-the-japan-thailand-train-deal-makes-sense/.

58. "Japanese Vow Backing for High-Speed Rail," *Bangkok Post*, March 8, 2019, www.bangkokpost.com/business/tourism-and-transport/1640924/japanese-vow-backing-for-high-speed-rail.

59. ESCAP, *Promotion, Development and Formalization.*

60. Suk-Won Lee and Jae-Keun Jeon, "Dynamic Relationships between Mega Projects and Official Development Assistance: Case of South Korean Infrastructure Construction Projects in ASEAN's Developing Countries," *Sustainability* 10, no. 12 (2018): 1–22.

61. Kwak Sungil, "South Korea's Development Assistance and Economic Outreach toward Southeast Asia," *Joint U.S.-Korea Academic Studies* 26 (2015): 153–79.

62. Lee Hyo-sik, "KR to Lead Global Railway Market," *Korea Times,* August 26, 2012, http://www.koreatimes.co.kr/www/tech/2019/03/693_118255 .html.

63. Korea Rail Network Authority (KR) website, http://english.kr.or.kr/sub /info.do?m=020501&s=english.

64. KR website.

65. Song Jung-a, "South Korea Has Big Target in Sight for Its Bullet Trains," *Financial Times,* December 19, 2016, www.ft.com/content/7563339a-bd27–11e6–8b45-b8b81dd5d080.

66. Song Jung-a, "South Korea."

67. However, because of Korea's advanced operational know-how and its cutting-edge wireless train control system and in-train communications networks, KR reportedly expressed confidence that it could still compete in global HSR markets "with attractive terms for technology transfer because we are well aware what is needed for these emerging countries." See Song Jung-a, "South Korea."

68. Mitsuru Obe and Kim Jaewon, "South Korea's Rail Dreams Face Harsh Realities," *Asian Nikkei Review,* January 9, 2019, https://asia.nikkei.com/Spotlight/Cover-Story/South-Korea-s-rail-dreams-face-harsh-realities.

69. "S. Korea's CJ Logistics Opens Up Iron Silk Road Linking Asia, Europe," Xinhua, March 6, 2018, www.xinhuanet.com/english/2018–05/09/c_137166783.htm.

70. From the very inception of AIIB, Beijing has seen the United States as opposed to both the bank and the larger BRI project, seeing Washington's skepticism as a lingering "Cold War mentality" and part of an effort to "tout values diplomacy, sowing discord." See, for instance, Zeng Peiyan, "'The Belt and Road Initiative': A Path Towards a Common Dream of Prosperity," *Qiushi* 7, no. 25 (October-December 2015): 98.

71. "India Refuses to Be Part of China's Belt-Road Initiative," *Business Standard* (India), May 13, 2017, www.business-standard.com/article/news-ians/india-refuses-to-be-part-of-china-s-belt-road-initiative-117051300941_1.html.

72. "India's 200 Mph Bullet Train Can't Get Started," Star Online, https://www.thestar.com.my/business/business-news/2018/10/17/india-200-mph-bullet-train-cant-get-started/#e1mLM50gCTJfAsp1.99.

73. "India's 200 Mph Bullet Train."

74. "Survey to Connect India-Myanmar with Railway Completed," *United News of India,* March 2, 2019, www.uniindia.com/survey-to-connect-india-myanmar-with-railway-completed/east/news/1516280.html.

75. Prabir De, *India's Emerging Connectivity with Southeast Asia: Progress and Prospects,* ADBI Working Paper, no. 507 (Tokyo: Asian Development Bank Institute, December 2014), 21. Also, email with Prabir De, February 23, 2020.

76. "India Hands Over Last Batch of Locomotives to Myanmar," Xinhua, March 20, 2018, www.xinhuanet.com/english/2018–03/20/c_137052903.htm.

77. De, *India's Emerging Connectivity,* 21.

78. Suyash Desai, "ASEAN and India Converge on Connectivity," *The Diplomat,* December 19, 2017, https://thediplomat.com/2017/12/asean-and-india-converge-on-connectivity/. See also Institute of Peace and Conflict Studies, "Linking South East Asia and India," February 2008, www.files.ethz.ch/isn/93333/IPCS-Special-Report-50.pdf.

79. Indian Railway website, http://www.indianrailways.gov.in/railwayboard/view_section_new.jsp?lang=0; "Our International Clients," IRCON International Limited, https://www.ircon.org/index.php?option=com_content&view=article&id=88&Itemid=479&lang=en.

80. "Completed Projects," IRCON International Limited, https://www.ircon.org/index.php?option=com_content&view=article&id=40&catid=2&lang=en&Itemid=410.

81. "India to seek Malaysian Expertise to Modernize Train Stations," Star Online, June 7, 2017, www.thestar.com.my/business/business-news/2017/06/07/india-to-seek-malaysian-expertise-to-modernise-train-stations/#QJOVClrRcHAYHcLi.99.

82. "India: contributions at a glance, 2006–2011," ESCAP, https://www.unescap.org/sites/default/files/IND_contributions_2006–2011.pdf.

83. Desai, "ASEAN and India Converge."

84. Desai, "ASEAN and India Converge." See also Chitresh Shrivastva, "Railway Diplomacy: China versus India," South Asian Voices, February 9, 2018, https://southasianvoices.org/railway-diplomacy-china-versus-india/; "China-Myanmar Railway Line a Threat to India's SE Asia Plans," Shillong Times, December 22, 2018, www.theshillongtimes.com/2018/12/22/china-myanmar-railway-line-a-threat-to-indias-se-asia-plans/.

85. "European Group to Bid for Malaysia-Singapore High-Speed Train," Jakarta Post, February 12, 2018, www.thejakartapost.com/seasia/2018/02/12/european-group-to-bid-for-malaysia-singapore-high-speed-train-.html.

86. Srinivas Mazumdaru, "Europe Faces China, Japan in High-Speed Rail Battle in Asia," Deutsche Welle, February 14, 2018, www.dw.com/en/europe-faces-china-japan-in-high-speed-rail-battle-in-asia/a-42589008.

87. Mazumdaru, "Europe Faces China."

88. "Malaysia, Singapore Reach Compromise over HSR Postponement," New Straits Times, September 2, 2018, www.nst.com.my/news/nation/2018/09/407466/malaysia-singapore-reach-compromise-over-hsr-postponement.

89. Erich Parpart, "High-Speed Rail Needs Help to Make an Impact," Bangkok Post, January 7, 2019, www.bangkokpost.com/business/news/1606654/high-speed-rail-needs-help-to-make-an-impact.

90. "CP-Led Group Closes In on Three Airport Rail Link Deal," Bangkok Post, December 22, 2018, www.bangkokpost.com/business/news/1598742/cp-led-group-closes-in-on-three-airport-rail-link-deal.

91. "CP-Led Group."

92. "CP Consortium to Build High-Speed Airport Rail Link," Bangkok Post, April 27, 2019, www.bangkokpost.com/business/tourism-and-transport/1667736/cp-consortium-to-build-high-speed-airport-rail-link.

93. Agatha Kratz and Dragan Pavlićević, "China's High-Speed Rail Diplomacy: Riding a Gravy Train?" Lau China Institute Working Paper Series (London: King's College London, 2016).

94. Chris Devonshire-Ellis, "The EU Commission's 'EU-Asia Connectivity Strategy' Omits China," China Briefing, October 16, 2018, www.china-briefing.com/news/eu-commissions-eu-asia-connectivity-strategy-omits-china/.

95. European Commission High Representative of the Union for Foreign Affairs and Security Policy, "Connecting Europe and Asia: Building Blocks for an EU Strategy," September 19, 2018, https://eeas.europa.eu/sites/eeas/files/joint_communication_-_connecting_europe_and_asia_-_building_blocks_for_an_eu_strategy_2018-09-19.pdf.

96. Fraser Cameron, "Europe's Answer to China's Belt and Road," *The Diplomat,* September 19, 2018, https://thediplomat.com/2018/09/europes-answer-to-chinas-belt-and-road/.

97. "EU Launches Asia Strategy to Rival China's 'New Silk Road,'" *Business Times,* September 26, 2018, www.businesstimes.com.sg/government-economy/eu-launches-asia-strategy-to-rival-chinas-new-silk-road.

98. Dana Heide, Till Hoppe, Stephan Scheuer, and Klaus Stratmann, "EU Ambassadors Band Together against Silk Road," *Handelsblatt,* April 17, 2018.

99. Heide et al., "EU Ambassadors."

100. Cameron, "Europe's Answer."

CHAPTER EIGHT. IMPLICATIONS FOR CHINA, ASIA, AND THE WORLD

1. Thai businessperson, interview by David M. Lampton, Selina Ho, and Cheng-Chwee Kuik, Khon Kaen, Thailand, June 3, 2017.

2. Malaysian researcher, interview by David M. Lampton, Cheng-Chwee Kuik, and Ithrana Lawrence, June 27, 2016.

3. Yasuo Onishi, "One Belt One Road Initiative: Impacts on Asia and the World" (presentation at the IDE International Symposium: *China at a Crossroads,* Intercontinental Hotel, Tokyo, February 22, 2019).

4. David J. Bulman, "Sustaining the US-China Economic Relationship to Avoid a Two Bloc Global Economic Order" (paper presented at Pacific Community Initiative Conference in Hong Kong, April 2019).

5. The Santiago Principles, or the generally accepted principles and practices for Sovereign Wealth Funds, is a set of widely accepted voluntary guidelines concerning best practices.

6. The Paris Group consists of six very large sovereign wealth funds that have agreed to consider climate risks as part of their investment strategies in furtherance of the Paris climate change agreement.

7. Pechnipa Dominique Lam, "Will Thailand's Chinese High-Speed Railway Be Worth It?" *The Diplomat,* March 6, 2019, https://thediplomat.com/2019/03/will-thailands-china-built-railway-be-worth-it/.

8. An excellent article by Raffaello Pantucci makes the case that Westerners, in their effort to reinforce the idea of Beijing's "debt-trap diplomacy," underestimate the ability of Beijing and its partners, particularly in Pakistan and Malaysia, to reshape and adapt projects. Pantucci cites a study by RWR Advisory Group asserting that about 14 percent of BRI projects have encountered issues. See Raffaello Pantucci, "China's Belt and Road Hits Problems but Is Still Popular," *Financial Times,* November 15, 2018, www.ft.com/content/814b39ea-e8cd-11e8-a34c-663b3f553b35.

9. Treasury Secretary Jack Lew, interview by David M. Lampton, June 4, 2015.

10. "OPIC Board Approves Nearly $900 Million to Development Projects in Africa, Asia and Latin America," OPIC, www.opic.gov/press-releases/2018/opic-board-approves-nearly-900-million-development-projects-africa-asia-and-latin-america; David M. Lampton, notes from interview with very

senior US Department of Transportation officials, Washington, DC, March 21, 2019, 7.

11. "U.S. Pledges Nearly $300 Million Security Funding for Indo-Pacific Region," Reuters, August 3, 2018, www.reuters.com/article/us-asean-singapore-usa-security/u-s-pledges-nearly-300-million-security-funding-for-indo-pacific-region-idUSKBN1KP022.

12. Raul Dancel, "Beware of China 'Debt Trap', Malaysia's Mahathir Tells the Philippines," *Straits Times* (Singapore), March 7, 2019, www.straitstimes.com/asia/se-asia/beware-of-china-debt-trap-malaysias-mahathir-tells-the-philippines.

13. John D. Donahue, Karen Eggleston, and Richard J. Zeckhauser, "The Dragon, the Eagle, and the Private Sector: Public-Private Collaboration in China and the United States," forthcoming manuscript, especially chapter 3, "Railroads."

14. William S. Greever, "A Comparison of Railroad Land-Grant Policies," *Agricultural History* 25, no. 2 (April 1951): 86. Cited in Karen Eggleston, "Railroads," chap. 3 in "Dragon," ed. Donahue et al.

15. Samuel P. Huntington, *The Third Wave: Democratization in the Late Twentieth Century* (Norman, OK: Oklahoma University Press, 1991).

16. Francis Fukuyama, *The End of History and the Last Man* (New York: Avon Books, 1992).

17. Huntington and Fukuyama, however, in their institution building work, drew upon the still earlier work of "functionalists" such as Gabriel Almond, scholars who argued that all governing systems were interlocking sets of institutions that needed to perform specific tasks well if polities were to function at all, much less be democratic or stable civic societies. See, Gabriel A. Almond and G. Bingham Powell, *Comparative Politics: A Developmental Approach* (Boston: Little, Brown and Company, 1966).

18. Francis Fukuyama, *Political Order and Political Decay* (New York: Farrar, Straus and Giroux, 2014), 23.

19. J. Linn, "The Role of World Bank Lending in Middle Income Countries," The OECD Conference on the Effectiveness of Policies and Reforms (Washington, DC: The Brookings Institution, 2004), cited in Francis Fukuyama, Michael Bennon, and Bushra Bataineh, "Chinese and Western Approaches to Infrastructure Development," working paper, February 2019, 22–23.

20. "$27.7 Billion Requested in Foreign Assistance for FY 2019," www.foreignassistance.gov/.

21. Tim Panzarella, "A Rising China Bets Big on Infrastructure Spending Overseas, as U.S. Wavers," Reason Foundation, December 5, 2017, https://reason.com/blog/2017/12/05/a-rising-china-has-its-benefits.

22. James Politi, Sam Fleming and Mark Vandevelde, "The Sudden Departure of World Bank President Jim Young Kim Has Triggered Confusion among Staff . . .," *FTWeekend*, January 12–13, 2019.

23. Czeslaw Tubilewicz and Kanishka Jayasuriya, "Internationalisation of the Chinese Subnational State and Capital: The Case of Yunnan and the Greater Mekong Subregion," *Australian Journal of International Affairs* 69, no. 2 (2015): 185–204.

24. Leading Chinese academic, interview by Selina Ho, Singapore, December 7, 2018.

25. Barry Naughton, "Decline of Central Control over Investment in Post-Mao China," in *Policy Implementation in Post-Mao China*, ed. David M. Lampton (Berkeley: University of California Press, 1987), 51–79.

26. David M. Lampton, notes on meeting with think-tank delegation from China, Washington, DC, June 14, 2017, 3.

27. Pantucci, "China's Belt and Road."

28. Think-tank researcher, interview by David M. Lampton, Washington, DC, June 16, 2017.

29. Senior former Thai leader, interview by David M. Lampton, Selina Ho, and Cheng-Chwee Kuik, Bangkok, Thailand, May 30, 2017.

30. Thai professor, interview by David M. Lampton, Cheng-Chwee Kuik, and Ithrana Lawrence, July 27, 2016.

31. Former Malaysian diplomat, interview by David M. Lampton and Cheng-Chwee Kuik, June 28, 2016.

32. Foreign policy official, interview by David M. Lampton, Hanoi, Vietnam, January 29, 2018.

33. David M. Lampton, Selina Ho, and Cheng-Chwee Kuik, notes on meeting with social scientists, Hanoi, January 6, 2017, 2.

34. Ministry of Foreign Affairs of Japan, "Official Development Assistance (ODA)," https://www.mofa.go.jp/policy/oda/page18_000076.html.

35. Senior Cambodian People's Party official, in conversation with David M. Lampton, Selina Ho, and Cheng-Chwee Kuik, August 24, 2018.

36. Senior Vietnamese official, interview by David M. Lampton, Selina Ho, and Cheng-Chwee Kuik, Hanoi, January 6, 2017.

37. Lampton, notes from interview with very senior US Department of Transportation officials, March 21, 2019, 2, 7.

38. "Belt and Road Initiative Cooperation a New Highlight in Sino-Singapore Ties: Teo Chee Hean," *Straits Times*, July 5, 2018, www.straitstimes.com/asia/east-asia/belt-and-road-initiative-cooperation-a-new-highlight-in-sino-singapore-ties-teo-chee.

39. "China Allowing 2,000 Ethnic Kazakhs to Leave Xinjiang Region," Associated Press, January 9, 2019, apnews.com/6c0a9dcdd7bd4a0b85a0bc96ef3dd6f2; see also James Griffiths, "China Is Becoming an Election Issue in Asia. And That's Bad News for Beijing," CNN, April 4, 2019, www.cnn.com/2019/04/04/asia/china-indonesia-election-influence-asia-intl/index.html.

40. Former Southeast Asian official, interview by David M. Lampton, Cheng-Chwee Kuik, and Ithrana Lawrence, July 26, 2016. Quotations indicate direct quotes, while the rest of the excerpt is close paraphrase.

41. Senior foreign diplomat, interview by David M. Lampton, Vientiane, Laos, June 5, 2017.

42. Senior Indo-Pacific diplomat, interview by David M. Lampton, Vientiane, June 5, 2017.

43. Researcher and bureaucrat in Ministry of Commerce, interview by David M. Lampton, Beijing, March 28, 2017.

44. Senior Vietnamese economic adviser, interview by David M. Lampton, January 29, 2018.

45. In his masterful volume entitled *China's Quest: The History of the Foreign Relations of the People's Republic of China* (London: Oxford University Press, 2016), John W. Garver explains the dramatically different eras of Chinese foreign policy by referring to a corresponding and driving change in the legitimating rationales that different Chinese leaderships have employed to ground their rule domestically. As one leadership era has given way to the next, legitimating rationales have also changed, setting the stage for changed foreign policy.

46. Vietnam Institute for Economic and Policy Research (VEPR), "BRI Projects in Viet Nam," PowerPoint presentation, photocopy, released in Manila, Philippines, November 29–30, 2018.

47. Thai academic, interview by David M. Lampton, Selina Ho, and Cheng-Chwee Kuik, Bangkok, May 31, 2017.

48. "Myanmar, Having Warmed to the West, Turns to China Again," Associated Press, May 28, 2017, www.apnews.com/934850a3df5d4d63add4b8fa5b2db633.

49. Hein Ko Soe and Thomas Kean, "Myitsone's Moment of Truth," *Frontier*, November 29, 2018, https://frontiermyanmar.net/en/myitsones-moment-of-truth.

50. "China, Myanmar Sign MoU on Feasibility of Muse-Mandalay Railway," Xinhua, www.xinhuanet.com/english/2018-10/23/c_137550972.htm.

51. VEPR, "BRI Projects in Viet Nam."

52. Transportation researcher, interview by David M. Lampton, Cheng-Chwee Kuik, and Ithrana Lawrence, Bangkok, July 26, 2016.

53. Pham Sy Thanh, VEPR, "BRI Projects in Viet Nam."

54. Zhou Taidong, China Center for International Knowledge on Development, Development and Reform Commission (China), "Progress of Connection Projects of the Mainland Southeast Asia Economic Corridor under BRI," presented in Manila, November 2018.

55. Internal fissures in the EU over whether or not member countries should participate in BRI are an example. In March 2019, just as President Xi Jinping arrived in Rome to have Italy sign on to Beijing's BRI, "the leaders of France, Germany, and the European Union huddled in Brussels hoping to strengthen the Continent's defenses against what they considered to be China's economic incursion." Jason Horowitz and Steven Erlanger, "Italy Welcomes China's Leader, and Vast Infrastructure Project," *New York Times*, March 23, 2019.

56. Secretary of State Michael R. Pompeo, "Interview with Laura Ingraham of the Laura Ingraham Show," www.state.gov/interview-with-laura-ingraham-of-the-laura-ingraham-show/; Kinling Lo, "Xi Vows to Boost Ties with Uruguay Amid US Warning: President's Pledge Comes after US Secretary of State Warns Region against 'Predatory Actors,'" *South China Morning Post* (Hong Kong), February 4, 2018.

57. "U.S. Pledges Nearly $300 Million."

58. Senior policy adviser, in conversation with David M. Lampton, Hanoi, January 29, 2018.

59. Kinling Lo and Sidney Leng, "Chinese factory in Myanmar ransacked by hundreds of angry workers," *South China Morning Post*, February 23, 2017, www.scmp.com/news/china/diplomacy-defence/article/2073775/chinese-factory-myanmar-ransacked-hundreds-angry.

60. Southeast Asian corporate official, interview by David M. Lampton, Selina Ho, and Cheng-Chwee Kuik, Southeast Asia, May 29, 2017.

61. Lampton et al., notes on meeting with social scientists, Hanoi, January 6, 2017, 3.

62. Bulman, "Sustaining the US-China Economic Relationship."

63. Alex Barker and David Keohane, "EU Probes Mergers as China Threat Looms," *FT Weekend*, January 12–13, 2019.

64. Nicholas R. Lardy, *The State Strikes Back: The End of Economic Reform in China?* (Washington, DC: Peterson Institute for International Economics, 2019), 41.

65. Pompeo, "Interview with Laura Ingraham."

66. Senior former US official, interview by David M. Lampton, January 15, 2019.

67. David M. Lampton, "Reconsidering U.S.-China Relations: From Improbable Normalization to Precipitous Deterioration," *Asia Policy* 14, no. 2 (April 2019): 43–60.

68. Robert McCartney, "Senators to Metro: No More Federal Funding If You Buy Chinese Rail Cars," *Washington Post*, April 13, 2019, www.washingtonpost.com/local/trafficandcommuting/senators-to-metro-no-more-federal-funding-if-you-buy-chinese-rail-cars/2019/04/13/99d22b7a-5cab-11e9-9625-01d48d50ef75_story.html; Jeff Davis, "Key Senators Introduce Bill Banning Transit Agencies from Procuring Rolling Stock from China-Based Manufacturers," *Eno Transportation Weekly*, March 14, 2019, www.enotrans.org/article/key-senators-introduce-bill-banning-transit-agencies-from-procuring-rolling-stock-from-china-based-manufacturers/.

69. Very senior former official, interview by David M. Lampton, Selina Ho, and Cheng-Chwee Kuik, Southeast Asia, May 31, 2018.

70. Former senior official, interview by David M Lampton, Selina Ho, and Cheng-Chwee Kuik, "Interview, Former Senior Official," Kuala Lumpur, Malaysia, May 31, 2018, 9–10.

71. Senior Vietnamese official, Hanoi, January 6, 2017.

72. Former Chairman of the China Banking Regulatory Commission Liu Mingkang, Johns Hopkins—SAIS, March 29, 2016. As recorded in David M. Lampton's notes.

Index

Founded in 1893,
UNIVERSITY OF CALIFORNIA PRESS
publishes bold, progressive books and journals
on topics in the arts, humanities, social sciences,
and natural sciences—with a focus on social
justice issues—that inspire thought and action
among readers worldwide.

The UC PRESS FOUNDATION
raises funds to uphold the press's vital role
as an independent, nonprofit publisher, and
receives philanthropic support from a wide
range of individuals and institutions—and from
committed readers like you. To learn more, visit
ucpress.edu/supportus.